Early Modern History: Society and Culture

Series Editors

Rab Houston
School of History, The Scores
University of St Andrews
St Andrews, Fife, United Kingdom

Edward Muir
Department of History
Northwestern University
Evanston, Illinois, USA

This series encompasses European topics in the areas of social, political and cultural history from 1400 to 1800. It will also include colonial subjects where the themes and methodologies have direct relevance to, and influence on, European history.

More information about this series at
http://www.springer.com/series/15033

Cecilia Cristellon

Marriage, the Church, and its Judges in Renaissance Venice, 1420–1545

palgrave
macmillan

Cecilia Cristellon
Max Planck Institute for European Legal History
Hansaallee 41, 60323 Frankfurt am Main, Germany

Translated by Celeste McNamara from the Italian edition: La carità e l'eros. Il matrimonio, la Chiesa, i suoi giudici nella Venezia del Rinascimento (1420-1545) (Annali dell'Istituto storico italo-germanico in Trento. Monografie, 58) Bologna: il Mulino 2010.

Early Modern History: Society and Culture
ISBN 978-3-319-38799-4   ISBN 978-3-319-38800-7   (eBook)
DOI 10.1007/978-3-319-38800-7

Library of Congress Control Number: 2016956492

© The Editor(s) (if applicable) and The Author(s) 2017
This work is subject to copyright. All rights are solely and exclusively licensed by the Publisher, whether the whole or part of the material is concerned, specifically the rights of translation, reprinting, reuse of illustrations, recitation, broadcasting, reproduction on microfilms or in any other physical way, and transmission or information storage and retrieval, electronic adaptation, computer software, or by similar or dissimilar methodology now known or hereafter developed.
The use of general descriptive names, registered names, trademarks, service marks, etc. in this publication does not imply, even in the absence of a specific statement, that such names are exempt from the relevant protective laws and regulations and therefore free for general use.
The publisher, the authors and the editors are safe to assume that the advice and information in this book are believed to be true and accurate at the date of publication. Neither the publisher nor the authors or the editors give a warranty, express or implied, with respect to the material contained herein or for any errors or omissions that may have been made. The publisher remains neutral with regard to jurisdictional claims in published maps and institutional affiliations.

Cover illustration: © Adam Eastland Art + Architecture/Alamy Stock Photo

Printed on acid-free paper

This Palgrave Macmillan imprint is published by Springer Nature
The registered company is Springer International Publishing AG
The registered company address is: Gewerbestrasse 11, 6330 Cham, Switzerland

for Alexey

Foreword

Canon law is a system of regulations binding throughout Christendom. The judge who decides a case in an English ecclesiastical tribunal and an episcopal vicar who presides over an Italian court are acting within the same juridical framework found in Spain, France, and the former lands of the Holy Roman Empire. This institutional continuity – which was not called into question even by the Protestant Reformation – has guaranteed European nations a rich and systematic set of documentation that sheds light on many crucial areas of social life and that is astonishing in its continuity. Preserved in massive quantities in ecclesiastical archives (or, outside of Italy, in the public archives that have inherited them), the cause records of the bishops' tribunals allow us to reconstruct and analyze, from a comparative viewpoint and over several centuries, the most important of the components of social life: the matrimonial alliance. The terrain thus opened up to scholarly investigation is of unparalleled fecundity, not only for the sheer quantity of the series and their spatial ramifications (not all of them, as yet, accessible to researchers) but also for the polyphonic character of these cause records, which captures social phenomena not in a static phase but in the dynamic one of conflict and presents them from the diverse and contradictory viewpoints of the protagonists and their attendant figures.

The Centre of Italo-Germanic Historical Studies, which publishes Cecilia Cristellon's monograph in one of its series, has promoted a cycle of studies that has enabled Italy to regain much of the territory previously lost in exploring of this category of sources – the Italian ones excelling both in quantity and quality over the rest of Europe – and to host a series of conferences that have opened up new channels of international scholarly communication.

By now that cycle has produced a series of volumes (nine in number) and an equally substantial number of journal articles that make the Centre an internationally recognized authority in the study of marriage, both from the viewpoint of the social sciences and legal studies.

In the series of publications that are the lasting result of this cycle as well as four other collaborative research projects, Cecilia Cristellon's monograph represents a high point. For the first time, an Italian matrimonial tribunal has been subjected to an investigation that is both analytical and systematic – not through documentary surveys, not by selecting this or that phenomenon, not for periods restricted to a few years, but for 125 years in that crucial period that runs from the beginnings of serial documentation in Venice to the momentous changes marked by the convocation of the Council of Trent. What Anne Lefebvre Teillard did for French ecclesiastical tribunals, Richard Helmholz for English ones, and Charles Donahue Jr. did for five medieval tribunals in French-speaking territories and in England (which he studied in comparative fashion), Cristellon now does for an Italian tribunal, one that has bequeathed us a documentary patrimony immeasurably richer than any of those studied hitherto.

The extraordinary explorative energy that this labor demanded, the intellectual courage that underlies the endeavor, and the tenacity shown in overcoming difficulties both technical and otherwise make the final result one of the highest excellence. This book is set to become a point of reference for all future research on the structure and praxis of the matrimonial tribunals and on the emotional tempests and affective equilibriums that the matrimonial experience upsets or produces. The character of the primary research and the freshness of the sources that are here interrogated for the first time manifest themselves in results that resist summarizing in a simple and univocal conclusion: despite the clear normative and procedural parallels that this book reveals with other parts of Europe – I am thinking especially of France – the Italian case reveals deep and fundamental divergences regarding the social role of the tribunals, their presence in the community (the numbers of cases heard), the judges' authority and culture, their interaction with the surrounding society, and the social features of the "tribunals' clients." Such divergences pose a real challenge to future research, because they confront it with new and unforeseen questions.

For students of history, institutions, and law, Cecilia Cristellon now supplies, along with a clear outline of its procedure, a systematic analysis of the reference parameters and moral values that underlay the decisions of one ecclesiastical tribunal on the cusp between the medieval and the early modern world. "One" tribunal? The patriarchal tribunal of Venice is not comparable to the other Italian tribunals. A strong research team of 30–40 scholars, who for a decade have regularly met to compare their experiences working in 11 different ecclesiastical archives throughout the country, has concluded that the tribunal of Venice represents a special case in Italy. The Venetian *matrimonialia* stand out in the Italian landscape for the documentary density of individual cases, for the evocative power of court transcripts, and for the immediacy of lived experience that the notaries' pens managed to capture. The extraordinary quality of the Venetian case records the reflection, in documents, of an institutional reality which the reader will find illustrated in detail in the following pages – that is to say the particular political, social, and cultural physiognomy of the Venetian church. For the Venetian patriciate's reluctance to appeal to Rome in cases of spiritual matter, for the role as a court of appeal that the patriarchal tribunal procured from Rome in relation to the other episcopal tribunals of the Republic of St. Mark, for the high theological and theologico-canonical competence of the patriarchs and their extremely close links – though never subordinate – with the ruling class, for the linguistic expertise that a solid humanistic education conferred on its officials and clerks, the Venetian tribunal stood out in the landscape of proto-Renaissance and Renaissance Italy as a lively center of political, juridical, theological, and literary culture (and it will shine more brightly still when some extremely industrious scholar, possibly the author of this book herself, subjects those extraordinary documents that are the decisions of the courts – personally composed by the patriarchs – to a rigorous analysis of *Kulturgeschichte*).

The fact that the first systematic investigation of an ecclesiastical tribunal should be centered on Venice is one of those fortuitous events whose providential character is perceived only *a posteriori* by the scholars concerned. This monograph is the result of a choice made many years ago, the wisdom of which could have been grasped neither by Cecilia Cristellon (who at that time was completing her higher education) nor the writer of these lines (who was then the coordinator of a national research project financed by the Ministry of Universities and Research) nor the other scholars engaged in the project. The favor of Clio has ensured that the only Italian archive of *matrimonialia* that has been explored in systematic fashion thus far should also be the one that is most exciting for scholars, the one that most boldly challenges the reader's literary sensibility and most strongly appeals to his or her empathy: where else do we find a clerk who records the blushes of a hermaphrodite or the bold replies of an interrogated female witness (p. 233)? The happy result of Cecilia Cristellon's undertaking has been aided by the presence of a supremely professional archivist, Francesca Cavazzana Romanelli, as the scholarly director of the Archivio Storico del Patriarcato, by the flexibility of the archive's opening hours, by the competence and courtesy of its staff, and by the generous spirit with which the archive has been, and still is, run.

Cecilia Cristellon's is an austere book. She has worked on material endowed with immense seductive power. Stories of passion and deception, incantation of love and violence, sensuality and patrimonial interests, intrigues and kidnappings, false identities, family strategies, and the pride of a patriciate class unequalled in Europe for its riches and prestige: the fascination that emanates from these documents and holds the researcher rooted to the desk is not without its risks. Some historians who have examined these records, including the present writer, have failed to resist the temptation of storytelling, and in some cases have abandoned themselves to the pure pleasure of telling a story for its own sake, or else have selected from the ocean of stories those that support a preconceived thesis.

Not so with the author of this book. Cristellon rigorously follows the scheme of her four chapters, which are arranged primarily according to institutional topics: the tribunal and its procedure; testimony as a juridical problem and as an expression of social networks; the figure and role of the judge; and the substance, form, and perception of consent. She pursues this scheme without deviations, developing in the course of this study a sobriety of language and clarity in argumentation that mark her as a scholar endowed with great maturity of judgment and one who has achieved her own personal style. Possibly as a result of this rigor, the monograph that emerges confronts the specialist and non-specialist with thrilling results. Among these I might mention the portrait of the judge as confessor (chap. 4, § 4) and the theme of "conscience" as a parameter in the interrogation especially of young women (chap. 4, §§ 7–8). These are previously unexplored areas of research, pages in which the originality of this young scholar attains what in my view is a truly remarkable level of penetration. Her ability to enter into syntony with the documents produces pages of vibrant density.

In this austere book, which makes no attempt to flatter the reader, the buried voices that the author has for many years compressed into brief entries (so as to supply the reader with a quantitative picture) and the diverse stories she has turned her eyes away from (to be able to classify them into categories) erupt on every page. It is everyday experience that gives life and tension to this reconstruction. The book has hundreds of personalities. Clara Marcello, Elisabeth di Pietro di Fiandra, Hieronimo Mudazzo, Margherita de Amicis... each and every one of them is at the center of a dramatic story that the author has rapidly evoked in a few lines or even – as with Elisabeth di Pietro di Fiandra, Giandomenico Ceti, Andrea Filocampo, Teodoro di Giovanni ... – condensed into a phrase or note. These figures, brought into sharp focus before sinking back into the shadows of a choral ensemble, animate the drier material with the sharpness of their profiles, with an incisive phrase or an impulsive reply. A special instrument was needed to orchestrate these remote voices. This book, which will be returned to again and again as a point of reference, is a document of profound and vibrant humanity.

Silvana Seidel Menchi

Acknowledgments

I would like to thank the editor at Il Mulino – FBK for permission to publish the English version of my book for Palgrave Macmillan.

This work was developed as a part of the project "I processi matrimoniali degli archivi ecclesiastici italiani" ("Marriage cases of the Italian Ecclesiastical Archives"), coordinated by Silvana Seidel Menchi and Diego Quaglioni at the University of Trent (2001–2005). I am indebted to the organizers of the seminar and to the scholars who participated in it for the exceptional opportunity for intellectual exchange which they offered me.

The Archivio Storico del Patriarcato di Venezia directed by don Diego Sartorelli and before him by don Bruno Bertoli and don Gianni Bridi provided an ideal working environment, for which I am very grateful. To Francesca Cavazzana Romanelli, the scientific supervisor of special projects at the same archive, and to the archivists Manuela Barausse, Laura Levantino, and David Trivellato, as to Paola Benussi of the Archivio di Stato di Venezia go my sincere thanks for their professionalism, availability, cooperation, and friendship over the years.

The book was developed from a doctoral dissertation conducted at the European University Institute in Fiesole under the kind supervision of Gerard Delille and owes much to the later recommendations for reflection in the final phase by Anthony Molho.

Various institutions have supported the research that forms this project with research contracts and fellowships: the University of Trent, the Fondazione Michele Pellegrino in Turin, the Newberry Library in Chicago, the University of Pisa, and the Institut für Europäische Geschichte in Mainz. To their directors, as to all the personnel at their libraries, I would like to express my most sincere gratitude. Likewise, I thank the prefect of the Vatican Secret Archives monsignor Sergio Pagano and the personnel there, the former director of the Archivio Storico Diocesano of Padua monsignor Claudio Bellinati, the director of the Archivio Storico of the Diocese of Verona don Franco Segala, the personnel of the Archivio di Stato di Venezia, and Dr. Giuseppe Ellero of the Archivio dell'Istituto di Ricovero e Educazione in Venice.

Stanley Chojnacki, Giovanni Ciappelli, Charles Donahue Jr., Emlyn Eisenach, Daniela Lombardi, Luca Faoro, Chiara La Rocca, Julius Kirshner, Sara McDougall, Laura Prosperi, Mark Adrian Roberts, Kirsi Salonen, Ludwig Schmugge, and Heide Wunder were all, in various phases of this research, valuable interlocutors. Richard Helmholz, a font of inspiration for all scholars of *matrimonialia*, has greatly encouraged my work with his characteristic kindness. To Regina and the late Rosanne Schwartz, William Davis, and Edward Muir I would like to express thanks that go beyond the professional sphere.

I am particularly grateful to Fernando Chavarría Múgica and Ermanno Orlando for their repeated readings and our open, gracious, and constant dialogue. Ottavia Niccoli read the entire manuscript and enabled me to improve it with her advice. Anne Jacobson Schutte never denied me prompt counsel. I wish to thank Jenny McCall, Emily Russel, Rowan Milligan and their associates at Palgrave Macmillan for their accuracy, and their efficiency, as well as the anonymous reviewer for useful commentary.

My work has continually taken me to various countries and cities. To my parents I owe the precious sensation of always having a home to return to for me and for my family.

Among the many debts of gratitude I have contracted with Silvana Seidel Menchi, I wish to mention specifically the most rare virtue in a teacher and thank her for the discretion with which she has followed my research, allowing me to become a historian.

I am profoundly grateful to Edward Muir for encouraging and supporting the translation of this book into English. To have such a brilliant scholar and friendly colleague as Celeste McNamara as its translator was an honor and a great pleasure. Having Charles Keenan revise the text with great competence and sensibility was a true privilege. I would like to thank both warmly for their very precise and fine work.

Alexey never left me on my own. This book is dedicated to him.

Contents

1 Introduction   1

2 **The Matrimonial Tribunal and the Procedure in Marriage Litigations**   33
    1 *Composition of the Tribunal and the Parties in a Cause*   33
    2 *The Petition*   36
    3 *The Citation*   36
    4 *Contumacy*   37
    5 *Postponements*   39
    6 *Exceptions*   39
    7 *The Formal Joinder of Issue: The* litis contestatio   42
    8 *The Positions*   42
    9 *The Proof*   47
    10 *The Sentence*   58
    11 *The Appeal*   59
    12 *The Execution of the Sentence*   60
    13 *The Summary Procedure*   60

3 **Witnesses and Testimony**   77
    1 *The Deposition and Report*   77
    2 *The Witnesses' Oaths*   79
    3 *The Formation of Testimony*   80
    4 *Perjury: An Open Question*   83
    5 *The Burden of Testimony*   84

4 The Office of the Judge: Mediation, Inquisition, Confession — 111
  1. *The Office of the Judge* — 111
  2. *Mediation* — 114
  3. *Inquisition* — 118
  4. *Confession* — 120
  5. *From Confessor to Judge* — 123
  6. *Confessors "in Place of the Judge"* (in vice iudicis) — 125
  7. *Judges and Women* — 127
  8. *From the Conscience of the Judges to the Conscience of the Women: The Oath* — 131

5 "Maybe so": Marriage and Consent in Pre-Tridentine Venice — 159
  1. *"Consent Makes Marriage"* (Consensus facit nuptias) — 161
  2. *The Expression of Consent* — 164
  3. *"The Bond Between Man and Woman That Cannot Be Dissolved Except by Death"* — 166
  4. *From Plural Marriage to Polygamy* — 169
  5. *Separation Between a Private Fact and "the Gravest Thing"* (res gravissima) — 172
  6. *Conditions and Errors* — 174
  7. *The Age of Consent* — 181
  8. *Consent and Parental Coercion* — 187

6 Venetian "Matrimonialia": A Quantitative Analysis (1420–1500) — 219

7 Conclusions — 227

Abbreviations — 237

Manuscript Sources — 239

Print Sources	243
Bibliography	245
Index	277

CHAPTER 1

Introduction

In Venice on 20 November 1515, the nobleman Francesco Barbaro "solemnly" gave his daughter Marietta, a "chaste maiden," in marriage to Matteo Giustinian. This occurred in the presence of witnesses and the notary, Daniele Zordan, who united the couple in matrimony "in the name of the Holy Trinity, the Father, Son, and Holy Spirit, of the glorious Virgin Mary, and the entire celestial court," registering the dowry contract stipulated by the parties.[1] The rigid formality of the nuptial contract, similar to many others preserved in notarial archives, provides little insight into Marietta and Matteo's marriage. The period's prescriptive literature about, and the historiographic image of, noble marriage would lead us to believe that this story is about a socially endogamous union (since both parties were nobles) and that it was blessed by their families (as Marietta was given in marriage to Matteo by her father). The fact that the bride was defined as "pudica domicella" (a chaste maiden) and that the groom had lost his father suggests a union conforming to the ideals of noble marriage described about a century earlier by the patrician humanist, Francesco Barbaro. In *"De re uxoria"* he had described a marriage built on the principle of marital supremacy assured by the tender age and inexperience of the bride, sweetly inclined to submit to a more mature and experienced husband who, as an independent man, was capable of protecting her.[2]

Our understanding of this marriage is completely altered by the matrimonial litigation that followed the conclusion of the contract. This cause is conserved in the Archivio Storico del Patriarcato di Venezia, which holds the documentation related to the ecclesiastical management of matrimonial conflict in the diocese of Venice and the dioceses under the jurisdiction of the Patriarch. In the process, Matteo is described as a youth who may not have reached the age of 14, who was possibly affected by psychiatric disturbances, and who was probably unaware of the significance of the act he was carrying out. A more scrupulous notary than Zordan had refused to preside over such a marriage, an event which none of Matteo's relatives attended. His family claimed that they had not even known about the match and so they prevented Marietta's father from registering the nuptials in the patrician matrimonial register of the Avogaria di Comun.[3]

Marietta and Matteo's story brings up many of the problems that will be confronted in this book: What were the elements that rendered a marriage valid? What transferred the event into the sacred sphere? How many different and often contrasting conceptions of the nuptial bond and consent existed? Which powers were the interpreters? What elements did the judge consider to decide upon one sentence over another? And to what extent are litigation documents trustworthy? Above all, this case reveals the importance of marriage litigations for the study of marriage practices.

This book investigates the actions of the Venetian marriage tribunal from 1420 until the opening of the Council of Trent. Both in terms of subject and chronology, it is the first such study for Italy, but it has been preceded by some works on English, French, and German tribunals, with which this book intends to establish a constant dialogue.[4] As a subject relevant to the health of the soul, matrimony was under the jurisdiction of the Church, which had assumed a juridical monopoly over marriage since the eleventh century.[5] At times the Church operated in harmony with secular authorities, and at others there was conflict due to the civil consequences of marriage – primarily regarding the legitimacy of children.[6] Technically, secular tribunals had jurisdiction over patrimonial questions between spouses, though the Church at times inserted itself into these matters either directly, by substituting itself for the secular authority,[7] or indirectly, by influencing Rulings through their own sentences.[8] The lay magistratures, for their part, somewhat eroded the authority of ecclesiastical tribunals by continuing to exercise autonomous jurisdiction over marriage, particularly regarding marital separations and offenses connected to the bonds of marriage and its definition, including adultery, bigamy, and rape.[9]

During the period under consideration, Venice experienced important institutional changes in both the civil and ecclesiastical realms. The definition of nobility became more limited through rigid rules of membership based on the purity of blood and legitimate birth. New legislative provisions related to marriage, dowries, and descent assigned women a pivotal role in the patrician family, denying fathers the possibility of guaranteeing through their own status the status of their children, whether legitimate or illegitimate.[10] It required the registration of patrician marriages at the Avogaria di Comun and declared that only sons born to parents whose marriages were registered in the Avogaria could be admitted to the Consiglio and therefore be eligible for a political career. The patrician class dealt with the problem of its own survival through matrimonial politics, but this could be threatened by the *mesalliances* favored by the ecclesiastical doctrine of consent, which required only the agreement of the couple to constitute a juridically valid marriage.[11]

In the same period the Venetian Church underwent changes as its bishopric became a patriarchate. Instituted in 1451, the patriarchate assumed jurisdiction over the parishes of the ancient marine diocese of Castello, to which was added the patriarchate of Grado under the guidance of Lorenzo Giustiniani.[12] The diocesan tribunal over which he presided, first as bishop of Castello and then as patriarch, was a consolidated structure, aware early on of its own role in marital conflicts. The records of these litigations are no longer entrusted to the notarial archives as they once were (and still are in other dioceses)[13] but are now jealously conserved within the registries of the curia, which mediated and documented its own activity.[14]

Jurisdiction over marriage offered the Church an exceptional instrument of social control starting from the nucleus of society itself, as it permitted the Church to have access to the most intimate personal sphere and influence the formation and dissolution of the family.[15] In Venice this jurisdiction extended in practice to all social classes: Venetian marriage causes involved the highest representatives of the nobility (who in other dioceses favored extrajudicial solutions to their conflicts), but also slaves, whose use of the tribunal is rarely documented elsewhere.[16] The presence of non-Catholic communities in Venice and the prevalence of immigration there make the activities of the patriarchal court particularly vivid. Its efficacy can be measured by its capacity to interact with multiple customary laws and to assume a flexible attitude towards liturgical experimentation, among other things.[17]

A study dedicated to the Venetian patriarchal tribunal is interesting not only for what makes it exceptional but also what makes it representative of other trends: not so much because the tribunal extended its jurisdiction over a city located at the center of international affairs, influencing its social and sometimes its political life (and being influenced by those same things in turn), but because it was representative both of diocesan tribunals more broadly (as a site of first judgment) and as a central institution of the Church (as a court of appeal).

Analyzing its *modus operandi* offers points of comparison that extend beyond Europe, as canon law guided the tribunal in Venice as in the rest of Catholic Europe, and was carried to and readapted in the New World. Even after the Protestant Reformation, it continued to be applied in the tribunals of reformed churches.[18] Beyond representing a "factor of unification for European law"[19] canon law inspired and contained elements of common law,[20] with which it shared flexibility, creativity, and versatility.[21]

In conducting this research, I have examined all types of sources relative to the management of marriage in the Venetian diocese – from pastoral visits to acts of the episcopal inquisition, from registers of the curia to synodal constitutions. Moreover, I have extended the field of inquiry to include the notarial records of the state archive, the documentation of some dioceses under the patriarch's jurisdiction, and the records of the Congregation of the Council preserved in the Vatican Secret Archives. But the main source base for the book is the series of matrimonial causes debated in the patriarchal curia. This book aims primarily to be a study of the history of this institution and its functions while at the same time examining the attitudes of those who sought its assistance. It therefore makes a contribution to the history of Venetian society and the history of mentalities. Rather than using only normative documents, it is primarily based on sources that combine the concrete actions of the tribunal and its users, thereby placing practices and norms in conversation with one another.

Analyzing the activity of the matrimonial tribunal allows us to paint a strongly representative picture of the interaction between a society and a juridical-institutional system. The Venetian documentation allows such analysis based on an extremely well-preserved collection, which I will briefly describe below.

1. The documentation related to matrimonial conflicts is conserved primarily in four series in the archive of the patriarchal curia.

    – The series *Causarum matrimonium*, an impressive source, preserves the records of individual marriage causes beginning in 1452. The individual causes are extraordinarily rich in both

quality[22] and quantity: there are about 1,000 litigations from 1452 to 1810.
- Other processual materials, which should be examined in context with the suits of *Causarum matrimonium*, are found in the series *Actorum, mandatorum, praeceptorum*, which contains registers of acts relevant to the litigations – mostly civil – discussed before the patriarchal curia (or, until 1451, the bishop of Castello). Marriage causes were included beginning in 1420.[23] This series is important because it allows one to identify a precise number of matrimonial conflicts that the ecclesiastical tribunal was called to settle, clarifying how many cases reached sentencing and how many began but were likely settled by an agreement between the parties. These registers also document cases in which parties approached the ecclesiastical tribunal but had no juridical justification for a matrimonial litigation. This helps us to understand the differences between lay and ecclesiastical conceptions of marriage. The *Actorum, mandatorum, praeceptorum* also allows for a detailed study of the procedural aspects of marriage litigations, providing a glimpse of the functioning of the ecclesiastical tribunal. It clarifies how many marital separations were *de facto*, in which the ecclesiastical judge simply reacted to the prior abandonment of one spouse, and how many were granted through a suit. As we will note, this allows for a reshaping and reinterpretation of how and why women resorted to the courts.[24]
- The series *Filciae causarum*, beginning in 1446, contains, among other things, acts of matrimonial causes, generally depositions of testimonies, and sometimes sentences.
- The series *Sententiarum*, starting in 1464, collects together the sentences of various litigations including sentences from marriage cases.

No work on Venetian marriage litigations has yet made use of all these series. The attention of scholars has thus far been directed at the cause records and the sentences; the registers of the curia have been almost completely ignored.[25]

2. The majority of Italian episcopal archives preserve ample collections of marriage litigations, collecting the records of conflicts between spouses from the late medieval through the early modern periods (i.e., the twelfth through eighteenth centuries).

For decades French- and English-language historiography has noted the relevance of these records for the history of the family, the history of mentalities, women's history, as well as for the history of institutions (e.g., ecclesiastical tribunals), the relationship between church and state, and for the history of law.[26] German historiography has also paid significant attention to these documents, originally as part of the history of reformed churches,[27] and later following social history by focusing on themes of female honor and the construction of gender identity,[28] emotions as a fundamental element of family life,[29] the status of women in Protestant families,[30] the control of sexuality as a key to the formation of the state,[31] or by comparing the *modus operandi* of Catholic and Protestant judges.[32] More recently, Christina Deutsch has analyzed the activity of the tribunal of Augsburg, while Ludwig Schmugge, in a study of the petitions addressed to the Apostolic Penitentiary of the Holy Roman Empire, has for the first time compared the *modus operandi* of certain local tribunals with those of the central institutions of Catholicism.[33]

Italian historiography has for the most part been reluctant to attribute the dignity long granted to political and economic topics of research to the private sphere and subjective subjects. It has only recently discovered the value of these documentary collections even though the Italian documentation is richer and more articulated than most of the transalpine records and could perhaps be equaled only by the Spanish collections.[34]

During the 1980s, growing interest in social history – particularly the history of the family, women's history, and gender history,[35] – as well as the renewed tension around the narrative aspects of history writing[36] helped to spark the interest among Italian historians in this type of source base.[37] Marriage litigations have formed the documentary foundation for works related to themes of honor,[38] the formation of the modern consciousness,[39] social discipline,[40] the dialogue between church and state on matters relating to marriage,[41] and female agency.[42] There were some historiographical precedents for these studies, though they were articles of limited scope, which focused above all on institutional history.[43]

In the last decade, as part of the project "The Marriage Cases of the Italian Ecclesiastical Archives" coordinated by Silvana Seidel Menchi and Diego Quaglioni (1996–2001), four volumes were published. The first three were dedicated to separation, pre-modern marriage, and cases with mixed fora (in which ecclesiastical and secular tribunals were equally competent). The fourth volume dealt with themes of marital norms, symbolism, and rituals; parental control and freedom of consent; sexuality; and the contractual and sacramental aspects of the marital bond, in comparison with the situation across the Alps.[44] Based on sources that privileged social practices, these contributions provide a counterpoint to the images of the agnatic family founded on the arranged and insoluble marriage presented by earlier historiography, which was primarily based on prescriptive and normative sources.[45]

Using the marriage cases of the ecclesiastical archive of Florence – placed in context with theological and juridical tracts – Daniela Lombardi has published a volume dedicated to the history of marriage from the late medieval period to the end of the eighteenth century. It analyzes the competition between church and state for control over the formation of couples and sheds light on the resistance put in by the faithful and of subjects to this form of discipline.[46] Joanne Ferraro has drawn from the causes for separation and annulment in Venice to tell the stories of these cases, which underline female agency in ending failed marriages. Following the psychologist Mary Gergen and Natalie Zemon Davis, Ferraro read the narratives of those involved in these suits as the fruit of reappropriation and re-elaboration of a cultural patrimony shared by the community.[47] Daniela Hacke's volume, also focused on Venice, analyzes the marriage politics of lay and ecclesiastical institutions and examines the use of gender by those who appealed to the Venetian tribunal.[48] Emlyn Eisenach, in her book on marriage litigations in Verona, examines the practices of concubinage, clandestine marriage, and the informal dissolution of marriage as they related to gender and social status.[49] Chiara La Rocca's book, dedicated to the phenomenon of separation in eighteenth-century Livorno, compares the practices followed by church and state, while Ermanno Orlando reconstructs, for the late medieval Veneto, the interaction between formal marriages and various other irregular or spurious behaviors, such as clandestine, fake, or mixed marriage.[50]

> 3. As the diversity of these studies attests, these documents allow for investigations of a multitude of fields. Many of these are completely or mostly unexplored but could be quite profitable.[51] These sources can have a disorienting effect precisely because of their richness. My work analyzes them from the point of view of the institution that produced them, since knowledge of the institution's *modus operandi* is necessary prior to a critical evaluation of the documentation and essential before proceeding to a comparative analysis.[52]

Beginning in the 1970s, historians developed a growing interest in judicial sources, aware that they permit access to sectors of society otherwise unavailable to researchers (like members of lower classes and women).[53] The growing use of trial documents was accompanied by a lively methodological debate. One side underscores the polyvalence of these sources and the need for an approach that "transcends" this, to avoid "a history of pragmatically-inspired crime."[54] The other side reiterates the documents' "natural and necessary function, which is to be first of all a source for its environment," a source base for the history of justice.[55] While one side affirms that the trial only constitutes a primary source for the institution that produced it,[56] the other insists that the trial can also provide information on the people the institution disciplined and repressed, and on the matters it regulated.[57] The structure of this book is based on the premise that, for marriage causes, these two methodological approaches are complementary.

Although they have been neglected by research, marriage litigations constitute the source base *par excellence* for the history of the ecclesiastical tribunal, especially in Italy, since they quantitatively and qualitatively represent one of the most significant aspects of the tribunal's activity.[58] These documents allow us to outline the characteristics of the institution; reconstruct the tribunal's organization and the suit's structure; analyze the methods of proceeding and determine the typology of cases subject to the tribunal's judgment; understand the tenor of sentences and the culture of the judges, including the ways in which they conceived of their role and valued their work; and probe the conformity or divergence between norms and practices.

In the Venetian case, the reconstruction of the tribunal's activity can take advantage of rare and precious documents: sentences that demonstrated the judge's reasoning. Although judges generally pronounced their verdict without mentioning the legal principles they were following, in exceptional cases they produced explanatory sentences, which revealed the logical path followed by the magistrate in question and mentioned the juridical authorities on which his decisions were founded. Such sentences help us to understand analogous cases and augment our logical and juridical instruments for the analysis of various causes.[59]

Far from documenting only deviation and marginality,[60] marriage litigations provide access to aspects of married life that are rarely documented and only revealed during a suit, when those who were called to testify on a controversial union placed it in the context with a sanctioned union.[61]

The stories told by these parties were often fine-tuned by legal experts who adapted them to the prescriptions of canon law to obtain a favorable sentence. The fact that litigation sources are codified as are all other sources does not imply that they preclude access to the reality of marriage. During the suit entire networks of relatives and neighbors were called to testify and evaluate the controversial union compared to customary parameters, which had great value as evidence for the tribunal. Both the witnesses and the parties involved in the cause often restated a conception of marriage and of the couple's relationship that contrasted with the type of marriage advocated by the Church, expecting that the magistrate's sentences would conform to them. As a result, these documents constitute not only an important source for the study of the marriage tribunal but also for the history of marriage.[62] My work progressively shifts attention from the tribunal to the people involved, from the suit to the matters that it investigated. This analysis will take into account the dialogic nature of the sources and investigate conflicts between the ecclesiastical hierarchy's conception of marriage and the more versatile lay conception of marriage. What will emerge is a much more fluid image of marriage than has been outlined by the historiography of marriage in Italy, which has privileged the use of normative sources and has taken as a principle object of study the marriage of the ruling classes.[63] This type of marriage was monolithic and celebrated in a precise moment; it was the fruit of familial alliances,[64] was monogamous and indissoluble, and was "the exclusive place for the exercise of sexuality and legitimate procreation." With respect to this image the previous historiography has defined phenomena like bigamy, concubinage, and "rape" (*stuprum* – in its juridical significance of the defloration of a virgin or the seduction of an honest widow, even with consent)[65] as transgressive experiences, thereby imposing a rigid post-Tridentine and moral classification on a relational and emotional universe characterized by flexibility, adaptability, and experimentation.[66]

Avoiding moral classifications taken from the decrees of the Council of Trent, I propose to reread the experiences of bigamy, concubinage, and "rape" in their actual social manifestation and to analyze the perceptions of these transgressions held – or more often not held – by the users of the tribunal and the community to which they belonged.[67]

4. The inclusion of marriage causes in international social history has a strong foundation thanks to Lawrence Stone's work on England. The narrative structure of two of his widely circulated monographs

has been influential.[68] Stone has declared the work of the historian to be restoring life to the past, a responsibility that, for him, justifies the practice of narrative history.[69]

The narrative potential of marriage causes has led some historians to use these sources to reconstruct suggestive case studies,[70] sometimes without taking account of their historical[71] and juridical[72] context. The extrapolation of a single case from its legal context, in particular, has been subjected to methodological criticisms that have influenced more recent work.[73] Critics warn against a naïve approach to the sources, inviting scholars to consider the legal elements of the case as well.[74]

This appropriate methodological warning sometimes gives way to a general affirmation of the discursive nature of litigation sources and a simple negation of a "sharp dividing line between history and fiction."[75] This approach is more defeatist than critical. It avoids the analysis and critique of the source base in relation to the institution that produced it rather than creating a methodology. It also satisfies itself with speculating about the reasoning of the litigation and the decisions of the magistrates even when they are documentable and legally motivated. This indiscriminately extends the range of historical possibilities in play by hiding behind the unattainability of the truth.

The 750 litigations I have analyzed lend themselves to telling captivating and often dramatic stories, but I read them in context, aiming to reconstruct the tribunal's *modus operandi*. When I use a single case, I choose it because it is representative, and I use it to reconstruct the historical context.

By analyzing the procedures that structure the cause as a document, I propose first of all to develop methodological instruments for the hermeneutics of these sources. I use both the documents and their lacunae to reconstruct the activity of the tribunal. I seek to interpret the significance of a document's preservation in the archives, the failure to have produced a document at all, as well as a document's destruction. The premise of this way of proceeding is that a "fact" does not exist solely as a text.

5. Renata Ago and Simona Cerutti have stressed that studies of the history of justice have focused above all on criminal trials and examined its procedure only in relation to proof, integrating themselves into a tradition of studies about the rights of the accused.[76] Social historians have used judicial documentation in ways that privilege

themes of repression and social control or themes of deviance or popular culture.[77] They have generally ignored procedural aspects of trials, considering them undeserving of specific treatment if not obstacles to research altogether.[78] Only recently has trial procedure become an object of study in itself in "new social history," which is interested in the interactions between individuals and institutions more than in conflict, repression, and the disciplining of deviance.[79]

In this work, the procedure of marriage suits is considered imperative for understanding the dialogues between judges and users of the tribunal and between the ecclesiastical hierarchy and the faithful. The judge's active or passive attitude during the cause, the spontaneous, mediated, or forced appearance of the parties and witnesses in court, the requests made to the magistrates, the parties' willingness to respect the ecclesiastical judge's dictates and their capacity to influence his decisions, the arrangement of the sentences and the payment of litigation costs, and the adoption or the suspension of punitive measures on the part of the tribunal – all of these determine the tone of this dialogue. Judges and users actively participated in, and contributed to, the creation of the juridical system in which they acted.[80]

6. In the dialogue between judges and users of the tribunal women were privileged interlocutors.[81] It is often emphasized that trial records constitute one of the few source bases capable of restoring the voices of women to historians, albeit "distorted by the structure of the interrogation and the pen of the notary." Women otherwise risk being members of "a silent group," particularly if they were part of the lower social classes, who rarely left anything they wrote themselves.[82]

The recovery of female voices happens in a particular manner during a marriage litigation, not only because the procedure allowed for ample female testimony (unlike other suits)[83] but also because when judges conducted interrogations they generally chose to question the woman.[84] In particular, this happened when the vicar found himself confronted with young girls, often with children, who were strongly influenced by familial pressures. On such occasions the magistrate sought to establish a dialogue with the young woman, to gain her trust and shorten the distance between them. He addressed the young people with a familiar tone, often calling them by name; he invited them to abandon "any respect"[85]; and he proposed the relief that sincerity would bring[86] or else threatened a destiny of eternal damnation.[87] He might interrogate the young women in different places and times.[88] He presented himself as knowledgeable of the pressures to which they were subjected, disclosing his own suspicions,[89] and probing their inclinations, — asking one bride claimed by two husbands, for example, with whom she would rather stay.[90] The girls sometimes revealed their souls to the vicar, though only in exceptional cases did they avail themselves of the possibility offered by the tribunal to follow their own inclination to escape their family's wishes. The procedures adopted by Venetian patriarchs to remove children from familial influence, the tone chosen by vicars when they interrogated young wives, and the tricks used to encourage women to express their own choices or preferences reflect anxieties of conformity,[91] infantile trepidations,[92] and fears of abandonment[93] that the tribunal sought to combat – usually in vain – in the name of free expression of nuptial consent and in the end to gain better control over marriage.

7. The interpretation of marriage litigations in terms of women's history and gender history, stimulated by Anglo-American historiography, has been fully absorbed by lively debates over the Italian sources. The (often female) interventions in these debates have pushed historians to interpret these sources in terms of agency, rather than through the lens of victimization common to the historiography of the 1970s and 1980s.[94]

Such an interpretive approach is not only encouraged by the quantitative aspects of female initiative. The female protagonists of these causes used multiple strategies, making informed and sometimes unscrupulous use of the law and constructing an image of themselves that respected or transgressed conventional canons of the honest and fragile woman. One woman faced three consecutive suits over the validity of her marriage after the death of her husband to ensure the legitimate succession for her children.[95] Another battled strenuously to obtain recognition of her marriage to a man from whom she had already separated in order to obtain the restitution of her dowry.[96] A courtesan used her dense network of relations to prevent her husband and brother-in-law from taking possession of her rich inheritance, using her own reputation to demonstrate that she had been involved with her husband's brother before the marriage to obtain an annulment on the basis of incest. Afterward, she changed strategies and dressed in the clothes of a "good and obedient daughter" before secular magistrates to contest her mother's will who had disinherited her in favor of her own sister.[97]

Many of the protagonists of the causes analyzed in this book challenge the image of the "kept woman " presented by pastoral literature.[98] They were often resourceful organizers of their own marriages, autonomous workers,[99] young women ready to get out of unions imposed by their relatives or capable of fleeing from the convent,[100] and youths free to go out unaccompanied to attend parties and balls according to their own desires.[101] Even the attitude they assumed in court revealed their strong personalities. The obstinate refusal of one young woman to present herself in court and the reaction of another described by the notary as "audacious" when the magistrate exhorted her to respect the promise of an unpleasant marriage support the positions of those who see the birth of individuality in conflict, resistance, and refusal.[102]

The historiography seeking to overturn the image of women as victims by instead exalting their initiative and creativity, however, risks overlooking the fact that these things were principally "reactive solutions" in a system where negative elements of the female condition were real and prevalent.[103] For each girl who took the chance offered by the tribunal to continue in a marriage she wanted but was undesirable to her family, there were many more who were passively inclined to submit to the will of their families. The episodes that are exemplary of female will and individuality do deserve to be mentioned and analyzed, however, as they illuminate the development of "hidden possibilities,"[104] the range of solutions and strategies which were historically possible, even if they were not often used.

8. Giulia Calvi has underlined how the use of categories that historians of gender have borrowed from anthropology – categories such as strategies, mediation, networks of relations, and so on, – has contributed to "construct a historiography of consent and not of conflict."[105] In this interpretive lens the tribunal is considered as an instrument users could take advantage of rather than as an instrument of control and/or repression in the hands of authorities.

Many historians have argued that women primarily used ecclesiastical tribunals to protect their own interests and well-being because they found allies and protectors in the ecclesiastical magistrates.[106] This may be true above all in suits for separation, in which a clear majority of causes (it should be noted) were initiated by women.[107] This position must be contextualized with quantitative data, which demonstrates the prevalence of male success in court.[108] They must also be reread in light of the *favor matrimonii*, the juridical principle that was supposed to guide the magistrates' decisions during the acquisition of evidence and at the moment he issued the sentence.

The data relative to the prevalence of suits initiated by females in cases of separation, which in Venetian studies has been gleaned only from the litigation records,[109] is here corrected and reinterpreted in light of the curial registers. These registers document phases of conflict preceding, or alternative to, a suit, such as orders issued by the vicar at the request of the abandoned spouse to restore cohabitation. Separation causes generally began with these mandates from the vicar. Only in a few cases did women respond to the tribunal's injunction by requesting a judicial proceeding. Based on the new documentation examined here, female-initiated suits do not represent recourse to a philo-female authority, but rather reaction of a clearly dominant masculine judicial initiative, which itself was caused by the woman's unquantifiable extrajudicial action – the abandonment of the marital house.[110]

The norms of canon law are formally structured around traditional categories of gender, according to which the models of accusation and defense were formed in the tribunal.[111] But insofar as Christianity ideally ignores the category of gender, canonical norms should have valued men and women equally, as lawyers did not hesitate to stress (in favor of the party they represented).[112] In this work I propose to determine to what extent the dominant categories of gender influenced the magistrates' decisions and to what extent they were instead nullified by the potentially sanctioning force of canon law. The picture that emerges corresponds, in part, to dominant social constructions (in the case, for example, of female fragility (*fragilitas sexus*), and in part it strongly contrasts with them (as in the very rare cases of separation for male adultery).[113]

9. With regards to criminal justice, Mario Sbriccoli has emphasized the distinction between a "negotiated" justice – based on community membership, regulated by the norms and practices shared by this community, and ending with reparations and oral agreements – and a "hegemonic" or "bureaucratic" justice – responding to laws pro-

duced by an authority, based on subjection, finishing with the punishment of the guilty and being formalized in writing. For Ancien Regime society, only the first type of solution for conflicts – the combination of practices constituted by strongly ritualized vendetta and retaliation,[114] renunciations, peace, pardons, accords, and remissions[115] – was capable of effectively rendering justice (rendering the commonly used term "infrajustice" inappropriate[116]). The justice of the state apparatuses was considered "residual,"[117] to the point that it sometimes followed the rituality of vindictive justice to make itself more acceptable.[118]

This book aims to determine whether, and to what extent, the marriage tribunal was considered by its users as an expression of community justice or instead as an institution extraneous to the community that inserted itself into their lives and their rules to influence, modify, and control them.[119]

I argue that the institution analyzed here was an expression of mixed justice, which assumed a particular judicial character according to the individual case and the marital problem under investigation (the magistrate's attitude, for example, was different when he had to adjudicate presumed marriage or separation). This mixed nature particularly characterized the period considered here, which constituted a moment of transition between a phase in which the tribunal was primarily one of the actors of negotiated justice to a phase in which it became a creator and instrument of hegemonic justice. This transition altered the procedure and stabilized the responsibilities of the tribunal, even reducing the functions that were its own and assigning the repression of new crimes and new sins to new institutions, while the roles that originally belonged to both judges and confessors were restricted to the exclusive realm of the confessor.[120] Some of the elements that distinguished the first phase – in particular the adoption of the summary procedure, the *arbitrium* of the judge, and the recourse to the mediation of friars and parish priests – constitute elements that made the passage from one type of justice to the other possible.[121]

Just as with negotiated justice, the jurisdiction of the marriage tribunal rested on consensus, as the suit began at the request of the parties. By means of the doctrine of reserved cases – that is, those sins (among which were some regarding marriage) which could only be absolved by a bishop – the Church laid the foundation to force couples to present themselves in court.[122]

In the pre-Tridentine age confession was not particularly common and, the Easter requirement notwithstanding, it remained in the end a voluntary act the faithful could undertake before a priest of their own choosing.[123] Those who practiced it could be induced to present themselves to the vicar for the resolution of their marital disputes. The confessor became a mediator between the parties as well as between them and the tribunal, for the most part still respecting the rules of the community.[124] After the Council of Trent the Church started an aggressive policy to impose and spread confession,[125] indoctrinating the secular clergy[126] and seeking to educate them to lead a lifestyle that would distinguish them from their flocks.[127] Without formally changing the voluntary character of recourse to the ecclesiastical court in cases of matrimonial conflict, they appeared to make this recourse obligatory thanks to the intervention of confessors, whom the faithful could not avoid without falling under the suspicion of heresy.[128]

In the pre-Tridentine period, the subject of marriage was managed according to various juridical systems that intertwined, interacted, and often collided. Canon law, which is already a multifaceted law on its own, had to face lay statutory laws and unwritten laws backed by custom.[129] In judging a controversial union, a judge could assume the role of arbitrator conferred on him by the community and make himself the interpreter. He could do this while respecting canon law, which assigned significant evidentiary value to local customs, considering clues and presumptions (that is, artificial proof) of marriage.[130]

Institutionally, the judge had two instruments at his disposal to make himself the interpreter of the community's voice: the summary procedure and the *arbitrium*. When interpreted through the lens of an Enlightenment critique, which are interested in defending the supremacy of the law and defining crime and punishment, the summary procedure and *arbitrium* have a strongly negative connotation in scholarship primarily interested in criminal trials. They are associated with a justice that acts in secret with inquisitorial procedures, sacrificing the rights of the accused at the discretion of the judge; it is described as a system of justice that avoided recourse to lawyers, limited the number of witnesses, and left ample space for oral exposition.[131] In a civil trial, which did not presume a criminal opposite an examining judge but was configured as "an act of three people" (the parties and the judge),[132] the summary procedure represented a simplification of the ordinary procedure, which was even accessible to those who were not legal professionals. The Church created an abbreviated ritual prompted by the cases submitted to its jurisdiction. The legislation relative to the summary process, fixed in 1306 with Clement V's decretals *Saepe* and *Dispendiosam*, sanctioned the formal recognition of a process which was quite common at the local level.[133]

In a marriage litigation the summary procedure could coincide with the ordinary procedure and be applied only in certain phases of the proceedings, making it flexible and therefore accessible to the users of the tribunal. This use of the summary process was the institutional response to specific needs of the community. It provided access to those normally deprived of juridical capacity (minors, slaves, excommunicates).[134] It was begun with a request from the parties, who could invoke it to avoid the delays and costs of an ordinary proceeding, and it assumed an informal structure similar to that of an arbitrated case, giving a judge deemed acceptable by the parties ample space to make a decision. This happened more frequently when the case was delegated to a parish priest, as he was better able to guide the mediation between two disputants who came from the same community that had elected him.[135]

The *arbitrium* is the instrument that places juridical ideals and practical realities in conversation.[136] Common law is a system based on "juridical pluralism," a term that designates the coexistence of different sets of norms each having their own legitimacy and distinct contents,[137] and of varying conceptions of what is right and the modes for affirming it.[138] The scope of justice is not to reduce the plurality of norms to unity but to harmonize them: elements of each of system are understood more as "prospective solutions to the case" than as precepts. Things not defined by the law are referred to the judges, who should select the norms most appropriate among those at their disposal for the case before them, "furnishing an arbitral solution that can come as close as possible to creating harmony."[139] To this end the judge should avoid altering certain norms on the basis of others and abide by the *stylus curiae*, that is the procedure of the tribunal in similar cases.[140] In the end, norms adapt to practices, and the court's procedures become norms.

As we have noted, the matters related to marriage were not only regulated by canon law but also by written and unwritten customary norms. Regarding the stipulation of the marital bond, the Church, although recommending the publication of the union above all through a priest's blessing, recognized that the simple consent of the bride and groom had the power to effect a marriage, without the need for precise formalities.[141] Anyone who wanted to prove the celebration of a marriage could often only do this indirectly, through evidence and presumptions: he should demonstrate the expression of consent according to a customary ritual, or rather attest to having experienced with his partner a union considered nuptial according to the community and class-specific standards of affection.[142] Evidence and presumptions constituted artificial proof of marriage, which did not guarantee the decisions of the magistrate but were to be valued according to his *arbitrium*. The judge could then choose to make himself a spokesman for the community by declaring valid a marriage that the community validated, thus reconciling canonical norms and customary law, or he could intervene in customary practices to censure them and affirm a law extraneous to the community.

In the pre-Tridentine period, guided by *favor matrimonii*, the judge would most often choose to reconcile customary and canon law, especially in cases regarding the verification of nuptial consent.[143] The Tridentine dispositions established legislation relative to marriage and imposed a single ritual on the marital celebration, thus depriving the law of the Church of its own jurisprudential creativity[144] and the judge's *arbitrium* of the necessary space to explain itself.

The scope of the marriage suit was not to punish a crime but to determine the existence of a bond or the legitimacy of a separation – ideally, to guide the course of publicizing a union that was useful for public order, to restore cohabitation, or to avoid separation.[145] Many procedures did not end with a sentence.[146] This fact is not necessarily due to a lack of documentation (which is the case in a minority of causes) but rather is because it was possible to reach an accord between the parties, a desirable end for the litigation.[147] The consensual solution of the disagreement did not impair the efficiency of the tribunal but testified on the contrary to its capabilities in the realm of mediation, aimed at social concord.[148] The suit constituted one aspect of a negotiation to resolve a conflict without a sentence, which could aggravate the conflict if it did not represent the bureaucratic sanction of an agreement between the parties.[149]

When the sentence was pronounced, the *arbitrium* of the judge became relevant with respect to the *aequitas canonica*, which called for a flexible application of the law and even, if necessary, for the law not to be applied in consideration of human fragility (*humanae fragilitates*).[150] This happened, for example, when the judge pronounced his own verdict based on intentions rather than proof after having personally interrogated a girl, or when he exempted someone who was unknowingly part of a double marriage, from paying the cause expenses.[151] Only the perception of socially transgressive behavior induced the judge to greater severity: a man guilty of having publicly married three women in a short period of time was punished severely, while a woman who had contracted a second marriage was treated benevolently because of "womanly fragility" (*fragilitas sexus*), her reverential fear of her relatives, and her presumed ignorance of the norms.[152] This *modus operandi* conforms to negotiated justice, which acts with severity only when faced with the incorrigible or recidivist.[153]

The question of whether the judge expressed the voice of the community or if he made himself the interpreter of bureaucratic justice does not have a single answer. The material handled in court cannot be approached in a single manner. The action of the magistrates should always have been guided by *favor matrimonii*, which resulted in different methods of dealing with cases of betrothal or pretended marriage compared to those of separation or annulment. While in cases of pretended marriage magistrates often adopted the parameters of customary law, which the users and witnesses fought for strongly in court, in cases of the dissolution of marriage the lay and ecclesiastical conceptions were irreconcilable. To end an unpleasant marriage the users of the tribunal had to adhere strictly to the theory of impediments developed by the canonists, which meant that the motivations given in court rarely corresponded with the real reasons for the litigation.

The community into which the tribunal's jurisdiction extended was socially heterogenous and differently open to the mandates of canon law. This often varied with regards to class and gender: the doctrine of consent only required the consent of the spouses for a valid marriage, a principle that extended to all marriages – including any socially unequal ones or *mesalliances* – and gave children the ability to marry even if their relatives disapproved of it. Proud noble families considered these unions as an affront equal to that of a homicide, and by civil laws these unions constituted a crime punishable by loss of dowry, disownment, and jail. Canon law considered both female and male adultery as valid reasons for separation, but the two offenses were not considered equal in the rules of the community. The office of judge was in the middle of legal systems that were different and often irreconcilable. My work seeks to recover that tension.

This volume is divided into two main sections, followed by an appendix (Chap. 6) that presents the quantitative results of my research. The first section (Chaps. 2 and 3) concerns the organization of the tribunal. The second chapter is dedicated to the procedure of the litigation and the methods of acquiring proof. As marriage causes gave precedence to testimonial proof, this constitutes the subject of the third chapter, which examines the methods of deposition and record-keeping, and the criteria by which the admissibility and credibility of witnesses were determined. It discusses the objective criteria tied most often to gender, status, and age, or relative to this, the criteria related to the connections that linked witnesses to the parties in the cause (including kinship, patronage, friendship, or enmity), which were valued differently based on the status of those who presented them to testify.

The second section (Chaps. 4 and 5) is dedicated to the dialogue between judges and users of the tribunal regarding the subject of matrimony. The fourth chapter examines the office of the judge, including his role as mediator and also as confessor and inquisitor. The assumption of one role or another implied different conceptions of truth (internal or external to the suit) and the assumption of the responsibility for the litigation's development on the part of the judge, or its assignment to the parties. The fifth chapter analyzes the conceptions of marriage held by the ecclesiastical hierarchy and by the laity, concentrating in particular on the question of consent. My analysis emphasizes the changes that the Council of Trent imposed on a centuries-old marriage practice, relegating it to the experience of marginality and deviance.

Notes

1. "Solennemente," "pudica domicella," "in nome della santa Trinità Padre, Fiol, et Spirito Sancto, della gloriosa Verzene Maria e de tutta la corte celestial." A copy of the contract is conserved among the acts of the matrimonial cause cited in note 3. The original acts of the notary who drafted the document are available in ASV, Notarile Atti, b. 2555, notary Daniele Zordan.
2. F. Barbaro, *De re uxoria liber in partes duas*. The necessary reference regarding the Venetian nobility and its familial politics is S. Chojnacki, *Women and Men*.
3. ASPV, *CM*, vol. 17, Marietta Barbaro *vs* Francesco Giustinian, 1516 and ASPV, *FC*, vol. 2.
4. R. Helmholz, *Marriage Litigation*; F. Pederson, *Marriage Disputes in Medieval England*; A. Lefebvre Teillard, *Les officialités a la veille du Concile de Trente*; C. Deutsch, *Ehegerichtsbarkeit im Bistum Regensburg*; also, for a comparison of the procedures of English

tribunals and those in the Franco-Belgian region, see C. Donahue Jr., *Law, Marriage and Society*.
5. J. Gaudemet, *Il matrimonio in Occidente*, p. 106; M. Maccarone, *Nuovi studi su Innocenzo III*, pp. 47–8, 108–10.
6. C. Donahue, *Law, Marriage and Society*, pp. 41–2.
7. See *infra*, ch. 4, § 2.
8. See *infra*, ch. 5, § 4, and, in particular, the document cited there in note 101.
9. In Venice four magistratures had jurisdiction over marital issues. The Avogaria di Comun in conjunction with the Quarantia Criminale focused on violations of adultery, bigamy, and pre-matrimonial sexuality. The Giudici del Procurator fixed the alimony for separated wives and ended up decreeing separations, eroding the jurisdiction of the patriarchal curia. Beginning in 1577, the Esecutori sopra la Bestemmia assumed jurisdiction for the offense of seduction following a promise of marriage. See G. Cozzi, *Note e documenti sulla questione del «divorzio»*. On the activity of the Giudici del Procurator see A. Rigo, *Interventi dello Stato veneziano nei casi di separazione*. On the jurisdiction of the Esecutori contro la Bestemmia on charges of seduction with promise of marriage, see G. Derosas, *Moralità e giustizia a Venezia nel '500–'600*, pp. 431–528.
10. See the bibliography cited *infra*, note 11. For legitimation in common law, see T. Kuehn, *Illegitimacy in Renaissance Florence*, pp. 49–59.
11. S. Chojnacki, *Women and Men*, pp. 53–75. But Venice had a policy of reintegrating illegitimate daughters of the nobles, who were among the most favored candidates among those who asked the Avogaria di Comun for permission to marry Venetian patricians in deference to the laws of the Republic. Natural sons born of relations with concubines frequently came to be accepted as citizens. This allowed them to enter the bureaucracy at very high levels or to work as notaries. See A. Cowan, *Marriage, Manners and Mobility in Early Modern Venice*.
12. On the passage of the see of Castello to the patriarchate of Venice, see S. Tramontin, *Dall'episcopato castellano al patriarcato veneziano*. On the patriarchate see P. Prodi, *The Structure and Organization of the Church in Renaissance Venice*. On Lorenzo Giustiniani, G. Cracco, *Il periodo vicentino di San Lorenzo Giustinani*; Idem, *Prefazione*, pp. 4–7 and *Esperienze di vita canonicale*; S. Tramontin (ed.),

Venezia e Lorenzo Giustiani; P.H. Labalme, *Religious Devotion;* F. Cavazzana Romanelli, *Leggere i santi entro la storia.* Regarding the patriarchate of Grado, which had under its jurisdiction the Venetian parishes of San Silvestro (where the patriarch of Grado lived), San Matteo di Rialto, S. Giacomo dell'Orio, S. Bartolomeo, San Canciano and San Martino, see also ASPV, *Patriarcato di Grado, Atti,* b. 1 and F. Cavazzana Romanelli, *Archivio storico del Patriarcato di Venezia,* pp. 286, 294; A. Niero, *Dal patriarcato di Grado al patriarcato di Venezia;* D. Rando, *Una chiesa di frontiera,* pp. 21–34, 73–98; and E. Orlando, *Tribunali di curia.*

13. See Orlando *Tribunali di curia,* where the author analyzes some fragments of processes from the thirteenth and fourteenth centuries discovered in the notarial series of the Archivio di Stato di Venezia, in particular p. 139 for the citation. In the Florentine diocese matrimonial cases of the fourteenth century are probably conserved among the papers of ecclesiastical notaries, as is the case in the trial studied by G. Brucker, *Giovanni and Lusanna.*
14. See *infra,* § 1. For marriage litigations within the register of the curia in Asti, see E. C. Pia, *La giustizia del vescovo,* pp. 101–119.
15. Significant examples are in ASPV, *CM,* vol. 9, Michele Leoni *vs* Faustina Foscarin, 1507; ASPV, *CM,* vol. 7, Andrea de Ballinio da Brixia *vs* Helisabeth filia Petri de Flandria, 1504, and in P. Scaramella, *Il matrimonio legato.* See also *infra,* ch. 4, in particular § 7.
16. The only marriage causes to my knowledge that involve slaves are those cited by P. Erdö, *Eheprozesse im mittelalterlichen Ungarn,* which mentions some annullment cases on the basis of servile condition; C. Donahue Jr., *Law, Marriage and Society,* p. 113; R. Helmholz, *Marriage Litigation,* pp. 212–4; and ASV, CC, *Synopsis,* vol. 2, c. 77 (1698). Regarding the nobility's presence in the tribunal, Venice is different from the example of Florence, where the nobility did not resort to the episcopal tribunal: see D. Lombardi, *Matrimoni di Antico Regime.* On the generalized tendency of the nobility to avail itself of extrajudicial solutions to conflicts, see O. Niccoli, *Storie di ogni giorno in una città del Seicento,* pp. 153–172.
17. On the celebration of marriage on the part of a Jew, for example, see *infra,* ch. 5, § 1. Roni Weinstein offers many brief comparisons with hebraic ritual in *Marriage Rituals Italian Style.* For inter-confessional and interfaith commingling in Venice see E. Orlando,

Mixed Marriages. The presence of Greek Orthodox Christians in Venice influenced both the nuptial ritual and the ritual of the litigation (relative to the issuance of oaths): see respectively *infra*, ch. 5, § 1 and ch. 4, § 8. Regarding the relationship between plural marriage and immigration and geographic mobility see *infra*, ch. 5, § 3. On the Greek community and church in Venice see M.I. Manussacas, *La comunità greca e gli arcivescovi di Filadelfia*.

18. R. Helmholz, *Roman Canon Law*; J. Harrington, *Reordering Marriage*; and P. Prodi, *Una storia della giustizia*, in particular chapters 5–6, pp. 219–324. Regarding the colonies see P. Latasa, *La celebración del matrimonio*; also B. Albani, *In universo christiano orbe*. Regarding the process of adaptation of canon law to the realities of the New World and to the reformed lands, see P. Broggio – C. de Castelnau-L'Estoile – G. Pizzorusso (eds.), *Administrer les sacraments*.
19. A.M. Hespanha, *Introduzione alla storia del diritto europeo*, p. 106.
20. Ibid., p. 110 and note 18 and 19. On the influence of the Church in the history of penal trials, see G. Alessi, *Il processo penale*.
21. P. Grossi, *L'ordine giuridico medievale*, p. 13.
22. See the preceding paragraph.
23. ASPV, *AMP*, b. 1, fragments of matrimonial causes up to the final decades of the fourteenth century conserved in a non-serial manner.
24. See *infra*, § 7 and *infra*, ch. 6.
25. Regarding work on Venice see J. Ferraro, *The Power to Decide*; Eadem, *Coniugi Nemici;* Eadem, *Marriage Wars*; D. Hacke, "Non lo volevo per marito in alcun modo"; Eadem, *La promessa disattesa;* Eadem, *Von der Wirkungsmächtigkeit des Heiligen;* Eadem, *Women, Sex and Marriage;* V. Hunecke, *Der venezianische Adel;* S. Chojnacki, *Il divorzio di Cateruzza;* Idem, *Valori patrizi nel tribunale patriarcale*. Chojnacki's work has also made use of the *AMP*, but he looks at a restricted number of cases, related only to the nobility. Also Hacke and E. Orlando, *Sposarsi nel medioevo*, has used this documentation as a sample.
26. See, beyond the bibliography cited *supra*, note 4: R. Houlbrooke, *Church Courts*; L. Stone, *Road to Divorce*; Idem, *Uncertain Unions*; J. Bailey, *Unquiet Lives*; B. Capp, *When Gossip Meet*; Idem, *Live, Love and Litigation;* T. Stretton, *Marital Litigation*, B. Gottlieb, *The Meaning of Clandestine Marriage*; A. Lottin, *La désunion du*

couple; J.L. Flandrin, *Les amours paysannes*; J.R. Farr, *Authority and Sexuality*. See also S. McDougall, *The Punishment of Bigamy*; Eadem, *Bigamy*.
27. W. Köhler, *Zürcher Ehegericht und Genfer Consistorium*.
28. S. Burghartz, *Jungfräulichkeit oder Reinheit?* Eadem, *Geschlecht, Körper, Ehre*; Eadem, *Zeiten der Reinheit*; R. Van Dülmen, *Tribunali matrimoniali*; S. Mohle, *Ehekonflikte und sozialer Wandel*.
29. J.R. Watt, *The Making of Modern Marriage*.
30. L. Roper, *The Holy Household*.
31. U. Sibeth, *Eherecht und Staatsbildung*; U. Strasser, *State of Virginity*.
32. T.M. Safley, *Let No Man Put Asunder*.
33. See the bibliography of C. Deutsch cited above, note 4, also L. Schmugge, *Ehen vor Gericht*.
34. Early attention to the private and subjective spheres in Italian historiography was undertaken by L. Accati – V. Maher – G. Pomata (eds.), *Parto e maternità*. The richness of the Spanish sources is reflected in F.J. Lorenzo Pinar, *Amores inciertos*; Idem, *Actitudes violentas*; *Conflictivedad social*; Idem, *La mujer y el tribunal diciocesano*; M.J. Campo Guinea, *Comportamientos matrimoniales*; A. Dyer, *Seduction by Promise of Marriage*; R. Barahona, *Sex, Crimes, Honour*; J.M. Usunáriz, *"Volved ya la riendas, porque no os perdáis"*; Idem, *El matrimonio y su reforma*; Idem, *El matrimonio como ejercicio de libertad*; Idem, *Marriage and Love*; E. Porqueres I Gené, *L'autonomia dei figli minorenni*; and M.I. Falcón Perez, *"Processos per causas matrimoniales."* M. Charageat, *"La delinquence matrimoniale*.
35. Among the first works that approached the history of women and gender on a theoretical level were M. Zimbalist Rosaldo – L. Lamphere (eds.), *Women, Culture and Society*; G. Rubin, *The Traffic in Women*; N. Zemon Davis, *Women's History in Transition*; R. Radford Ruether, *Sexism and God Talk*; J. Kelly, *Women, History and Theory*; and J. Scott, *Gender*. Regarding the historical and anthropological studies of the family and marriage, among the first to appear between the late 1960s and 1980s were F. Robin, *Kinship and Marriage*; J.L. Flandrin, *Parenté, maison, sexualité*; M. Mitterauer – R. Sieder, *Vom Patriarchat zur Partnerschaft*; D. Herlihy-C. Klapisch Zuber, *Tuscans and their Families*; M. Anderson, *Approaches to the History of the Western Family*; G. Duby, *Le chevalier, la femme, et le prêtre*; A. Borguière, *Histoire de*

la famille; J. Goody, *The Development of the Family;* G. Delille, *Famille et propriété;* and D. Herlihy, *Medieval Households.*
36. L. Stone, *The Revival of Narrative.* The narrative potential of the Italian marriage litigations found an early proponent in G. Corazzol-L. Corrà, *Esperimenti d'amore.*
37. For an ample panoramic of research on Italian marriage and a comparison with the relevant research in English, German, and French, see S. Seidel Menchi, *I processi matrimoniali come fonte storica.*
38. S. Cavallo-S. Cerutti, *Onore femminile.*
39. O. di Simplicio, *Peccato, penitenza, perdono.*
40. L. Ferrante, *La sessualità come risorsa;* Eadem, *Differenza sociale e differenza sessuale;* Eadem, *Il matrimonio disciplinato;* Eadem, *Il valore del corpo;* Eadem, *Legittima concubina.*
41. D. Lombardi, *Il matrimonio;* see also Eadem, *Intervention by Church and State;* Eadem, *Fidanzamenti e matrimoni.*
42. See the bibliography of D. Hacke, J. Ferraro, S. Chojnacki cited *supra,* note 25.
43. P. Rasi, *L'applicazione delle norme del Concilio di Trento,* and Idem, *La conclusione del matrimonio;* G. Cozzi, *Padri, figli e matrimoni clandestini;* Idem, *Il dibattito sui matrimoni clandestini;* Idem, *Note e documenti sulla questione del «divorzio».*
44. See the bibliography cited *supra,* notes 25 and 28; also S. Seidel Menchi-S. Quaglioni (eds.), *Coniugi nemici;* Iidem, *Matrimoni in dubbio;* iidem, *Trasgressioni;* iidem, *I tribunali del matrimonio.*
45. I will limit myself to citing M. Barbagli – D. Kertzer, *Storia della famiglia in Europa* and the considerations of G. Pomata, *Family and Gender.*
46. D. Lombardi, *Matrimoni di Antico Regime.*
47. J.M. Ferraro, *Marriage Wars;* M. Gergen, *The Social Construction of Personal Histories;* and N. Zemon Davis, *Fiction in the Archives.*
48. D. Hacke, *Women, Sex and Marriage.*
49. E. Eisenach, *Marriage, Family, and Social Order.*
50. C. La Rocca, *Tra moglie e marito;* E. Orlando, *Sposarsi nel medioevo.*
51. For the fields of inquiry that seem most promising to me, see *infra,* ch. 7.
52. The necessity of an approach to the matrimonial causes that gives attention to the procedural aspects with the aim of making comparative analysis possible is emphasized by D. Lombardi, *Matrimoni di*

Antico Regime, p. 12. Donahue's volume, cited *supra* in note 4, constitutes an exemplary work of comparative analysis.
53. A. Blauert-G. Schwerhoff, *Vorbemerkungen.*
54. E. Grendi, *Per lo studio della storia criminale,* and *Premessa.*
55. M. Sbriccoli, *Fonti giudiziare e fonti giuridiche.* To Sbriccoli's article, in relation to the contributions of Grendi mentioned *supra,* note 54, follows E. Grendi, *Sulla «storia criminale».*
56. A. Del Col, *Alcune osservazioni sui processi inquisitoriali,* and Idem, *L'inquisitione romana.*
57. C. Ginzburg, *The Inquisitor as Anthropologist.*
58. For example, C. Donati, *Curie, tribunali, cancellerie episcopali,* does not make mention of marriage causes.
59. Examples of argumentative sentences are also in L. Faoro, *Il giudice e il principe,* pp. 333–334; D. Lombardi, *L'odio capitale,* pp. 342, 361, 367. On the theme of motivation of sentences, see F. Mancuso, *Exprimere causam in sententia;* M. Ascheri, *Il processo civile,* p. 359. See also G.P. Massetto, *Sentenza.*
60. The hypothesis that marriage causes document marginal and deviant experiences of marriage is proposed again by F. Pedersen, *Marriage Disputes in Medieval England,* p. 23.
61. S. Seidel Menchi, *I processi matrimoniali come fonte storica,* p. 21. Observations on the fact that the exceptionality documented in the trial sheds light "on a reality elusive in the documents" are found in C. Ginzburg, *Prove e possibilità,* p. 134.
62. The argument for the adequacy of marriage litigations as a source for the history of marriage is discussed and sustained by T. M. Safley, *Let No Man Put Asunder,* pp. 6–8, and has recently found significant support in C. Donahue Jr., *Law, Marriage and Society,* in particular pp. 8–12, 51.
63. See for example the first important synthesis on marriage M. de Giorgio – C. Klapsich Zuber (eds.), *Storia del matrimonio.*
64. A. Molho, *Marriage Alliance.*
65. Violence was not a necessary element, but it aggravated the violation. See C. Povolo, *Il processo Guarnieri,* p. 34.
66. See the observations of S. Seidel Menchi – D. Quaglioni, *Introduzione,* p. 7 for the citation. That deriving continuity and stability from the norm can obscure "the wide variety of historical forms that marriage has taken" is underlined also in D. M. Luebke, *Introducion* in *Mixed Matches,* p. 2. For a clean distinction between licit, marital sexuality finalized by procreation and illicit pre- or

extramarital sexuality, capable of satisfying passions and guaranteeing sensual pleasure, see G. Ruggiero, *The Boundaries of Eros*.
67. See *infra*, ch. 5.
68. See the bibliography of the author cited *supra*, note 26.
69. L. Stone, *Uncertain Unions*, p. 3.
70. There are very interesting cases, for example, in J.M. Ferraro, *Marriage Wars*.
71. T. Cohen – E.S. Cohen, *Words and Deeds*.
72. G. Brucker, *Giovanni and Lusanna*; G. Corazzol – L. Corrà, *Esperimenti d'amore*.
73. The volumes curated by S. Seidel Menchi and D. Quaglioni, cited *supra*, note 44, unite historical-social and historical-juridical analysis. Individual cases are sometimes objects of different contributions on the part of historians and historians of law. See also, among the more recent works of D. Lombardi, *Matrimoni di Antico Regime*; C. La Rocca, *Tra moglie e marito*; C. Donahue, *Law, Marriage and Society*.
74. T. Kuehn, *Reading Microhistory*.
75. J.M. Ferraro, *Marriage Wars*, p. 11. See also A. White, *The Fiction of Factual Representation*; P. Novick, *That Noble Dream*. For a critique of White's claim that discourse creates its object, and of Barthes, according to which "Le fait n'a jamais qu'une existence linguistique," see C. Ginzburg, *Unus testis*; Idem, *Aristotele, la storia, la prova*; Idem, *History, Rhetoric, and Proof*.
76. R. Ago – S. Cerutti, *Premessa*; S. Cerutti, *Giustizia Sommaria*, pp. 11–13.
77. A. Blauert – G. Schwerhoff (eds.), *Kriminalitätsgeschichte*. Regarding marriage causes in particular, the reading of them as a key to the history of criminality, deviance, and social control has been the focus mostly in German scholarship, influenced by the particular institution, as the consistorial tribunals operated also as tribunals of good behavior. Some examples: S. Breit, *"Leichtfertigkeit"*; L. Roper, *Oedipus and the Devil*; U. Gleixner, *"Das Mensch" und "der Kerl"*; K. Schreiner-G. Schwerhoff (eds.), *Verletzte Ehre*; O. Ulbricht (ed.), *Von Huren und Rabenmuttern*.
78. In the first Italian edition of a marriage cause the procedural steps are omitted, a testimony, to my mind, of the fact that the procedure has been considered as a framework irrelevant to the interesting historical facts. See G. Corazzol – L. Corrà, *Esperimenti d'amore*.
79. M. Rospocher, *Recensione*.

80. Sparks of the contribution of individuals to the creation of cultural systems in E.P. Thompson, *Whigs and Hunters*. Stimulating observations in M. Rospocher, *Recensione*.
81. See *infra*, ch. 4.
82. G. Pomata, *La storia delle donne: una questione di confine*, pp. 1441, 1453.
83. See *infra*, ch. 3, § 6.
84. See *infra*, ch. 4.
85. ASPV, *CM*, vol. 12 Clara Marcello *vs* Francesco de Orlandis, 1512; ASPV, *CM*, vol. 16 Marinum filum magistri Iohannis Cercheri *vs* Serenam, 1515. See chs. 4–5 for the cases cited here and in the following notes.
86. ASPV, *CM*, vol. 9, Marco Antonio de Stefani *vs* Lucretia q. Simonis Vacha, 1506–1507.
87. ASPV, *CM*, vol. 13, Elena de Stefani *vs* Girolamo Marangon, 1513.
88. Even in the vicarial residence: ASPV, *CM*, vol. 16 Marinum filum magistri Iohannis Cercheri et Serenam, 1515.
89. See the document cited *supra*, note 86.
90. "Cui eorum cupit magis adherere." ASPV, *CM*, vol. 6, Maffeo da Conegliano *vs* Angela de Mestre, 1491.
91. See the document cited *supra*, note 86: "I want what mine want." ("Io voglio quello che vogliono li mei.")
92. ASPV, *CM*, vol. 11, Helisabeth Cristophori textoris *vs* Jacobo de la Zotta, 1510.
93. See ASPV, *CM*, vol. 12 Clara Marcello *vs* Francesco de Orlandis 1512.
94. D. Hacke, *Women, Sex and Marriage*; J.M. Ferraro, *Marriage Wars*; S. Chojnacki, *Il divorzio di Cateruzza*.
95. See *AMP*, registers 15, 22, 23, Caterina Gaiato *vs* Battista Giusto, 1459–1461.
96. S. Chojnacki, *Il divorzio di Cateruzza*.
97. C. Cristellon, *Ritratto di una cortigiana del Cinquecento*. The citation is in AIRE Ve, Zit. E. 31, 1 c. 20. Through the relation with the brother of her future husband, Caterina had contracted an "affinity *ex copula illicita*" with him. Either a prior marriage with a person related to the prospective spouse or an extramarital relation with a prospective spouse's relative constituted a diriment impediment, according to Pauline principle (1 Cor 6, 16) for which "qui adhaeret meretrici una caro efficitur cum ea." See *Thomae Sanches disputationum*, pp. 217–218.

98. C. Casagrande, *La donna custodita*.
99. L. Ferrante, *Gli sposi contesi*.
100. See *infra*, ch. 4.
101. ASPV, *CM*, vol. 2, fasc. 15, Franceschina Britti *vs* Francesco Agnus Dei, 1461.
102. N. Zemon Davis, *Histoire tout feu tout flamme*; G. Calvi, *Chiavi di lettura*, p. XII. For the examples cited, see *infra*, ch. 2, § 2 and ch. 4, §2.
103. See the observations of E. Brambilla, *Dagli sponsali civili al matrimonio sacramentale*, p. 1005.
104. The citation, originally referring to culture, is extracted from C. Ginzburg, *Il formaggio e i vermi*, p. XX.
105. G. Calvi, *Chiavi di lettura*, pp. XXVI–XXVII.
106. H.R. Schmidt, *Hausväter vor Gericht*.
107. J.M. Ferraro, *Marriage Wars*; D. Lombardi, *Famiglie di Antico Regime*, p. 209. S. Burghartz, *Zeiten der Reinheit*, in particular p. 26 disagrees with the prevalent interpretation that considers the magistrates as benevolent in their interactions with women.
108. See *infra*, ch. 6.
109. J.M. Ferraro, *Marriage Wars*, does not give quantified data, but speaks generically of the prevalence of female initiative. The quantitative analysis of D. Hacke, *Women, Sex and Marriage*, pp. 43–55, is based predominantly on the causes and the sentences but does also explore a sample of the curial registers.
110. See the quantitative analysis *infra*, ch. 6.
111. U. Gleixner, *"Das Mensch" und "der Kerl,"* and Eadem, *Sexualisierung der Geschlechterverhältnisse?*; D. Hacke, *Women, Sex and Marriage*, p. 5. There are stimulating observations on the role of "juridical representation" in court in M. Sbriccoli, *"Deterior est condicio foeminarum,"* pp. 81–83.
112. See for example the document cited *supra*, note 3.
113. See respectively *infra*, ch. 4 §§ 1 and 8; ASPV, *CM*, vol. 4, Teologia Baffo *vs*. Francesco Baffo, 1475.
114. E. Muir, *Mad Blood Stirring*.
115. O. Niccoli, *Rinuncia, pace, perdono* and Eadem, *Perdonare*.
116. Although not a common term in English, "infrajustice" is a term taken from French historiography (infrajudiciaire) and rendered into Italian as "infragiustizia." It refers to a justice considered only semi-legitimate, which is practiced by the community and includes

practices of vendetta, peaces, pardons, and so on. Although considered illegitimate by the authorities, it was considered the "true justice" by the community. B. Garnot (ed.), *L'infrajudiciaire*.

117. M. Sbriccoli, *Giustizia negotiata, giustizia egemonica* regarding "negotiated" justice, and pp. 360–364 regarding hegemonic or bureaucratic justice.
118. E. Muir, *Ritual in Early Modern Europe*, pp. 109–111.
119. The fact that a public authority was in charge of the resolution of the controversy did not necessarily change the physiognomy of negotiated justice, as the judge assumed a function mostly of arbitrator, in order to resolve the conflict between "subjects equal in terms of negotiating." See M. Sbriccoli, *Giustizia negoziata, giustizia egemonica*, p. 357 for the citation. Also M. della Misericordia, *Giudicare con il consenso*; O. Niccoli, *Perdonare*.
120. See *infra*, ch. 5: each paragraph retraces this evolution according to different matrimonial issues.
121. See *infra*, ch. 4, §§ 5 and 8.
122. See *infra*, ch. 4, §§ 5–6.
123. On the lack of an effective territorial penitential jurisdiction before the Council of Trent, and on the effective non-observance of Easter confession, see R. Rusconi, *L'ordine dei peccati*, p. 47.
124. See *infra*, ch. 4, §§ 5–6.
125. G. Romeo, *Ricerche su confessione dei peccati e Inquisizione*, pp. 35–61.
126. See *infra*, ch. 4, § 6 and note 136.
127. O. Niccoli, *Storie di ogni giorno in una città del Seicento*, pp. 23–42.
128. See *infra*, ch. 4, §§ 6 and 8.
129. See *infra*. ch. 5.
130. See *infra*, ch. 2, § 9.
131. See the observations of S. Cerutti, *Giustizia Sommaria*, pp. 11–32 and M. Meccarelli, *Arbitrium*, pp. XVII–XXXII.
132. K.W. Nörr, *Iudicium*.
133. G. Salvioli, *Storia della procedura civile e criminale*, pp. 299, 333–334; C. Lefebvre, *Les origines romaines*; R. Helmholz, *Marriage Litigation*, p. 120. See also *infra*, note 137 and ch. 4.
134. See *infra*, ch. 2, §§ 6 and 13.
135. See E. Orlando, *Tribunali di curia*, pp. 143–145 for an example from 1250.
136. M. Meccarelli, *Arbitrium iudicis und officialis im Ius commune*; and Idem, *Arbitrium*.

137. P. Grossi, *L'ordine giuridico medievale*, pp. 29–35; A.M. Hespanha, *Introduzione alla storia del diritto europeo*, pp. 115–116.
138. S. Cerutti, *Giustizia Sommaria*, p. 29.
139. A.M. Hespanha, *Introduzione alla storia del diritto europeo*, p. 119.
140. Ibid., pp. 125–126. The judges made explicit reference to the *stylus curiae*, for example, when they admitted all the witnesses to depose and decided to ascertain their credibility after having excused them. See *infra*, ch. 3, § 2.
141. See *infra*, ch. 5, § 1.
142. The cohabiting of two people of the same social class, for example, constituted presumption of marriage. See *infra*, ch. 2, § 9.
143. See *infra*, ch. 5, in particular §§ 1–2.
144. Such creativity would be limited by the interpretation of the passage of *Tametsi* that required the presence of the parish priest at weddings. See, *infra*, Conclusions.
145. See *infra*, ch. 4, § 2.
146. In the period from 1420 to 1500 only 253 of the 706 cases of marital conflict catalogued, or 36%, concluded with a sentence. The data relevant for the seventeenth century presented by D. Hacke in *Women, Sex and Marriage*, p. 51 are not very useful because the quantitative analysis is based largely on the causes and sentences, but explores only a few samples of the curia registers.
147. Regarding extrajudicial agreements in seventeenth- and eighteenth-century Venice, see *ibid.*, pp. 62–64.
148. B. Capp, *Live, Love and Litigation*, p. 77; and D. Lombardi, *Giustizia ecclesiastica*. On the fact that judges considered their conciliatory activity prestigious, see M. Dinges, *Usi della giustizia*, p. 295.
149. According to N. Castane, *Justice et repression*, p. 70, the function of the law was to favor the availability of agreement among the parties. According to M. Dinges, *Usi della giustizia*, pp. 293–4, the tribunals became implicated only to increase their own contractual capacity in the extrajudicial seat.
150. P. Grossi, *L'ordine giuridico medievale*, pp. 210–213.
151. See respectively *infra*, ch. 4, § 4 and ch. 5, § 4.
152. See *infra*, ch. 5, § 4.
153. I take this point from the reflexions of M. Sbriccoli, *Giustizia negoziata, giustizia egemonica*, p. 349.

CHAPTER 2

The Matrimonial Tribunal and the Procedure in Marriage Litigations

When we consider the late medieval matrimonial tribunal in general and the Venetian tribunal in particular, we must set aside the institutional image evoked by the term tribunal. The institution had rules and constants, which will be explained in the following pages, but it also had a flexibility and a plasticity that allowed it to adapt to specific situations and assume approaches appropriate to the case, either by acting creatively in the absence of norms, or in contradiction to the same norms. The reasons for these variations seem to be related to the judge's pastoral vocation, which will be explored more fully in Chap. 4, "The Office of the Judge."

1 Composition of the Tribunal and the Parties in a Cause

With the Church's jurisdictional monopoly over marriage, the bishop was ordinarily the judge in charge of resolving marital conflicts among Catholics.[1] As noted, since the passage of the episcopacy to the patriarchate in 1451,[2] the Venetian ecclesiastical tribunal was the seat of marriage litigations in both the first and second instance. First instance causes were those in which at least one of the two parties came from the diocese of Venice. Second instance cases, which the Venetian tribunal had jurisdiction over by papal delegation, were appeals. They began with an appeal presented either at the end of a litigation of the first grade debated in the

Venetian diocese or at the end of cases that had been concluded in a diocese under patriarchal jurisdiction.[3]

The tribunal was staffed by various members of the curia. The post of the patriarch was almost exclusively reserved for members of the Venetian nobility, chosen by the Pope from a list proposed by the Venetian Senate.[4] The marriage tribunal was presided over by the patriarch – or by his vicar – as judge. The chancellor or notary of the curia was supposed to verbally register every act conducted before the judge or by him, as required by a decretal of Innocent III,[5] under penalty of the nullification of that act.[6] At least two witnesses had to be present at the various phases of the procedure: they were usually clerics or servants of the bishop, but on occasion they could be two people who were waiting outside the court room for the hearing of their own case.[7]

Two procurators of the curia had the duty and right[8] to defend the cases debated in the patriarchate, each in favor of a different party in the cause: if the procurators wanted to defend the same disputant, the judge required one of them to defend the other party under pain of excommunication.[9] The procurators active in the Venetian curia remained in their posts for many years, so they were familiar with the *modus operandi* of the tribunal, the judges who presided, and those who represented the opponent in judgment.[10] They were doctors of law *in utroque iure* (in both canon and civil law). Their qualifications, rather than the frugality of parties in the case, provide the most likely explanation for the fact that they were also frequently used as lawyers in the same cases. Finally, the nuncio of the curia was charged with sending each injunction of the tribunal to the parties involved in the litigation.

In the opening of the suit, practices diverged from the doctrine. In practice, Venetian marriage causes handled between 1420 and 1545 were begun only at the request of one party, never by a third-party denunciation or *ex officio*. This is generally what happened in England and German territories, but different from the Franco-Belgian region.[11] Teaching, however, distinguished between causes that could have been initiated only by the parties in the case and causes that could have been initiated by a third-party denunciation. Litigations dealing with lack of consent, impotence, sexual immaturity, and *separation of bed and board* had to be initiated by one of the parties involved. Causes regarding kinship and affinity, solemn vows, previous marriages, disparity of cult –that is, a marriage between a Christian and someone who was not baptized– and crime – that is, the promise exchanged by adulterers to marry if the betrayed spouse died (such marriages would be nullified independently because of the relationship they had had at the time of the spouse's death) – all of these causes could be initiated by a third party.[12]

The parties involved in a marriage cause were:

- the plaintiff, who initiated the litigation by denouncing to the judge a behavior considered to be harmful, and who had the burden of proof.[13]
- the defendant, who was called to respond about his or her behavior, considered harmful by the plaintiff.[14]

The plaintiff and defendant could be supported in court by someone whom they presented or was cited "in their interest" or "if he or she considered that the cause was in his/her interest." It was possible, for example, for a man to begin litigation asking for a woman to cease defaming him – cease, that is, claiming to be his wife – with a woman whom he had publicly married ("before the church") at his side.[15] Alternatively a woman beginning a suit for alleged marriage might accuse a man who had publicly married another woman: that woman would then be invited to intervene in the litigation next to her husband.[16]

In addition to the procurators of the curia, the parties could avail themselves, at their discretion, of lawyers. This was sometimes a matter of there being better jurists on the market, active in the nearby University of Padua, of the caliber of Bartolomeo Cipolla.[17] The parties were also almost always represented by members of their families: generally the father,[18] brothers,[19] uncles,[20] son,[21] and sometimes the mother.[22] Whoever acted on behalf of the party in court had to have a procuratorial mandate, drafted by a notary. A suit could be delayed as one party contested the legality of the notary who had written the document, which made the intervention of the doge himself necessary to attest that the notary in question was an imperial notary of "good condition and reputation."[23]

A notary of the curia – who was sometimes also the chancellor – recorded every act of the cause in triplicate. One copy remained in the tribunal, while the others were given to the parties in the case. The delivery of the acts of the litigation to the parties was called the "publication of the cause" (*pubblicatio processus*).

The marriage litigation began at the initiative of one party.[24] Only those with juridical capacity (men over the age of 14 or women over the age of 12[25] who were of a free condition[26]) could initiate a marriage litigation. Major excommunication, which was delivered by the bishop and "excluded [the excommunicate] from the church and the community," depriving those under this sentence "of civil and juridical rights of baptismal-recorded membership in the civil-religious community," also caused a person to lose juridical capacity.[27]

2   The Petition

The litigation began with the presentation of a petition (*petitio*) by the plaintiff, which could be written (formalized in a libel) or oral. In the latter case the petition began with the formula "The petition [is presented] not in the form of a solemn book but in such a manner."[28] The petition had to be very precise or it would be inadmissible, and it had to contain the names of the plaintiff and defendant, indicate the judge to whom it was presented, the request, and the law which justified it.[29] It could be modified until the formal joinder of issue (*litis contestatio*).

Having seen the book or heard the petition, the judge cited the defendant. If the defendant admitted that the information in the petition was true, he or she was obligated to satisfy the plaintiff's requests, subject to the respect of *favor matrimonii*. If instead the defendant contested the petition, the suit began.

In cases of defamation litigation could occur even if the defendant confirmed the plaintiff's story. When a certain Marino received a mandate from the vicar that ordered him to stop claiming that Ludovica Calbo was his wife or to present himself at court to prove the marriage, he denied both the defamation and the marriage. As a witness attested to the defamation, an embarrassed Marino declared to the nuncio that he had been "joking" (*buffonizzato*), again denying the marriage. He complained to the nuncio of the curia that he was surprised the vicar wanted to proceed against him for a joke and he continued to deny the marriage ("Sir Father Bernardino, I am amazed by your actions, I will tell you again what I have said once already.")[30] Nevertheless, the cause proceeded in the absence of the defendant and he was sentenced to "perpetual silence," ordered to stop the defamation forever.[31]

3   The Citation

A citation was an order to appear before the tribunal sent to the parties by the judge. By rule the initial citation was written, while later citations were usually oral and delivered at the end of each audience. The first citation had to be delivered to the defendant at home. Sometimes if he or she were not available it would be entrusted to a relative. Understandably, the citation caused unpleasant reactions. One woman, for example, tore up the bulletin presented to her.[32] Others apparently refused to come to court, leaving everything to the decision of the magistrate: "I do not want to come, the patriarch will make justice...the vicar will apply reason"[33]; "I do not want to come, tell the vicar that he can do what is right and what he pleases... I do not want to come, do what you please and I do not want to come any more."[34] Sometimes the nuncio had to find more creative ways to deliver the citation. After having searched in vain for a man "in the *piazza* and the basilica of San Marco, the Rialto, and in all the public places, among friends and family," the nuncio threw the document – which his relatives had refused to take – through an open door of the man's house.[35] If the defendant was, in the end, unavailable, the citation was affixed to the parish church door[36] or sometimes to the door of the defendant's house.[37] When the person cited lived in another diocese, the Venetian judge delivered the citation with the assistance of the bishop of that diocese.[38]

The citation had to contain the names of the executor, the person cited, and the amount of time he or she had to present her/himself in court. Usually the defendant had three juridical days to appear – three days, that is, when audiences of the ecclesiastical tribunal occurred, which in Venice were usually Monday, Wednesday, and Friday. If the citation was delivered on a Monday, for example, the defendant had to present himself in court by the following Friday. In the case of a peremptory citation, defendants had to present themselves in court immediately.

The citation was recorded in the registers of the curia. If after three citations or after a peremptory citation the person did not come to court, he or she was declared to be contumacious.

4 Contumacy

Contumacy was the crime of not observing the obligation to appear in court after three citations or after a peremptory citation; or of leaving without the judge's permission after having presented oneself; or of refusing to swear an oath.[39] Contumacy could be actual or presumed. Actual contumacy was committed by those who, having received a citation, announced they would not appear in court, thus authorizing the court to proceed without another citation.[40] False (*ficta*) or presumed (*praesumptiva*) contumacy was committed by those who declared they would present themselves in court but then did not actually appear. Before the court could proceed against them, they had to be cited three times. False contumacy could also be committed by those who were unavailable each of the three times the court tried to deliver a citation.[41]

Contumacy carried the penalty of major excommunication, which, as noted, excluded the excommunicate from both church and community and deprived him or her of civil rights.[42] Excommunication was rarely executed: it was exceptional for a person to be declared excommunicated for contumacy by affixing the mandate of excommunication on the doors of the parish church and notifying the community of the faithful.[43] Probably for this reason, such sanctions did not usually provoke timely respect for the tribunal's decrees. In each case punishment was suspended as soon as the excommunicate appeared in court or provided valid reasons – an illness, for example – why he or she had not observed the citation.[44]

Contumacy became a strategy to prolong litigation. Its effects varied depending on whether the plaintiff or defendant was contumacious and if the *litis contestatio* had occurred. If the plaintiff were contumacious – though this was very rare – and if the *litis contestatio* had not yet occurred, the judge dismissed the defendant and charged the plaintiff for court expenses.[45] In a case that involved a certain Nicolò and Isabetta, for example, the vicar gave the plaintiff eight days to prove his marriage to Isabetta; at the end of this period, at her request, he was declared contumacious and "Isabetta was freed from Nicolò."[46] After the joinder of the suit, moreover, a judge who believed he had sufficient information could decide to deliver a sentence even if the plaintiff were contumacious.

If the defendant were contumacious, however, the judge could use excommunication to allow the cause to proceed. But it should be noted that as much as contumacy could slow litigation, rarely did it constitute an effective obstacle to its progress: in a marriage cause the judge could proceed against the contumacious party up to sentencing[47] based on the assumption that the absence of the defendant "is made up for by the presence of God".[48] A defendant could obtain an annulment of the sentence of the first instance cause, however, through an appeals process if he could show that he had been declared contumacious but was not properly cited. A certain Pietro Cortese, for example, was able to prove during the first instance cause through witnesses that he was not, as his wife had claimed, a "vagabond," as he had been seen "publicly…in his house with the apothecary and his goods." A sentence of the second instance annulled the preceding sentence as he had not been cited, "or at least it was not done legitimately."[49] After the formal joinder of issue, contumacy of the defendant usually caused a judge to pronounce a definitive sentence.

Dossiers of nullity for a previous marriage record the contumacy of defendants with great frequency. These dossiers consist of suits against people who were absent from Venice, those about whom all news had been lost or who had been separated from their families for a long time. This type of defendant was often unavailable and was not interested in appearing in court to defend a marriage to which he or she no longer attached any value. Contumacy thus often reveals a way in which the laity contrived to legally end a marriage that was already defunct.[50]

5   Postponements

Requests for postponement were frequently made by both parties for a variety of legitimate reasons. They could be requested to have time to appoint a procurator, to collect evidence, to inform themselves about testimony presented by their opponent to direct cross-examination, and for political appointments or professional obligations of the procurators or the parties involved.[51] By rule the judge received the request *sua solita humanitate* (by his customary humanity) or *nolens recedere a sua solita urbanitate* (not wishing to withdraw from his customary urbanity).[52] The party who requested the postponement needed to take an oath *de malitia*, having to guarantee that he or she was not seeking to delay the litigation for a specific strategic purpose.[53]

6   Exceptions

During the marriage litigation objections could be raised that could invalidate the proceeding. Exceptions could be dilatory or peremptory. Dilatory exceptions had to be raised before the contestation of the suit and could be related to either the incompetence of the plaintiff or the judge.[54] The defendant, for example, could contest the juridical capacity of the plaintiff on the grounds of minority, servile condition, or excommunication. In Venetian cases, this last objection was the one raised most frequently. A dramatic example is provided by a Paduan-Venetian case from 1455 to 1458. The suit was opened by Giorgio Zaccarotto, who claimed

Maddalena di Sicilia, then living in a convent under the name of Sister Giustina and perhaps not yet 12 years old, as his wife. The procurator contested his right to take this to court because Giorgio's father, during the solemn investiture of the girl, had brusquely interrupted the consecration. He had ordered the priest to put down the host and then read a statement of protest from a notary.[55] For this very grave act, Zaccarotto had incurred major excommunication *ipso facto* because he had disturbed the divine service (*propter turbam divinorum*).

Absolute or relative exceptions could be presented against the judge. Absolute exceptions were those that could exclude him from his office (e.g., excommunication). We have never encountered any cases like this. Relative exceptions, however, rendered the judge unsuitable to preside over a specific suit, for geographic limit to his jurisdiction territorial incompetence or because of his connections with one of the two parties – for example, in cases of consanguinity or affinity.[56] The judge himself generally preempted any exceptions that could be raised: in the suit between Vittore Pisani and Candida Bollani, the patriarch himself declared that he could not preside over the cause as he was "united in the third degree" to Vittore, and with the consent of the parties, he delegated the case to his vicar Niccolò delle Croci.[57]

Direct attempts to recuse the judge were exceptional.[58] In the conflict between Giorgio Zaccarotto and Maddalena di Sicilia, the plaintiff successfully requested that the cause be transferred from Padua to Venice by papal delegation. The request was made because the bishop of Padua, Fantino Dandolo, the territorially competent judge, was "in the position of lord" over Maddalena since she had entered the novitiate. This rendered the Paduan prelate suspect of protecting the material interest of the convent that had received the very rich dowry of the novice and future nun Maddalena, calling his objectivity into question.[59] Once he had obtained the transfer of the litigation from Padua to Venice, patriarch Maffeo Contarini decided to take the case himself. Despite the fact that Zaccarotto sought to influence his choice, proposing the names of some prelates, parish priests, and finally of the patriarchal vicar Niccolò delle Croci, Maffeo Contarini chose the vicar Domenico de Groppis.

To this point, the exceptions presented by Zaccarotto constituted a real frontal attack on the judge. He systematically tried to delegitimize the magistrate, acting on a double binary. On one side, in fact, he accused the bishop of Padua, Fantino Dandolo, of partiality. According to these accusations the bishop had personally sought to convince Maddalena to become a nun and had made her visit a midwife loyal to him to ensure the girl was a virgin and could therefore enter the convent without the approval of her husband.[60] Before the publication of the suit he had ruled that the girl was released from any marital bond and was free to become a nun; to induce her to carry out this act he had influenced the girl's will with the assistance of the abbess, a consistent defamer of both Giorgio and his father, whom she accused of having poisoned his wife and of having passed down his uxoricidal instinct. Finally, when the case was taken from his jurisdiction, the bishop went many times to Venice to convince the patriarch not to take on the role of judge.

On the other side, Zaccarotto first implied the suspicion and then openly formulated the accusation that the patriarch and his vicar were conspiring with the bishop of Padua and were therefore partial. He argued that their complicity with the bishop was manifest in the patriarch's refusal to appoint the vicar proposed by Giorgio as judge and in his permission that Maddalena, in spite of Giorgio's objections, remain in the convent of San Mattia in Padua and be interrogated there, where Fantino Dandolo exercised great influence. Such collusion would have only been veiled by the guise of legality, when the patriarchal vicar allowed Giorgio to talk to the girl and had let him see the acts of the litigation in Padua, not yet published.

Giorgio therefore asked that they elect arbitrators, who would need to establish whether or not the patriarchal vicar was a suspect judge. Proposing that one of the arbitrators be elected by the vicar himself, Zaccarotto openly demonstrated that he regarded the magistrate as an adversary in court, from the moment that, according to the rules, the arbitrators should have been chosen in equal numbers by each of the parties.[61]

The exceptions raised by Zaccarotto did not compromise the progress of the case only because, based on the pontifical decision that had assigned it to the Venetian patriarch, it had to be conducted according to summary procedure, which excluded dilatory exceptions. Dilatory exceptions could only be raised before the contestation of the suit and in regard to the incompetence of the plaintiff or the judge. Peremptory exceptions, however, could be invoked at any point in the procedure and constituted a perpetual obstacle to the judge. Malice, *metus* (fear), and *res iudicata* – the sentence passed in judgment (which marriage causes excluded) – were peremptory exceptions. In the Venetian documentation I have not found any peremptory exceptions.[62]

7 THE FORMAL JOINDER OF ISSUE: THE *LITIS CONTESTATIO*

The *litis contestatio*[63] was the phase of the suit when the plaintiff presented the petition (*libellum*) to the defendant, who contradicted it with the formula "I deny what you affirm and I oppose the requests you have advanced."[64] If either of the two parties was missing, the *litis contestatio* was rendered invalid, because the petition – the object of contestation – was established from the narration of facts and the formulation of a request.[65] At the moment of the *litis contestatio* the defendant could ask that any eventual ambiguity be removed from petition or could contest the validity of the cause. Girolamo Mathei, for example, contested the action brought against him by Caterina due to the lack of substantial elements (*substantialibus a iure requisitis*). He argued that she had not specified when their presumed marriage had occurred and that the time was "the substance and foundation of the entire suit" (*substantia et fundamentum totius litis*). But the witnesses, who Caterina expected would prove her version of the facts, were unreachable, blocked while the wall of Padua was besieged (1509). This was a moment in which we see the tragedy of the Republic interacting with the individual dramas of its subjects: only after Caterina had specified the date of the supposed marriage – and the tenacious resistance of the city had ended the siege – could the legal action proceed.[66]

The *litis contestatio* defined the limits of the controversy, entailed the definition of the judge's competence, prevented the defendant from producing new dilatory exceptions, and conferred on the procurators or the representatives in general the *dominium litis* (competence for the suit).[67] The *litis contestatio* was the foundational moment of the Roman canonical procedure, but in the marriage litigation it could be omitted if summary procedure were applied.[68]

8 THE POSITIONS

After the *litis contestatio*, the plaintiff presented some positions that summarized his or her version of the facts and often swore to believe that these assertions corresponded to the truth (*iuramentum de veritate dicenda*). Generally spontaneous,[69] rarely requested by the judge,[70] sometimes simply hypothesized,[71] or passed under silence,[72] this oath, although called for by the doctrine that ruled the processual structure,[73] does not seem to have been expected by the norms specific to marriage litigations. With only one exception, I have never found cases during which the procurator of the defendant – typically zealous and quick to take any occasion to hinder the development of the case – availed himself of the lack of an oath by the plaintiff to invalidate the regularity of the procedure.[74]

The positions defined the material on which the defendant would be interrogated. He or she would respond to each position, either confirming it by saying *credit*, denying it by saying *non credit*, or correcting it by saying *non credit prout ponitur*. As this was a fundamental act of the procedure, I present as an example the positions of a legally sophisticated case: the aforementioned Paduan-Venetian case that involved Giorgio Zaccarotto and Maddalena di Sicilia. The positions that follow were presented by the presumed husband.[75]

Giorgio: 1. First of all I affirm that a marriage between myself and the said Maddalena, my wife, was contracted and consummated while her father, Signor Cosma was alive, who was then sick with the malady that killed him.

Maddalena: *Non credit.*

Giorgio: 2. I then affirm that before the death of her father, Maddalena came to me, that I awaited her in the house of Nicolò Grezoti, her guardian, according to agreements among us.

Maddalena: *Non credit ut ponitur.*

Giorgio: 3. Then I sustain that, when Maddalena came to me, she was stopped by a son of Giovanni dalla Minutaria who took her by force to his own house against the young woman's will, and she clearly declared "Let me go to my husband" (*Lassatime andar da mio marido*).

Maddalena: *Non credit ut ponitur.*

Giorgio: 4. Then I affirm that, when she was taken to that house, Maddalena openly and clearly confessed in the presence of many people that she had contracted marriage with me, that she was my wife to all effects, that she had married me with a ring (*veretta*) that was there.

Maddalena: *She said that she was married with a ring to someone unknown to her, after she had been tricked by her sister. She denies the rest.*

Giorgio: 5. I also affirm that after this, many worthy people asked Maddalena for news of this marriage and its consummation. She confessed to being my wife and to having consummated the marriage.

Maddalena: *Non credit.*
Giorgio: 6. Also, I affirm that Maddalena said to the person with whom she spoke that she would rejoin me voluntarily if only she could, if she were free and not kept as she was, and she said this lamenting, crying, and affirming to love me very much.
Maddalena: *Non credit.*
Giorgio: 7. I sustain also that I, Giorgio, married Maddalena for the first time in her father's house, while he was still alive, in the presence of many worthy witnesses, in 1455 around the 18th of June.
Maddalena: *Confirmed that in that house a ring was placed on her finger by that same man she did not know. She denied the rest.*
Giorgio: 8. I also sustain that, after all of this, Maddalena spoke with me and my father at Nicolò Grezoti's house, and, asked by us her age, she told us that she would turn twelve on the next feast day of Santa Maria Maddalena.
Maddalena: *Confirmed that she had said she was twelve when asked by Giorgio's father, as her sister Giovanna had told her to say this, and she did not know otherwise.*
Giorgio: 9. I then sustain that, when we knew of her age, we decided that, to reinforce the marriage, I would marry her again after the day of Santa Maria Maddalena, and then I consummated the marriage with her, and so I agreed with them because she came to lunch in her guardian master Nicolò's house, where her sister Giovanna also was.
Maddalena: *Non credit ut ponitur.*
Giorgio: 10. Also I sustain that the same day the aforementioned Giovanna asked Maddalena's mother to allow her to go to lunch with Maddalena and thus she let her go. Maddalena knew that my father and I were there.
Maddalena: *Confirms, to the extent that she had heard the order given to Giovanna, but she did not know that Giorgio would also be there.*
Giorgio: 11. The day of San Lorenzo, before lunch, after we had said many things between us, I married her again, in the presence of my father and many others. Afterwards my father went away and I remained with her for lunch.
Maddalena: *Confirms that she did this according to Giovanna's advice.*
Giorgio: 12. After lunch everyone left and she and I remained before the hearth to my pleasure and we consummated the marriage.

Maddalena: *Non credit ut ponitur.*
Giorgio: 13. After the consummation, because of the fear she had demonstrated, she looked upset and blushed, so much that her face revealed the sign of its carnal knowledge (*signa ipsius cognitionis*).
Maddalena: *Non credit.*
Giorgio: 14. Giovanni dalla Minutaria, the abbess of San Mattia, other nuns, and many other people, with the intention of influencing Maddalena, told her that me and my relatives were poor and of evil life, and that nothing good would happen to her if she were to live with me, convincing her to not come with me, and claiming that if she came, she would have lived little with me, because I would kill her. With these conversations they made her become a nun, but they succeeded in their intentions, also saying that I lacked hands and that if she came with me, she would have to dress me and put on my shoes and feed me, and that my father had poisoned my mother.
Maddalena: *She believes that Giovanni dalla Minutaria, the abbess, and other nuns often told her, that if she had consummated the marriage, she could not have become a nun. She denies the rest.*
Giorgio: 15. Maddalena did not believe these malices. She was certain that such words were false and that if she were with me she would be well treated by me and mine, like other women of her class, well-dressed, that she would have servants and everything that she needed. She would have been content to come and be with me.
Maddalena: *Non credit.*
Giorgio: 16. Maddalena was sequestered in that convent as a protection from the marriage, not so that she would become a nun. She had no intention of becoming a nun, if it were not for the negative influence of Giovanni dalla Minutaria, the abbess, the nuns of San Mattia, and other people speaking on their behalf.
Maddalena: *She confirms that then she did not intend to become a nun, but then, guided by God, after having been in the convent, she received the spirit to become a nun – guided by Him, however, and not persuaded by anyone.*
Giorgio: 17. When Maddalena's father died, Giovanni dalla Minutaria took her to his house and held her in his strict custody against her will, so that no one could see her or talk to her.
Maddalena: *Non credit.*

Giorgio:	18. In the same way, the abbess of San Mattia held her under maximum custody, warning her not to talk to me or any of my relatives, and she did not let me or anyone else in my name speak to her. If any of us went to her, she said every bad thing possible about us, insulting us and despising us.
Maddalena:	*Non credit.*
Giorgio:	19. The same abbess always allowed Giovanni dalla Minutaria and all of his people to talk to Maddalena at their pleasure.
Maddalena:	*Non credit.*
Giorgio:	20. While Maddalena was at Giovanni dalla Minutaria's house, these people, knowing that there had been carnal relations between us and intending to destroy our marriage so the truth could not be proven, promised money and other goods to find someone who could treat Maddalena so it would not appear that she had been deflowered and that she would appear to be a virgin. With various promises he sought someone who could create hatred between Maddalena and me with magic, to the point that she would not want to hear my name, nor I hers.
Maddalena:	*Non credit.*
Giorgio:	21. Giovanni dalla Minutaria made Maddalena practice many astringent ablutions, so that it could not be proven that she was deflowered.
Maddalena:	*Non credit.*
Giorgio:	22. All of this is *publica vox et fama* (public knowledge).
Maddalena:	*Non credit.*

While plaintiffs could legitimately, according to the form already illustrated, delegate to procurators the presentation of their version of the facts to the judge, the defendant had to intervene personally – the only moment in the suit when his or her presence was obligatory – to reply to the *positiones* of the plaintiff under oath.[76] Judges were extremely reluctant to allow exceptions – although allowed by legislation[77] – even in cases where the danger of subornation was very remote,[78] or when the party conferred the faculty of conducting all juridical acts in his or her stead, including the issuing of the oath, to his or her own procurator by mandate.[79] The obligation to present oneself to depose personally – in the presence of the judge (or, in his place, the chancellor) and the notary alone – guaranteed the possibility of deposing free of external pressures and conditions. The solemn ritual of the oath, which placed the deposition in the sphere of the sacred, set the fear of God against those constraints.[80]

This oath was imposed also on those who, according to doctrine, were not actually able to take a valid oath: those who were not yet 14 years old, for example.[81] A party's young age could be invoked by a lawyer as a pretext to avoid a personal appearance in court. In the case between Iacopo Franco and Agnesina de l'Orsa – the former claimed the existence of a marital bond, the latter denied it and hoped to marry another man – the girl's procurator sought to remove Agnesina from the interrogation, arguing that she had been duped because of her young age. In this way the lawyer recognized the girl's capacity to express free consent required for marriage – for this it was sufficient that Agnesina was over 12 – but not to respond to the positions of her adversary without being pressured – for this she had to be at least 14.[82] The judge rejected the lawyer's request.

The interrogation of witnesses was outlined and took shape based on the answers of the defendant to the plaintiff's *positiones*. The *positiones* admitted by the defendant, in fact, were considered a confession (the proof *par excellence*), though judges still might act in *favor matrimonii*, as we will see. The contested positions were transformed into articles (*articuli*) or chapters (*capituli*), about which the witnesses presented by the plaintiff were interrogated.[83]

9   The Proof

Common law recognized, with regards to evidence, a distinction between real (non-artificial) proof (or *probatio vera*) and artificial proof (*probatio ficta*).[84] *Probatio vera* directly represented a fact, without being mediated by a jurist or orator; this included confession, testimony, and oaths. Artificial proof, instead, "leads one to knowledge of the truth through reasoning or judgment." Included in this category were clues and presumptions.[85] Juridical doctrine of common law distinguished between three full proofs – sufficient on their own to demonstrate the truth of a fact – and semi-full proofs or insufficient proofs, which could consist of either a direct proof compromised in some way (like direct testimony from only one witness[86]) or circumstantial evidence. While proof bound the decision of the judge, the valuation of clues and presumptions was left to his *arbitrium*. For the medieval jurist, this strictly legal notion was tied to those of *aequitas, ratio,* and *iustitia*, through which the discretionary power entrusted to the judge "was balanced by heavy responsibilities."[87]

9.1 The Confession

Canon law considered a confession given in court as proof *par excellence*,[88] as long as it was free, spontaneous, and given by a "capable" person.[89] In marriage cases, whose procedures were shaped by *favor matrimonii*, the confession of marriage was considered full proof, as was a confession of behaviors that implied separation, as long as it did not compromise the subsistence of the marriage bond. The confession of the invalidity of the bond, however, had to be supported by the testimony of witnesses and sometimes even by an oath of the parties involved.[90] If in the case of a purported marriage, for example, the defendant confirmed the story of the plaintiff and admitted the marriage, the judge simply ordered them to solemnize the bond and begin living together.[91] The same result occurred if the plaintiff could in any way prove the same claims through witnesses "for greater clarity and to remove any suspicion of collusion."[92] Only if the confession of marriage prejudiced a later marriage and the rights of a third person, would the vicar demand proof of the first union and revoke the order to cohabit.[93] When an Albanian woman named Lucia, for example, confessed that she had contracted a marriage with Giovanni da Rodi before witnesses, the judge gave the order for cohabitation within eight days under the penalty of excommunication for both her and whomever hosted her. Lucia was only able to remove the sanction by arranging to prove through witnesses that Giovanni had already been married.[94]

Although the confession of marriage generally constituted a full proof, if a man asked for an annulment because his wife had previously contracted a marriage he had not known about, the woman's confession was not sufficient on its own to dissolve the bond. Witnesses had to be interrogated *ad probandum*.[95] In spite of the obligation to present evidence to sustain the preceding bond, annulment cases for previous marriages often amounted to expedients to end a union that had become onerous: for the most part the real motive for the cause – which the party sometimes admitted – had nothing to do with the discovery of a previous marital bond of the husband or the wife.[96] In this type of litigation the probability of collusion between the spouses was high, and lawyers sometimes brought up this danger.[97]

Attributing the value of "full proof" to a confession of marriage was not only due to *favor matrimonii*. It was also provided for by the doctrine of consent, which said that consent of the parties was sufficient to declare marriage: by admitting to being married, the parties in a suit celebrated marriage. The confession of marriage given in court was comparable to a recurring nuptial formula where, instead of displaying the intention to contract a marriage, one attested to the reality of the fact. The husband saying "you are my wife" and taking the hand of the bride constituted a marriage.[98]

9.2 Testimonial Proof

Since the twelfth century, with the elaboration of Roman canonical procedures, testimonial proof acquired primary importance in ecclesiastical tribunals.[99] Concordant testimonies from two exemplary witnesses (*omni exceptione maiores*) constituted a full proof. The deposition of a sole exemplary witness constituted a semi-full proof. The Venetian tribunal attributed a greater value to testimonial proof than to documentary proof, which was only accepted in support of the first.[100] The valuation of testimonial proof was up to the judge based on rigid casuistry in concert with doctrine.[101] We will not linger further here on the analysis of testimonial proof, as it will be treated specifically in the next chapter.

9.3 The Oath

As we have already seen, oaths were included among "true or non-artificial" proofs. Oaths could have a decisive value if taken by the party who had already provided a semi-full proof. The oath could be decisive or supplementary. The former occurred at the request of the opponent, the latter occurred at the request of the judge.[102] As we will later emphasize, judges tended to request an oath most often from women, even though doctrine considered them less trustworthy witnesses. Legally it would seem preferable to request an oath capable of determining the end result of a case from men, while women would have had to abstain.[103] As we will see, the oath was therefore an instrument that could influence decisions of the magistrate in a decisive manner; it was also revealed as an instrument capable of dissuading the opponent, by virtue of its connection to the sacred sphere.[104]

9.4 Clues and Presumptions, or Nuptial Customs in the Tribunal

Artificial proofs, those proofs that bring out knowledge of the truth through a logical method based on reasoning and judgment, include clues and presumptions. The clue has a factual consistency but is interpretable in several ways: the pallor of a bride, for example, could indicate the absence of her consent to the marriage, but it did not necessarily imply this,[105] just as turmoil and blushing could indicate that defloration had occurred (as we saw in the *positiones* presented by Giorgio Zaccarotto against Maddalena di Sicilia).

Presumption is an argument in favor of a fact that is based on the proof of another fact: in the case of cohabitation of suspect people, there was a presumption of sexual intercourse.[106] Presumption could be temerarious, probable, or necessary. Temerarious presumption was a product of malevolence, in which something that could be (and therefore should be) interpreted positively was interpreted negatively: if, for example, a priest hugged a woman, according to doctrine one should presume that he intended to bless her or exhort her to penitence. A different presumption was temerarious and as such invalid, and should have been excluded from judgment and should not have influenced the spirit of the judge.[107] Probable presumption (*praesumptio probabilis*) could not persuade the judge to deliver a sentence on its own, but it could be placed alongside a presumption of equal value or the oath of the person whom the presumption favored, which could be demanded by the judge. Probable presumption could be opposed by a proof. Among the probable presumptions of marriage were the prolonged cohabitation of a man and a woman belonging to the same social class[108] or the consummation of marriage in the case of two spouses who had lived together for a long time.[109] It so happened, for example, that two men whose spouses brought suit for an annulment of marriage based on non-age underlined the fact that the wedding had been followed by 18 months of cohabitation in one case, and cohabitation and the payment of alimony in the other. Both advanced the long cohabitation as presumption of sexual intercourse (*copula carnalis*). This, based on canonical principle for which *carnalis malitia* makes up for age (*supplet aetatem*),[110] would have rendered the declaration of nullity much more difficult.[111] The presumption of the consummation of marriage in the case of prolonged cohabitation between spouses could, however, be negated by the proof of the woman's virginity.[112] Finally, necessary presumption determined the tenor of the sentence. Sexual relations following the expression of consent in the future (henceforth called *matrimonium presumptum*) or of conditional consent (*sub conditione*) constituted a necessary presumption of marriage.[113]

In the pre-Tridentine tribunal, presumption and clues of marriage were of primary importance because of the extreme diversity of marriage practices and celebrations, which often made it very difficult to prove the bond. Only the consent of the couple was required for a valid marriage. The publication of the union, though encouraged for "honesty" (*ad honestatem*), was not necessary for the marriage to be valid or sacramental. Consent could be expressed in a public, private, or secret form: it did not have to be expressed verbally, and it could be explained in successive phases, even implicitly by the continual frequenting or cohabitation of the couple.[114] The boundaries between betrothal, marriage, and concubinage were ephemeral. A man could deny a marriage after many decades, one fulfilled by the birth of children recognized as legitimate, by indicating his wife as "consorte" in his will.[115] Another man, asked whether he was married to a woman he claimed as his wife, responded uncertainly: "maybe so."[116] Precisely because the expression of consent was often difficult to prove, the ecclesiastical tribunal preferred to investigate the signs of affection (*affectus*) rather than the moment of the expression of consent,[117] sometimes considered unimportant in the constitution of the bond (it is possible, e.g., that a woman could bring a case of alleged marriage without mentioning the wedding).[118] By canon law, the fundamental distinction between concubinage and marriage (*coniugium*) was determined by affection, the sentiment appropriate to marriage, which was capable of transforming concubinage into marriage.[119] The daily behavior of the couple, their networks of relations, and the relations maintained with each other's families were examined and interpreted by the judge according to a customary semantic code that was able to identify nuptial consent even if it had not been expressed punctually. The wife could be differentiated from the concubine by the role the husband attributed to her within the family and tasks entrusted to her in the management of the household.[120] Lay and ecclesiastical conceptions of marriage converged on the subject of clues and presumptions: the community's judgment on the formation of a couple held significant weight in the tribunal.

In the period under examination, cohabitation was often equated with marriage by both the laity and the ecclesiastical hierarchy. The Church tended to equate cohabitation with "clandestine" marriage, as the Church was inclined to presume that cohabitation, especially between people from the same social class, was an outward manifestation of private consent that created an unbreakable bond. Civil law supported this interpretation: Bartolo, for example, held that cohabitation between a man and woman of equal social class constituted presumption of marriage. Likewise, Baldo noted that "by custom a free woman kept in a house in nuptial shape, order and honor is presumed to be married unless a contrary declaration is raised."[121] Unless cohabitation was explicitly indicated as concubinage, perhaps formalized as such before a notary, it could be submitted to the judgment of the ecclesiastical judge with a good chance of being declared a real marriage.[122] This caused more than one man to present himself to the vicar to register the declarations of his concubine, who admitted to not being joined to him by any nuptial bond and assured him that, in the future, she would not bring suit for marriage.[123]

As mentioned above, according to canon law, affection (*affectus*) distinguished marriage from concubinage. Affection was defined as a moderate sentiment that should not cross into unrestrained passion, which could certainly be manifested by the man at the beginning of the relationship, but which should be restrained by the woman to make it develop into an honest union. Physical passion, for example, could be the motive that pushed a very young man to marry an older woman, or a member of a lower social class, who would have been seen as using her sexuality as a social and economic resource.[124] "Drunk on love," the man could not contain his feelings or control his erotic impulses, which caused him to transgress the most common norms of the social code in force.[125]

The love that characterized a union that was socially congruous in terms of age and status of the partners[126] did not exclude passion but manifested it delicately. Not "drunk on love," in this case, but "captured by love,"[127] the enamored man began the ritual of courtship. Frequenting a street he had previously rarely been on showed that he "used the street" for love, even before he decided to make an "act or sign or any signal… as youths do."[128] The normal site for the first encounter between youths was a party.[129] The closeness allowed by dancing favored the expression of signs clearly identified as "signs of love," such as hands that were held rather than touched fleetingly.[130] The dance was so clearly associated with pre-marital courtship that the post-Tridentine moralizers, intending to repress the customary practices connected with it, sought to stop it with the assistance of the secular government (as in Tuscany) or identified it as a reserved case, the type of sin that could only be absolved by the bishop (as in Borromeo's Milan). The ban on weddings for two years for those who danced together, desired by Borromeo, is a further confirmation of the immediate perception of dancing as an act belonging to the sphere of pre-nuptial courtship and the rituality of pre-Tridentine betrothals (*sponsalia*).[131]

In the period that followed weddings and sometimes preceded cohabitation (though not necessarily the consummation of the marriage), the familiarization between the new spouses happened in the midst of conviviality and celebration. In these occasions, nicknames and gestures that to our eyes seem only friendly were instead interpreted as clear signs of "great love," as when Francesco Toscano addressed his companion "saying 'my old one' as young people captured by love do," and giving her pats on the back "as lovers are accustomed to do."[132] It is important to note that these gestures and words were not from a witness who could appear specious, but from the wife who intended to prove the marriage.

Music and song played an important role during the wedding feast: in the period after the wedding these constituted a method of communication between spouses beginning the ritual of familiarization.[133] The husband passed by the house of his wife three or four days in festive company.[134] Common meals were accompanied by songs sung by the husband, who was joined by some of those present (for example, one of his cousins) but not by the wife, who instead guided the melody according to her preferences ("Do you know that song?" she asked her husband as he sang to her).[135] This dialogue between spouses was interpreted, in the judgment of the community, as a sign of consent to the union. The minute description of these events should not be interpreted as a mere concession to the narrative temptation or as a simple purpose of creating "a real effect."[136] The accurate noting of facts was a sign of the importance of these details for judgment and qualified them as clues and presumptions which the magistrate would be able to value in terms of their symbolic value and juridical consequence.[137]

Months or even years could pass before a couple began stable cohabitation, so non-cohabitation did not necessarily indicate that a marriage was not valid. In the meantime the husband had free access to his wife's house, where he often slept and ate in her company. The common meal, in particular, assumed a very important symbolic valence of the representation of nuptial trust (*fides*).[138] Eating together remained significant for at least two more centuries: in 1701 the Congregation of the Council, an institution founded in 1564 to resolve, among other things, doubts that arose from the interpretation of the decrees of the Council of Trent,[139] declared valid a marriage that the spouse had challenged affirming that he had been forced into it by proxy by the episcopal curia. At the moment of the wedding he found himself in jail as one night he had "violently" (*violenter*) kissed the woman he was then forced to marry. This was a grave act, immediately ascribable to pre-Tridentine nuptial rituals, and generally done to attest nuptial rights over the woman, though sometimes to impede her marriage to another man. In the post-conciliar period such a gesture became severely punished: in the Kingdom of Naples it was punishable by death, and in the Papal States by lashing, the loss of goods, and the prohibition of marriage between the kisser and the kissed.[140] In our case, however, the man was incarcerated and required to marry her, which gave him the chance to challenge the validity of sustaining a bond that was contracted by force (*per vim*).[141] The Congregation of the Council, however, rejected his case because while he was in jail, he had accepted food that the woman had prepared for him and a bed that she had furnished (it should be noted, moreover, that the bed constituted one of the household furnishings for the common house generally provided by the wife.)[142]

From the moment cohabitation began, the figure of wife was distinguished from that of concubine based on the attitude she assumed in relation with her husband, the type of relationship that tied the couple to the families of their respective partners, and the role played by the woman in the management of the house.[143] When the woman belonged to an inferior social class with respect to her husband's, each element that demonstrated the man's will to raise her to his status constituted a presumption of marriage in the eyes of the community: the clothing and jewelry worn distinguished a wife from a concubine, as did the fact that she was admitted to the company of noblewomen; or that, importantly, she knew how to read.[144]

Among the jewelry a presumed wife presented to prove a marriage, the wedding ring had particular symbolic importance. The ring ceremony, a Roman tradition, was used in the Christian West by the ninth century and was traditionally associated with the moment of the promise of marriage. Since the eleventh century the Church sought to associate this ceremony with the solemnization of the bond, to the marriage understood as a "public, solemn, and ecclesiastical event."[145] In Venice the ring ceremony assumed a subordinate role to the touch of the hand, an essential gesture of matrimonial consent. The conferring of the ring, however, constituted presumption of marriage by canon law, which defined the ring as a "sign of love" (*signum amoris*). A decretal of Alexander III mentioned the term "to pledge" (*subarrhare*) as a synonym for "to marry" (*desponsare*), and the community considered a woman wearing rings more likely to be a wife than a concubine.[146] Precisely because the ring constituted tangible proof and a symbol of marriage, a man who after 20 years decided to cast off his wife to contract a more socially advantageous marriage tore off of her finger that ring which she desperately tried to keep as a symbol of her status. A girl forced into marriage by her relatives always refused to wear the ring given to her by her husband. And a mother who disapproved of the marriage of her 13-year-old daughter held on to the ring given by the girl's husband as a sign of her control over the union.[147]

The wedding ring could be a simple band called "the true" (*la vera*), made of gold, simple or gilded silver, or even of brass (*laton*).[148] The material was always specified whenever it was mentioned as proof of marriage. A gold ring had particular symbolic value: Guillaume Durant argued that the ring should be made of gold as that metal was distinguished from the others as love distinguished itself from all other sentiments.[149] And in fact, during a marriage cause for a marriage celebrated in Feltre, a witness was asked if a man had given a ring to the presumed spouse as one in love would give to a future spouse or wife. He responded that the man had certainly given it to her as a wife, as otherwise he would not have given her a gold ring. He certainly would not have done so in the presence of her father and brothers, nor would they have been able to accept that the girl received the ring as a "future spouse."[150]

The stone set in the ring was also duly mentioned by witnesses and accurately registered by notaries: rubies, sapphires, emeralds, diamonds, and turquoise were among the most frequently mentioned jewels in the cases. In Venice, as in Florence, the gift of these stones was not the prerogative of the upper classes.[151] The precise mention of the stones was not coincidence: in the period under examination they were considered to have magical and medical properties. The ruby had the power to disperse poisons in the air and guaranteed love and fortune. According to Altieri this symbolized the body, the seat of the heart: the husband who gave his wife a ruby thus gave her his heart. The sapphire was the vehicle of the soul. The emerald, beyond protecting one from various maladies, spells, demons, and madness, shielded the chastity of whoever wore it and protected women during childbirth. Diamonds and pearls were considered at the time symbols of purity and capable of warding off various maladies.[152] Precisely for their magical-therapeutic properties, not only because they were precious, these stones constituted a nuptial gift, as was noted by witnesses who mentioned them and by judges called to value their symbolic worth. Moreover, magical value was not just attributed to the stone but also to the ring itself: it was attested that a woman should put the ring in her shoe to prevent frigidity, and that a man should urinate through his wife's wedding ring to cure impotence.[153]

The ring that the presumed wife presented to the judge was sometimes engraved with the spouses' names. At times she presented the ring that her husband usually wore on his finger, with his family's crest. Laura Pascetto, to demonstrate that she was married to Girolamo Priuli, showed the vicar a ring with Girolamo's name and her own and another with the Priuli crest and Girolamo's name.[154] The ring, in this case, constituted a very strong presumption of marriage: not only because the jewelry incontrovertibly showed its origin, but because it attested that there had been a ring ceremony which, above all in the sixteenth century, was assumed to constitute the bond of marriage. In Venetian documents, in fact, the woman was said to be married "by the putting on of the ring" (*per anuli immissionem*). If the husband lacked a ring, a woman present at the wedding would loan her own, which would be returned at the end of the ceremony: it did not seem to be necessary for the wife to receive a ring as a gift, but she did have to be married by means of a ring.[155]

If the ring constituted a presumption of marriage in favor of the woman, the handkerchief, given by the bride to the groom, was an important object which the man could present to demonstrate the marital bond. In 1506 young Marco Antonio managed to marry a 13-year-old girl, Lucrezia, who was under her mother's control. Balanced on a ladder leaning against a window covered by a grate, he put a ring with a ruby on her finger. Having received the ring, Lucrezia gave him a woman's handkerchief of Cambrais fabric, "worked around the edges in black silk" as a "sign of their true and legitimate marriage."[156] When the girl, ceding to familial pressure, denied the marriage, the young man produced the object as proof to the ecclesiastical judge. The handkerchief fringed with black silk, on display during the various phases of the litigation, contributed to the determination of the sentence in favor of the marriage.

In Venice as in Friuli, in the territory of Bormio as in Florence, a silk or linen handkerchief embroidered or fringed with lace was a customary nuptial gift that was a material sign of the young woman's consent and symbolized her purity. A Florentine suit studied by Daniela Lombardi attests to the material and strongly symbolic utility of the handkerchief as a sign that consummation had occurred; this sometimes assumed a magical valence (in Piacenza, for example, it was recognized that this nuptial gift was capable of warding off sorcery and evil magic).[157] In the realm of nuptial rituals, furthermore, the handkerchief was one of the objects that the wife sometimes gave to witnesses, to intermediaries at the wedding, or to those who congratulated her. In other words, she gave these objects to those who guaranteed the publicity of the union, which was beneficial for public order, and for which neither the validity nor the sacramentality of the bond was necessary. If a groom barged into the bride's bedroom in the middle of the night to contract a marriage with her, he reassured the servants of his good intentions by celebrating the wedding before the image of the Madonna and Child and by giving them a handkerchief.[158] The symbolic valence of this object was such that the theft of a handkerchief from the hands and the belt of a young woman carried a very severe penalty (four years of banishment and a fine of 1,500 lira) – as happened in Venice both at the end of the fifteenth century and in 1530. A more lenient response would provoke comments from contemporary witnesses, helping us to decipher the symbology of that act of theft as a violation of the woman.[159]

The nuptial union was also distinguished from concubinage by the attitude of the man towards his companion's family: the fact that he washed her mother's hands before they sat together at the table and that he addressed her with the title "madona," for example, was put forward as presumption of marriage.[160] Conjecturally the care taken by the woman for her husband's physical appearance – the cut of his hair and the trim of his beard[161] – and the management of the household were likewise elements that distinguished the figure of the wife from the concubine. The servants hastened at her command; she controlled the meals (even if the husband slept with a concubine, e.g., he ate with his wife, or he would send someone to get the meal prepared by her)[162]; and she managed the pantry and kept the keys. Just as many fifteenth-century prints represent the matron with the keys at her belt, so too in marriage litigations the fact that she kept the keys contributed to prove marriage.[163]

Beginning in the sixteenth century the existence of a conjugal bond became validated not just by these deferential rituals executed by various members of the family, which attested to the role and status of each within the family, but also by the practice of the sacraments, which were permitted for spouses but denied to concubines.[164] These are also indices of a growing control by the Church over nuptial and para-nuptial practices enforced through confessions, foreshadowing post-Tridentine control.

It was understood that while a woman sought to prove a marriage by demonstrating her own strong religiosity – which she expressed by making alms, confessing her sins, and taking the Eucharist at the required times (practices evidently not conforming to those who lived "as a concubine" *more uxorio*) – the husband sought to refute the bond by attesting he did not practice the sacraments at their required times because the woman in question was his concubine, not his wife. This expedient became useless when the wife demonstrated he did not take the sacraments because he had another woman as his concubine.[165]

Based on the declarations of the parties that, regardless of their veracity, appeared plausible, it seems that sometimes the will to be readmitted to the practice of the sacraments pushed the woman to end an affair and convince the man to transform their relationship into marriage. When Lucrezia Scaletaria took leave of her lover, saying "Domenego, go with God, I do not want to make this life anymore, I want to confess and communicate, for this reason I want to marry," he immediately got ready for the wedding: "I accept you as my wife."[166] I have not compared similar declarations in the fifteenth century, when the criminalization of concubinage in Europe began. This process was realized in 1514, during the Fifth Lateran Council, in the first universal norms that prohibited such practices – norms that remained a dead letter for a long time, at least in Italy.[167]

In the sixteenth century, the practice of confession was not only an indication of the fact that the debated union was nuptial instead of concubinatory, it also became a moment of spiritual preparation for the wedding and corroborated the proof of matrimony. When a woman named Isabetta went to demonstrate her marriage to Francesco, she told the judge that Francesco had declared "I have confessed and communicated with this intention… I believe that you understood that I love you and therefore I want you… now for my true and legitimate wife."[168]

10   The Sentence

During the cause the judge could issue interlocutory sentences. These did not end the litigation but contained the judge's provisions pertaining to it. This kind of sentence was issued, for example, to arrange for the custody of an alleged wife in a convent, to remove her from influences that could compromise the outcome of the litigation[169]; or to allow evidentiary delays, permitting the interrogation of a witness in his or her own house rather than in the tribunal, and so on.[170] The interlocutory sentence did not necessarily have to be registered; it could simply be summarized among the procedural acts.[171]

When the probatory phase of the suit ended, the judge issued a definitive sentence, which had to be recorded in writing. It began with a divine invocation (eventually also to the Madonna or to some saint, according to the devotional inclination of the judge); it mentioned the judge, the parties in the case and their respective procurators; and it presented a brief summary of the procedural phases. At the end came the pronouncement. The judge had to respond to all of the plaintiff's claims, to condemn or absolve the defendant, to condemn one or the other party to pay the litigation costs (which could also be split between the parties or be remitted "for the good of peace"[172]), to establish the amount of that payment, or to reserve the right to set it later. As the sentence was recorded in Latin, sometimes it had to be translated for the parties by the nuncio of the curia.[173]

The sentence was executed immediately and the parties were obligated to respect it under penalty of excommunication. It should be noted, however, that for consistency with the principle of *favor matrimonii*, the sentence that declared a marriage non-existent was never reexamined, and sometimes the judge who pronounced it transferred responsibility to the conscience of the parties,[174] leaving open the path to a reunion if the parties would be united in matrimony "before God and the Church triumphant."[175]

Many marriage causes lack a sentence.[176] This is not always attributable to a lacuna in the documentation.[177] Ostensibly the opening of the litigation, used as an instrument of pressure on the opposing party, favored reaching an agreement that ended the dispute, even though (based on canonical norms) the marriage suit could not conclude without a sentence from the ecclesiastical judge. Moreover, the substitution of the judge with arbitrators was technically not allowed.[178] In practice, however, the judge tended to assume the function of mediator, avoiding emitting a sentence if the parties could agree, in conformity with the rules of pre-modern justice.[179]

11   The Appeal

If the sentence seemed unjust, it could be brought up on appeal. The appeal had to be presented to the same judge who had pronounced the original sentence (*iudex a quo*). The appeal was divided into three phases: the presentation or denunciation (as soon as the sentence was pronounced the loser protested *viva voce de appellando*),[180] the filing of the appeal, and finally, the execution or justification of the appeal. If the juridical terms were not respected (which in Venice were generally for three months), the right to appeal was lost.

During the appeal the judge who had issued the sentence was asked to answer the *apostoli*, which were formulas of complaint to the judge of the appeal. The *apostoli* could be dimissory, reverential, or refutatory. In the case of dimissory *apostoli* the judge simply remitted the case to a superior magistrate, such as the Pope, or to the competent judge if one of the two parties had raised founded objections to the magistrate's competence. Reverential *apostoli* remitted the case to the superior judge, who then delegated the suit to another seat with apostolic commission (but in Venice it often stayed within the patriarchal tribunal, as it was the court of appeal). Refutatory *apostoli* did not allow for appeal, however; instead the appellant had the right to send the *apostoli* directly to Rome.[181]

12   The Execution of the Sentence

The execution was for the most part tacitly left to the discretion of the parties. It was likely, in the face of resistance, that the tribunal was almost powerless to make people respect its decrees.[182] From the systematic examination of the curial registers it does not seem that the tribunal took advantage of coercive instruments to ensure the execution of matrimonial sentences, with the exception of excommunication, which was the greatest sanction issued by the Church and had grave implications that went beyond the spiritual sphere, as the excommunicate was also deprived of civil and juridical rights.[183] Excommunication against someone who did not respect the provisions of the sentence rarely happened and was done by the request of the winner of the litigation, as when Maria di Negroponte presented herself to the vicar with her daughters and asked him to enforce the sentence issued several years earlier against her husband, requiring him to fulfill his obligations as husband and father.[184]

If the parties did explicitly make a request, the tribunal could assume the role of intermediary in the execution of the sentence, coordinating, for example, the process of *transductio*, a rite through which the bride installed herself in the marital house.[185]

13   The Summary Procedure

In the introduction we analyzed the function of the summary procedure within a process of simplification of classical Roman canonical procedures, the complex development of which entailed considerable time and cost in addition to a specialized knowledge of the law. The abbreviated process also had an important function in the realm of arbitral justice.[186] I will limit myself here to present its strictly formal characteristics.

According to the summary rite the litigation could be started without written petition (*libellum*), with an oral exposition of the material under contention. The counter party could be called to court through a peremptory citation (which, as we have seen, required his or her immediate appearance in court) that explained the object of the plaintiff's request. Summary procedure did not require the contestation of the suit; it provided for proceeding within a week (*tempore feriarum*); it excluded dilatory exceptions (regarding, that is, the incompetence of the plaintiff or the judge); it put limits on the disputes between the parties, the lawyers, and the procurators; and it limited the number of witnesses.[187] As we will note later, the summary procedure, which also allowed those who were excluded, like excommunicates, slaves, and minors, to act in court, encouraged the magistrate to assume an active role.[188]

Notes

1. R. Helmholz, *Marriage Litigation*, p. 141 and note 1; Gulielmi Durandi, *Speculum iudiciale*, book II, partic. I, § 1, n. 1.
2. See *supra*, ch. 1.
3. Of the 706 cases of marital conflict catalogued relative to the period 1420–1500, 22 were cases of appeal. See *infra*, ch. 6.
4. S. Tramontin, *Dall'episcopato castellano al patriarcato veneziano*.
5. X 2.19.9. The obligatory verbalization of litigation acts was sanctioned by the Fourth Lateran Council of 1215. See G. Alberigo et al. (eds.), *Conciliorum Oecumenicorum Decreta*; *Concilium Lateranense IV-1215*, 38, *De scribendi actis, ut probari possint*, p. 252.
6. W.M. Plöchl, *Geschichte des Kirchenrechts*, p. 354. On judicial notaries See C.J. Duerr, *The Judicial Notary*, pp. 12–25.
7. For example, see ASPV, *CM*, vol. 2, fasc. 7, Ursina Basso *vs* Alvise Soncin, 1462 for the presence of the bishop's servants.
8. ASPV, *CM*, vol. 3, fasc. 9, Giovanni Nascimbeni *vs* Ursolina, 1473, c. 6; ASPV, *CM*, vol. 6, fasc. 15, Maddalena Fontana *vs* Zuane Andrea Fragonà, 1497–1498; ASPV, *AMP*, reg. 46, 27 February 1493, Pro domino Jacopo de Parleonibus.
9. ASPV, *CM*, vol. 12, Anthea Ariano *vs* Thoma Michiel, 1512.
10. Employing the same procurators for marriage causes was common practice in other dioceses as well. See for example R. Helmholz, *Marriage Litigation*, p. 120 regarding Hereford, Rochester, and York; and for Padua, see M. Alexander, *Paduans*.

11. R. Helmholz, *Marriage Litigation*; C. Donahue Jr., *Law, Marriage and Society*; C. Deutsch, *Ehegerichtsbarkeit in Bistum Regensburg*; L. Schmugge, *Ehen vor Gericht*. For the comparison of various tribunals See *infra*, ch. 7, and the observations of Donahue on pp. 622–632.
12. W.M. Plöchl, *Geschichte des Kirchenrechts*, p. 362. About *crimen*, See C. Donahue Jr., *Law, Marriage and Society*, pp. 26–7. As was already noted in the introduction, and as will be explained in greater detail *infra*, ch. 4 § 5, if the marriage litigation was initiated by one party it is possible that the complainant was sent by a confessor as a condition of receiving absolution.
13. See Gulielmi Durandi, *Speculum iudiciale*, book II, partic. I, De actione seu petitione, nn. 7–8, p. 369.
14. Ibid., partic. II, De reo.
15. *In facie ecclesie*. The expression *in facie ecclesie* reflects a much more varied and ample reality than the statement "in the front of the church" implies. See *infra*, ch. 5.
16. These causes were very numerous. See for example ASPV, *CM*, vol. 5, Regina de Colbrusato *vs* Ioanne Cornelio de Como, 1484, in which Puccino da Prato was called beside Regina, "si putat suo interesse"; ASPV, *CM*, vol. 7, Bernardina de Garzonibus *vs* Bernardino conte de Collalto, 1500, in which Andriana Tron was called beside Bernardino; ASPV, *CM*, vol. 4, fasc. 3, Soprana Bonavita *vs* Antonio Dolfin, 1475–1476, where a certain Caterina was called beside Antonio.
17. A case of this sort was analyzed in C. Cristellon, *Ursina Basso contro Alvise Soncin*. On the *concilium* of the jurist elaborated in favor of Ursina in this cause see G. Marchetto, *Il «matrimonium meticulosum»* and the bibliography cited here on p. 248, note 5 on Cipolla. On the procurators and the episcopal court, in particular in Padua, see M. Alexander, *Paduans*.
18. ASPV, *CM*, vol. 3, fasc. 4, Paolo Gabrieli *vs* Isabella Bartolomei, 1470; *CM*, vol. 6, fasc. 10, Elisabetta Simoni *vs* Natale da Cattaro, 1496; *CM*, vol. 4, fasc. 5, Domenico de Medulis *vs* Marietta, 1476: in this case the woman's procurator was her stepfather.
19. ASPV, *CM*, vol. 6, Comina Bonsignori *vs* Stefano Verdelli, 1496.
20. ASPV, *CM*, vol. 6, Giovanni Luchini a Serico *vs* Cassandra de Marconibus, 1492–1493.
21. ASPV, *AMP*, reg. 15, Pietro Cortese *vs* Santuccia q. Bartolomei Platarii, 23 March 1453– 4 July 1453.

22. ASPV, *CM*, vol. 12, Adriana Nigro *vs* Pietro Bontremolo, 1512–1514.
23. "Bona conditione et fama." ASPV, *CM*, vol. 12, Theodosia de Grandis *vs* Antonio Entio, 1512.
24. The phases of the procedure occurred consecutively following the structure described in A. Lefebvre-Teillard, *Les officialités à la veille du Concile de Trente*, pp. 46–70, relative to civil causes. On the procedure of the classic civil canonical cause see also W.M. Plöchl, *Geschichte des Kirchenrechts*, pp. 353–359; K.W. Nörr, *Zur Stellung des Richters*. On the procedure of marriage litigation see also R. Helmholz, *Marriage Litigation*, pp. 113–140 for English cases; also C. Donahue Jr., *Law, Marriage and Society*, pp. 33–41.
25. See Gulielmi Durandi, *Speculum iudiciale*, book II, partic. II, De actore, § 1, n. 9, p. 168. In Lucca, for example, a girl who was declared a minor at her first court appearance was ordered by the judge to return after she had turned 12, because as she was too young to contract a marriage she was also too young to break the bond in court. See C. Meek, *Liti matrimoniali*, pp. 117–118.
26. See Gulielmi Durandi *Speculum iudiciale*, book II, partic. II, De actore, § 1, respectively n. 13, p. 168 and n. 17, p. 169. Minor excommunication, however, "non repellitur ab agendo": Ibid., n. 13, p. 168.
27. E. Brambilla, *Confessione*, pp. 497–500 regarding judiciary excommunication, and p. 499 for the citation. Judiciary excommunication was called "ab homine" in canon law to indicate that it was pronounced by a single ecclesiastical judge against a single individual. See Ibid., p. 498. See also Eadem, *Battesimo*. On excommunication see also R. Helmolz, *Excommunication*. On Ecclesiastical censure See also T.D. Albert, *Der gemeine Mann*, pp. 47–52.
28. "Non in modo et formam solemnis libelli sed talis qualis petitio." For examples of petitions not presented in *libellum* but instead as an oral denunciation see ASPV, *CM*, vol. 2, fasc. 11, Matheus Barilarius *vs* Margardia, 1462, c. 17. See also R. Helmolz, *Marriage Litigation*, p. 121 and n. 29.
29. W.M. Plöchl, *Geschichte des Kirchenrechts*, p. 355: "quis petat, a quo, quid et qualiter et coram quo."
30. "Messer prè Bernardino, me meraviglio del fatto vostro, quello ve ho dito una volta v'el digo de rachao."
31. "Perpetuo silenzio." ASPV, *CM*, vol. 11, Ludovica Calbo *vs* Marino da ca' Viniani.

32. ASPV, *AMP*, reg. 8, Giovani Catani *vs* Barbarella, 15 January 1440.
33. "Non voglio venir, il patriarca faza iustitia....il vicario faza rason." ASPV, *CM*, vol. 13, Alovisii Basilio *vs* Adriana di Treviso, 1514.
34. "Non voglio venir, disè al vicario che faza quello li par e piaza... non volgio venir, faza quello li piaza e non voglio venir più." ASPV, *CM*, vol. 11, Domenico Santurini *vs* Elisabeth filia Simonis Piva, 1510–1511; also ASPV, AMP, reg. 46, Niccolò di Zara *vs* Nicoletta, 6 February 1493, where the woman who was presented with the petition said she did not want to respond beyond "what may be just."
35. "Per plateam et ecclesiam Sancti Marci et Rivum Altum et alia loca publica...et inter amicos et cognatos." ASPV, *CM*, vol. 7, Caterina Minoto *vs* Marco Abramo, 1500; C. Meek, *Liti matrimoniali*, p. 132, mentions a woman who fled her house as soon as she saw the nuncio arriving on horseback, because the citation was not delivered in court. R. Helmolz, *Marriage Litigation*, p. 118 and n. 13, mentions the case of a man who threatened to split the heads of the nuncio and anyone else who came to cite him.
36. ASPV, *AMP*, reg. 9, Caterina Ungara *vs* Antonio di Treviso, 29 August 1442; *AMP*, reg. 9, Maria Martini *vs* Giovanni da Mencastro, 12 August – 1 October 1442; *AMP*, reg. 10, Vittorella *vs* Niccolò da Corfù, 28 January-1 February 1443.
37. ASPV, *AMP*, reg. 10, Rosa *vs* Raffaele, 3 June– 31 July 1444.
38. ASPV, *AMP*, reg. 10, Domenico Fanten *vs* Caterina filia Nicolai de Vanzon, 1443.
39. See Gulielmi Durandi *Speculum iudiciale*, book 2, part. 1, De contumacia, § 1, p. 448.
40. On true or presumed contumacy See Ibid., n. 2, p. 448. See for example ASPV, *CM*, vol. 11, Domenico Santurini *vs* Elisabeth filia Simonis Piva, 1510–1511.
41. Gulielmi Durandi, *Speculum iudiciale*, book II, part. I, De contumacia, § 1, notes 2 and 3, p. 450.
42. See the bibliography of Brambilla cited *supra*, note 27.
43. ASPV, *AMP*, reg. 10, Meneghina *vs* Zanino veludario, 4 December 1443.
44. ASPV, *CM*, vol. 29, Pelegrina linarola *vs* Dominico linarolo, 1530–1531.
45. See Gulielmi Durandi *Speculum iudiciale*, book II, partic. I, De contumacia, § 2, n. 1, p. 450. See ASPV, *AMP* 11, Zanfrancesco di Antonio di Cipro *vs* Luchina, 13 January 1455.
46. "Liberavit Isabetam ab ipso Nicolao." ASPV, *AMP*, reg. 2 Nicolao Cerdone *vs* Isabetta, 24 January 1421.

47. The judge could proceed against the contumacious party up to the definitive sentence also when the contestation of the suit had not occurred. See R. Helmholz, *Marriage Litigation*, 1974, pp. 124–126, and p. 125, note 49.
48. ASPV, *AMP*, reg. 34, Cattarino Sutore *vs* Bona da Strana. The sentence, not published, was delivered "in contumacia dicte Bone, cuius absentia Altissimi presentia suppleatur." This was not dated, but the register in which it was recorded is from 1475. An analogous case is found in R. Helmolz, *Marriage Litigation*, p. 126 and note 50.
49. "Publice... ad domicilium suum cum apotheca et bonis suis." "vel saltem non legitime". ASPV, *AMP*, reg. 15, Pietro Cortese *vs* Santuccia Platari, 23 March – 4 July 1453.
50. See *infra*, ch. 5, § 3.
51. ASPV, *AMP*, reg. 24 Franceschina Venier *vs* Paolo Priuli, 7 January 1463.
52. ASPV, *CM*, vol. 11, Clara Brano *vs* Baldassare Penzino, 1511.
53. ASPV, *CM*, vol. 13, Johannis de Masonibus *vs* Polissena Vidutiis, 1513. See Guliemi Durandi *Speculum iudiciale*, book II, *De iuramento calumnie*, § 1, n. 6, p. 571.
54. A. Lefebvre-Teillard, *Les officialités à la veille du Concile de Trente*, p. 51.
55. "Ste' firmi, mìtti zuso!" ASPV, *CM*, vol. 1, fasc. 13, Giorgio Zaccarotto *vs* Maddalena di Sicilia, 1455–1458.
56. For territorial incompetence, see for example ASPV, *CM*, vol. 5, fasc. 8, Regina de Colbrusato *vs* Ioanne Cornelio de Como, 1484.
57. "Coniuncto in tertio grado." ASPV, *CM*, vol. 7, Vittore Pisani *vs* Candida Bollani, 1500.
58. Recusing a magistrate was an exceptional act that I have found in only two other cases: ASPV, *AMP*, reg. 29, *Quinternus sententiarum*, and *AMP*, reg. 33, Niccolò a Bulzia *vs* Paula, 5 October 1474. On the recusing of the judge see L. Fowler, *Recusatio iudicis*; I. Pérex de Herédia y Valle, *Die Befangenheit des Richters*.
59. See G. Minnucci, «*Simplicier et de plano*», p. 178 and note 6. On Maddalena's dowry see P. Benussi, *Oltre il processo*, pp. 160–161.
60. On the basis of applicable canonical legislation, one of the spouses could take religious vows even against the will of the other if the marriage had not been consummated. See X 3. 32. 2.
61. On arbitral jurisdiction see G. Cozzi, *La politica del diritto*, in particular p. 108; G. Ferri, *L'arbitrato tra prassi e sistemazione teorica*

nell'età moderna, Roma 2012, in particular pp. 23–59. Regarding juridical norms see Gulielmi Durandi *Speculum iudiciale*, book I, partic. I, De arbitro et arbitratore, §§ 1–10, pp. 102–132.

62. A. Lefebvre-Teillard, *Les officialités à la veille du Concile de Trente*, p. 51. On the fact that in marriage litigations the sentence did not proceed in judgment, see *infra*, §10.
63. On *litis contestatio* in the twelfth through eighteenth centuries see S. Schlinker, *Litis contestatio*.
64. "Nego narrata prout narrantur et dico petita fieri non debere." See Gulielmi Durandi *Speculum iudiciale*, book II, partic. II, De litis contestatione, § 2, n. 2, p. 563.
65. Ibid., n. 4, p. 564.
66. ASPV, *CM*, vol. 11, Catherina Iohannis Petri de Vincentia *vs* Hieronimo Mathei de Pergomo, 1509–1510. See also *CM* vol. 12, Anthea Ariano *vs* Thoma Michael, 1512. Defeated at Agnadello by the League of Cambrai (1509), Venice lost dominion over all the cities of the terrafirma. Padua, once reconquered, was the front for the siege by imperial troops whom they were able to resist thanks to the intervention of mercenaries and Venetian volunteers led by Andrea Gritti. See F.C. Lane, *Storia di Venezia*, pp. 284–288.
67. See Gulielmi Durandi, *Speculum iudiciale*, partic. II, De litis contestatione, § 6, pp. 569–570.
68. ASPV, *CM*, vol. 7, Caterina Minoto *vs* Marco Abramo, 1500.
69. The spontaneity of such oaths seems to contradict the norm according to which "iuramentum nunquam est praestandum antequam exigatur." See Gulielmi Durandi *Speculum iudiciale*, lib. II, De iuramento calumnie § 2 n. 4, p. 573. Examples of spontaneous oaths: ASPV, *CM*, vol. 1, fasc. 8, c. 3. Leonardo Marangon *vs* Onesta Blanco, 1453; *CM*, vol. 1, fasc. 9, c. 6, Natale da Castelfranco *vs* Clara Restia; *CM*, vol. 1, fasc. 11, f. 5.
70. For example in ASPV, *AMP*, reg. 46, Matteo d'Austria *vs* Maria di Niccolò da Padova 29 March 1493; *AMP*, reg. 46, Domenico da ca' Mauro *vs* Caterina di Niccolò, 17 April 1493.
71. ASPV, *CM*, vol. 3, fasc. 1, c. 18, Antonio Pasetto *vs* Samaritana, 1468; vol. 3, fasc. 2, c. 2, Margherita Manica *vs* Giuliano de Sanctis, 1468. In both of these cases the plaintiffs quickly said they would swear to present their positions without the intention of lying, but they did not say an oath, nor were they asked to do so.

72. ASPV, *CM*, vol. 2, fasc. 16, Maria Sanador *vs* Dioniso Gabrieli e Allegretto, 1465; *CM*, vol. 3, fasc. 7, Antonio da Genova *vs* Suor d'Amor Malabotta, 1471.
73. See Gulielmi Durandi *Speculum iudiciale*, lib. II, partic, II, De positionibus, § 5, n. 14.
74. The only exception is ASPV, *CM*, vol. 25, Diana Minio *vs* Alvise Caravello, 1526–1527.
75. See *supra*, § 6. The author translated here from the Latin the text which she transcribed in the original in *Appendice documentaria* in S. Seidel Menchi – D. Quaglioni (eds.), *Matrimoni in dubbio* (CD-ROM).
76. See Gulielmi Durandi *Speculum iudiciale*, book II, § 6, n. 5. Doctrine required that the plaintiff's version would also be presented under oath, taken by him or herself or by the procurator *in animam principalis* (the moral responsibility for the oath rested on the soul of the instigator). Ibid., book II, partic. II de positionibus, § 5, n. 14, p. 587.
77. The possibility of representing one's own client in the obligation of responding to the *positiones* is recognized by the same jurist, which diminishes the strength of the regulation mentioned before. Ibid., book II, partic. II de positionibus, § 6, n. 18, p. 588.
78. ASPV, *AMP*, reg. 24 Franceschina Venier *vs* Paolo Priuli, 7 January 1463. The defendant was a nobleman, absent from Venice on business, and his representative in court was not a relative, but the ordinary procurator of the curia.
79. ASPV, *CM*, vol. 6, Giovanni di Luchino a Serico *vs* Cassandra de Marconibus, 1492–1493.
80. On the ritual of the oath and the emotional hold of the act see *infra*, ch. 4, § 8, and the documentation and bibliography cited there.
81. Fourteen was the minimum age required by the decree for the issuance of a valid oath. See C XXII, q. V. See also *infra*, ch. 4, § 8 and note 162.
82. ASPV, *AMP*, reg. 9, Jacopo Franco *vs* Agnesina de l'Orsa, 4 October 1441.
83. See Gulielmi Durandi *Speculum iudiciale*, book. II, partic. II, De confessionibus, *additio*, p. 603.
84. I. Rosoni, *Quae singula non prosunt collecta iuvant*; A. Giuliani, *Il concetto di prova*.

85. G. Marchetto, *Il «matrimonium meticulosum»*, pp. 250–1; also L. Turchi, *Adulterio*, pp. 332–3.
86. See Gulielmi Durandi *Speculum iudiciale*, book I, partic, IV de teste § 11, n. 7, p. 335. For exceptions to the case see *ibid.*, n. 8, pp. 335–6. The literature consulted considered the deposition of a single witness valid proof of marriage if it was combined with very strong presumptions of marriage. See C. Valsecchi, *«Causa matrimonialis est gravis et ardua»*, p. 477. On testimonies in ecclesiastical tribunals see C. Donahue Jr., *Proof by Witnesses*.
87. A. Giuliani – N. Picardi, *La responsabilità del giudice*, p. 30. See also U. Nicolini, *Il principio di legalità*, p. 119; D. Quaglioni, *La responsabilità del giudice*; G. Marchetto, *Il «matrimonium meticulosum»*, pp. 250–1. The analysis of criteria through which testimonial proof was built and how the credibility of witnesses was valued is found in chapter 3. Explicit reference to the discretion of judges in marriage cases in ASPV, *CM*, vol. 9, Isotta filia adoptiva magnifici Aloysii Michael *vs* Marco Antonio Caravello; See *infra*, ch. 3, n. 28. On the role of *arbitrium* of the judge in marriage cases, see also *supra*, ch. 1, point 9 and the bibliography cited there.
88. See Gulielmi Durandi *Speculum iudiciale*, book II, partic. II, De confessionibus, § 1, p. 604 and § 3, n. 7, p. 608. On the role of confession within the system of legal proofs see P. Marchetti, *Testis contra se*; I. Rosoni, *Quae singula non prosunt collecta iuvant*; C. Povolo, *L'intrigo dell'onore*. On confession from its foundation in Canon Law from the middle ages to the contemporary penal trial see P. Brooks, *Troubling Confessions*.
89. See Gulielmi Durandi *Speculum iudiciale*, book II, partic. II, De confessionibus, § 1, p. 604, p. 606, n. 7.
90. C. Valsecchi, *«Causa matrimonialis est gravis et ardua»*, pp. 483–484, and note 171. ASPV, *AMP*, reg. 8, Alessio di Scutari *vs* Monica, 17 July 1439.
91. ASPV, *AMP*, reg. 28, Giovanni di Francia *vs* Brigida de Alemannia, 14 March 1466.
92. ASPV, *CM*, vol. 11, Cecilia di Asolo *vs* Angelo Badoer, 1509–1510.
93. ASPV, *AMP*, reg. 10, Benedetto *vs* Venturina, 3–6 July 1443; *AMP*, reg. 15, Blasio de Albania *vs* Maddalena, 5 April 1454; *AMP*, reg. 17, Falcone q. Giovanni da Pergamo *vs* Beatrice Francigena, 21–23 January 1456. See also C. Donahue, Jr., *Law, Marriage and Society*, p. 37.

94. ASPV, *AMP*, reg. 13, Giovanni da Rodi *vs* Lucia albanese, 14 January–27 March 1450.
95. According to Andrea Barbazza and Bartolomeo Camerario, for example, a couple had to consent to continue in "comercium matrimoniale" also in cases of a cause for the annulment of a preceding bond. See C. Valsecchi, *«Causa matrimonialis est gravis et ardua»*, p. 492, note 214.
96. See *infra*, ch. 5, § 3.
97. ASPV, *AMP*, reg. 34, Pietro Chemeto *vs* Maria di Scutari, 16 January 1475.
98. "Tu è mia moiér." On nuptial rituals see *infra*, ch. 5, §§ 1–2.
99. J. Brundage, *Law, Sex and Christian Society*, pp. 319 and 345; C. Donahue Jr., *Proof by Witness*.
100. See ASPV, *AMP*, reg. 10, Niccolò da Conegliano *vs* Polissena di Pietro, 20 November 1444; ASPV, *CM*, vol. 13, Filomena Tinelli *vs* Angelo e Franceschina, 1514. See also R. Helmholz, *Marriage Litigation*, p. 127.
101. See A. Giuliani, *Il concetto di prova*, pp. 175–189. On the doctrinal aspects see D. Quaglioni, *Diritto e teologia*.
102. See R. Provinciali, *Giuramento decisorio*, in particular p. 107.
103. See *infra*, ch. 4, §§ 1 and 8.
104. Ibid.
105. ASPV, *CM*, vol. 12, Clara Marcello *vs* Francesco de Orlandis, 1512.
106. See Gulielmi Durandi *Speculum iudiciale*, book II, partic. II, De praesumptionibus, p. 736.
107. Ibid., § 2, n. 1, p. 737.
108. As according to Bartolo. See J. Brundage, *Law, Sex and Christian Society*, p. 436; L. Ferrante, *«Consensus concubinarius»*, p. 109, note 3.
109. Another probable presumption was fornication in the case of a man and woman surprised in the nude in bed or in a secluded and hidden place (*secretis locis et latebris*): see Gulielmi Durandi *Speculum iudiciale*, book II, partic. II «De praseumptionibus», § 2, notes 2 and 3, p. 737.
110. R. Helmholz, *Marriage Litigation*, p. 98, C. Donahue, *Marriage, Law and* Society, p. 99. A particularly significant case is in E. Orlando, *Pubertà e matrimonio*. On this theme see more diffusely infra, ch. 5, § 7.
111. ASPV, *CM*, vol. 5, Luca Semitarius *vs* Lucia Jacobi a Fenestris, 1488; ASPV, *CM*, vol. 6, Cassandra Badoer *vs* Niccolò Venier, 1491.

112. X 4. 2. 18.
113. See Gulielmi Durandi *Speculum iudiciale*, book II, partic, II, De praesumptionibus, § 2, nn. 5 and 6, pp. 738–739. Regarding influenced marriage see *infra*, ch. 5, § 6.
114. S. Seidel Menchi, *Percorsi variegati, percorsi obbligati*.
115. ASPV, *CM*, vol. 7, Bernardina de Garzonibuz *vs* Bernardino conte di Collalto, 1500–1501.
116. "Forsi che sì." See *infra*, ch. 5.
117. J. Brundage, *Law, Sex and Christian Society*, p. 297; L. Ferrante, «*Consensus concubinarius*».
118. C. Cristellon, *Ursina Basso contro Alvise Soncin*.
119. J. Brundage, *Law, Sex and Christian Society*, p. 297, and notes 182–183. To justify the fact, the author of *Summa Parisiensis*, who was the first to resolve the problem of concubinage distinguishing between concubinage with and without marital affection (the first of which constituted marriage, the second merely fornication), recalled Salic Law. Other authors, including Sicardo da Cremona or Uguccione, made this distinction themselves and identified concubinage with clandestine marriage. See also J. Gaudemet, *Il matrimonio in Occidente*, p. 116 and note 25, p. 382; D. Quaglioni, «*Sacramenti detestabili*», p. 65 and note 14. For an analysis of the juridical significance of *affectus maritalis* see also F. Pedersen, *Marriage Disputes in Medieval England*, pp. 153–175.
120. On the rituals of behavior and deference and the ceremonies of recognizing social roles as part of social order, see A. Bergensen, *Die rituelle Ordnung*, in particular pp. 60–62.
121. "In consuetudine liberae mulieris tentae in domo in schemate, in ordine et onere nuptiali matrimonium praesumitur nisi in contrarium interveniat protestatio." For Bartolo, see J. Brundage, *Law, Sex and Christian Society*, p. 436. For Baldo, see C. Valsecchi, «*Causa matrimonialis est gravis et ardua*», p. 491.
122. Regarding concubinage stipulated before a notary see G.L. Barni, *Un contratto di concubinato*, p. 132; also A. Eposito, *Convivenza e separazione*.
123. ASPV, *AMP*, reg. 32, 10 August 1472, Declaratio pro Vito toscano et Leonarda. The vicar interrogated the woman to ascertain that she made her declaration "nullo sibi metu incusso aut violentia sed sponte et libere." Similar cases are found in ASPV, *AMP*, reg. 10, Giovanni di Pergamo *vs* Isabetta, 30 March 1444; *AMP*, reg. 17, 14

April 1455, request of Giovanni q. Petri de la brazza, sclavone, *AMP*, reg. 32, 3 July 1472; *AMP*, reg. 32, 17 July 1472.
124. I am using the expression of L. Ferrante, *La sessualità come risorsa*.
125. ASPV, *CM*, vol. 21, Helisabeth filia Iohannis Buttarii *vs* Gaspare Ioannis Pistoris, 1522.
126. See on this subject S. Chojnacki, *Women and Men*, pp. 185–205; Idem, *Valori patrizi nel tribunale patriarcale*, pp. 207–8.
127. "Filocaptus" or "captus amore." ASPV, *CM*, vol. 10, Elena Rosso *vs* Ludovico Bono, 1508–1509.
128. "Us[a] della via," "Acto né cigno né signal alcuno... come suol far i zoveni." ASPV, *CM*, vol. 9, Alessandro de Pastis *vs* Marietta Zeno, 1506. On courtship rituals in the Italian Jewish community see R. Weinstein, *Marriage Rituals*, pp. 239–244.
129. ASPV, *CM*, vol. 7, Martino q. Baptiste Cursii *vs* Giovanna filia Iohannis liberalis de Arteno, 1507.
130. "Signa amoris." ASPV, *CM*, vol. 7, Maria q. Andree de Matheis *vs* Vincentio Dragano, 1503.
131. D. Lombardi, *Storia del matrimonio*, pp. 116–118. For laws against balls decreed by Cosimo III in Tuscany see E. Fasano Guarini, *Gli «ordini di polizia»*, pp. 83–4. For Borromeo's dispositions, see W. De Boer, *La conquista dell'anima*, pp. 72–75 and 241–251.
132. "Amorem magnum," "Dicendo 'vechia mia' prout faciunt iuvenes amore capti," "ut solent facere amatores." ASPV, *FC*, vol. 3, Helisabeth filia Marini hartaroli *vs* Franciscus Amizo, 1520. For an interesting analysis of marital sociability and the objects ascribable to this, see M. Ajmar Wollheim, *The Spirit is Ready, but the Flesh is Tired*.
133. S.F. Weiss, *Medieval and Renaissance Wedding Banquets*.
134. "De briga[ta]."
135. "Saveu la tal canzon?"
136. R. Barthes, *L'effet de reél*, also N. Zemon Davis, *Fiction in the Archives*; O. Niccoli, *Introduzione*, pp. XIX–XXII.
137. S. Seidel Menchi, *Cause matrimoniali e iconografia nuziale*.
138. See *infra*, ch. 5, § 2.
139. F. Romita, *Le origini della S.C. del Concilio*.
140. O. Niccoli, *Storie di ogni giorno in una città del Seicento*, pp. 109–129 and in particular p. 128. On the symbolic significance of the kiss see also *infra*, ch. 5, § 2 and the bibliography cited there.
141. On marriage *per vim* see *infra*, ch. 5, § 8.

142. ASV, CC, *Synopsis*, vol. 2, c. 80. On the fact that wives generally provided beds see R. Sarti, *Vita di casa*, pp. 49–50.
143. ASPV, *AMP*, regs. 26–29, Bartolomeo Alovixii draperius *vs* Maria de Andrea, 8 July 1465– 16 July 1466.
144. ASPV, *CM*, vol. 7, Bernardina de Garzonibuz *vs* Bernardino conte di Collalto, 1500. On the distinctive characteristics of wives and concubines, see also E. Eisenach, *Marriage, Family, and Social Order*, pp. 148–149.
145. S. Seidel Menchi, *Cause matrimoniali e iconografia nuziale*.
146. During the ring ceremony the groom could give the bride more than a ring. See for example the document cited *supra*, note 144. The gift of more than rings is also mentioned in C. Klapisch-Zuber, *La maison e le nom*, pp. 200–208.
147. ASPV, *CM*, vol. 7, Bernardina de Garzonibuz *vs.* Bernardino conte di Collalto, 1500; *CM*, vol. 9, Marco Antonio de Stefani *vs* Lucrezia q. Simonis Vacha, 1506.
148. For a silver ring see ASPV, *CM*, vol. 2, fasc. 13, Christophorus Batibambaso *vs* Catarina, 1462; for a gold one *CM*, vol. 1, fasc. 10, Armanno Theutonico *vs* Agnete, 1454.
149. E. Chénon, *Recherches historique*.
150. "Morosa"S. Seidel Menchi, *Percorsi variegati, percorsi obbligati*, p. 81.
151. See for Florence J. Kirshner, *'Li emergenti bisogni matrimoniali'* in *Renaissance Florence*, p. 88, and notes 26–27.
152. Ibid., p. 87, and note 24.
153. E. Muir, *Ritual in Early Modern Europe*, p. 41.
154. ASPV, *CM*, vol. 2, fasc. 6, Laura Pascetto *vs* Gieronimo de Priolis, 1461; also, relative to the same case, ASPV, *AMP*, 22, 17 August 1460.
155. ASPV, *CM*, vol. 20, Laurentii Tamburlini *vs* Maria da Mugla, 1521. On wedding rings see also I. Rossoni, *Anelli nuziali nel XVI secolo*; D. Lombardi, *Matrimoni di Antico Regime*, pp. 220–227.
156. "Muliebre… laboratum serico nigro circumcirca… segno di vero e legittimo matrimonio".
157. C. Corrain – P. Zampini, *Documenti etnografici*, p. 49; D. Lombardi, *Matrimoni di Antico Regime*, p. 209; also O. Niccoli, *Baci rubati*, p. 240.
158. ASPV, *CM*, vol. 2, fasc. 10, Catharina de Varda de Nigroponte *vs* Matteo Permarin, 1462–1465.

159. ASVe, *Consiglio dei X, Criminale*, fil. 6, 17 and 28 May 1530. M. Sanuto, *I diarii*, LVI, pp. 95–96. The documents are also cited by P. Molmenti, *La storia di Venezia nella vita privata*, and by P.H. Labalme – L. Sanguineti White – L. Carroll, *How to (and How Not to) Get Married*, pp. 65–66.
160. ASPV, *CM*, vol. 7, Bernardina de Garzonibuz *vs* Bernardino conte di Collalto, 1500.
161. L. Menegon, *I figli naturali*, p. 75.
162. See the document cited *supra*, note 160.
163. O. Ranum, *I rifugi dell'intimità*, p. 169. ASPV, *CM*, vol. 3, fasc. 3, Barbarella de Pastis *vs* Giorgio Zaccarotto.
164. See *infra*, ch. 3, § 6, the document cited above, note 160, and *infra*, ch. 4, note 131.
165. Ibid. In the "proof of nobility" procedures through which non-patrician women sought to obtain permission to marry Venetian noblemen, among the reasons for which witnesses were inclined to argue that a woman had the status of wife rather than concubine was the fact that she sat at the table with her husband and guests and gave orders to the servants, who obeyed her without reservation. See A. Cowan, *Marriage, Manners and Mobility in Early Modern Venice*, p. 130.
166. "Domenego, va con Dio, non voglio più far questa vita, me voglio confessar e comunegar, perciò me voglio maridar." "Mi te accepto per moier." ASPV, *CM*, vol. 18, Lucrezia Scaletaria *vs* Domenico Varotario, 1517–1522.
167. G. Romeo, *Amori proibiti*, in particular pp. 8–9. For the growing restrictions of the fifteenth century, see J. Brundage, *Law, Sex and Christian Society*, pp. 514–517; J. Harrighton, *Reordering Marriage*, pp. 123–124; and A. Esposito, *Adulterio, concubinato, bigamia*. From what appears in the actual state of research in Italy, in the early sixteenth century only Verona took up the spirit of this norm under the leadership of Gian Matteo Giberti, an exceptional bishop. See E. Eisenach, *Husbands, Wife and Concubines*.
168. "Io me ho confessà e comunicà cum questa intention…: io credo che vi haveti acorta che ve ho voluto ben et sì ve voglio… tuor adesso per mia vera et legitima mogier." Helisabeth filia q. ser Marini hartaroli *vs* Franciscus Amizo toscanus filius ser Sebastiani 1520. See also ASPV, *FC*, vol. 3, Giovanni di Cumo *vs* Paola Albanese e Albertino da Brescia, 1531.

169. For examples of confinement in a convent during the suit see *infra*, ch. 4, § 1.
170. ASPV, *CM*, vol. 2, fasc. 7, Ursina Basso *vs* Alvise Soncin, 1462.
171. A. Lefebvre-Teillard, *Les officialités à la veille du Concile de Trente*, p. 59 and note 79. In the acts of the curia of Venice, in fact, only the orders for interlocutory sentences were summarized.
172. "Pro bono pacis." ASPV, *AMP*, reg. 7, Antonio Sarasino *vs* Iacobella Trevisano mother of Isabetta, 12 January 1438 (the controversial marriage was between Antonio and Isabetta); ASPV, *AMP*, reg. 7, Giovanni Pansa *vs* Caterina de Luse, 4 February 1439.
173. ASPV, *CM*, Hieronima Quirini *vs* Andrea de Dominicis, 1512–1513.
174. Examples of reference to the conscience in ASPV, *CM*, vol. 7, Andrea de Ballinio de Brixia *vs* Helisabeth filia Petri de Flandria 1504; *CM*, vol. 7, Niccolò q. Dominici Cortesii *vs* Angela filia Sebastiani Cavazza, 1503–1508; *CM*, vol. 9, Isotta, filia adoptiva magnifiici Aloysii Michaael cum Marco Antonio Caravello, 1507; *CM*, vol. 9, Ludovica Calbo *vs* Marino da cà Viniani, 1509; *CM*, vol. 11, Andrea Marzari *vs* Bernardina Vincentina 1510; *CM*, vol. 11, Helisabeth Cristophori textoris *vs* Jacobo de la Zotta, 1510.
175. "Davanti a Dio e alla chiesa trionfante." See the most analyzed treatment *infra*, ch. 4, §§ 7–8.
176. See the quantitative data *infra*, ch. 6.
177. Sentences are always reported in the curial registers which, for the period 1420–1500, are almost completely preserved.
178. See Nicolai de Tudeschis *Commentaria in quinque libros Decretalium*, book I, tit. 43, can. 10, n. 1; also R. Helmholz, *Marriage Litigation*, p. 135. Regarding the conclusion of the process before the emission of the sentence and its significance within Ancièn Regime justice, see the observations *supra*, ch. 1, point 9.
179. See the data furnished *supra*, ch. 1, note 146.
180. ASPV, *CM*, vol. 2, fasc. 7, Ursina Basso *vs* Alvise Soncin, 1462.
181. W.M. Plöchl, *Geschichte des Kirchenrechts*, pp. 338–339; P. Fournier, *Les Officialités au Moyen-Age*. Examples of refutatory *apostoli*: ASPV, *AMP*, reg. 28, Pasqualina *vs* Guidone (Vito) Trevisano, interveniente Isabetta, 12 February 1466.
182. The absence of children born to a couple whom the judge had ordered to cohabit is sometimes considered as an indication that they had not executed the sentence. See A.M. Lazzeri – S. Seidel

Menchi, *«Evidentemente gravida»*, p. 327, n. 86; S. Chojnacki, *Valori patrizi nel tribunale patriarcale,* pp. 241–242.
183. For the absence of references to modes of coercion to ensure the respect of the sentence, see ASPV, *AMP*, regs. 2–37 (1420–1480) and reg. 46 (1492–1493). See also ASPV, *FC*, vols. 1 (1446–1498), 2 and 3 (16th century).
184. ASPV, *AMP*, 25, 19 December 1464; see also *CM*, vol. 29, Pelegrina linarola *vs* Domenico linarolo, 1530–1531.
185. See *infra*, ch. 4, § 2.
186. See *supra*, ch. 1, point 9.
187. See Clem. 2. 1. 2; Clem. 5. 11. 2.
188. See *infra*, ch. 4, § 8.

CHAPTER 3

Witnesses and Testimony

The preceding chapter emphasized the primary importance of testimonial proof for the elaboration of the Roman-canonical procedural system beginning in the twelfth century.[1] This chapter examines how testimonial proof was presented and received in the tribunal. It analyzes the criteria for choosing witnesses, investigates the instructions they received, discovers attempts at subornation, probes the ties that united witnesses and parties in the case, evaluates the strength of the bonds that they were subjected to (above all the oath), and illustrates how evidence was verbalized.

It begins, therefore, by illustrating the criteria for the admission of witnesses and how their credibility was evaluated, placing this in the context with the tribunal's practices and the juridical norms. This chapter has two parallel objectives. The first is narrative – the reconstruction of the system of deposition, of its weight and limits. The other is hermeneutic – the evaluation of the reliability and verifiability of narrative and biographic constructs placed before the judgment of the marriage tribunal.

1   THE DEPOSITION AND REPORT

In the marital litigation witnesses were almost exclusively biased towards one party.[2] The plaintiff and defendant presented their own versions of facts and a list of witnesses who could attest to them. The witnesses had to be presented after the formal joinder of issue, with rare exceptions for the expected absence of the witness if he or she were in danger of death and had certification from a doctor, or due to the "malicious" (*malitiosa*) absence of the defendant, who was then declared contumacious.[3] The judge was strict in this regard: in the case of a priest of "decrepit age" (he was over 60), the vicar refused to proceed to the interrogation before the correct time, as he had not "made faith" that, in spite of his white hair and his suffering from "the French disease," he should fear imminent death.[4] In another case, when a witness was interrogated before the joinder of issue because he had to leave the city, the judge rejected the deposition once he ascertained that the witness had still not left Venice eight days later.[5]

There were strict requirements governing the deposition of witnesses. Witnesses had to be summoned by the judge; spontaneously appearing to depose was considered suspicious.[6] Witnesses were interrogated on articles presented by the party who had called them. Based on the rules, any declarations that lay outside the same articles had no value.[7] Beyond the articles presented by the party who called them, witnesses could depose on a list of questions produced by the procurator of the counter-party, which were principally intended to undermine their credibility.

The judge was responsible for the interrogation of witnesses. The judge could, however, delegate to the notary or chancellor in civil cases, but not in criminal ones.[8] In fact, based on the sentences he issued it seems that the magistrate did not personally interrogate witnesses and was only familiar with their depositions through the filter of the notary's reports.[9]

At the end of the deposition the notary reread the record to the witness to confirm it and did not fail to note possible hesitations, which diminished his or her credibility.[10] Suits in other dioceses document both antagonistic reactions to the notary's choice of one term over another[11] and the complete faith in the report ("you do not need to read it again, because I heard and saw that which you have written and I confirm it.")[12] The Venetian documentation does not record reactions of witnesses to the reading of the report, but the substitution of one term for another could either be from a notary's error or clarification by the witness.[13] While the question was most often recorded in Latin, responses were generally recorded in the vernacular, especially by the sixteenth century. In a cosmopolitan city like Venice the depositions of some witnesses – mostly Greeks or Germans – had to be translated by an interpreter into Latin (*sermone latino*).[14]

Although the interrogation of witnesses generally happened in the patriarchal curia, "noteworthy" (*notabiles*), old, ill, and female witnesses could be interrogated in their houses by the chancellor or notary.[15] When some "Venetian patricians" refused to present themselves in Castello – the seat of the Curia – the magistrate, appeasing them, sent a notary to examine them in the Rialto.[16]

2   The Witnesses' Oaths

When witnesses presented themselves in court, they (and their necessary translators) had to take an oath to tell the truth (*de veritate dicenda*). Among the witnesses, no one seemed to be *a priori* exempt from the obligation of the oath, not even the chancery staff, who were also sworn in.[17] Nor was the patriarch's vicar exempt when he was called to depose before his own successor regarding a marriage that the couple had wanted to celebrate before a witness of unquestionable credibility (as was the vicar) and wanted it recorded in the curial register to avoid the opposition of the bride's relatives to the wedding.[18] The curial nuncio was not exempt[19]; nor was the notary, who in the litigation between Ventura di Francesco and Jacopo Polo (1446), for example, had to swear at the explicit request of Jacopo's procurator.[20] Only the chancellor seems to have been considered credible by virtue of his position. In the case between Alessandro de Pastis and Marietta Zeno (1506), Francesco Morandi, chancellor of the curia, is found among the witnesses. He was not a biased witness, however. Alessandro sought to demonstrate his marriage to Marietta through a series of evidence, including the dense amorous correspondence[21] he had maintained with the young woman thanks to the complicity of an intermediary. To this end, he presented a witness who had seen the intermediary give a letter to Marietta. After he had examined this witness, the patriarch – on the suggestion of the girl's father – ordered the chancellor to conduct an inspection to verify the truth of his affirmations. When the chancellor reported the results of his inspection in court, he was not required to take an oath; his declaration was put in the acts and the fact that he did not swear an oath was not highlighted in any way.[22]

Not all witnesses could swear when they were admitted to depose: representatives of the regular clergy could only take oaths with permission from their superiors, as they were bound by a vow of obedience that prevented them from testifying (and therefore from swearing oaths) without that permission.[23]

In one exceptional case, a witness refused to swear because he did not want to.[24] The laconic recording of the notary does not permit us to certify the method or motivation for this refusal, nor does it record the reaction of the judge. It was probable, however, that the vicar did not place particular pressure on the witness, nor did he investigate the motivations for his behavior,[25] so far as the refusal to take an oath was a serious act that could make whoever undertook it suspect of heresy.[26] The deposition of an unsworn witness was admitted. We cannot determine, however, what level of credibility was given to it – according to doctrine it had no value[27] – nor if it were decisive, since the party who had presented that witness won the case, but the deposition of the unsworn witness was bolstered by many others agreeing with it. The acceptance of an unsworn deposition was probably due to the custom of the Venetian tribunal to admit almost all witnesses to depose, evaluating their credibility after excusing them. This was a practice lawyers sought to oppose, since such depositions obviously risked influencing the judge, even if they were given by a witness declared not credible.[28]

Unlike what happened in criminal and inquisitorial trials[29] and sometimes in other dioceses,[30] in Venetian marriage litigations an oath of silence (*de silentio*) was rarely requested of the witnesses.[31] Thus, they were not obliged to be silent outside the court about their interrogations or about the declarations made in court. The lack of an imposition of an oath of silence – which was not required by doctrine[32] – had clear implications for the formation of testimony. Witnesses involved in marriage suits must have exchanged news and comments on what was discussed in court[33] (it should be noted that witnesses were often united to the protagonists of the case and to each other by ties of family, alliances, and neighborhoods), but the tribunal did not consider it necessary to prevent this occurrence. Witnesses could then legitimately contribute to spreading a version of facts through dialogue outside of the court. This version of the facts was structured by the articles and defined by the cross-examination, it was shaped during the proceedings, spread beyond the tribunal and then brought up again.

3   The Formation of Testimony

Pre-Tridentine nuptial practices strongly conditioned both how testimony was formed and the criteria of admissibility for witnesses adopted by the tribunal.

Marriages that landed in court were often contracted in a private or secret form. In the first case, those who had assisted were generally tied to one party by bonds of kinship or "familiarity." This rendered a witness less credible in court. When the marriage was contracted in secret, however, the couple could only produce circumstantial evidence. It was understood that before a suit for an alleged marriage, a woman would conduct preliminary investigations among the acquaintances of her presumed husband, hoping to find potential witnesses.[34] Not all potential witnesses were presented in court. The bad reputation of some[35] or the possible declarations of others threatened to invalidate the version of facts that the party intended to sustain. These could be revealed in extreme cases by witnesses examined ex officio because they were named by others as able to give context,[36] primarily by the same witnesses called by the parties.[37]

In the case that involved Ursina Basso and Alvise Soncin (1461–1462), for example, Alvise sought to obtain an annulment of their marriage by claiming the impediment of fear (*metus*).[38] Ursina sought to argue against his version of marriage by fear (*meticulosum*), declaring first of all that there were no reasons that could cause Alvise fear. As the only circumstance which could embarrass Alvise, the young woman mentioned a chance encounter that had occurred in the house between Alvise and her mother. Though he was not surprised in an intimate situation with Ursina, Alvise had felt the need to justify his presence there, presenting himself as the young woman's husband and claiming as his right the frequenting of her house. The situation was certainly not sufficient to frighten a "steadfast man" (a man who was not subject to baseless fears).[39] A witness presented in favor of Ursina, however, hinted at the young woman's pregnancy, which had not yet been mentioned. It is not surprising that Ursina sought to keep her pregnancy a secret. The circumstance, in fact, rendered her tale baseless, as it constituted a serious motive for Alvise to fear the violent reaction of the young woman's family. Keeping the pregnancy a secret was also a part of Alvise's strategy. He too had valid reasons to hide the fruit of their union: a child predisposed the judge to consider the bond between the parties as stable and freely made – and stability was often considered presumption of marriage.[40]

Because testifying could be inconvenient, it is not surprising to find statements to convince witnesses to present themselves in court that say that one of the parties in the case promised them gifts or recompense, which ranged from sums of money to plots of land.[41] Even the gift of shirts (*camisie*) figured among the incentives considered useful for encouraging a witness to depose.[42] Probably because they knew that paying witnesses constituted a form of compensation, some canonists did not automatically consider witnesses who had received recompense untrustworthy.[43]

It is very probable that, as happened in other episcopal tribunals,[44] lawyers and procurators in Venice had preliminary meetings with the witnesses, during which they prepared witnesses for interrogation with general proofs from the hearing in the tribunal without pushing them to manipulation and falsification of testimony. These meetings reflect an effort to avoid declarations that would diminish the witnesses' credibility. The witness, in fact, had to declare if he cared for one party over the other, declaring who he wanted to win or whom he considered to be right, to specify if he wanted to obtain a certain advantage from the deposition, and if he was tied to – or divided from – the parties by feelings of love or hate.[45] To express one's own opinion or to manifest one's own hopes about the case's result diminished the witness's credibility. The uniformity that characterized responses to the cross-examination – "he proves neither love nor hate for the parties," "he does not know towards which party reason leans," "he desires that the party in the right wins" – is suspicious to the historian. How can one believe, for example, that a person who had assisted at a wedding ceremony, a fact obstinately denied by one of the parties, could spontaneously affirm that he did not know which party was right? How can one believe that a mother presented as a witness for her daughter could declare that she did not prefer one party over the other? It is useful instead to consider these declarations necessary for establishing the credibility of the witness. Rare divergences from the script – "He prefers more the said Hieronima, and wants madonna Hieronima to win"[46]; "he wants the person who is right to win, and he believes that Salomona is right"; and "he would like Filippo to bring Salomona to his house as his wife"[47] – attest that the intervention of procurators was either not systematic or not always effective.[48]

If the preparation of testimony appears trustworthy, its manipulation is sometimes discovered in the same procedural files.[49] We find biased witnesses who, once under the bond of the oath, confessed to having been induced to depose falsely with the promise of considerable patrimonial advantages, "especially a Venetian house," or a field.[50]

The same positions (*positiones*) of the parties were sometimes articulated in such a way as to favor an appeal to complacent witnesses, as is discovered in the case that involved Cassandra de Marconibus and Giovanni di Luchino a Serico. The two young people were married by avoiding and somewhat defying the control of Cassandra's brothers, who then forced her into a convent.[51] When Giovanni addressed the ecclesiastical judge to claim his wife, he underestimated the girl's determination and tenacity: he presented a version that restructured the events on the foundation of recurring *topoi* in marriage litigations, the attempts of the young girl's relatives to impede the spread of knowledge of it. Recall that the defendant had to respond to the *positiones* with the formula *credit* or *non credit*, and that the contested positions were transformed into *capitula* about which witnesses were interrogated.[52] With a glaring infraction of the norms, which usually saw the defendant flatly deny the affirmations of the plaintiff, Cassandra substantially confirmed Giovanni's story: she confessed to the marriage, recalled how she had been terrorized by her mother and placed under the strict control of the nuns in her convent, but she flatly denied the conventional circumstances to which Giovanni had made recourse. The positions of the plaintiff were then revealed as contrivances that could only have been corroborated by willing witnesses.

4   Perjury: An Open Question

The principal weapon against false testimony at the disposition of the ecclesiastical tribunal was the oath, which was imposed on all witnesses through a very strongly emotional ritual.[53] Though this ritual sometimes had the effect of inducing witnesses and their parties to reveal legal constructs they had devised,[54] its power to prevent false declarations and immunize against a mortal sin that could bring excommunication was not absolute.[55]

Here we see open another gap between norms and practices. Although perjury constituted a mortal sin, the pre-Tridentine ecclesiastical tribunal did not adopt any repressive action against it. In the 253 sentences I examined the judge sometimes declared that the loser had not presented sufficient proof or that he or she had not presented "unexceptionable witnesses."[56] In other cases he praised the behavior of the winner or vigorously underlined the improper recourse of the loser to the tribunal.[57] But judges never accused the witnesses of lying, even when the false testimony was obvious,[58] nor did they mention the necessity that they be punished for perjury by the patriarchal tribunal or any other tribunal.

Whether the patriarchal tribunal adopted punitive measures against perjury and to what extent remains an open question.[59] Possible provisions were not documented in the sentences of marriage litigations or in the curial registers, which provide records of cases brought before the patriarchal tribunal, as well as of injunctions, mandates, threats, and declarations of excommunication. On one side it seems improbable that the judge proceeded against perjurers – either personally or by delegating it to the judgment of another authority – without making note of it in the sentence, because sentences often recorded indications about actions to be followed in a legal arena regarding other questions not strictly connected to the issue being contested in the marriage case, such as the dowry or the payment of court costs.[60] On the other side, both the gravity of the sin of perjury and the absence from the same curial registers of other types of suits (which are documented in other archival series)[61] do not allow us to completely rule out that such instructions were given and documented.[62]

The Inquisition's fight to impose their own jurisdiction over the crime of blasphemy, a crime which included perjury,[63] since the late Middle Ages[64] could also have resulted in the assumption of jurisdiction over the crime of perjury by this tribunal in Venice. This hypothesis however is not confirmed by the examination of the inquisitorial trials, in which – at least for the period which concerns us here – there are no recorded proceedings against perjurers.[65]

It is also possible that this documentary silence is due to the fact that patriarchs and their vicars proceeded against perjury in the internal forum (*forum internum*), allowing their pastoral role to take priority over their judicial role, particularly considering that in marriage cases accusations of perjury were sometimes explicitly raised by the other party.[66] Perjury was included among reserved sins that were under the bishop's jurisdiction and could not be absolved by a regular confessor, and which could only be absolved by compensation of the damage inferred by whomever had been harmed.[67] To be absolved of the sin of perjury – when the witness had claimed to be ignorant of a marriage he or she knew to exist – he or she would have to confess to the bishop, who would need to reopen a proceeding to declare in an external forum (*forum externum*) the validity of that marriage. No proceeding of this type is documented among the curial registers. In the current state of research, then, we still are not able to understand what, if any, measures were adopted by the Venetian ecclesiastical tribunal against perjury.[68]

5   The Burden of Testimony

Legally, the faculty to depose was considered an honor, as an index of credibility and good reputation.[69] In the Venetian documentation, it is clear that deposing was an onerous experience, sometimes discrediting or dangerous. People who presented themselves to depose lost precious time working for which they were not reimbursed. A woman named Lucia, when asked about her hopes of obtaining some "benefit" from her deposition, noted to the examiner that she would receive only harm, as "she loses time, and she makes a living working silk day and night."[70] Some witnesses who lived outside of Venice refused to present themselves to depose unless they would be reimbursed for the expenses they would incur by appearing in the tribunal.[71]

After having testified about the facts under debate in the litigation, the witness submitted to cross-examination which attempted to prove – or better, to challenge – his or her credibility. The witness's life and the lives of relatives were sifted through, digging up decades-old events[72]: his or her honor was in danger. In order to protect themselves witnesses sometimes begged discretion, presenting petitions to be exempt from the obligation to appear personally in court and to instead be interrogated in their own homes.[73]

A controversial marriage – because it was socially unequal, secret, or disapproved of by relatives – was a cause of social tension that emerged in the marriage suit. The tribunal was not always able to contain latent violence: a husband might unsheathe his sword in the presence of the judge,[74] witnesses of opposing factions might brawl,[75] lawyers might be threatened and abused.[76] Witnesses feared to present themselves in court because of the pressures they endured, whether generic intimidation ("keep your tongue inside your teeth, and mind your own business"),[77] threats that could be carried out through networks of alliances that extended beyond Venice,[78] or actual acts of physical violence.[79] In the face of looming violence, the prospect of ecclesiastical censure was not enough to cause reluctant witnesses to present themselves in court: "Because of excommunication I will go to the flames, but I do not want to be killed," replied a certain Luca to the vicar's threats of excommunication.[80]

To give testimony was an obligation that broke ties of solidarity. It could induce the magistrate to issue a verdict perceived by the witness as unjust because it was contrary to rules of the community and was sometimes destined to encounter strong resistance. For example, when a certain Alvise abandoned his sick wife after nine years of cohabitation, believing he could obtain an annulment since his wife, Margherita, had previously married another man, the witnesses, who were allied with her, refused to present themselves to depose.[81] In the eyes of the community, which, as we will see, perceived multiple marriages as legitimate as long as the first marriage was *de facto* ineffective,[82] Alvise and Margherita were bound by the conjugal bond and he had no right to abandon the sick woman. When he summoned them to testify about the former marriage, the witnesses would not appear in the tribunal. The judge could interrogate them only through the intervention of the secular arm.

Testifying could also create a crisis of conscience. Even if they could identify a bond as marriage with certainty based on the customary parameters, those who were called to depose sometimes led the judge to issue a sentence of annulment, as the judge could act based on another law, sometimes irreconcilable with the laws of the community. And if the discomfort of some witnesses can only be speculated,[83] others declared it openly. "It seems to me that it is right that dona Perina should win, because she is right, because this marriage is public and manifest," one woman declared, invalidating her own testimony with this declaration of partiality.[84]

For economic motives, for fear, in order to preserve their honor, or out of solidarity, many witnesses refused to appear in court and had to be forced to do so under threat of excommunication: "if one is asked to testify, one cannot refuse to tell the truth without incurring a mortal sin."[85] Often they were brought to the tribunal with the help of the secular arm. By invoking the coercive force of lay magistrates, an ecclesiastical judge recognized the weakness of his own moral authority.[86]

5.1 Credibility of Witnesses

In 1454, Isabetta, the daughter of a boatman addressed the patriarch, claiming to have contracted a marriage with Jacopo da Marignano. According to the young woman's story, during Lent Jacopo came to her house saying to her parents that he wanted her as his "spouse" (*fia*). Alarmed, her mother objected that Jacopo was eligible to receive a "great dowry" (*gran dote*), which Isabetta was in no place to provide. Jacopo replied that marriage with a poor girl offered him the opportunity to redeem himself from a life of sin and return to the practice of the sacraments: in fact, for ten years, he had kept a concubine. Finally cornered by her mother, who was worried that Jacopo's frequent visits would damage her daughter's reputation, he married the young woman before her parents, two women (Elena and Diana, a mother and daughter, respectively), a certain Bartolomeo, and a certain Luchina. At the ceremony the taking of hands and the exchange of the ring had occurred, and then there was a dinner and a dance.[87]

During the litigation, Elena and Diana were summoned to depose for Isabetta while Bartolomeo and Luchina were summoned for Jacopo.

All confirmed the ceremony, only disagreeing on how the consent was expressed. For Elena and Diana it had been verbal and gestural, but for Bartolomeo and Luchina only gestural: Isabetta's father, addressing Jacopo, had invited him to take his daughter's hand in the sign of matrimony; he had taken her hand but had not said any words. Fifty years later this marriage would likely have been declared "valid, legitimate, and contracted *in facie ecclesie*." At the time of this case, and for the entire fifteenth century in general, the Venetian tribunal tried to devalue the taking of hands (which constituted for the laity the most efficacious expression of consent) in favor of verbal consent.[88] Isabetta then needed to demonstrate that Jacopo had expressly declared that he wanted to take her as his wife.

The parties in the case could each count on two witnesses. Legally, the concurring testimony of two exemplary witnesses[89] constituted a full proof: therefore, whoever could diminish the credibility of the other's witnesses would win the case. The nature of marriage litigation, during which two distinct groups of witnesses were presented because they supported two contrasting stories, made the tenor of the sentence dependent on the credibility of the witnesses. As Richard Helmholz has noted, in marriage litigations there was little chance of success if one could not demonstrate that the opponent had used suspect witnesses or induced them to give false testimony.[90]

The procedure required that each of the two parties in the case give the other party the list of witnesses they intended to present in court, so the other side could conduct investigations about their reputation and compile a list of questions to address to them at the end of their deposition, to explore – or in practice, to damage – their credibility. The battle to delegitimize witnesses was rendered more bitter by the practices of the pre-Tridentine ecclesiastical tribunal, which saw the court assume a benevolent attitude in the face of witnesses presented to sustain the marital bond, out of respect for *favor matrimonii*.[91] This predisposition explains the imbalance that is found in some suits between the small number of probatory witnesses (*testes probatori*) presented by the plaintiff to prove his or her story and the dense crowd of reprobatory witnesses (*testes reprobatori*) intended to discredit the first witnesses, presented by the defendant. Sometimes the plaintiff presented his or her own witnesses to defame the reprobatory witnesses and rehabilitate the probatory witnesses.[92]

The result of the cause depended on demonstrating the witnesses' good or bad reputation. In the suit between Isabetta and Jacopo, the presumed husband had an advantage; he could bring at least nine witnesses to court, who were neighbors and as such more credible,[93] who testified about the terrible reputations of Isabetta's two witnesses, "extremely poor and of abject lives," (it should be noted that a poor witness was considered less credible because he or she was assumed to be more corruptible)[94] – whose house was frequented by men night and day. Diana, moreover, was pregnant but not married. Against the witnesses presented by Jacopo, the plaintiff could not demonstrate anything, "so, in doubt, they were presumed to be adequate."[95]

This example effectively attests to the importance of delegitimizing opposing witnesses to win a case. In this section, I propose to analyze the ways in which a tribunal evaluated witnesses' credibility. To this end I will also use some juridically motivated sentences, which will allow me to infer the reasons behind a judge's choices.

The credibility of a witness was evaluated based on gender, class, age, geographic provenance, and ties with the party who produced him or her, with respect to shared social values and their practice of the sacraments. Women's testimony was considered with suspicion, based on the principles of canon law – which ended up being generally applicable[96] – by which the words of a woman were fickle.[97] Overall, in marriage litigations, the positive testimony of two exemplary women was considered sufficient to prove the existence of a bond.[98] But if it were possible to raise objections against a female witness, the *qualitas sexus* rendered her more suspect.[99]

The subject of the litigation often entailed recourse to familial witnesses, often the only or the best-informed of the facts: even parents and siblings were found among the witnesses. Although procedure did not exclude familial witnesses *a priori*, especially in cases of alleged marriage, it attributed greater or lesser credibility to them based on whether the controversial union was socially congruous[100] and whether there had been sexual relations between the two parties, as these had an effect on the honor of the woman and could influence the credibility of her relatives. Doctrine actually proclaimed that only in the event of parity of social status between spouses and when there had not been sexual intercourse between them could relatives be considered trustworthy witnesses; otherwise their statements were intended to promote their own prestige or to avoid familial dishonor.[101] Parity of status, moreover, did not render familial witnesses above all suspicion.[102] The trustworthiness of familial witnesses was ultimately weakened by their possible cohabitation with the party who produced them. Cohabitation also threatened the weak credibility of servants and dependents.

Beyond "excessive affect" towards the producing party, "capital hatred" or enmity towards the other party also diminished a witness's trustworthiness: to have suffered blows for committing theft, to have been defamed, fired, or denounced before a judicial authority (and so on) were motives of enmity or capital hatred that undermined the credibility of the witness.[103] This could be mitigated by demonstrating that the conflict had been resolved, by attesting, for example, that they had shared a common meal and greeted one another, but lawyers objected that an enemy, even a reconciled one, should be excluded from testimony *a principio*.[104]

Direct involvement in the controversy between the presumed spouses – threats to the family of the contested bride ("Give Marino his bride if you don't want us to burn down your house"),[105] or a declared intention to spread the rumor of marriage ("Tell her then that if she wants to deny the truth I want to be the one who goes about saying that she is the wife of Marco Antonio.")[106] – denoted lack of balance and excessive involvement in the case and contributed to a witness's lack of credibility. According to Thomas Aquinas and Alessander of Hales, moreover, the disclosure of a "clandestine fact" that prefigured defamation constituted a sin and rendered the person who tarnished the other a suspect witness.[107]

Among the witnesses many marriage litigations included midwives (indicated in the examined documents as "matrone"), doctors, and surgeons to verify either the virginity of the woman or the impotence of the man.[108] Cases that involved midwives were much more common, as the certification of a woman's virginity often assumed a central role in suits for alleged marriage, for annulment to take the veil, and for annulment because of male impotence, sometimes verified by proving the woman's virginity rather than the man's sexual inability. According to canon law virginity was to be verified by three midwives of good reputation[109] who, in the cases examined here, were chosen by the judge or nominated by the parties.[110] The same happened with doctors and surgeons.[111] Except in unusual cases,[112] doctors and surgeons were not used to delegitimize midwives; midwives were considered credible "experts" (*periti*).

Expert testimony was primarily founded on observation, and regarding credibility in the tribunal, there was a hierarchy of senses that privileged sight: the only credible testimony was that *de visu*, while *de audito* testimony was not credible on its own, not even in the presence of the fact. Witnesses preventively hidden in the attic or behind the bed in a room where the bride intended to induce the husband to express his consent to the marriage had to affirm that they had seen – assisted by ample cracks – rather than heard the couple while they expressed *de presenti* consent.[113] Their testimony would otherwise be worthless despite their familiarity with the couple and their ability to recognize them by voice alone.[114]

Age was another variable that affected a witness's trustworthiness. In the cause between Marco Antonio Caravello and Isotta Michiel, the judge mentioned that among the qualities that rendered the testimony of one of Marco Antonio's witnesses unsuitable was that she was illegitimate and young – at that point 19, a legally adequate age for deposing in court. In marriage litigations we sometimes find witnesses who may not have been of a suitable age to testify. In the case that involved Ursina Basso and Alvise Soncin (1462), for example, it was objected that one of Ursina's witnesses, Margherita, was not yet 12 years old. When questioned about her age, the girl admitted that she was a minor when the facts of the case had occurred but insisted that she had since turned 12.[115] This made a substantial difference: a pre-pubescent (*impubes*) witness could not testify – probably because he or she could not take an oath[116] – but a witness who had reached the acceptable age (12 for girls, 14 for boys) could give testimony on what had happened before they were legally old enough to testify, just as a slave, once free, could testify on what had happened while he or she was enslaved, and a blind person could refer in court to things he or she had observed while still able to see.[117]

Foreign origin, often associated with indigence and suspect of connivance with the "Turks," could also be used against witnesses.[118]

Adopting the strategy of accumulating arguments, the Soncin family used another biographical fact that could negatively influence the magistrate: they emphasized Margherita's Slavic (*sclavona*) origins, countering her self-definition as "from Treviso (tarvisina)".

We have seen that the strategy for delegitimizing witnesses followed a preset script. There were several common accusations raised against witnesses in addition to those already mentioned. One was theft – in one case aggravated by the fact that the object stolen was infected by the plague, and thus the witness was also an infector.[119] Women were also frequently accused of sexual promiscuity and the practice of magical arts.[120] The accusation of practicing magic also allows us to speculate, for the period under examination, a connection between marriage litigations and inquisitorial trials, during which accusations were mostly for *herbaria*, use of magic philters, medicaments, and incantations used for amorous purposes.[121] Against male witnesses accusations of sodomy were sometimes raised.[122] More common were accusations of pandering or games of chance – with the elevated charge of being a cheat (*baro*) and of gambling "all night in the company of great gluttons."[123] These last accusations not only stressed the violation of patterns that regulated the economic life of the community but also the transgression of bodily ethics and cycles of time: the gambler managed his money in an immoral way and did not take account of the passing of time, whether natural (day-night), artificial (work-repose), or ritual (work-pray).[124] Excessive and disordered gesturing was connected to gambling, which often degenerated into fights with sometimes fatal consequences, potentially starting a vendetta.[125] The accusation of being a cheat, in particular, often designated criminals. At the end of a case a witness given to games of chance was rendered particularly suspect for the contiguity – commonly perceived – between gambling and blasphemy, which, as we have seen, was a sin/crime that included perjury. The person who was given to gambling, then, assumed in statutory literature the traits of a person who induced naïve people into the error of lying.[126] Inclined to excesses, disrespectful of the rules, a threat to social order, blasphemers and liars were potential perjurers; the gambler could therefore not be a credible witness.

Male witnesses were also accused of having a concubine and of necromancy. When accusing a man of having a concubine, the reprehensible fact that he led a "whore" (*putana*) to dancing was often emphasized.[127] This was likely mentioned because by doing this, he introduced the concubine to a social environment usually associated with courtship and the stipulation of nuptials.[128]

In cases of alleged marriage brought by women, the defendant could invalidate a male witness by arguing that he was in love with the plaintiff, that he had had sexual relations with her and was the promoter of the marriage she wanted to prove. The argument was considered logical and judicially effective because of the socially codified custom that obliged a patron to restore the honor of a young seduced woman or a stable concubine by furnishing her with a dowry and finding her a husband of equal condition at the end of the relationship.[129] The seducer or lover was not therefore an impartial witness, as he gained personal advantage from the proof of the marriage. By unwritten customary laws, in fact, restoring the honor of the seduced by placing her in the marriage market also protected the honor of the seducer.

A witness's practice of the sacraments was also included among the criteria for credibility. Practicing the sacraments proved one's obedience to the Church, which prescribed the practice of Easter confession and communion (the ritual question addressed to the witness was, in fact, "if you obey the Church every year") – a prescription which was, however, frequently disregarded in this period.[130] If a witness violated the Easter precept, he or she could refuse to describe the motive, like a certain Maria, who "this year has not taken the Eucharist 'because of a certain respect' that she does not want to explain, but she has confessed."[131] When the witness responded in a more detailed manner, furnishing explanations about abstaining from the sacraments, a truth that clearly revealed "the consequential connection between confession and pardon" emerged.[132] In fact, the reluctance to go to confession was often motivated by hate or enmity, and those who nurtured such sentiments preferred not to confess so that they would not be forced to pardon, as with the witness who had not confessed because of "the great hatred" that he still felt towards those "who brought the plague into my house last year, because of which eleven of my people died."[133]

Questions relating to confession were therefore intended to unmask possible breeches of the Church's requirements, as indicated by the reluctance to take the sacrament. This could be a double-edged sword, however, revealing unfounded attempts to discredit a witness. For example, the accusation directed at a witness of having a concubine was quickly retracted when it was proven that his presumed concubine had communicated and confessed regularly for at least 15 years, indicative of the fact that she was considered his wife. This condition, beyond that fact that it was considered unlikely that a man of 64 years old would have a concubine, rendered him exemplary.[134]

In the period we are examining, however, confession was not the widespread instrument of control it would become after the Council of Trent. When a procurator raised objections against a witness by accusing him of concubinage – and claimed to demonstrate it by proving that his parish priest had never administered the sacraments to him – the defendant objected that no one had proven he had not confessed in another parish or to some itinerant friar.[135] Such an objection caused the procurators to put forward more specific questions, ordering witnesses to specify in which church they had confessed and communicated, and before which priest.[136]

It seems evident that the criteria used to evaluate witnesses' credibility reflected the social hierarchies in force and contributed to reinforcing them, above all in cases regarding a socially incongruous marriage. This was in part mitigated by the principle of *favor matrimonii*, for which the court assumed a flexible attitude towards witnesses to help prove the bond, and thanks to which, in this period, nobles of the rank of Dandolo and Badoer were constrained by ecclesiastical sentences to maintain their socially incongruous marriages.[137]

5.2 Witness Credibility and the Parameters of Collective Morality

The Venetian documentation furnishes significant answers about how testimony and witness behavior was evaluated, and it reflects slippages in the parameters of collective morality. The first decades of the sixteenth century signal some novelties that snuck into cross-examinations intended to diminish the credibility of the witness – for example, questions that reflect the fear of Lutheran teaching or an increasing distance from the Jewish world, symbolized by the creation of the Venetian Ghetto in 1516. At this point, though sporadically, witnesses might be asked "if they frequent Jews or eat with them, or with Lutherans, heretics, and pagans."[138] At the same time it is possible to note a new firmness in regard to pre- and extramarital sexuality that heralded post-Tridentine tendencies[139]: here, in fact, witnesses were asked "if they are faithful to their wife," and celibate persons asked "if they live chastely."[140] Witnesses flatly denied any frequentation of Lutherans, while they showed themselves more or less open about contact with people of other faiths: "My business is to work in my shop and when I do not work in my shop I practice with good men, and not with Lutherans or Jews," and "I do not practice with similar people, but sometimes it happens that I speak with Jews and also with Turks," declared two of them.[141] The questions relating to one's sexuality came instead to be perceived as interference in the private sphere, which witnesses felt they had the full right to protect. Asked if he lived chastely, one witness responded stonily, "That is not of your business."[142]

NOTES

1. See *supra*, ch. 2 § 9.
2. Some exceptions in ASPV, *FC*, vol. 1, Giovanni Luchini a Serico *vs* Cassandra de Marconibus, 23 January 1493; ASPV, *AMP*, reg. 28, Bernardo Spagnolo *vs* Cristina, 27 January 1466; *AMP*, reg. 29, Quinternus sententiarum, Tadiolo Astoris *vs* Alterice Superantio, 15 December 1466; *AMP*, reg. 30, Iulianus de Sanctis *vs* Margherita Manica; ASPV, *CM*, vol. 16, Marinum filium magistri Iohannis cerchieri *vs* Serenam, 1515. See ch. 4, § 3.

3. Based on juridical norms witnesses could be interrogated before the formal joinder of issue in cases of fear of death, for illness, old age, in case of prolonged absence, or "cum agitur de matrimonio carnali et is qui convenitur, se malitiose absentat et contumax est." See Gulielmi Durandi *Speculum iudiciale*, book I, partic. IV, De teste, § 2, p. 304.
4. "Età decrepita," "fatta fede," "il morbo gallico." ASPV, *CM*, vol. 15, Vincenza filia Helene vidue *vs* Francesco Maraveggia, 1514.
5. ASPV, *CM*, vol. 14, Margherita da Traù *vs* Alexandro Aurio, 1514.
6. See Gulielmi Durandi, *Speculum iudiciale*, book I, partic. IV, De teste, § 3, n. 6, p. 307; ASPV, *CM*, vol. 10, Elena Rosso *vs* Ludovico Bono, 1508–1509.
7. See Gulielmi Durandi *Speculum iudiciale*, book II, partic. II, De probationibus, § 2, p. 623.
8. See Gulielmi Durandi *Speculum iudiciale*, book I, partic. IV, De teste, § 7, n. 2, p. 324.
9. According to R. Helmholz, *Marriage Litigation*, p. 129: "It is thus almost literally true that the medieval judge knew no more about the evidence of a case than the historian who picks up the depositions six hundred years later."
10. ASPV, *CM*, vol. 12, Antonia de Moretis *vs* Gaspare de Morandis, 1514–1515; *CM*, vol. 14, Margherita de Traù *vs* Alexandro Aurio, 1514 (the witness "relectum confirmavit" but "non videbatur constans"). For the effect of hesitations on credibility of the witness see Gulielmi Durandi *Speculum iudiciale*, book I, partic. IV, De teste, § 7, n. 4, p. 325.
11. L. Faoro, *Processi matrimoniali*, II.
12. "Non acade che legete altramente, perché ho sentito e visto ciò che avete scritto e lo confermo." ASDVr, ATE XI, *PM*, b. 7, Caterina de Medici *vs* Giulio Maffei, 3 September 1551.
13. For example in ASPV, *CM*, vol. 15, Vincentie filie Helene vidue *vs* Francesco Maraveggia, 1514, the sentence "even if she was the most evil woman in the world" (*si la fusse ben la più trista del mondo*) corrected the preceding sentence "even if she was a whore" (*si la fosse ben una putana*). It can be excluded in this case that the notary intervened to censor an expression considered too strong for the magistrate, as similar expressions were very common.
14. ASPV, *AMP*, reg. 24, Anna da Antivari *vs* Rado da Budua, 21 April 1494.

15. ASPV, *CM*, vol. 2, fasc. 7, Ursina Basso *vs* Alvise Soncin, 1462, c. 39. The possibility for the witnesses to be interrogated at home was provided for in the legal norms. See Gulielmi Durandi *Speculum iudiciale*, book I, partic. IV, De teste, § 3, n. 22, p. 310. In ASPV, *CM*, vol. 15, Hieronima Compostella *vs* nobilem dominum Franciscum de Mosto, 1514: "nec requiritur quod testes examinandi compareant coram iudice sicut solet fieri in criminali, quia ratio est diversa in causis matrimonialibus et criminalibus."
16. "Patrizi veneti." ASPV, *CM*, vol. 12, Johannis Dominicis Ceti *vs* Camilla e Angelica, 1512–1513.
17. The personnel of the chancellory had to take an oath when they took their place there.
18. ASPV, *AMP*, reg. 10, Niccolò da Conegliano *vs* Polissena di Pietro da Murano, 20 November 1444. In this case, moreover, the judge probably wanted to know precisely if the formula expressed at the moment of the conclusion of the marriage effectively created the bond. Such a formula was not transcribed in the curial register, in which it was simply noted that the marriage was stipulated.
19. ASPV, *CM*, vol. 11, Ludovico Calbo *vs* Marino da cà Viniani, 1509.
20. ASPV, *AMP*, reg. 11, Ventura di Francesco *vs* Jacopo Polo, 1446. The documentation relative to this last case does not allow us to determine if the notary had to swear as a witness or, as seems more likely, because of the absence of credentials – simply to be able to do his own job. An example of a notary as a (sworn) witness is found in ASPV, *CM*, vol. 13, Filomena Tinelli *vs* Angelo e Franceschina, sua moglie, 1514–1515. It should be noted that in this case, as in the case in which the vicar was interrogated about the marriage conducted before him in the curia and inserted into the acts, the declarations of witnesses seemed to have greater weight than notarial documents, which, as such, had public faith (*publica fides*). See *supra*, note 18 and ch. 2, § 9.
21. "Plures amatorias ambasiatas." The young man had sent Marietta "cantillenas seu rithmos."
22. ASPV, *CM*, vol. 9, Alessandro de Pastis *vs* Marietta Zeno, 1506.
23. See Gulielmi Durandi *Speculum iudiciale*, book I, part. IV, De teste, § 1, num. 29, p. 289. See for example Ambrosina de Blasonibus *vs* Marco Antonio Bacinetto 1509–1510. The obligation to swear only with the license of the superior can be connected in part also to the disposition of Gregory IX, who recommended extreme caution regarding the oath of ecclesiastics: X 4. 23. 26.

24. "Quia iurare noluit." ASPV, *FC*, vol. 1, Flornovella *vs* Vittore, 1458.
25. The interrogations and the warnings, whether repeated or less frequent – in this case completely absent – were generally recorded even if they were formulaic or in indirect discourse.
26. A gloss on the opinion of the canon of the *Decretum*, according to which the oath was not in contrary to divine precepts, specified that he who refused to swear was to be considered a heretic: c. 2, C. XX q I. Among those who sustained the illicit nature of oaths were the Waldensians, Cathars, Patarines, Nestorians, and Anabaptists. See respectively C. Casagrande-S. Vecchio, *I peccati della lingua*, p. 269 and R. H. Bainton, *La Riforma protestante*, p. 99. A. Prosperi, *Fede, giuramento, inquisizione*, p. 158, regarding the initial oath to which the criminal was subordinated in inquisitorial trials, underlines that the acceptance of the oath constituted on its own a proof of obedience to ecclesiastical authority, while refusing it was considered an open admission of heresy.
27. According to doctrine the witness "non valet nisi iuratus": See Gulielmi Durandi *Speculum iudiciale*, book I, partic. IV, De teste, § 1, n. 33, p. 290.
28. Witnesses were admitted to depose with the formula "salvis et servatis oppositionibus et exceptionibus tam contra dicta quam contra personas ipsorum testium." In ASPV, *AMP*, vol. 9, Isotta filia adoptiva magnifici Aloysii Michael *vs* Marco Antonio Caravello, 1507, the judge was more precise and, recalling the authority of Angelo Gambiglioni, also known as Aretino, affirmed to act in such a way "servato nobis arbitrio in fine cause deliberandi circa personas et dicta testium...., an et quanta fides tam coniunctim quam divisim illis esset adhinbenda." In ASPV, *CM*, vol. 11, Zinevra filia Nicolai barbitonsori *vs* Hieronimo Baldigara, 1509–1510, the magistrate admitted two witnesses, one of whom was the plaintiff's mother, "salvis et reservatis... oppositionibus et exceptionibus dicto Hieronimo competentibus etiam ab initio repellentibus... quod si probabuntur exceptiones contra predicta militantes, earum dicta non solum probationem non faciunt verum etiam nec inditium aut animum iudicis moveant..." The inherent danger in this modality of proceeding was clear to the lawyesr: see for example ASPV, *CM*, vol. 16, Cornelia Zabarella *vs* Buzacarino de Buzacarinis, 1515, where Buzacarino's procurator was opposed to the adoption of this practice "quia testes qui non debent examinari, si examinerentur et si

non plene probent et etiam possent repelli post examinationem, tamen possunt facere inditium et inducere maximam presumptionem in mentem iudicis, ex quo infertur gravamen irreparabile per appellationem a diffinitiva."

29. See G. Buganza, *Il potere della parola*, p. 128.
30. For example in Florence: see D. Lombardi, *Matrimoni di Antico Regime*, p. 151.
31. As in ASPV, *FC*, vol. 1, Giovanni Luchini a Serico *vs* Cassandra de Marconibus, 1492–3.
32. C. Donahue Jr., *Law, Marriage and Society*, pp. 40–41.
33. J. Ferraro, *Coniugi nemici*, p. 142; on the influence of gossip in Venice see G. Ruggiero, *Binding Passions*, pp. 60–61, 143–147; J. Ferraro, *The Power to Decide*, p. 505 and notes 38–39. On the circulation of information and its uses for favoring a marriage, the analyses of A. Goan, *Gossip and Street Culture* and Eadem, *Marriage, Manners and Mobility*, are particularly interesting. For the Jewish world see R. Weinstein, *Marriage Rituals*, pp. 213–261.
34. ASPV, *CM*, vol. 15, Helisabeth Gurgura *vs* Francesco de Nigris, 1514 (the woman conducted these preliminary investigations among her husband's acquaintances to check if they knew of the marriage stipulated between her and Francesco); ASPV, *CM*, vol. 11, Catherina Iohannis Petri *vs* Hieronimo Mathei, 1509–1510 (the plaintiff, after contesting the imprecision of the petition, in which the time of the presumed marriage had happened was not indicated, asked the judge for a delay to seek information).
35. ASPV, *CM*, vol. 16, Cornelia Zabarella *vs* Buzacarino de Buzacarinis, 1515 (someone on the plaintiff's side refused to serve as a witness, to avoid the attempted delegitimization put in place by the other side).
36. ASPV, *CM*, vol. 9, Isotta filia adoptiva magnifici Aloysii Michael *vs* Marco Antonio Caravello, 1507.
37. See for example ASPV, *CM*, vol. 14, Margherita da Traù *vs* Alexandrio Aurio, 1514; *CM*, vol. 15, Hieronima Compostella *vs* Francesco da Mosto, 1514.
38. On marriage by force (*per vim*), see *infra*, ch. 5, § 8.
39. "Vir constans." Only a threat that could instill fear in one who was not easily scared constituted cause for annulment. See D. 4, 2, 6.
40. C. Cristellon, *Ursina Basso contro Alvise Soncin*, pp. 299–301. For this reason many women brought up their children during marriage

litigations as proof of marriage, often without specifying sex, age, or number. Some examples in ASPV, *CM*, vol. 1, fasc. 7, Laura Piacentini *vs* Thadeo Quirini, 1452; *CM*, vol. 2, fasc. 11, Matteo barilario *vs* Margherita (in this case Margherita wanted to demonstrate that Matteo was already married to a certain Coletta, and presented among the evidence to this preceding marriage the fact that Matteo had a daughter with Coletta); *CM*, vol. 2, fasc. 12, Helena *vs* Alvise Cavazza, 1462–1463; *CM*, vol. 4, fasc. 8, Marina Burgi *vs* Nicolao Avonal, 1476–1477; ASPV, *FC*, vol. 1, Giovanni Gerliq *vs* Rosa, 1451 (in this case it was the husband who brought up this fact to prove that his wife was already married to another); *FC*, vol. 1, Agnese *vs* Francesco e Niccolò di Niccolò, 1455.

41. ASPV, *CM*, vol. 15, Hieronima Compostella *vs* Francesco da Mosto, 1514.
42. ASPV, *CM*, vol. 15, Helisabeth Gurgura *vs* Francisco de Nigris, 1515.
43. C. Donahue Jr., *Law, Marriage and Society*, p. 93.
44. L. Faoro, *Processi matrimoniali*, I, pp. 52, 53, 56.
45. See Gulielmi Durandi *Speculum iudiciale*, book I, part. IV, De teste, § 4, n. 1.
46. "Magis diligit dictam Hieronimam, e voria che madonna Hieronima venzesse," ASPV, *CM*, vol. 14, Hieronima Compostella *vs* Francesco da Mosto, 1514.
47. "Vellet iusticiam habentem vincere et credit domina Salomona habere ius." "Cuperet quod dicus dominus Philippus transduceret dictam dominam Salomonam tamquam uxorem suam." ASPV, *CM*, vol. 15, Salomona Salomono *vs* Filippo Minio, 1514.
48. See also the document cited *infra*, note 81, another cited in A.M. Lazzeri – S. Seidel Menchi, "*Evidentemente gravida*," p. 325, note 81, and another cited in J. Ferraro, *Marriage Wars*, p. 97.
49. See beyond the cases cited here, also A. Marchetto, *La dote contesa*, p. 65; F. Pedersen, *Did the Medieval Laity know the Canon Law Rules on Marriage?*, pp. 140–141.
50. "Presertim domum Venetiarum." See rispectively ASPV, *CM*, vol. 14, Margherita da Traù *vs* Alexandro Aurio, 1514; and *CM*, vol. 15, Hieronima Compostella *vs* Francesco da Mosto, 1514. Both witnesses so suborned had to confirm the existence of a marriage which they knew nothing about.

51. See ASPV, *FC*, Giovanni di Luchino a Serico *vs* Cassandra de Marconibus, 1492–1493; for a broader look at this case see *infra*, ch. 4, § 7.
52. See *supra*, ch. 2, § 7.
53. See *infra*, ch. 4, § 8, and the document from Feltre cited in S. Seidel Menchi, *I processi matrimoniali come fonte storica*, pp. 78–79: "To begin the witness was warned to be very careful about the tenor of his or her depositions. If, after the publication, the testimony turned out to be false, the same witness had wronged three people: in the first place God (and the offense to God would cost him or her seven years of penitence, in the course of which he or she would have to fast every year for the forty days of Lent, eating only bread and water); in the second place the judge (and the deception and lie to the judge would be punished at the discretion of the same judge according to the severity of the crime, the witness might be rendered infamous, might no longer be allowed to testify in other cases, might be denied the sacrament of the Eucharist until his or her death *exclusive*); and in the third place he or she had wronged the innocent party, to whom he or she would be required to compensate and reimburse for all the damages, expenses, and interests which the party had incurred because of the fault of this witness, at the risk of ending in eternal flames and perpetual torments." According to Gulielmi Durandi *Speculum iudiciale*, book I, partic. IV, De teste, § 7, n. 3, p. 324, the judge had to warn the witness in a particular format. In Venice the formula for the imposition of the oath was recapitulated by the notary, who noted that the witness was "warned by the conventional words to tell the truth." ("monito convenientibus verbis quod dicat veritatem.")
54. See the documents cited *supra*, § 3 with reference to witnesses, and *infra*, ch. 5, § 4, with reference to the parties.
55. The sin of perjury, closely tied to the sin of bearing false witness, transgressed both the second and eight commandments; beyond "directly offending God, it offends the neighbor," ("oltraggia direttamente Dio, offende il prossimo") and, violating the authority of the magistrate, "put the administration of justice in crisis" ("mette in crisi l'amministrazione della giustizia"): see C. Casagrande – S. Vecchio, *I peccati della lingua*, p. 266. See also M. Sbriccoli, *Crimen laesae maiestatis*, p. 358.

56. "Testes omni exceptione maiores."
57. In the appeal case between Caterina de Luse *vs* Giovanni Pansa, for example, the patriarch Lorenzo Giustiniani was indignant because of the new request for appeal made by the woman, who did not want in any way to accept the fact that she was married to Giovanni. Reiterating that he had delivered a "truly just and sound" sentence, the judge declared that, if Caterina did not want to live with her husband, her only option, as an alternative, was that she could enter a convent. ASPV, *AMP*, reg. 8, Caterina de Luse *vs* Giovanni Pansa, 20 June 1439.
58. See C. Cristellon, *Ursina Basso contro Alvise Soncin*, pp. 289–290, also ASPV, *CM*, vol. 12, Lucrezia Fosco *vs* Angelo Cima, 1512–1513. Cases of overt lying are also found in C. Donahue Jr., *Law, Marriage and Society*, pp. 47, 51; R. Helmholz, Marriage Litigation, p. 157.
59. According to P. Prodi, *Il sacramento del potere*, p. 221, cases of perjury "fill the episcopal and civil courts of the late Middle Ages and early modern age with their discussions in the competition between them." The author does not cite documents.
60. See *infra*, ch. 5, § 4 for examples of judges' instructions regarding dowries. Relative to the instructions regarding payment of court costs see ASPV, *AMP*, reg. 9, Jacopo Donato Bonacorso *vs* Andriola; *AMP*, reg. 14, Catarucia Blanco *vs* Jacopo de l'Albona. It does not even seem plausible that the magistrate would have considered it superfluous to reserve the right explicitly to himself – or to assume the burden – of proceeding in the future against one who had sworn to a lie, in the consideration that such a proceeding would have been up to him or to his successor anyway. And in fact practices that the judge reserved the right to himself in the sentence – with the formula *reservando sibi ius* – were to take additional or different provisions in the future for questions that were in his jurisdiction, as for example in the case of paying court costs.
61. This is the case, for example, with inquisitorial trials, preserved in ASPV, Archivio Segreto, *Criminalia SS. Inquisitionis*.
62. I consider it improbable that suits for perjury were deposited in an archival series on their own and that such documentation, unlike that of the inquisitorial trials, has been lost. Such a loss in this case likely happened before the eighteenth-century reorganization of the patriarchal archive led by archivist Giovan Battista Scomparin, who

did not mention them in his inventory, which instead listed numerous suits which have since been lost (e.g., the cases of the *Criminalia monalium*).
63. A. Prosperi, *Fede, giuramento, inquisizione*, p. 159.
64. C. Casagrande – S. Vecchio, *I peccati della lingua*, pp. 229–240; and Eaedem, *"Non sire falsa testimonianza contro il tuo prossimo."*
65. Following the documentation conserved in the Archivio Storico del Patriarcato di Venezia, see ASPV, Archivio Segreto, *Criminalia SS Inquisitionis*, vol. 1, 1461–1558. Regarding the documents of the Holy Office conserved in the ASVe, I thank Silvana Seidel Menchi, who has closely examined the documentation and informed me that no such cases are extant.
66. ASPV, *CM*, vol. 14, Margherita da Traù *vs* Alexandro Aurio, 1514.
67. E. Brambilla, *Confessione*, p. 494 and note 9.
68. On the magistrature that was concerned with blasphemy in Venice see G. Derosas, *Moralità e giustizia a Venezia nel '500–'600*, pp. 431–528; G. Cozzi, *Religione, moralità e giustizia a Venezia*; and S. Piasentini, *Indagine sulla bestemmia*. The studies on the documentation of marriage cases in other cities does not examine the actions of ecclesiastical judges against perjury. Based on the information available in D. Lombardi, *Matrimoni di Antico Regime*, p. 150, note 18, in Florence the marriage tribunal did not proceed against perjury and false testimony either.
69. See Gulielmi Durandi *Speculum iudiciale*, book I, part. IV, De teste, § I, n. 29: "Ferre enim testimonium est dignitas."
70. "Respondit quod non sed potius damnum quia amittit tempus ... vitam suam ducit in exercitio laborando serico die noctuque" ASPV, *CM*, vol. 27, Dianora Muscha *vs* Bernardino stringario, 1528. An example of an impatient witness also in D. Lombardi, *Matrimoni di Antico Regime*, p. 149.
71. ASPV, *CM*, vol. 10, Elena relicta Aloysii Barbitonsoris *vs* Aloysio a Brachio Aurifice, 1508.
72. ASPV, *CM*, vol. 10, Paola de Mastellis *vs* Michele Leoni, 1508–1510: against a one witness accusations were raised relative to things that had occurred more than 25 years before the cause.
73. ASPV, *CM*, vol. 11, Vincenzo de Iadra *vs* Magdalena ser Simonis de Tarvisio, 1510.
74. ASPV, *AMP*, reg. 28, Paola de Spalato *vs* Martino friulano, 9 May 1466.

75. ASPV, *AMP*, reg. 8, Thomeus Petri de Canareggio *vs* Cristina Nicole de Patrasso, 18 April 1440.
76. ASPV, *AMP*, reg. 10, Jacopo Foscareno *vs* Caterina Pizzolati, 4 November 1445–20 February 1445.
77. "Tegnì la lengua dentro dai denti, e fe' i fatti vostri."
78. ASPV, *CM*, vol. 7, Bernardina di Garzonibus *vs* Bernardino conte di Collalto, 1500–1501.
79. See ASPV, *CM*, vol. 3, fasc. 8, Andreola Vitturi *vs* Doctrina Vitturi, 1471.
80. See the document cited *supra* note 76. Other cases of terrified (*perterriti*) witnesses in ASPV, *CM*, vol. 9, Alessandro de Pastis *vs* Marietta Zeno, 1506; *CM*, vol. 2, fasc. 7, Ursina Basso *vs* Alvise Soncin, 1462.
81. ASPV, *CM*, vol. 12, Margherita de Amicis *vs* Alvise Battilauro, 1512.
82. See *infra*, ch. 5, §§ 3 and 4.
83. See for example the discomfort of witnesses in A.M. Lazzeri – S. Seidel Menchi, "*Evidentemente gravida*," p. 321 and note 64.
84. "El me pareria per el dover che dona Perina dovesse venzer, perché l'à raxon, perché questo matrimonio è pubblico e manifesto." ASPV, *CM*, vol. 16, Perina relicta q. ser Varisci Samitarii *vs* Benedictum Barbitonsorem, 1515.
85. "Attento quod non sine peccato mortali requisitus in testem potest recusare veritatem dicere." ASPV, *CM*, vol. 11, Vincenzo Quirino *vs* Caterina Mauro 1509–1512.
86. See the document cited *supra*, note 81.
87. ASPV, *CM*, vol. 1, fasc. 11, Isabetta *vs* Jacopo da Marignano, 1454.
88. See *infra*, ch. 5, § 2.
89. "Qui nulla possint exceptione repelli." On the sense of the expression "maior omni exceptione," see the gloss *maiores*, c. *Ex litteris, de consanguineitate et affinitate* (1. X. 4. 14): "illi dicuntur omni exceptione maiores, qui repelli non possunt aliqua exceptione."
90. R. Helmholz, *Marriage Litigation*, p. 156; T. Kuehn, *Reading Microhistory*, p. 532.
91. C. Valsecchi, "*Causa matrimonialis est gravis et ardua*," p. 477. On respect for *favor matrimonii* see also Gulielmi Durandi *Speculum iudiciale*, book II, part. II, De confessionibus, § 2, n. 5, p. 605.
92. For example ASPV, *CM*, vol. 9, Domenico a Lectis *vs* Andriana Bono, 1507–1509.
93. On the weight of neighbors' testimony see also *CM*, vol. 7, Argentina *vs* Agostino del Zonta, 1505. The declarations of neighbors had

particular weight in the establishment of "fama." See with regards to the declarations of the magistrate ASPV, *CM*, vol. 9, Ludovica de Comitibus *vs* Hieronimo de Verona physico, 1507, which contested the existence of reputation, in as much was noted "aliud necessarium....requisitum ad concludentem probationem fame, scilicet quot ita dici audiverint a maiori pare vicinie et aliorum qui verisimiliter de matrimonio huiusmodi asserto debuissent audire." See also Guliemi Durandi *Speculum iudiciale*, book II, partic, I, De notoriis criminibus, § 4, n. 5, p. 47 and § 3, n. 4, p. 46. On reputation in medieval juridical thought see F. Migliorino, *Fama e infamia*, in particular pp. 45–83. Very significant examples of social control exercised by neighbors, and in particular on the authority of the neighborhood on the subject of customs in J. Rossiaud, *La prostituzione nel medioevo*, pp. 42, 80–81. See also E. Shorter, *The Making of Modern Family*, pp. 42–47.

94. "Pauperrime et de abiecta vita." On the fact that a poor witness was considered less credible, see in particular the closing arguments of the lawyer in ASPV, *CM*, vol. 14, Margherita da Traù *vs* Alexandro Aurio, 1514, according to which spiritual and voluntary poverty was not "damnanda et vituperanda, quia Christus et apostuli fuerunt pauperes voluntarie, et dixit Christus nisi quis renuntiaverit omnibus que possidet non potest meus esse discepulus, et mandavi omnia vendi et dari pauberibus; sed paupertas in laico inducit presumptionem rapine et corruptionis ut dicunt doctores et canoniste." According to Alessandro Tartagni, however, one who, in spite of being "pauper," had good "mores" and was not of servile condition could not be considered "vile." See C. Valsecchi, *"Causa matrimonialis est gravis et ardua,"* p. 540 and note 344. On the theological and moral reflection of the late Middle Ages on poverty, see B. Geremek, *Il pauperismo nell'età preindustriale*, pp. 677–685, and more generally, Idem, *La pietà e la forca*.
95. "Unde ex dubio persona illorum presumuntur idonea."
96. E. Koch, *Maior dignitas*, p. 87.
97. "Varium et mutabile verbum saepe foemina producit." See Gulielmi Durandi *Speculum iudiciale*, book I, partic. IV, de teste, § 1, n. 15, p. 287. This adage is cited, for example, in ASPV, *CM*, vol. 1, fasc. 10, Hermani Teutonici *vs* Agnete, 1454. On the role of the woman in Renaissance jurisprudence and on her processual capacity, see A. Belloni, *Die Rolle der Frau*, pp. 55–58 and pp. 68–78 on female testimony; also G. Minucci, *La capacità processuale della donna;* and

T. Kuehn, *Figli, madri, mogli e vedove*, in particular p. 435. Catholic marriage causes, although they attributed less weight to female testimony, always admitted it. This was not the case for reformed tribunals: see K. Beck, *Zürcher Ehegerichtsprotokolle*. On the attitude towards female testimony in Venice in penal trials, see G. Buganza, *Il potere della parola*, in particular p. 132.

98. See C. Valsecchi, "*Causa matrimonialis est gravis et ardua*," p. 477.
99. ASPV, *CM*, vol. 9, Isotta Aloysii Michiel *vs* Marco Antonio Caravello, 1507.
100. ASPV, *CM*, vol. 9, Lucia de Ponticis *vs* Aloysio Bollani, 1507–1508, where the lawyer opposed the credibility of a witness, beyond the fact that he was the plaintiff's brother: "sic etiam allegatur ad effectum premissum disparitas inter ipsos litigantes." In this case the norm to which he referred was X 2. 20. 22. See also gl. "cum mater" in X 2. 20. 22.
101. See ASPV, *CM*, vol. 9, Ludovica de Comitibus *vs* Hieronimo de Verona physico, 1507. See also the case of 1600, cited in R. Helmholz, *Roman Canon Law*, p. 73, note 64; also ASPV, *CM*, vol. 9, Ludovica de Comitibus *vs* Hieronimo de Verona physico, 1507: the judge, at the moment of evaluating the deposition of the plaintiff's sister and brother-in-law, appealed to the authority of Giovanni d'Andrea and Alessandro da Imola. Recalling instead Felino Sandeo he affirmed that "inter fratres et sorores fit quadam comunicatio honoris et bone fame vel etiam infamie et vituperii et iniuriarum in vita civili et politica."
102. See Guliemi Durandi *Speculum iudiciale*, book I, part. IV: "de teste", § 1, n. 5, p. 283 and p. 286. For a concrete example: ASPV, *CM*, vol. 16, Helisabeth Gurgura *vs* Francesco de Nigris, 1514–1515.
103. "Nimia affectione," "odio capitale." ASPV, *CM*, vol. 7, Argentina *vs* Agostino del Zonta, 1505: one witness had been beaten by Agostino because he had defamed him. *CM*, vol. 15, Helisabeth Gurgura *vs* Francesco de Nigris, 1514–1515: one witness had been fired by Francesco for theft, and only the intermediation of some nobles had stopped him from taking legal recourse.
104. ASPV, *CM*, vol. 11, Helisabeth Christophori textoris *vs* Jacobo della Zotta, 1510. The vicar, considering that Cristoforo had publicly confessed that a year earlier he had made peace with the witness, and that afterwards he had often eaten and drunk with him and lived in

the same house, and that they also exchanged greetings in the street, decided to admit the witness, reserving oppositions and exceptions *tam contra dicta quam contra personam*. On the theme of resolving conflicts see O. Niccoli, *Perdonare*, in particular p. 83 regarding the common meal.

105. "Dage sua muglier a Marino se non [volete] che ve bruxeremo in casa." ASPV, *CM*, vol. 16, Marinum filium magistri Iohannis cercheri *vs* Serenam, 1515.
106. "Digli che dappoi che la vol denegar la verità io voglio mi esser quella che vada dicendo ch'è la muglier de Marco Antonio." ASPV, *CM*, vol. 9. Isotta Aloysii Michael *vs* Marco Antonio Caravello, 1507.
107. "Factum clandestinum." *Ibid.*
108. On the collaboration of "comari" or "mammane" (midwives), called "matrone" in Venice, see A. Pastore, *Il medico in tribunale*, pp. 129–148, in particular pp. 129–131 regarding the proof of virginity. Pastore's study refers to the penal tribunal. On obstetric examinations see also G. Pomata, *Barbieri e comari*. In the sixteenth century an eminent military surgeon, Ambroise Paré, contested the existence of the hymen and consequently, the trustworthiness of virginity examinations performed by midwives, upon which judges often issued sentences "committing a grave abuse." (*commettendo un grave abuso*). See G. Sissa, *La verginità materiale*, pp. 752–753. On the same subject see T. Sánchez, *De sancto matrimonii sacramento*, book VII de impedimentiis matrimonii, disputatio XIV, q. 1 (in quo consistat signaculum virginalem, an sit aliqua membranula).
109. See Gulielmi Durandi *Speculum iudiciale*, book I, partic. IV, de teste § II, n. 6, p. 335.
110. Some examples in ASPV, *AMP*, reg. 6, Anna *vs* Giorgio, 1437; *AMP*, reg. 9, Daniele de Laude *vs* Lucia, 9 February 1442–10 March 1442; *AMP*, reg. 10, Martino *vs* Nicolosa, 4 February 1443–20 November 1443; *AMP*, reg. 13, Battista *vs* Isabetta Rizo, 20 November 1450–22 March 1451; *AMP*, reg. 20, Pietro Bono *vs* Caterina Crosta, 18 May 1459–5 December 1459; *AMP*, reg. 22, Antonio da Pergamo *vs* Isabetta da Pergamo; *CM*, vol. 4, Adriana Coppo *vs* Niccolò Civetani, 1476–1477.
111. ASPV, *CM*, vol. 16, Perina q. ser Varisci sanitarii *vs* Benedictum barbitonsorum, 1515.
112. ASPV, *CM*, vol. 1, fasc. 13, Giorgio Zaccarotto *vs* Maddalena di Sicilia, 1455–1458.

113. ASPV, *CM*, vol. 11, Zinevra filia Nicolai barbitonsoris *vs* Hieronimo Baldigara, 1509–1510. Also C. Donahue Jr., *Law, Marriage and Society*, p. 92 mentions witnesses who attended a marriage through a crack. On the preeminence of *de visu* testimony see also S. Lepsius, *Der Richter und die Zeugen*, p. 10, and Eadem, *Von Zweifeln zu Überzeugung*, pp. 87–89.
114. ASPV, *CM*, vol. 11, Leonarda filia Bernardini da Bergamo *vs* Agostino de Tarsia, 1510–1511; ASPV, *AMP*, reg. 22, Oliviero *vs* Margherita, 27 July 1461.
115. ASPV, *CM*, vol. 2, fasc. 7, Ursina Basso *vs* Alvise Soncin, 1462.
116. As was already noted, unsworn testimony did not have value in court. See *supra*, note 27. From Soncin's declarations, in which he insisted that Margherita was not yet 12, it seems that the age requested for deposition was that of puberty (and also in the juridical text cited *pubes* or *impubes* witnesses are discussed). The age that canon law had fixed in the fourteenth century was 14 for boys and 12 for girls (see J. Gaudemet, *Il matrimonio in Occidente*, p. 147). In practice, however, the oath was imposed not only on children who had not yet reached 14 (see ASPV, *AMP*, reg. 9, Jacopo Franco *vs* Agnesina de l'Orsa, 4 Oktober 1441) but also on children who were doubted to have reached the age of 12. See ASPV, *CM*, vol. 1, fasc. 13, Giorgio Zaccarotto *vs* Maddalena di Sicilia, 1456–1457. According to G. Buganza, *Il potere della parola*, pp. 131–132, in Venetian penal trial witnesses younger than 14 were admitted to depose and the tribunal sometimes assigned a crucial weight to their declarations.
117. See Gulielmi Durandi *Speculum iudiciale*, book I, partic. IV, de teste, § 1, n. 35, p. 290. The Soncins however presented as negative the fact that witnesses deposed "de hiis que viderunt in pupillari etate." Incapable of putting forward proof of the girl's age, the Soncins asked the judge to declare her age *per inspectionem*, according to a juridically legitimate and reasonably common practice for the Venetian tribunal, in an epoch in which age was mostly known in an approximate way. Ibid, book I, De actore, § 1, n. 5, p. 167. See also P. Benussi, Oltre il processo, pp. 169–171 and E. Orlando, *Pubertà e matrimonio*.
118. "Turchi." According to the Soncins Margherita was "sclavona quondam Iohannis de Sclavonia, et ut sibi melius fides adhiberetur,... appellavit [se] in hac causa tarvisinam." On the fact that foreign

origin could be used to dishonor witnesses, see for example ASPV, *CM*, vol. 1, fasc. 13, Giorgio Zaccarotto *vs* Maddalena di Sicilia, 1455–1458, where the procurator for the defendant emphasized that the plaintiff had presented "many Albanian witnesses" (*plures testes albanenses*); see also *CM*, vol. 14, Margherita da Traù de convinio Sancti Martialis *vs* Alexandrio Aurio, 1514, where the opposition to witnesses "ne detur causa peccandi et periurii in producendo assertos testes viles et pauperes et nationis barbare que est. conterminans sive confinans cum Turchis," or *CM*, vol. 15, Helisabeth Gurgura *vs* Francisco de Nigris, 1514–1515, where it was said about some witnesses and the bride herself that they were "forenses, natione greca, et degens in hac civitate Venetiarum tamquam forensis et alienigena." Also N. Pizzolato, *"Lo diavolo mi ingannao,"* p. 467, cites a case during which, to the detriment of the witness, it was emphasized that he was "a vile son of a foreign man." (*vili figlio di homo de fuora*). Interesting observations in J. Eibach, *Versprochene Gleichheit-verhandelte Ungleichheit*. E. Orlando, *Migrazioni mediterranee. Migrazioni, minoranze e matrimony a Venezia nel basso medioevo*, Bologna 2014, pp. 481–484.

119. ASPV, *CM*, Anna Bergamese *vs* Vincenzo Marci, 1496: the accusation of having stolen objects infected by the plague was directed at a woman.

120. The accusation of practicing magic was sometimes raised against both witnesses and the parties in the case. Some examples of the accusation of *herbaria* in the course of marriage causes in ASPV, *CM*, vol. 1, fasc. 13, Giorgio Zaccarotto *vs* Maddalena di Sicilia, 1455–1458; *CM*, vol. 1, fasc. 14, Clara Matafar *vs* Michele Giustiniani, 1455–1456; *CM*, vol. 3, fasc. 1, Samaritana *vs* Antonio Passetto, 1468; *CM*, vol. 7, Bernardina de Garzonibus *vs* Bernardino conte di Collalto, 1500–1501; *CM*, vol. 10, Paola de Mastellis *vs* Michele Leoni, 1508–1510; *CM*, vol. 11, Leonarda filia Bernardini da Bergamo *vs* Agostino de Tarsia, 1510–1511, also the case cited by S. Chojnacki, *Il divorzio di Cateruzza*, p. 389.

121. It is not possible to establish a direct connection between marriage cases and inquisitorial trials. Relative to the period 1461–1518 I found 23 inquisitorial trials, 12 of which contained accusations of *herbaria*: see ASPV, *Criminalia SS. Inquisitionis*, vol. 1, Georgii clerici et Fraceschine, 1461; contra Caterinam Sclavonam, 1477;

contra Caterinam relicta Stephani Bontempo, 1477; contra Helisabeth Estensem, 1500; contra Maria mogier d'Etor Gradenigo, 1514; querella contra Antoniam Sclavonam 1515; contra Aloysiam Grecam 1516; contra Cristinam matrem et Tarsiam eius filiam, 1516; contra Marietam Perseghinam maleficam, 1516; contra Lucretiam, Florinam, Faustinam, et Thadeam, 1518; contra Catharinam et Luciam 1518; contra mulierem vocatam 'la Turca' 1518. Later examples, conserved in the archive of the Holy Office, in D. Hacke, *Von der Wirkungsmächtigkeit des Heiligen*. The ties between marriage and inquisitorial trials is illustrated, for the first half of the seventeenth century, in D. Hacke, *La promessa disattesa*. See also on this theme G. Ruggiero, *Binding Passions*; also R. Martin, *Witchcraft and the Inquisition in Venice*. On themes of "incantationes ad amorem" see M. Duni, *Tra religione e magia*, pp. 184–208.

122. ASPV, *CM*, vol. 6, Anna Bergomense *vs* Vincenzo Marci, 1496.
123. "Tutta la notte in compagnia di gran ghiottoni." ASPV, *CM*, vol. 10, Paola de Mastellis *vs* Michele Leoni, 1508–1510.
124. A. Degrandi, *Problemi di percezione*, pp. 117–119. The clash over the management of time, in the thirteenth century, brought an ethical legitimation to work time and a progressive closing of the spaces for wasteful uses of time, like games. On this theme see J. Le Goff, *Nel medioevo*.
125. Examples of the degeneration of gambling into violence in O. Niccoli, *Storie di ogni giorno in una città del Seicento*, pp. 52, 82–83; and E. Orlando, *Morire per gioco*, in particular 21–32 for examples of games of chance that degenerated into explosions of anger, often moral, or into brawls. On vendetta see E. Muir, *Mad Blood Stirring: Vendetta and Factions in Friuli During the Renaissance*; Baltimore and London 1993.
126. On the perception of the figure of the gambler see A. Degrandi, *Problemi di percezione*; and A. Zorzi, *Battagliole*, in particular pp. 86–107. On the association between blasphemy and perjury see *supra*, § 4.
127. ASPV, *CM*, vol. 8, Paola de Mastellis *vs* Michele Leoni, 1508–1510.
128. See *supra*, ch. 2, § 9.
129. Sometimes the reintegrating marriage did not end the preceding relationship, as is demonstrated in E. Eisenach, *Husbands, Wives and Concubines*, pp. 134–177. The prospect of an arranged marriage from the patron at the end of the relationship, sometimes with little

warning, could arouse lively reactions. See J. Ferraro, *Marriage Wars*, pp. 105–108.
130. "Si quotannis pareat ecclesiae." See *infra*, ch. 4, § 8, and Romeo, *Recensione*.
131. "Sacramentum eucharistiae hoc anno non sumpsit, propter certum respectum quem nolluit propalare, licet fuerit confessa." ASPV, *FC*, vol. 3, Damianus Masarachias *vs* Marieta filia Bone, 1525.
132. O. Niccoli, *Perdonare*, pp. 158–166.
133. ASPV, *CM*, vol. 7, Nicolò q. Dominici Cortesii *vs* Angela, 1507–1508. For confession as tribunal that not only pardoned but also obligated one to pardon. See O. Niccoli, *Perdonare*.
134. ASPV, *CM*, vol. 10, Paola de Mastellis *vs* Michele Leoni, 1508–1510.
135. *Ibid*.
136. ASPV, *CM*, vol. 18, Helisabeth filia q. ser Marini Hartaroli *vs* Franciscus Amizo toscanus filius ser Sebastiani, 1521.
137. A particularly significant example is found in S. Seidel Menchi, *Ritratto di famiglia in un interno*. See also ASPV, *CM*, vol. 15, Pietro Dandolo *vs* Quirina Bollani, 1515.
138. "An conversetur cum iudeis et comedet cum illis, vel cum luteranis, heretici[s] et pagani[s]." ASPV, *CM*, vol. 45, Rochum olim in regimine et gubernio q. magnifici d. Johannis Mauroceni *vs* Lucretiam filiam ser Thomasii de Grassonibus, 1545.
139. The stiffening with regards to sexuality became noticeable also in annulment suits for male impotence. In fourteenth-century cases a man accused of impotence could defend himself by bragging about numerous pre- or extramarital relations often with multiple women, which associated the exercise of sexuality with women who were not their wives or with prostitutes with male sociability: cfr, for example, ASPV, *CM*, vol. 4, Adriana Coppo *vs* Niccolò Civetani, 1476. In causes in the first half of the sixteenth century the defensive strategy decisively changed: the man did not mention sexual relations, but instead sought to depose a friend who could attest to his virility having casually observed him as he bathed in the river. See *CM*, vol. 45, Lucretia Bondumier *vs* Hieronimo Mudazzo, 1546. See C. Cristellon, *Public Display of Affection*. In the Venetian region the new moralizing wave did not quite have the proportions evident in Germany, where, in roughly the same years – the 1540s – eight

young men from Frankfurt were sentenced to a month in prison for being surprised bathing nude in the river. See J. C. Bologne, *Histoire de la pudeur*, p. 34, cit. by S. Matthews Grieco, *Corpo, aspetto e sessualità*.

140. "Si servant fidem uxori" and "Si vivant caste." ASPV, *CM*, vol. 45, Rochum olim in regimine et gubernio q. magnifici d. Johannis Mauroceni *vs* Lucretiam filiam ser Thomasii de Grassonibus, 1545.

141. "La mia pratica è atender a la mia botega et quando non attendo a la mia botega pratico cum homeni de ben, et non cum lutherani né zudei," "Io non pratico con simil persone, ma ben quando el me acade parlo cum iudei et anche cum turchi." *Ibid.*

142. "Di questo non vi ho da render conto." *Ibid.*

CHAPTER 4

The Office of the Judge: Mediation, Inquisition, Confession

1 THE OFFICE OF THE JUDGE

Two alleged Venetian spouses addressed the vicar of the patriarch of Venice as "arbiter and amicable arranger," a title emblematic of the function that both canonical norms and petitioners to a tribunal attributed to the judge of marriage.[1] A marriage suit, with procedures based on Roman canonical procedures, conceived of the judge as a mediator.[2]

As noted, the plaintiff either personally or through a procurator presented an articulated petition (*positiones*) that the judge accepted without conducting any investigation regarding its veracity, respecting the formality required *de iure*. The defendant was interrogated on the *positiones*, which he or she either confirmed or denied by saying *credit* or *non credit*. The tribunal would find for the plaintiff on those that were confirmed and those that were denied would be turned into the points on which the plaintiff's witnesses would be questioned. The burden of proof rested entirely on the plaintiff, while the magistrate limited himself to the reception and evaluation of the evidence.[3] The assumption of this *modus operandi* was that what emerged from the case was not "the" truth but rather a procedural truth – that is, a negotiated[4] and self-reflexive truth.[5]

As was the case in civil causes,[6] marriage suits did not provide for varied or more exhaustive interrogations of the defendant. Sometimes, however, the judge did not limit himself to the enforcement of practices, but assumed an active role asking the parties – but usually only the woman – questions modeled in tone and style after those asked in confession. These interrogations were allowed by the rules[7] but were not often part of the normal procedure that a judge, at least in other dioceses, felt justified in using.[8] They occurred in the presence of the chancellor or notary alone and in a secure place – generally a monastery, less often the house of some honest person (*honesta persona*), and sometimes even the vicar's dwelling – so the parties would not be under external pressures or influences.[9]

As said, women were the privileged interlocutors of the magistrates, considered more fragile because of their nature and therefore as having greater need for protection. A precise norm of canon law established that whenever free consent to a marriage was investigated, the woman should be placed in a condition to express herself freely.[10] As with all canonical dispositions, this norm was supposed to be applied indiscriminately to men as well, but in practice that did not happen, even if lawyers insistently requested it. The feminine condition, which magistrates and witnesses indicated as *fragilitas sexus* or *fragilitas muliebris* (fragility of sex or fragility of women), could not be attributed to men even if they were very young.[11]

The interrogations of women sharpened in the sixteenth century, when magistrates used this norm to remove the interrogated person from danger of subornation as well as for informative purposes, before witnesses were interrogated.[12] It was also used when the tenor of a sentence depended solely on the declarations of the parties because of the weakness of testimonial proof.[13] In the absence of probable truth the judge followed his own personal convictions through dialogue with the woman being questioned – "Until the mind of the said girl ... is investigated,"[14] "wanting to carefully investigate the soul and mind of the same,"[15] "for information on his mind,"[16] "for the investigation of the truth,"[17] – as the magistrates noted time and again.

Such formulas are clues to the various roles played by the ecclesiastical judge. In fact, "for the protection of substantial justice"[18] the judge assumed the role not only of mediator but also of inquisitor and confessor. These different functions – certainly familiar to magistrates who presided at times over the diocesan tribunal in civil and criminal cases, who were pastors of their own dioceses and sometimes also had *cura animarum* of important parishes[19] – were not contradictory. Instead, they mutually complemented and legitimated one another, in an equilibrium maintained by the interaction between judges and parties in the case. To analyze them is the primary goal of this chapter.

The devices used by ecclesiastical judges to remove women from familial influence; the tenor of interrogations of very young brides terrorized by the prospect of being abandoned or even just reprimanded by their relatives[20]; adolescents afraid to harm their souls[21] by disappointing maternal expectations of a marriage – all of these show us magistrates protecting the free expression of matrimonial consent and promoting what has been defined as "feminine self-consciousness."[22] It is not, however, feminine individuality that this chapter intends to bring to the fore (based on the interrogations in marriage suits) but rather the role played by the ecclesiastical judge in the formation of women's conscience and accountability.

The interrogations of the female party, intended to offer her the possibility of autonomous expression, were conducted mostly after a period of solitude. They were punctuated by frequent warnings to tell the truth, references to conscience, and invitations to "examine [your] soul."[23] This imposed on the woman an introspection that was translated into responsibility, implicit in the fact that she was only interrogated on decisive questions for the case and explicit in the warnings that evoked the prospect of eternal damnation as well as the threat of shame and social marginalization that extended beyond her to her entire extended family. The woman became the principal person responsible for the outcome of the case through these interrogations and the oath, ensuring either the continuation or invalidation of the marriage and, consequently, the formation or dissolution of the family.

Daniela Lombardi – and before her Adriano Prosperi and Gabriella Zarri – have detected the origins of that privileged relationship between men of the Church and women in the Council of Trent and in the subsequent ecclesiastical policy of controlling individuals' and families' behavior. This relationship was founded on the clergy's ability to "penetrate their hearts"[24] and form consciences "in the enclosure of judicial halls, like in the secrecy of the confessionals."[25] It was the fruit of the growing attention paid by ecclesiastical culture to the female world beginning in the twelfth century and a function of the role of mediator clerics attributed a wife as a "preacher" and "missionary" to her husband.[26] This connection between women and church men is evident in the Venetian marriage suits beginning in the fifteenth century. In the tribunal, this was manifested through an act of protecting a woman to the disadvantage of familial authority, which was intended to weaken the power binding her to her family of origin in favor of the family being formed.[27] This action found its most clear expression -and most effective means – in the interrogations of the female party. Conducted with a tone that alternated between persuasive and threatening, these interrogations – on one side – pushed women to reveal their souls to the vicar, encouraged them to reveal their personal inclinations, to confide their fears, and even confess contrived legal constructions. On the other side, these interrogations consolidated a judicial practice that made women privileged interlocutors, to the point that magistrates generally chose to demand a supplementary oath from them, making them capable of determining the suit's outcome,[28] which was technically a man's responsibility.[29] The analysis of this process is the second objective of this chapter.

2 Mediation

2.1 "Favor Matrimonii"

As we have seen, the procedure in marriage litigations principally expected the judge to act as a mediator; for the purposes of the marriage case, that he did not seek to punish an offense but to ascertain the validity or invalidity of a bond, or the legality of a separation.[30] Mediation, which was favored by the pastoral function of the ecclesiastical judge, and characterized by *favor matrimonii* and the doctrine of consent, sometimes occurred in a phase that preceded – and avoided – litigation. In these cases, spouses presented themselves to the magistrate in an informal manner, advancing their requests and explaining problems of a private nature that could not be legitimately used to initiate a suit. For example, a woman confessed to the vicar that she simply did not want her husband[31] and one couple declared that the wife, "discontent" with her husband, wanted to separate from him after 40 days of cohabitation. The judge limited himself to sending them away, ordering the reinstatement of cohabitation.[32] Similarly, a certain "greek" named Arsenio, married to a certain "skinny but pretty" Jacobina, who "had a dishonest life," asked "the vicar if for this reason he could leave her and marry." The vicar explained that "if he had given his hand, even if she did not lead a good life, he could not separate them nor could one leave the other, and that no one but God could end this marriage."[33]

Such requests might astonish the reader familiar with juridical norms of the time, which allowed separation only for very serious motives such as adultery and violence and which clearly distinguished between the cases that could lead to separation and the impediments that required the annulment of the bond.[34] However, one should not marvel at magistrates confronted with popular marital practices that were reluctant to assimilate to the principle of a marriage's indissolubility; that saw the value of honor strictly tied to control of female virginity and a wife's faithfulness; that considered separation as a private matter; and that balked at accepting the impossibility of contracting a new marriage if the first husband had abandoned the conjugal house for some time or if the wife committed adultery.[35]

Pre-Tridentine judges reacted, on one side, with censorial synodal dispositions – though only regarding cases of private separation.[36] On the other, they used episodes of conjugal conflict to explain the nature and finality of marriage, as well as on the competence of ecclesiastical authority in matrimonial matters, whether in the phase that preceded – or avoided – a suit, through interrogations of the parties in the litigation,[37] or at the moment of sentencing,[38] especially when the sentence was juridically motivated.[39] But in this practice the magistrates also reacted by exercising a certain discretion, characterizing their actions as *favor matrimonii* rather than as an imposition of norms. When the magistrate declared to the "skinny but pretty" Jacobina's husband that even if his wife conducted a "dishonest life" the two could not be separated "nor could one leave the other," for example, he in fact exercised a certain discretion. Although adultery was not included among reasons for annulment, it was among the reasons for separation (*divortium quoad thorum et mensam*), and in fact, it was among the most frequently invoked reasons for it.[40] Facing a husband ignorant of the norms, however, the magistrate avoided the possibility of a separation. Indeed, it was typically in cases of *divortium* that the magistrate's role as mediator reached its greatest intensity. One arrived at separation only after every other attempt at reconciliation had failed. Most of these suits concluded with a sentence that, even in the most serious cases, denied the separation (usually requested by women) with an agreement stating that the husband guaranteed, under penalty of an enormous fine, to "treat his wife well." In this pact he promised not to use violence, to assure her a lifestyle suitable to her status, and to trust her with the management of the house.[41] To arrive at this type of agreement the judge used intermediaries who had to provide surety for the husband and guarantee with their own goods that the conditions imposed by the tribunal would be respected. The sureties were often from priests: required to pay personally for any violations by the husbands, they became instruments (and actors) of ecclesiastical control over marriage.[42]

2.2 Freedom of Consent: Suits for Betrothals

Although Alexander III (1159–1181) had bestowed binding value only on a sworn promise of marriage, canonists attributed such value to any type of marriage promise.[43] The obligatory value of betrothal, however, contradicted the fundamental principle of Christian marriage, freedom of consent. In the rarest suits for betrothal, those which debated the obligation to stay true to a promise of marriage, the Venetian magistrates (in contrast with what happened in other dioceses) made themselves guarantors of the free expression of consent rather than promoters of the binding power of betrothal. As one of them affirmed, "marriages, in order to arrive at a good end, should be free."[44] When one of the two parties changed their mind, magistrates always granted the dissolution of the betrothal. These suits were generally easy and quickly resolved.[45] Only the doubts that the words exchanged between the two were stated in the present and not the future or that the promise was followed by sexual relations induced the magistrate to conduct a more detailed investigation, as the spouses might then be united by an indissoluble bond.[46] As much as the judges were more respectful of the principle of consent than to any promise made, though, they did try to mediate in betrothal litigations: "Why don't you want him?" the magistrate asked young Raimunda Sicula, who had promised to marry Antonio Busatto if he would only wait two months, later changing her mind.[47] The terse response of the young woman – "I don't want him and I will not marry him" – was followed by the judge's warning about the promise's value, but a new short and firm refusal from Raimunda – "It is up to me to decide if I want to marry him, and I do not want him" put an end to any other attempts at mediation.[48]

2.3 Social Mediation

The majority of pre-Tridentine marriage litigations regarded cases of presumed marriage.[49] When the magistrate issued a sentence of validity for a secret or clandestine marriage, he took on an institutionally recognized function of social mediation, since he became a promoter and guarantor of the union's solemnization. The formalization of the union was beneficial to public order and therefore requested "for decency" (*ad honestatem*), although it was not necessary either for the validity or the sacramentality of the bond, which were assured by the simple consent of the couple.

In some cases the judge did not limit himself to deciding on the validity of the marriage but pushed himself beyond his role, seeking to reconcile canonical norms with the material needs of the disputants. It was understood, for example, that a husband would contest an alleged marriage or justify the breach of obligations connected to a marital bond's stipulation with a missing dowry payment. Some magistrates ignored these reasons, limiting themselves to require that the union – which was valid by the exchange of consent – had taken effect.[50] Others, however, made themselves intermediaries for such requests to the bride, and, after ascertaining the bride's ability to satisfy her husband's demands, invited them to begin cohabitation. Only the relapse of the spouse would lead the judge to impose excommunication.[51]

Even the sentence, which often sparked an appeal or lively reactions, was not always perceived by the parties as an imposition. It might also be the culminating phase of a negotiation or a moment capable of clarifying and disentangling an unmanageable situation. For example, one magistrate was practically entrusted with choosing a wife for a man claimed by two women, who declared himself disposed to accept as his wife whichever one the vicar "assigned" to him.[52]

The execution of the sentence, mostly tacitly left to the discretion of the parties,[53] could be mediated by the tribunal if the disputants explicitly requested it. For example, when a husband finally obeyed the judge's sentence after an initial reluctance to begin cohabitation, he could ask the magistrate to guide the process of installing his wife in the marital house by having the judge inform her that her husband was willing to receive her.[54]

Following requests from the disputants, an ecclesiastical judge could even take over the role of secular authorities and become a mediator in negotiations regarding reparations for rape (*stuprum*)- a crime that fell under the jurisdiction of the Avogaria di Comun and the Council of Forty.[55] This happened at the end of the case of alleged marriage brought by Elena Simoni against Alvise Cavazza (1462–1463), which the woman lost because Alvise was able to demonstrate that he was compelled to marry her "by force and fear."[56] However, as Alvise did not deny that he had had a relationship with Elena that resulted in the birth of a baby girl, the parties entrusted the vicar, as *arbiter et amicabilis compositor*, to fix the amount of the restitution owed Elena. Despite the fact that he had won the suit, Alvise was obliged to pay the court costs and to reimburse Elena for the costs she incurred during the litigation, to dower her with 200 gold ducats, and to give her another 40 in hand as consolation; finally, he was obliged to pay 50 ducats to Elena's father to educate the child. He thus avoided a conflict before the Avogaria di Comun, which, although it would not have ensured Elena a better result, would have certainly been more unpleasant for Alvise.

3   Inquisition

As noted, judges in marriage cases mostly took on the function of mediation. Strict interrogations of women, however, bring up the problem of mixing accusatory and inquisitorial procedures within marriage litigation. In effect, the interrogation of a party was not part of civil procedure but of criminal procedure, which followed the inquisitorial rite. The final aim of the marriage cause, "the health of souls,"[57] justified in the eyes of judges and jurists the adoption (even if limited, as we will see) of techniques from the summary process. This included the interrogation of the parties. Characterized by the formula *simpliciter et de plano, sine strepitu ac figura iudicii*, the summary process took less time and reduced the costs of the accusatory procedure inherited from Justinian law, as well as giving the judge ample probatory power.[58] Precisely to avoid inconveniences, the parties sometimes invoked the adoption of this procedure.[59]

The application of techniques from summary procedure was evidence of a different conception of the truth from what underlay the common procedure of the marriage suit. This manifested itself in the formula "*ad inquisitionem veritatis*" (to find the truth) which sometimes preceded the interrogation of a party. The "argumentative nature" of truth in accusatory procedure gave way to a truth "[based on] presumed theological, even dogmatic and operative criterion" in the inquisitorial trial.[60] In other words, the truth resided in a precise place and the judge needed to find it.[61] It is surprising to find him in the trappings of an inquisitor while he proceeded to verify what was affirmed in the petition,[62] examine witnesses *ex officio*,[63] demand secrecy in depositions,[64] and proceed to extrajudicial controls,[65] even while threatening to torture reticent witnesses.[66] In this last – and truly exceptional – case,[67] the magistrate had to have been well aware that he was crossing the boundaries of his mandate, because he was concerned about preventing the recording of his threats: this is only noted thanks to the lively reaction of the plaintiff, who did not hesitate to recuse the judge.[68]

Having made an exception for interrogations of the party, the resistance of plaintiffs and the caution of magistrates confined inquisitorial procedures to the margins of marriage litigation. Excessive intervention by the judge – as is seen in the case of threatening to torture witnesses – raised vivid reactions from the parties. In one case, a magistrate who found himself presiding simultaneously over matrimonial and inquisitorial suits that involved the same couple and that were superimposed on one another clearly distinguished between the two proceedings.[69] In another case, the excessive zeal of a judge incurred the censure of a superior magistrate.[70]

Interrogations, even if stringent, followed a rather rigid schema based on the positions presented by the opposing party; the questions followed one another without taking account of the answers given,[71] in contrast to what happened in criminal trials, where the questions were modified according to the testimony. Interventions and warnings from the judge were intended to convince interrogated persons to freely express themselves and tell the truth, but not to depose against themselves, according to the principle that a party should not become "a weapon of offense in the hands of his adversary."[72]

In the aforementioned case that involved the young Paduan Ursina Basso, Ursina availed herself of all the instruments guaranteed by law to counteract excessive interventions by the magistrate and shape how the case would develop.[73] In the 1460s, Ursina came before the bishop of Padua to be recognized as the wife of fellow Paduan citizen Alvise Soncin. She lost the first case and appealed to the tribunal of Venice. As the events had taken place in Padua and all the witnesses were Paduan, the patriarch entrusted the enforcement and evaluation of the witnesses, as was practice, to the bishop of that city, reserving to himself the evaluation of evidence and, naturally, the issuing of the sentence. The elements in favor of Ursina were extremely weak and her hopes of victory were practically nonexistent, despite the fact she was helped by Bartolomeo Cipolla and Henry of Saxony, respectively, the best jurist and the fiercest legal professional available on the market.[74] To corroborate her version of the facts Ursina called obliging witnesses, who at least in some points in their testimony made glaringly false declarations.[75] The young woman was called to respond in court about the production of these witnesses. Her declarations were considered insufficient and the bishop demanded another interrogation to persuade her to confess. Ursina's position was difficult: she could be accused of inducing her witnesses to perjury.[76] Aware that they were faced with an anomaly, Ursina's lawyers presented an appeal to the patriarch against the bishop of Padua's decision to enforce their attendance. The patriarch immediately intervened with an injunction against the Paduan prelate to stop him from acting in a manner prejudicial to the young girl and to recall jurisdiction to himself over every phase of the suit. Ursina was not subjected to further interrogations.

4 Confession

4.1 The Judge as Confessor

While interrogations in which the magistrate assumed an active role are a sign of marriage causes borrowing from the procedures of inquisitorial and accusatorial interrogations, the measures chosen by the ecclesiastical judge to remove young people from parental influence, the tones adopted by vicars in the enforcement of the parties, their inquiry into intentions, and their frequent appeals to conscience[77] introduce the figure of the confessor. This role was not contradictory to that of the inquisitor but was rather attached to it and sometimes superimposed on it.

Judges who imposed confinement in a monastery and a period of relative solitude on a woman about to be interrogated believed – as did inquisitors and authors of confession manuals – that this favored confession.[78] The intermittent warnings given during the interrogation – phrases like "discharge your conscience," "tell the truth, because doing otherwise would cause the eternal damnation of your soul," and "abandon every respect," – alternatively reflect the "objective," "rigid," and "sweet" approaches of the ideal confessor according to contemporary manuals.[79] In particular, the invitation to abandon "every respect" recognized that shame and modesty (respect is synonymous with modesty in Venetian dialect) were obstacles to a full and sincere confession, especially in women's confessions, a fact that was also recognized by the authors of manuals and by preachers.[80]

In assuming the role of confessor, a judge pushed himself to the point of superimposing the internal (penitential) and external (judicial) fora. Such overlapping characterized a case in 1512 that involved the young Clara Marcello, an orphan of illegitimate birth. During this cause the judge assumed the role of the confessor to the extent to which Clara bestowed it upon him. She asked for the annulment of her marriage because it was performed by force and fear (*vis* and *metus*), but her version of the story lacked the necessary pretexts required by law to win the case. And yet she won.

Invited by the vicar to let every "respect" fall away and to tell the truth for the benefit of her soul, Clara recalled how, finding herself in the monastery of San Zaccaria, she was sent to call on her paternal uncles, her tutors, and conducted to their house. In a room together with a group of people that included a chaplain, was the young Francesco de Orlandi. Seeing him, the girl suddenly realized that her uncles planned to give her to him in marriage, upon which she "was seized by a fit".[81] Seeing tears in her eyes, her uncles took her to another room but did not ask her for explanations, nor did she provide them. "Standing there a while, this accident passed," and Clara was taken to the room where the guests were.[82] Although the girl did not "show it on the outside, in her heart she was very distressed," anyway proceeded to the ceremony.[83] The young woman, who twice was not able to respond to the request of consent from the chaplain, finally spoke, pushed by a "respond, do you not have a tongue?" from her uncle.[84]

From the declarations of the young woman it was clear that Clara did not have any juridical motivation to request the annulment of her marriage. The fear demonstrated at the moment of the marriage, in fact, was of a reverential nature, a sentiment to which doctrine did not grant any ability to delegitimize the bond. Contrary to what juridical norms required, the young woman not only had not opposed to the wedding, but she had even sought to keep her anguish internal. Furthermore, in the period after the ceremony, she accepted Francesco's visits both in the parlor of the monastery where she was still living and later in her uncle's house. She had not refused her husband's kisses (which carried heavy symbolic value),[85] even if "done against her will," because "this was not by consent to take him as her husband."[86] This case is very different from the scenes of crude violence and open rebellion displayed in the more common annulment cases made on the grounds of *vis* and *metus*.[87] And in fact the vicar who interrogated Clara was surprised: "What fear was that which pushed you to say yes if your will was contrary to it?"[88] Clara explained: "I feared that my uncles would not believe me, and that they would think that I had fantasies about other people."[89] The judge again asked for an explanation: "And even if your uncles had scolded you, what harm and what evil for this would have happened by you telling them you were not content to take the said Francesco?" Clara explained: "I imagined they would think I wanted another, and I thought that if I did non consent to Francesco, they would abandon me and would not have taken care of me anymore."[90]

The sentence that annulled Clara Marcello and Francesco de Orlandi's marriage was clearly due to the magistrate's mixing of the penitential and judicial fora. Legally there was an important distinction between "the essential elements, which should have value because they constitute a valid marriage, sacred and indissoluble on the spiritual plane, and the valuation of such elements accomplished in the suit."[91] The vicar, then, should not have valued what Clara proved "in her heart" but only what she had "demonstrated outwardly," as the decision should have been based on a truth that could be proven. A judge could not accommodate the young woman's requests, but a confessor could.[92]

The case of Clara Marcello is not an isolated one. Women interrogated by ecclesiastical judges often revealed things as if they were confessors or confidants. Among these were the young women who, unsatisfied with their marriages, wanted to abandon their husbands without advancing any juridical motivation to sustain their request; or a woman who responded to the magistrate's questions in a confidential manner, asking for and obtaining the promise that her declarations would not be put in the record.[93] For young women inclined to obey their relatives, and for girls unaccustomed to being interrogated about their own will and preferences, the dialogue with the vicar sometimes developed into bitter venting: "[my father] sent me to [my husband] too early, I should at least be twenty years old," confessed a 13-year-old bride, revealing a perception of herself and of periods of life that contrasted with those that contemporaries viewed as socially acceptable.[94]

The overlapping roles of confessor and judge were not only implicit in the confidential approach they often used. It became clear – and perhaps instrumental – in the declarations of women that asserted the veracity of their own declarations. One said: "I told the truth as if I were before my confessor"; another: "so God help me that I am telling and will tell the truth as if I were on the brink of death." Others used less explicit variations on such statements.[95]

In Venetian marriage suits, therefore, judges sometimes assumed the role of the confessor to manage the procedure and, above all, for the tone of the interrogations of the parties (in particular when they spoke with women). Elsewhere they went as far as administering sacramental confession. So, for example, during a cause of separation that occurred in Zara, a man refused to declare his reasons for the failed fulfillment of the conjugal debt except under the seal of confession.[96] When accommodating another request, indulging a woman who wished to give her deposition in confidence or issuing a sentence based more on her intentions than her proof, ecclesiastical judges made themselves interpreters of the *aequitas canonica* that allowed for a flexible application of the norms and sacrificed "formal cogency, orderliness, and unity" for "human fragility."[97] To use their own words, judges acted with "humanity" and "urbanity,"[98] the latter being a quality counted among the "ten prospective parts" of the cardinal virtue of justice.[99] The *modus operandi* of the magistrates – that was clearly justified by the peculiarities of canon law – in fact created the prerequisites for challenging a case. In particular, by accommodating confidential declarations or those under the seal of confession, a judge not only lessened his function as a public figure by his own imposition, to arrive "publicly to knowledge of the truth"[100] but issued a sentence "that did not even merit the name of a sentence."[101] Such sentences lacked any foundation, as "that which did not happen on the record is not in the world,"[102] as a decretal of Innocent III declared the recording of any act that happened before the judge or by the same judge.[103]

5 From Confessor to Judge

This approach that promoted confidence, flexibility of the norms, and attention to the concrete cases leads us to believe that the parties presented themselves spontaneously to the ecclesiastical judge. Thus, when the young Maria, daughter of mastro Francesco, told the vicar that she wanted to consult him to exonerate her conscience, because "conquered by inducements of the flesh and human frailty" she had secretly married someone despite an earlier vow not to get married, it is not difficult to believe that the magistrate was seen as a confidant to whom it was easy to present oneself, even if only to have clarity and obtain relief.[104] In this case, however, the young woman had no choice: the stipulation of marriage with the violation of a vow, in fact, was among cases reserved to the bishop, making this among those sins which could not be absolved by a confessor, only by the bishop or his vicar.[105] The nature of confession makes it impossible to prove this hypothesis,[106] but the quality of the sin leads us to believe the young woman was directed to the ecclesiastical tribunal by her confessor with a suspension of absolution. In the tribunal, she declared herself willing to stay with her husband if she could do it "with good conscience" and without "divine offense."[107] A similar case where the presence of the confessor was obvious strengthens this hypothesis. In 1513, a certain Bartolomeo, asking for an annulment of his marriage to a woman named Adriana, declared to the judge that he had not been absolved in confession because he had married this woman in spite of earlier sexual relations with her mother, to whom he was united "by great love."[108] In fact, Bartolomeo's confessor did not have the faculty to absolve him, because Bartolomeo and Adriana had contracted an incestuous marriage by affinity *ex copula illicita* through the previous union of Bartolomeo with his mother-in-law – another reserved sin.[109]

Cases like these,[110] along with many marriage suits that involved confessors and spiritual fathers but also prescriptions to ministers of penitence,[111] require us to examine the problem of the relationship – sometimes collaborative, sometimes antagonistic – between confessors and judges of marriage. They raise a question that we are not capable of answering: how many marriage causes, apparently conducted with the free initiative of the plaintiff, were actually begun under the imposition of the confessor?[112]

Venetian marriage litigations show us confessors and spiritual fathers who were social mediators in cases of contested marriage and indoctrinators about the nature and purpose of the marriage bond. Mediation could happen at different levels: between spouses, among spouses and their families, and among the spouses and the judge.

At the first two levels their function was mostly as pacifier and guarantor of social order. In cases that involved people from the more educated regular clergy, the action of the confessor tended to reconcile the lay conception of honorable marriage – which placed an active role on the family in marital negotiations and considered the deflowering of a virgin the same way as an "assassination"[113] – with Catholic doctrine that only required the consent of the spouses for a marriage to be valid.

We thus find confessors in several roles that united the social with the pastoral, and this became an occasion to defend the official doctrine of marriage. They acted as mediators between spouses who had contracted a marriage in secret, encouraging them to solemnize the marriage, and if necessary imposing such solemnization on them they were trusted to get the agreement of the groom's father to honorably celebrate a marriage that had already been contracted without his knowledge[114]; and they even made themselves ministers of marriages at the last moment to control potential violence.[115] Adopting these roles allowed the clergy to decrease the importance placed on consummation in order to secure the stipulation of a marriage; to reshape, for example, the relationship between the contraction of a marriage and its consummation: "do not put these heresies in your head, because only pure consent makes a marriage, not copulation"[116] – said one friar, in a period when, on the contrary, the "equation between marriage (*connubium*) and sexual relations (*concubitus*)",[117] established by the laity is found clearly in the expression of "Don't you want to be my wife?" directed by a husband to a reluctant wife.[118]

When a spiritual father became involved in a marriage *in facinore*) – that is, in a marriage that followed the discovery of two lovers *in flagrante* by the bride's relatives, who were usually armed – he assumed a peacemaking function and, consequently, became a guarantor of the marriage's validity. Beyond offering "accommodating and spiritual" words, he took this opportunity to remind them of the binding power of the words of consent – to which the laity did not grant equal importance[119] – and to underline the necessity that a marriage be contracted freely: "watch what you say, because you should do these things voluntarily and not forced."[120]

6 Confessors "in Place of the Judge" (*in vice iudicis*)

Confessors, particularly those who were regular clergy, often took on the role of a social mediator and worked to spread teachings about, and promote the ecclesiastical tribunal's authority over, the subject of marriage. But in other cases, particularly when they were secular clergy, they became participants and often actors in a procedure in the internal forum in the resolution of a couple's conflicts. They freely interpreted the doctrine of matrimonial consent, taking into account the fragility of unions contracted in a moment of passion, and they were persuaded that a "changed will"[121] justified the creation of a new bond. Some confessors believed they had the authority to dissolve marriages (provided they were contracted in secret) and grant licenses to the couple to contract new, public nuptials. "A hundred weddings in this way are done per day, you may well marry": with these words the parish priest of San Jacopo de Luprio briskly dispelled the "concern" of Marietta, who was uncertain of what she was doing and fearful of getting in trouble if she married Damiano Masarachia. Earlier, in fact, the woman had secretly been united in matrimony to Agostino Penzino, with whom she had come "to blows," however, in spite of having loved him "for a long time."[122] In the eyes of a confessor the dissolution (but the term used, significantly, was "absolution" of a marriage in which the distance of the spouses meant that the marriage was ineffective allowed for them to avoid scandal, in the form of a bad example given to the neighborhood.[123] To Giorgio da Zara, for example, who for 14 years had received no news of his wife, the priest of San Fantin granted license – or rather advice – to marry Elena da Spalato, who had been his concubine for years, "with good conscience." According to the confessor, in this way Giorgio would be reintegrated in the community of the faithful and again allowed to receive the sacraments.[124]

Similar declarations about the role played by confessors in dissolving marriages to end unions that had become burdensome cannot be verified. Hints of this practice sometimes appear in court, however, because they could be interpreted by the magistrate as analogous to a *de facto* practice. The admonitions of one judge, who reminded a woman claimed as the wife of an alleged husband that marriage, even if secret, could not be dissolved by any confessor, are clues to such practices.[125] Cases conducted in other dioceses lead us to hypothesize that this was a common practice.[126]

The infrajudicial action of the confessor could have various motives, which can be traced to the closeness of the secular clergy to the laity, whose values they shared and with whom, often, they shared an ignorance of doctrinal subtlety,[127] even on the subject of marriage. And even when the action of the confessor was in line with that of the ecclesiastical judge – when a priest claimed that a man "married" a woman with whom he had had sexual relations following a promise of marriage, for example – the confessor referred to lay values of honor more than the canonical grounds of marriage. "You cannot leave, it is advisable that you restore her honor as you have taken it" one priest suggested to a reticent spouse, instead of mentioning that, before the Church, he was united to the woman by an indissoluble bond of marriage because the *copula carnalis* had transformed the promise of marriage into a marriage in all respects.[128]

When a priest granted a license to marry a concubine to a man who had not heard from his wife in many years, or when he endorsed the matrimonial plans of another who had thrown his first wife out of the house after he discovered she was already married, the priest, like most laity, had neither completely accepted the principle of a marriage's indissolubility nor an ecclesiastical judge's competence on the subject of marriage. Like the laity, the confessor considered it superfluous to approach a magistrate in cases of evident resolution or agreement between the parties. Ecclesiastical judges were aware of this fact, even praising some on their recourse to the tribunal in certain types of cases and rewarding them by waiving the costs of the suit.[129] Studies by Anna Esposito on Rome and by Linda Guzzetti on Venice document a practice strengthened by consensual separations,[130] practices of which the patriarchs had become aware in the course of their pastoral visitations[131] and to which they reacted with censorious synodal dispositions,[132] but that – as I understand it – did not create judicial interventions.[133] The very high number of suits for the annulment of a spouse's previous marriage reveals that the laity did not conceive of marriage as an indissoluble bond, but, for the most part, as a union that could be contracted and dissolved according to the social context in which they found themselves at different times. Sometimes those who confessed a marriage, because they were already cornered, defeated by the evidence put forward by their opponent, revealed that the dissolution of marriage was not perceived as a sin and did not make the community ostracize them.[134]

In the next chapter we will discuss more thoroughly the free initiative sometimes taken in dissolving a marriage. We will also investigate the diffusion of a conception of marriage that considered the marital bond valid only as long as consent lasted between the couple.[135] For now it is only important to underline that these practices and views were sometimes supported by confessors. And if in the pre-Tridentine period Venetian patriarchs do not seem to have adopted measures on this subject, after Trent their reaction to such practices was probably part of a wider process of indoctrinating the secular clergy, a task which, by Priuli's 1592 constitutions, was entrusted to the regular clergy, who were especially asked to teach cases of conscience.[136]

7 Judges and Women

7.1 Attack on Parental Authority

In marriage litigations, women were the privileged interlocutors of the magistrates. This was allowed by a canonical norm intended to protect their freedom of expression and was directly connected to the importance of consent in creating a marital bond. Interrogations of women who were physically removed from family control and placed under the protection of the Church[137] seem first and foremost like an attack on parental authority.[138]

Based on the canonical disposition that – in contrast with secular norms[139] – recognized only the consent of the couple as having the power to constitute a marriage, the attack on families' authority was explicit in interrogations that investigated alleged marriages, when vicars invited the young women to tell the truth without concern for anyone[140] or showed themselves aware of the pressures young girls might be under. For example, one magistrate asked: "Did any of your relatives with threats or in any other way seek to induce or persuade you that you should say anything other than the truth?".[141] Identifying in parental authority a limitation of freedom of expression and an obstacle to telling the truth (which they claimed coincided with freedom[142]), a judge sought to avoid it, offering the young person the protection of the Church. One vicar, for example, said: "It seems just to me that for a few days you should be sequestered in the monastery of San Servulo or in some other observant monastery, so that you can be outside of the power of your relatives, and that you can more freely and perhaps with greater sincerity respond with the truth about these things. Are you content to obey me?"[143] Confronted with fear of abandonment, anxieties of conformity, and reverential fear, the magistrate – as we have seen – sought to diminish the influencing power of parental reactions: what harm would really come to Clara Marcello if her uncles did yell at her for refusing the man they wanted her to marry?[144] That the ecclesiastical tribunal offered an opportunity to remove oneself from the imposition of relatives, to express oneself and have a choice, and that this was not merely a formality but a concrete opportunity was clearly attested to by the case in which a young woman, Cassandra de Marconibus, resolutely availed herself of the opportunity the tribunal offered her to make her own choice and oppose what her family sought to impose on her by every means. I briefly present this case, which is representative of the possibilities that were opened by being summoned to court.[145]

Cassandra and Giovanni di Luchino a Serico were married and well aware that her family did not approve of their union. Being certain of the validity of their marriage, made with an exchange of consent, they made a game out of the family's opposition: "If your brothers tell you that you should become a nun, tell them that they should become monks, and that you do not want to become a nun because you have a husband," Giovanni said, provoking the laughter of his young wife.[146] The lightheartedness of the young woman did not last long: a little while after, in fact, we find her in the monastery of San Jacopo di Murano, with the name Filippa. Having decided to assert his rights and aware of the influence that her family could exercise over the young woman, Giovanni asked and obtained from the ecclesiastical judge that Cassandra be transferred to a Venetian monastery. Being wary of the possibility of resistance from his wife – and perhaps advised by lawyers who often saw very young brides disposed to deny contracted marriages – he presented to the judge a version of the facts enriched with a series of tropes common to marriage suits. He was trying to demonstrate both the public knowledge of the marriage and the attempts of her relatives to hinder the diffusion of this knowledge, while also preparing for an eventual recourse to favorable witnesses.[147] This last expedient turned out to be useless. The strategy of Cassandra's family, in fact, had been successful as long as the young girl remained in the convent in Murano, the same in which two of her sisters were nuns, entrusted to care for her and control her. When Giovanni came to the grate to talk to his wife, she had confessed her fear and her decision to renounce the marriage. Having left the convent and arrived in the presence of the vicar, however, Cassandra was ready to talk: even though resolutely denying the tropes Giovanni had used, she confessed the marriage and described the terror she endured, the threats of death made by her mother, and the strict control under which her sisters had placed her.

Her kin did not back down when faced with these revelations: all of them – mother, sisters, relatives – attempted to take her back under their control through meetings and conversations and to take over the case in her place, composing an appeal to present to the Holy See. The judge, however, did not make any decision without consulting Cassandra – without asking her, face to face, if she expressed herself in full liberty. The young woman, meanwhile, was adamant in confirming her own declarations and in refusing to meet with her relatives; she had absolutely not wanted to enter the monastery and desired instead to go to live with her husband. The magistrate respected her decision, and the appeal was not forwarded to the pope.[148]

We will not linger therefore further on the fact that the tribunal offered a concrete opportunity to oppose parental authority. Instead, we will seek to demonstrate the role of these interrogations in the formation of women's consciences and in the process that made them principal keepers of, and responsible parties for, marriage and the family.

7.2 Introspection and Appeals to Conscience

The interrogations – often repeated – were preceded and punctuated by periods of solitude passed mostly in the monastery, which imposed an introspection on the woman meant to favor confession.[149] With the cell door closed, the conscience became a battleground, the control of which guaranteed control of the marriage.[150] Feminine solitude without occupation – a condition that pastoral and didactic literature deplored for containing every type of trap[151] but in which ecclesiastical judges saw possibilities[152] – was feared by both relatives and alleged spouses. They raced to attempt to prevent it and bend the young woman's will to their own ends through furtive conversations during mass allowed by complicit nuns, through appeals to the pope, or through actual attacks on the monastery. Magistrates sought to protect this solitude with the weapon of excommunication, by strengthening control over the convent, and transferring the woman to be questioned to various convents.[153]

If, through custody in the monastery, vicars limited themselves to ensuring women the time and space to organize their consciences, during interrogations they promoted it. The appeal to female conscience assumes here a significance in contrast to the very rare interrogations of men.[154] While the interrogations of women took advantage of the conditional power of the oath, they excluded every possibility of comfort except that which the truth would bring. The questions were spaced out with warnings to "examine your soul" and "unload your conscience," while to a man, the magistrate said "you are asked" "to tell the truth on that which you are interrogated."[155] For example, during an interrogation when Marco Antonio Caravello was asked to prove his marriage with Isotta Michiel and to declare it "with every truth," it was followed by the questioning of his alleged wife, which was of a very different tenor:

> Warned with suitable words to tell the truth, informed that this goes towards the salvation of the soul, and having imposed the corporal oath,[156] the petition and requests of Marco Antonio were read for her clear understanding, and then she was interrogated and warned that she should respond under the bond of the oath taken whether her intention – about the marriage and the circumstances pertinent to it, as Marco Antonio had reconstructed them –, were true, either in all or in part, and having been warned often, she responded denying everything.
>
> Afterwards she was asked if there were words or taking of hands between her and Marco Antonio, or any other sign that had importance for the constitution of marriage, and she, being consistently and many times interrogated and warned, said no. And she was informed that she should be truly careful, for if she had by chance been secretly united in marriage with Marco Antonio, in such a way that the marriage could not be proven, nevertheless she would be and would remain bound to him before God and in the forum of conscience; she could not be absolved of this bond by any confessor or penitentiary with a plenary indulgence, not even by the pope, and that therefore she should be careful not to hide the truth, as it would cause the irredeemable loss of her soul.[157]

7.3   *Empowerment*

The attribution of responsibility to the woman is therefore implicit in the fact that only she was asked questions that could decide the case, and that the questions put to her were asked in very different tones than those used for men. The empowerment of women becomes manifest, however, in the appeals to conscience that evoke, beyond the prospect of eternal damnation (the consequence of perjury), the concrete threat of social margination (the consequence of lying):

> Daughter, examine well your soul that you do not perjure yourself and that you are not the cause that this Hieronimo, if he is your husband, takes another, that the children will be illegitimate, and similarly, if you take another, you will be in the most mortal sin and your children will be bastards, and you will not be able to receive the sacraments of the church, and you will be continually excommunicated and you will still be able to suffer temporal punishment with great harm and shame to you.[158]

With these words the magistrate addressed Elena de Stefani, claimed by a certain Domenico, who asserted to have married her before Girolamo. The judge did not only present the personal consequences of Elena's declarations to her; he also added the effects they would have for the people tied to her. If Elena lied to the judge, thereby being allowed to live with Domenico even though she was married to Girolamo, she would push Girolamo to seek another companion, leading him to mortal sin and causing the illegitimacy of his children. She would also live in mortal sin, subject to excommunication, harm, and shame, and these same repercussions would fall upon her children as well.

8 From the Conscience of the Judges to the Conscience of the Women: The Oath

The empowerment of the woman reached its peak with the imposition of the supplementary oath, which constituted additional proof according to doctrine, and which could therefore determine the tenor of the sentence in cases of doubt.[159]

For many judges the imposition of the oath constituted a problem of conscience. While some of them imposed it without hesitation, others were very cautious and requested it only after repeated interrogations, during which the woman, who had been warned many times to tell the truth, always repeated the same version of facts.[160] The scruples of the judge regarding the oath peaked during the interrogation of the weaver Elisabeth di Eustacchio (1510). After having examined the young woman, the vicar, seeing her disposed to confirm her declaration under oath, decided not to push her to that point, "lest she make a worse error."[161] Probably, worrying that Elisabeth was lying, the magistrate intended to save her from the danger of committing mortal sin.[162] Based on the norms of canon law, which draw on passages from the Book of Wisdom (Wis 1: 6–11), if she were lying she would have irretrievably compromised her salvation. Assuming she had made a false declaration, being disposed to confirm it under oath would have been perjury *ipso facto*: whoever was disposed to commit perjury, in fact, had already done so before swearing the oath, as God does not judge actions as much as one's thoughts and heart.[163] The judge, however, having noted Elisabeth's disposition, avoided making her pronounce the oath, demonstrating and declaring that he attributed different weight to the intention – a sin on its own – and the action – the error that would have aggravated the preceding sin.

The behavior of the magistrate – perhaps influenced by contemporaneous debates about oaths, which resulted in the proposal of the Camaldolese monks Querini and Giustiniani to eliminate it from public life as an occasion for some other sin,[164] – could also be due to magistrates' preoccupations about saving their own souls. Based on doctrine, in fact, anyone who makes another person swear an oath knowing that person will swear falsely is also a perjurer, and thus commits a sin worse than homicide, because he causes the damnation of the soul of his own soul as well as that of the person who perjured himself, instead of simply causing the death of a body.[165] A person who perjures kills himself, but a person who induces him to perjury gives him the weapon.[166] The norms, therefore, give precise indications of the implications of inducing someone to perjury, if someone could clearly predict it. But even in a case in which the lie remained hidden – and in our case the judge was not certain – doctrine did not completely relieve the conscience of the judge. Certainly, he who induced someone to perjury without knowing it did not commit a sin; ignorance, however, did not exclude doubt and suspicion: and in these nested human temptation. In such cases the judge had to make a decision with his conscience. Our magistrate decided not to impose the oath. We can see the full significance of this decision by correlating it to the approach taken by the same magistrate – and all the judges I have found in the Venetian documentation – towards the swearing of witnesses. Witnesses were required to swear an oath when they presented themselves to testify in spite of the very strong possibility that they might make false declarations, and therefore make themselves perjurers, since, as we have seen, a marriage suit exclusively allowed for partial witnesses and did not exclude parents and siblings of the parties from testifying.

The doctrinal prescription that imposed the oath on witnesses would have rendered judges who did not request it culpable of negligence, while at the same time allowing them to avoid the co-responsibility for perjury. According to the reflections of Alexander of Hales, Thomas Aquinas and Bonaventure, "only he who personally constrains another to swear can eventually be co-responsible for his perjury, while he who demands the oath from official need" does not incur guilt "unless he can predict that the oath will be false."[167] Such directives explain why the same magistrates who regularly made all witnesses swear an oath adopted a very different attitude at the prospect of imposing the oath on the parties in a case during interrogation. Such imposition, which to the eyes of some of them was completely legitimate based on what the rules allowed, posed a serious problem of conscience for others because it was not prescribed by the same norms.

The oath did not only constitute a crucial moment for attributing responsibility to the woman: it also signaled the moment in which moral responsibility passed from the judge to the party under interrogation. We have seen how, sometimes, the figure of the confessor and the magistrate could coincide, as the pastoral office was superimposed onto the judicial one. This *modus operandi*, conforming to the principle of *equitas canonica*, went against what prevailed during the twelfth and thirteenth centuries[168] and often evoked by magistrates, by which the judge could not decide according to his own conscience but only according to what had been alleged and proven.[169]

Nevertheless, before imposing the oath the judge affirmed that he was acting "for the exoneration of his conscience,"[170] thus betraying the interior distress of one who (with the doubt that the woman may have lied) accepted a clear distinction between the internal and external fora, even though he was only responsible for managing the external forum. At the moment of pronouncing the sentence the pastor clearly abdicated in favor of the judge: his conscience was mollified by the rite of the oath.

I will briefly describe this rite, which seems to highlight the emotional hold of the act. The oath was taken on the Gospels, a tangible sign of the presence of the divine[171] and to which doctrine attributed a quasi-magical power.[172] The reverential fear that the sacred book instilled was expressed in the reactions of two witnesses who interspersed their depositions with oaths to God and the Virgin Mary and with invocations for divine curses on them and their children if they were lying – but they refused to touch the Scriptures.[173] The judges knowingly availed themselves of the symbolic and suggestive power of the sacred text becoming suspicious of those who asked to swear on other objects. So, when a "Greek" woman asked to swear on the image of the Virgin, the magistrate granted her request only after verifying that this effectively corresponded to Greek Orthodox traditions: he clearly intended to use a ritual that ensured effective symbolism and to guard against the danger of validating any expedient that was meant to deprive the oath of its binding power. Similarly, the suggestive power of the ritual itself (rather than the act's juridical value) gave magistrates incentive to impose the oath on minors, even though the norms of canon law required the witness to be at least 14 in order to take a valid oath and did not consider children who made false statements under oath as guilty of perjury.[174]

8.1 Fear of the Sacred: Instruments of Dissuasion and Means of Legitimation

The solemn ritual just described proved more effective with women than men. The refusal to swear an oath, for example, was a female prerogative: even if not denying her own claims, a certain Pasqua da Cherso refused to swear an oath, requesting that this be asked of her husband.[175] Men showed more flippancy towards the invocation of the divine: sometimes they pronounced the ritual formula with an irreverence that came close to blasphemy. We find in the mouths of men, or attributed to them, expressions like "to the blood of the Virgin Mary"[176] and "swearing on the blood of God,"[177] which were compared to non-heretical blasphemy (a typically masculine sin/crime)[178] and punished as such. One witness expressly declared that he feared private retaliation but not ecclesiastical censure[179]; another would be defined as "a blasphemer of God and the saints who took a false sacrament for a penny."[180] Lastly, only when men were cross-examined did the question of "if they blaspheme or curse God or the saints" appear.[181]

Even the perception of the sinfulness of false deposition was clearer in women. One of them, revealing to the judge a contrived legal construct, declared that she wanted to dissociate herself because "the sin of withholding the truth" would harm her more than abandonment on the part of her husband.[182] The reverential fear shown by women towards the oath had a double effect: on one side, it became an instrument of dissuasion in the hands of their adversaries; on the other, it constituted a point of strength for the women, who asserted their own sincerity simply by recalling the oath they took, which they claimed had an intrinsic value that legitimated and confirmed their declarations. Some women responded to the vicar who investigated the truthfulness of their depositions by describing their testimony in sacramental terms: "By the sacrament that I said above," "I told the truth as if I were in front of my confessor,"[183] "I have not deposed for other motives if not by having been cited and put under the sacrament by the archpriest," and "So God help me that I have told and will tell the truth as if I were at the point of death."[184] (Here it is important to note the use of the term "sacrament" for "oath" which reveals, in the Cinquecento, the persistence of a sacramental conception of the oath that comes from the high Middle Ages.[185]) Appeals to conscience, which we find in the mouths of vicars during interrogations, are also found in women's declarations to prove their truthfulness, when they highlight that they have spoken "only for their conscience" or "about their conscience."[186] Isotta, the adoptive daughter of Alvise Michiel and whose demanding interrogation was conducted by the patriarch himself, claimed that "in truth she never contracted a marriage with Marco Antonio, and that if it were true that by fragility she had allowed herself to be persuaded to contract it, she would want to exonerate her conscience and tell the truth."[187]

It is not my intention to argue that women did not succumb to perjury. I intend only to highlight that the practice of female interrogation, which originated in the desire to furnish women with a possibility of expression and free choice, was transformed into an instrument of control and empowerment, and ultimately created a privileged relationship between judges and women. If, on one hand, this pushed the vicar to reveal his own soul, to confess to having begun the suit with a false declaration,[188] and even to manifest anxieties and desires that were not written down in the records, on the other it nourished the magistrate's faith in female sincerity – an effect of that fragility which, to their eyes, was rendered softer in court.[189] This caused them to make women their privileged interlocutors. Because of this orientation there was in some cases a true gap between the *modus operandi* of the tribunal and the norms that considered women untrustworthy witnesses – "always fluctuating and changeable."[190] By doctrine, if the oath were to determine the outcome of the case, it should be given to the man.[191]

In the pre-Tridentine period the trend of the episcopal forum's passivity on the subject of marriage alternated with phases of activism. During matrimonial litigation the judge could assume the traits of mediator, inquisitor, and confessor. These diverse functions were familiar to the judge because he was the pastor of his own diocese, he presided over the ecclesiastical tribunal in civil and criminal matters, and he sometimes had responsibility over important parishes. He was in the position to control marriage practices through various paths: he could come to know them in the course of his pastoral visits and in the tribunal, endorse them or oppose them in court, and promote or censure them with synodal dispositions.

For the entire fifteenth century the documentation of visitations and diocesan legislation shows us vicars who intervened in marital matters only to oppose *de facto* separations. Marriage suits, instead, reveal attentive observers of marital practices. In the development of their office, they did not limit themselves to recording marriages: they intervened to modify the marriage ritual, promote the doctrine of pure consent, and affirm the competence of the patriarchal tribunal over marital conflict. From the first decades of the sixteenth century the sources jointly register some changes to the ecclesiastical management of marriage. A synodal disposition imposed the registration of nuptials with the parish priest, and legal documentation attests to the growing presence of priests at weddings. The intensification of ecclesiastical control over marriage is also reflected in the assumption of a more active role on the part of the magistrate. Greater activism was accompanied by the renunciation of some previous rigidity: in terms of ritual, for example, magistrates tended to assimilate what they could not oppose.[192]

In the development of his office, a judge of marriage found both allies and antagonists among confessors. In the first case, which involved above all members of the more educated regular clergy, confessors became mediators among spouses, families, and the vicar, contributing to spread the canonical doctrine of marriage and promoting – sometimes imposing with the suspension of absolution – the authority of the ecclesiastical judge regarding marriage. In the second case confessors exercised a *de facto* jurisdiction over marriage that eroded a vicar's competency. These were mostly secular clergy, who shared a common ethic and ignorance of doctrinal subtleties with the laity, even on the subject of marriage. Perhaps also because they were invested in their traditional function as notaries, they felt authorized – precisely as the latter[193] – to conclude and dissolve marriages. In the pre-conciliar period Venetian patriarchs do not seem to have adopted any measures to oppose the interference of confessors in marriage. After the council, they probably responded to this erosion of competence through a general plan to indoctrinate the secular clergy. Secular clergy were entrusted to the regular clergy of the city, who were especially deputized to teach cases of conscience. At the same time, the intense action carried out by the post-Tridentine Church to impose respect of Easter precepts and to conquer the traditional reticence towards confession[194] rendered collaboration between ecclesiastical judges and confessors more intense and effective, as it favored the disciplining of reserved cases,[195] among which were various sins connected to marriage.[196] Through the suspension of absolution – made most grave because it brought with it suspicion of heresy – confessors became promoters of the ecclesiastical tribunal's authority on marriage.

Above all, the judge assumed an investigative function in interrogations of women. These interrogations reveal an ecclesiastical instrument for controlling the behavior of individuals and families, in this case through the promotion and control of the consciences of women, which would acquire unprecedented proportions after the Council of Trent. At the same time, they also guaranteed women the possibility of interfering with the decisions of magistrates and, in some cases, the possibility of determining those decisions through the oath-taking. Some tribunals across the Alps that excluded women from taking oaths precluded this possibility.[197]

Notes

1. "Arbiter et amicabilis compositor."
2. ASPV, *CM*, vol. 2, fasc. 12, Helena *vs* Alvise Cavazza, 1462–1463, c. 80. However, as we have seen, during the marriage cause the judge could assume an arbitrator's role, but the judge could not be substituted by arbitrators. See *supra*, ch. 2, § 10.
3. See *supra*, ch. 2.
4. See on this theme M. Sbriccoli, *Giustizia negoziata, giustizia egemonica*.
5. The tribunal did not proceed to the verification of the *petitio*, which defined the material of the defendant. The principal instrument at the judge's disposal to determine an objective truth was the oath. According to doctrine, in fact, the plaintiff, before presenting his or her petition, had to swear that whatever he or she said was true. In practice, however, this oath was not always imposed. See ASPV, *CM*, vol. 3, fasc. 1, c. 18, Antonio Pasetto *vs* Samaritana, 1468; *CM*, vol. 3, fasc. 2, c. 2, Margherita Manica *vs* Giuliano de Sanctis, 1468; *CM*, vol. 2, fasc. 16, Maria Sanador *vs* Dioniso Gabrieli e Allegretto, 1465; *CM*, vol. 3, fasc. 7, Antonio da Genova *vs* Suor d'Amor Malabotta, 1471.

Regarding the legal norms, see Gulielmi Durandi *Speculum iudiciale*, book II, partic. II de positionibus, § 5, n. 14. Lawyers and procurators also had to swear not to proceed with *animo calumnie*. False declaration in court was also a subject investigated in confession. See G. Savonarola, *Cum gratia et privilegio*, book I "de iudicibus," c. 40v-41r. See also M. Turrini, *La coscienza e le leggi*. Lawyers who believed that their assistants had made false declarations sometimes worried about the health of their souls. See ASPV, *AMP*, reg. 34, Pietro Chemeto *vs* Maria di Scutari, 16 January 1475: "Presentibus...domino Georgio et domino Antonio de Sicilia et dicentibus quod per ea, que percipere possunt, partes ipse colludunt, et ideo fatiunt dictum dominum vicarium advisatum, nec per collisionem habitam inter dictam partes feratur iniqua sententia. Et hoc denotant ad exonerationem conscientie sue." It should also be noted that sentences of annulment were never passed in final judgment, a sign of the respect for *favor matrimonii*, certainly, but also an expression of the will to guarantee the correspondence between processual and substantial truth.

6. J.C. Maire Viguer, *Giudici e testimoni a confronto*, p. 109.
7. Gulielmi Durandi *Speculum iudiciale*, book II, part. I, De interrogationibus, § 1, p. 543.
8. For example, a magistrate from Feltre said: "Et quoniam, sicut dixit, officium iudicis debet exuberare in huiusmodi causis matrimonialibus, ubi de periculo animarum agitur, ideo duxit interrogandum et interrogavit dictum Domenicum," cited by A.M. Lazzeri – S. Seidel Menchi, "*Evidentemente gravida*," p. 312, n. 23.
9. "Ut securiori animo possit respondere veritatem" noted in ASPV, *CM*, vol. 16, Marinum f. magistri Iohannis cercheri *vs* Serenam, 1515; "ut in libertate ibi constituta liberius veritatem manifestare valeat": ASPV, *AMP*, reg. 30, Paula q. Dominici Balbi, 8 January 1467. Other cases of confinement in a monastery during the litigation: ASPV, *CM*, vol. 3, fasc. 9, Giovanni Nascimbeni *vs* Ursolina, 1473; *CM*, vol. 4, Stanetta *vs* Alberto, 1476; *CM*, vol. 4, Giovanni Antonio Venedego *vs* Tarsia de Bertapaglia, 1477. Regarding custody in a private house see ASPV, *AMP*, reg. 30, Bartolomeo Trevisano *vs* Lucia, 14 January 1467; *CM*, vol. 6, Francesco da Avila *vs* Elena Grinerio, 1495: in this case the defendant was held "with an honest woman, in a secure location." ("apud honestam mulierem, loco tuto.")
10. See X 4. 1. 14.

THE OFFICE OF THE JUDGE: MEDIATION, INQUISITION, CONFESSION 139

11. An emblematic example of different attitudes assumed by the ecclesiastical tribunal towards men, even if very young and in obvious danger of being suborned, is in ASPV, *CM*, vol. 17, Marietta Barbaro *vs* Matteo Giustinian, 1515–1517. During this cause Marietta's procurator, recalling the norm cited *supra*, note 10, and emphasizing that this should also hold for men, asked insistently that Matteo, a minor of 14, be physically removed from familial influence and placed in a secure location. The procurator's request was not granted. On the construction of feminine *fragilitas*, see A. Belloni, *Die Rolle der Frau*, with ample citations from the juridical records; see also J. Kirshner, *Donne maritate altrove*, in particular p. 399; T. Kuehn, *Figlie, madri, mogli e vedove*, in particular pp. 434; H. Wunder, *Herrschaft*, p. 32, note 25; and E. Koch, *Die Frau im Recht der Frühen Neuzeit*, p. 83, note 24. For the Roman origins of the construction of female *fragilitas*, see J. Beaucamp, *Le vocabulaire de la faiblesse féminine*; S. Dixon, *Infirmitas sexus*; and A.J. Marshall, *Ladies at Law*, pp. 51–54. Explicit reference by the magistrate to *fragilitas sexus* in ASPV, *CM*, vol. 13, Elena de Stefani *vs* Hieronimo Marangon, 1514.
12. ASPV, *CM*, vol. 7, Marietta q. Andree de Matheis *vs* Vincentio Dragano, 1503.
13. The assumption of a more active role during sixteenth-century marriage litigations can probably be explained by the contemporaneous attempt to impose stronger ecclesiastical control on marriage. See *infra*, ch. 5, § 1.
14. "Donec et quousque mens dicte puelle....indagetur." ASPV, *CM*, vol. 12, Marietta q. Petri Bon tuschani *vs* Federicum Petri de Fornariis, 1512
15. "Volens perscrutari animum et mentem ipsius." ASPV, *CM*, vol. 12, Lucretia Fosco *vs* Angelo Cima, 1512.
16. "Pro informatione mentis sue." ASPV, *CM*, vol. 12, Camilla de Dardanis *vs* Alovisio Donati, 1512.
17. "Ad inquisitionem veritatis." ASPV, *CM*, vol. 7, Marietta q. Andree de Matheis *vs* Vincentio Dragano, 1503.
18. M. Damaska, *I volti della giustizia*, pp. 341–342. The same canonical norm that legitimated these interrogations justified them in the name of *aequitas*. See *supra*, note 10.
19. The vicar Domenico de Groppis, for example, was the parish priest of San Barnaba for a long time while serving as ducal chancellor.

See ASPV, *AMP*, reg. 23, Graziosa Azzalina *vs* q. Niccolò Orsini, 1464, where he was mentioned as parish priest of San Barnaba, also in the sources cited by P. Benussi, *Oltre il processo*, p. 168, note 63, where he was indicated in this role in 1507. For the jurisdiction and activity of the episcopal forum in the fifteenth century, see B. Mariani, *L'attività della curia arcivescovile milanese*. On criminale procedure of the venetian ecclesiastical tribunal N. Gillen, *Nur Gott vor Augen*.
20. See *infra*, § 7.
21. ASPV, *CM*, vol. 7, Andrea de Ballinio de Brixia *vs* Helisabeth filia Petri de Flandria, 1504.
22. "Autocoscienza femminile." See S. Seidel Menchi, *Percorsi variegati, percorsi obbligati*, p. 28; D. Lombardi, *Matrimoni di Antico Regime*, pp. 245-262; and C. Cristellon, *La sposa in convento*, pp. 140-146.
23. "Vardar l'anima."
24. D. Lombardi, *Matrimoni di Antico Regime*, p. 259.
25. Ibid., p. 260; A. Prosperi, *Tribunali della coscienza*, p. 520. See also G. Zarri, *Recinti*.
26. On the growing attention paid to the female world by ecclesiastical culture since the twelfth century, see J. Delarun, *La donna vista dai chierici*, in particular pp. 42-52. On the function of mediation by women, who were supposed to be "preachers" and "missionaries" to their husbands: S. Vecchio, *La buona moglie*, in particular pp. 130, 140-143; C. Casagrande, *La donna custodita;* see also G. Dominici, *Regole e governo di cura familiare*; and Bernardino da Siena, *Le prediche volgari*. The attention to women was emphasized also because of the greater prestige granted to marriage – and consequently to women – in the fifteenth century both because of new demographic emergencies and because of marriage's reevaluation by humanists persuaded of the existence of a direct link between the conjugal state and the active or civil life that valorized the female role of mediation between two lineages, emphasizing the active function of valorizing kinship understood as the main nucleus of any society played by women: see L. Fabbri, *Trattatistica e pratica dell'alleanza matrimoniale*, in particular pp. 92-99. A. D'Elia, *The Renaissance of marriage*. See also L. Accati, *Soggeto collettivo*. These studies emphasize the fact that the cleric attributed to the woman a mediating role between clerics and their own

families. The documentation that we have examined attests to the fact that the family valued female mediation for informal requests to priests: during a marriage litigation, for example, the defendant was excommunicated for contumacy. During all the phases of the cause he was represented by his brother, and although his father was living, his mother was the one who presented herself before the judge to beg him to suspend the excommunication of her son. See ASPV, *CM*, vol. 29, Pelegrina linarola *vs* Dominico linarolo, 1530–1531.

27. See in particular ASPV, *CM*, vol. 6, Giovanni di Luchino a Serico *vs* Cassandra de Marconibus, 1492–1493; *CM*, vol. 15, Pietro Dandolo *vs* Quirina Bollani, 1515. On parental control of marriage J. Kirshner, *Baldus de Ubaldis*.
28. Sometimes the parties did not have sufficient proof and the judge could choose to ask one of them to take a supplementary oath, that could determine the outcome of the litigation. On the supplementary oath see the outlines in G. Provinciali, *Giuramento decisorio*, in particular p. 107.
29. It is sufficient to cite here Andreas Tiraquellus, *De legibus connubialibus et de iure maritali*, gl. I, l. 9, n. 54, p. 135, cited by E. Koch, *Die Frau im Recht der Frühen Neuzeit*, p. 85. The lesser value of a woman's oath places it in a larger context of women's inferior juridical capacity; see G. Minnucci, *La capacità processuale della donna*. See also *supra*, ch. 3, § 6.
30. D. Lombardi, *Matrimoni di Antico Regime*, p. 156.
31. ASPV, *AMP*, reg. 20, marinaio da Signa *vs* Isabetta di Georgii, 11 May 1459.
32. "Male contenta." ASPV, *AMP*, reg. 10, Pietro di Antonio Zagabria *vs* Maria da Valacchia, 4 April 1444. The appearance of spouses did not begin a suit; for this we only have records from the registers of the curia that recorded not only processual acts but also sometimes requests – that were more or less juridically sound – addressed to the ecclesiastical judge. See *supra*, ch. 1, point 1.
33. "Greco," "magrolina ma bella," "tegniva vita inhonesta," "a misser vicario se per tal causa lui la podeva lassar e maritarsse," "se lui li haveva dado la man, etiam che non la menasse bona vita, i non se podeva separar né partirse l'uno da l'altro, et che altri cha solo Dio non poteva partir questo matrimonio." ASPV, *FC*, vol. 2, Jacobina *vs* Giovan Battista Donati.

34. Confusion between the juridical motives valid for bringing suit for separation and those valid for bringing suit for annulment also in ASPV, *CM*, vol. 12, Johannis Dominici Ceti *vs* Camilla e Angelica, 1512–1513. For a review of the norms on separation and the reconstruction of the institution according to the lines of development of civil and canon doctrine of the middle age, see A. Marongiu, *Divorzio*, p. 182–507; G. di Renzo Villata, *Separazione personale dei coniugi*; and G. Marchetto, *Il 'divorzio imperfetto.'* On separation in the Ancien Regime, see S. Seidel Menchi – D. Quaglioni (eds.), *Coniugi nemici*; B. Borello, *Trame sovrapposte*, pp. 157–194; and C. La Rocca, *Tra moglie e marito*. On separation in post-Tridentine Venice see J. Ferraro, *Marriage Wars*. On the impediments that required the annulment of the bond, see J. Gaudement, *Il matrimonio in occidente*, pp. 146–165.
35. See *infra*, ch. 5, §§ 3–6.
36. See *Constitutiones et privilegia patriarchatus et cleri Venetiarum*, primae part., tit. Tert., cap. XXIV, Ex const. Andrea Bondumerio patriarcha, pp. 50–51.
37. See for example the interrogation of the woman in ASPV, *CM*, vol. 9, Isotta filia adoptiva magnifici Aloysii Michiel *vs* Marco Antonio Caravello, 1507 on the validity and indissolubility of clandestine marriage.
38. See for example the sentence of ASPV, *CM*, vol. 9, Michele Leoni *vs* Faustina Foscarin, 1507, on the competence of the ecclesiastical judge on the subject of annulment of marriage.
39. See for example the sentence of the document cited *supra*, note 37 on the division between the internal and external fora.
40. See *infra*, ch. 6.
41. "Bene tractando". ASPV, *AMP*, reg. 23, Elena Contarini *vs* Benedetto Erizo, 5 March–17 November 1462. In *AMP*, reg. 13, Anna *vs* Matteo Trevisano, 17–18 September 1451, the vicar granted Anna separation as long as her husband "neglected to adequately protect [his wife's goods and person] from damage and insecurity in a satisfactory and sufficient manner agreeable to the lord vicar of Castello" ("non satisderit idonee et sufficienter ad libitum domini vicarii castellani de indemnitate et securitate"). In *AMP*, reg. 16, Ermanno teutonico *vs* Agnete, 5 June 1454, the vicar established that Agnete was not required to return to live with her husband, "most extensively opposing his cruelty, for which he did not give

warning" ("obstante permaxima sevitia, pro qua cautionem non dedit"). See also S. Chojnacki, *Il divorzio di Cateruzza*.

42. See for example ASPV, *AMP*, reg. 9, Jacopo Donato Bonacorso *vs* Andreola, 12 February e 2 March 1444; Jacopo guaranteed, under penalty of 100 gold ducats, to treat Andreola well and the priest of San Geremia provided surety for him. There are cases of ecclesiastical sureties (made e.g., to guarantee the payment of court costs) also in various types of marital litigations: *AMP*, reg. 10, Jacopo Foscari *vs* Caterina Pizzolati, 15–17 February 1445; *AMP*, reg. 10, Donato Donati *vs* Paolucia, 20 April 1444; *AMP*, reg. 10, Bartolomeo del Memo *vs* Lucrezia di Giovanni Guernerii, 28 January 1443; and *AMP*, reg. 16, Ermanno Teutonico *vs* Agnete, 3 April 1454. In *AMP*, reg. 14, Caterina Gaiato *vs* Battista Giusto, 11 January 1454, father Giorgio of Santi Apostoli was distrained for the fee of the court costs, for which he had provided surety. *AMP*, reg. 1, 15 May 1452, the vicar asked father Jacopo Rixo to prove that he was absolved of the surety given in the marital case between Vittura Vitturi and Marco Zen, debated before the patriarchal curia of Grado.

43. J. Gaudemet, *Il matrimonio in Occidente*, pp. 123–127; and D. Lombardi, *Matrimoni di Antico Regime*, p. 133. The sworn promise of marriage was very widespread, so much so that in some places betrothals were called *iura*. See C. Klapisch, *La famiglia e le donne*, p. 117; D. Bizzarri, *Per la storia dei riti nuziali*, p. 618.

44. This was affirmed by the judge who annulled a betrothal in ASPV, *CM*, vol. 32, Baptistina de Bossis *vs* Marino Trono, 1532. The approach of magistrates was different, for example, in the dioceses of Florence, Pistoia, and Trent – but these are also all post-Tridentine cases. Regarding Tuscan dioceses see D. Lombardi, *Matrimoni di Antico Regime*, pp. 290–301, 294–295, which mentions cases of recourse to incarceration of the groom as long as he had not consented to the marriage (1552–1553 and 1559). Regarding the diocese of Trent in the 17th and 18th century see L. Faoro, *Il ricorso alla carcerazione*. Regarding Burgundy, where the royal tribunal had jurisdiction for cases of seduction following promise of marriage, see J.R. Farr, *Authority and Sexuality*, which mentions sentences that required the seducer to marry the seduced upon complaint by the seduced and her father: the execution of the sentence was ensured through incarceration and the man was brought to the church in chains for the ceremony.

45. See the quantitative data *infra*, ch. 6.
46. A. Esmein, *Le mariage en droit canonique*, I, pp. 245–262. For examples of particularly stringent interrogations to discover if the betrothal was followed by sexual relations see *infra*, ch. 5, § 7.
47. "Perché non el vostu?"
48. "E non el voglio e sì non el torò." "El starà a mi s'il vorò tuor, ma e non el voglio." ASPV, *FC*, vol. 2, Antonio Busatto *vs* Raimunda Sicula, 3 June 1510.
49. See *infra*, ch. 6.
50. ASPV, *AMP*, reg. 9, Anna di Giorgio *vs* Michele da Corfù, 26 November 1442; reg. 23, Paolo Georgii da Cividale *vs* Gentilina Amedei de Lando, 13 May 1462.
51. ASPV, *CM*, vol. 29, Pelegrina linarola *vs* Dominico linarolo, 1530–1531.
52. ASPV, *AMP*, 23, Alvise Arduino *vs* Pellegrina de Capitibus Vacharum, 22 November 1463.
53. See *supra*, ch. 2, § 12.
54. ASPV, *CM*, vol. 16, Perina relicta q. ser Varisci samitarii *vs* magistrum Benedictum, 1515–1516.
55. On the definition of rape see *supra*, ch. 1, point 3 and note 66. Crimes of a heterosexual nature were subject to investigation by the Avogaria di Comun, while the Council of Forty decided guilt and imposed a punishment. See G. Ruggiero, *Patrizi e malfattori*, pp. 51–66, and Idem, *The Boundaries of Eros*, pp. 16–44.
56. "Per vim et metum." See *infra*, ch. 5, § 8.
57. "La salute delle anime." P. Fedele, *La responsabilità del giudice*; and A. Padoa-Schioppa, *Sur la conscience de juge*. See also ASPV, *CM*, vol. 11, Vincenzo Quirino *vs* Caterina Mauro, 1508–1512; *CM*, vol. 11, Ambrosina de Blasonibus *vs* Marco Antonio Bacinetto, 1509–1510; and ASPV, *AMP* 46, Magdalena famula Ludovici Contareno *vs* Antonio Samitario: "attento quo causa est matrimonialis, et agitur de peccato." Also in A.M. Lazzeri-S. Seidel Menchi, "*Evidentemente gravida*," p. 312, note 23, the judge explicitly declared that he proceeded to interrogate the party in the marriage cause because "it leads to danger of the soul" (*de periculo animarum agitur*).
58. The process "simpliciter et de plano..." was authorized by Clement V in 1306: *Clem.* 2. 1. 2; *Clem.* 5. 11. 2. The abbreviated procedure was most commonly used. See *supra*, ch. 1, point 9, and the bibliography cited there in notes 135 and 137.

59. ASPV, *CM*, vol. 11, Zinevra filia Nicolai barbitonsoris *vs* Hieronimo Baldigara, 1509–1510. Zinevra's procurator asked that they proceed rapidly "because the cause on its own and by its nature demands and requires this, and mostly in that in which danger pursues the soul"("quod causa ex se et ex sui natura hoc expostulat et requirit, et maxime in ea in qua anime venatur periculum"). See also *CM*, vol. 7, Caterina Minoto *vs* Marco Abramo, 1500. In *CM*, Giovanni Mammoli *vs* Lucia d'Este, 1513, the summary proceeding was explicitly applied because of the poverty of the parties.
60. "Presupposto teologico, fine dogmatico e criterio operativo."
61. M. Sbriccoli, *Tormentum*, p. 24.
62. ASPV, *CM*, vol. 11, Ludovica Calbo *vs* Marino di Cavagnano, 1509. ASPV, *CM*, vol. 12, Adriana Nigro *vs* Pietro Bontremolo.
63. See *supra*, ch. 3, note 2.
64. ASPV, *FC*, vol. 1, Giovanni Luchini a Serico *vs* Cassandra de Marconibus, 23 January 1493: secrecy was imposed on two witnesses, under penalty of excommunication. This was an exceptional procedure: see *supra*, ch. 3, § 2.
65. ASPV, *AMP*, reg. 33, Isabette da Brixia *vs* Luchino ianuensis samitarii, 9 December 1474; ASPV, *CM*, vol. 11, Zinevra filia Nicolai barbitonsoris *vs* Hieronimo Baldigara, 1510.
66. ASPV, *AMP*, reg. 33, Niccolò a Bulzia *vs* Paula, 5 October 1474.
67. I have not found any analogous cases in the Venetian documentation I have examined. The only analogous case I know of is Florentine: T. Kuehn, *Reading Microhistory*, pp. 530–531.
68. On the recusing of a judge see *supra*, ch. 2, § 5 and n. 58. In the Florentine case recorded by Kuehn, (see *supra*, n. 67), the witnesses threatened with torture retracted their depositions, affirming that they had made false declarations "under fear of penalty, to remove the punishment" (timore pene, videlicet supplicii tollendi).
69. ASPV, *CM*, vol. 21, Helisabeth filia Iohannis Buttarii *vs* Gaspare Iohannis Pistoris, 1522.
70. ASPV, *CM*, vol. 2, fasc. 7, Ursina Basso *vs* Alvise Soncin, 1462.
71. D. Lombardi, *Matrimoni di Antico Regime*, p. 151–152.
72. "Un'arma di offesa nelle mani del suo avversario." M. Damasca, *I volti della giustizia e del potere*, pp. 217–218.
73. See *supra*, ch. 3, § 3, and the bibliography cited relative to this case.
74. On Bartolomeo Cipolla see *supra*, ch. 2, § 1, note 17 and the bibliography cited there.

75. One witness mentioned, among other things, that she had witnessed certain facts from a balcony that was revealed to be nonexistent.
76. On inducement to perjury, see *infra*, § 8.
77. ASPV, *FC*, vol. 2, Benedicta filia ser Novelli *vs* Antonio Donato, 1516 and the document cited *supra*, note 37.
78. See respectively A. Prosperi, *Tribunali della coscienza*, pp. 196–202 and R. Rusconi, *Manuali milanesi di confessione*, p. 120, relative to the confessional of Bartolomeo Caimi.
79. "Descarga la tua coscienza." "Dì la verità, perché altrimenti facendo tu resteresti in continua dannazion dell'anima tua." "Abbandona ogni rispetto." A. Jacobson Schutte, *Consiglio Spirituale e controllo sociale*, p. 52. About the approach assumed before women in confession, BNF, P.6.10, Antonino (S.) Vescovo di Firenze, *Incipit summula confessionis*, tractatus II, pars II "de confessione," ca. VIII, c. 60; on the alternation between sweetness and hardness, c. 60 r. Regarding studies of manuals for confessions see the ample bibliography of E. Brambilla, *Alle origini del Sant'Uffizio*, p. 118, note 16 and p. 225, note 1–5. On the reassuring and consolatory aspect of confession, T.N. Tentler, *Sin and Confession*, and J. Delumeau, *La confession pour tranquilliser*. On the confession of sins and the sacrament of penitence see also R. Rusconi, *L'ordine dei peccati*.
80. See respectively Petrus Pictaviensis, *Summa de confessione*, c. 47, *De impedimentis confessionis*, p. 60; Antonino da Firenze, *Opera*, "Il modo di domandare," c. 9, and *Sermoni del beato Bernardino*, 1: "De integritate confessionis," pp. 326–7; Ibid., "De qualitate confessoris," pp. 334–335.
81. "Vene uno acidente grande."
82. "Stando lì uno pezo, e passado questo acidente."
83. "Mostrasse de fuora, nel cuor era molto adolorata."
84. "Responi, non hastù lengua?" According to S. Chojnacki, *Valori patrizi nel tribunale patriarcale*, p. 231 and note 83, the initial rejection of the bride is part of the Venetian matrimonial ritual. See also M. Seidel, *Hochzeitsikonographie im Trecento*.
85. A long juridical tradition "considered the kiss as one of the signs of nuptial consent." The kiss was also considered a prefiguration of the consummation of the marriage. See O. Niccoli, *Baci rubati*, p. 225.
86. "Malvolentieri faceva," "non era stà de [suo] consenso de tuorlo per marito."

87. See *infra*, ch. 5, 8.
88. "Che paura fu quella che mosse a dir de sì si la vestra voluntà era in contrario?"
89. "Io haveva paura che i dicti mi' barbani non me cridasse, et che i non pensasse che havesse in fantasia ad altre persone." Barbani is Venetian dialect for uncles.
90. "Si ben vostri barbani ve havesse cridato, che danno et che malo per questo havesseu habudo digandoli vui che non eri contenta de tuorulo el dicto Francesco?" "Io ideaizava che loro se haveria pensado che volesse ben a qualche un altro, et sì pensava che se non havesse consentido in Francesco, che i non me havesse abandonada et non se havesse più impazado de mi." ASPV, *CM*, vol. 12, Clara Marcello *vs* Francesco de Orlandis, 1512.
91. C. Valsecchi, *"Causa matrimonialis est gravis et ardua,"* p. 420 and the sources cited in note 22.
92. It is not possible for me to interpret the magistrate's decision using documentation external to the cause. The notarial documentation about Clara's relatives named in the litigation has been lost or does not make mention of Clara. Clara herself does not appear in the documentation of the convent of San Zaccaria, where she was before her marriage and where one of her aunts lived. See ASVe, *Notarile Testamenti*, b. 192, n. 29, b. 1213, nn. 908 and 922, b. 1207, n. 188, b. 1220, n. 20; ASVe, *Corporazioni religiose soppresse, S. Zaccaria*, bb. 4 and 76. On the division of the two fora see also the citation of G. Savonarola, *Prediche sopra l'Esodo*, pp. 59–60 in D. Lombardi, *Matrimoni di Antico Regime*, p. 130, where, with likely apologetic intent, the friar attributes greater authority to the confessor in the internal forum than the bishop in the external forum. Savonarola later became the spokesman of the canonical position on the division of the two fora in his *Cum gratia et privilegio*, book I, part II De sacramento matrimonii, c. 25 v.
93. ASPV, *CM*, vol. 12, Camilla de Dardanis *vs* Alovisio Donati, 1512. See also *CM*, vol. 16, Perinam relictam q. ser. Varisci Samitarii *vs* magistrum Benedictum barbitonsorem, 1515, in which the defendant declared that the marriage was null for canonical impediment, which he did not want to explain "ex rationalibus causis" but about which the vicar could be informed *ex officio*.
94. "[Mio padre] el me ha mandà [a marito] tropo a bonora, almen ch'io abesse habudo venti anni." ASVP, *CM*, vol. 7, Andrea de

Ballinio de Brixia *vs* Helisabeth filia Petri de Flandria, 1504. See *infra*, ch. 5, § 7 and the bibliography cited there.

95. "Ho dicto la veritade como si fosse davanti el mi' confessor." "Cussì Dio mi adiuti che sto per dire e dirò la verità como se adesso fuosi al punto dela morte."
96. ASPV, *CM*, vol. 11, Vincenzo da Iadra *vs* Magdalena filia Simoni da Tarvisio, 1510.
97. "Logicità, sistematicità, unitarietà formali" "humanae fragilitates." See P. Grossi, *L'ordine giuridico medievale*, pp. 119–120.
98. "Humanitate" and "urbanitate." ASPV, *CM*, vol. 11, Clara Brano *vs* Baldassare Penzino, 1511.
99. "Dieci parti potenziali." Antonino da Firenze, *Opera*, III parte, c. 67 r, "delle 7 virtù": "iustitia."
100. K. Pennington, *Il diritto dell'accusato*, p. 40. On the separation between private and official knowledge in the administration of justice: K. W. Nörr, *Zur Stellung des Richters*, pp. 43 and 71.
101. "Minime nomen sententie mereri." ASPV, *CM*, vol. 11, Vincenzo da Iadra *vs* Magdalena filia Simoni da Tarvisio, 1510: the sentence of the first causa should be considered null "iuxta vulgarem regulam non credatur iuditio nisi quantus in actis constat."
102. W.M. Plöchl, *Geschichte des Kirchenrechts*, p. 335.
103. X 2. 19. 9. The obligatory recording of the suit acts was ratified by the Lateran Council of 1215. See G. Alberigo et al. (eds), *Conciliorum Oecumenicorum Decreta*, p. 252: *Concilium Lateranense IV-1215, 38, De scribendi actis, ut probari possint*.
104. "Victa stimulis carnis et fragilitate humana." ASPV, *FC*, vol. 2, Maria q. magistri Francisci *vs* Pietro Antonio da Soledo, 5 October 1502.
105. Antonino da Firenze, *Opera*, c. 11 v.
106. Regarding reserved cases, Bartolomeo Caimi in his *Interrogatorium sive confessionale* considered that the confessor would send the penitent to a superior judge, or if he was confronted with a "simple" (simplex) person, the confessor would write to the episcopal vicar: see E. Brambilla, *Alle origini del Sant'Uffizio*, pp. 234–235, in particular p. 235, note 16. In such cases, the confession of sin left documentary traces: so for example among the civil acts of the Paduan curia we find a "Frater Bartolomeus de Ancona" who asked the bishop of Padua for permission to absolve "a poor little woman" ("una poveretta donna") of killing her children, another reserved sin. See ACV, *Curia, Actorum civilium*, b. 35, loose paper, 1462.

107. "Cum bona conscientia" "offensione divina." See E. Brambilla, *Confessione*, p. 502, note 27.
108. ASPV, *FC*, vol. 2, Bartolomei de Monte Tuschani *vs* Andriana filia ser Antonii Balbi, 1513.
109. See E. Brambilla, *Confessione*, pp. 493–494 and note 9. Regarding affinity *ex copula illicita* see *supra*, Introduction, note 98.
110. See also the case presented by A.M. Lazzeri – S. Seidel Menchi, *"Evidentemente gravida"*, p. 318, and the post-conciliar cases analyzed by J. Ferraro, *Marriage Wars*, pp. 57–58, 71–85, and in particular p. 75, and by S. Luperini, *La promessa sotto accusa*, p. 372.
111. See for example P. Pictaviensis, *Summa de confessione*, XXVI, "De confessione laicorum," p. 29.
112. See in particular the words of the confessor in ASPV, *AMP*, reg. 26, Bartolomeo Alovixii draperius *vs* Maria de Andrea, 28 July 1465: "I can absolve you of past sins, but the separation you seek between you and Bartolomeo will be seen at the court of the most reverend lord patriarch or his vicar, in this I cannot support you." ["De peccatis preteritis possum te absoluere, sed quantum ad separationem quam petis inter te et Bartholomeum hoc spectat ad forum reverendissimi domini patriarche vel eius vicarii, in hoc non possum tibi suffragari."]
113. See the "You have made this girl dead to me" ("Tu me ha assassinà a questa tosa"), aimed by the mother of a girl from Cittadella to the young man surprised in the act with her daughter (1560), cit. by L. Megna, *In margine ad alcune carte processuali*, p. 320.
114. ASPV, *CM*, vol. 9, Marco Antonio de Stefani *vs* Lucretia q. Simonis Vacha, 1506–1507: "He needed to convince the young man's father to ask our family for the girl's hand in marriage for his son, but without informing us that the marriage had already been contracted, to preserve our honor."
115. ASPV, *CM*, vol. 11, Ambrosina de Blasonibus *vs* Marco Antonio Bacinetto, 1509–1510.
116. "Non ve mete' in testa queste heresie, perché el solo e puro consenso fa el matrimonio, non copula." See the document cited above, note 114.
117. "Equazione fra connubio e concubito" S. Seidel Menchi, *Percorsi variegati, percorsi obbligati*, p. 31.
118. "Non vostu esser mia moglier?" ASPV, *CM*, vol. 7, Nicolò q. Dominici Cortesii *vs* Angela Sebastiani Cavazza, 1503–1508. See

also ASDVr, ATE XI, *PM*, b. 7, Caterina de Medici *vs* Giulio Maffei, 28 April 1551, where the term "copularla" (to copulate with her) became used as synonymous with "sposarla" (to marry her).
119. See *infra*, ch. 5, § 2.
120. "Guarda quello che tu di', perché queste cose se vuol far voluntarie e non sforzadi." See the document cited *supra*, note 115.
121. "Semotis arbitriis." ASPV, *FC*, vol. 3, Damianus Masarachias nauta *vs* Marieta filia Bone sclavone, 1525.
122. "Cento matrimoni a questo modo se fa al dì, tu te puol ben maridar." "fastidio" "entrigarse" "ad rixam" "per multa tempora" Ibid.
123. Preachers and the authors of confessors' manuals lingered on the greater gravity of public sin than hidden. See respectively *Sermoni del Beato Bernardino*, p. 322 and F. Chavarría Múgica, *Mentalidad Moral*, pp. 730–731.
124. "Se absentavit," "cum bona conscientia." ASPV, *CM*, vol. 18, Georgii de Iadra *vs* Lena de Iadra, 1516.
125. See below, the interrogation of Isotta Michiel. That the faithful directed themselves to a confessor with the pretense of obtaining the dissolution of a marriage is also attested to in ASPV, *AMP*, reg. 26, Bartolomeo Alovixii draperius *vs* Maria de Andrea, 28 July 1465: Maria "bearing a privilege of plenary indulgence... seeks plenary absolution for herself," not only from sins, but also from marriage. ("Portans privilegium indulgentie plenarie...petebat se absolui plenarie").
126. In Bologna, the judge interrogated a woman – who had secretly married a man with whom she had two daughters and then was forced by her father to marry another, a marriage which she did not consummate – about the reaction of her confessor to the event: according to the woman's deposition her confessor absolved her without problems, from the moment that she did not have sexual relations with the second husband. See L. Ferrante, *Il matrimonio disciplinato*, p. 924 (the document is not dated).
127. L. Allegra, *Il parroco*, in particular p. 915. The fact that priests were not always capable of distinguishing between sins that could be absolved in confession and those that warranted excommunication (those of episcopal competence) is demonstrated by the declarations of some of them during pastoral visitations. See for example ASPV, *Visite*, 1461–1558, fasc. 3, 1495: "About the first chapter of the second chapter he responded with sound honor that he did not

know how to make absolution from excommunication and from sin and also he did not know how to respond about such things." (Super primo capituolo secundo capitulis recte respondit salvo quod nescit facere absolutionem ab excommunicatione et a peccatis et etiam nescit respondere circa alia etc.) See also ASPV, *Visite*, 1461–1558, fasc. 1 and 2.
128. "Tu non te puol partir, el convien che tu ge fazi honor, così como tu ge ha facto vergogna." ASPV, *CM*, vol. 15, Salamona Salamono *vs* Agostino Minio, 1514. See A. Esmein, *Le mariage en droit canonique*, I, pp. 245–262. On Florence D. Lombardi, *Matrimoni di Antico Regime*, p. 290: a priest who, called in the middle of the night to help in a marriage that had to happen at any cost, because the woman was pregnant, said to the deflowerer: "Either you will take her or you will be killed" – unequivocal adhesion to customary ethics.
129. ASPV, *CM*, vol. 9, Michele Leoni *vs* Faustina Foscarin, 1507.
130. See respectively A. Esposito, *Convivenza e separazione*, and L. Guzzetti, *Separation and Separated Couples*.
131. ASPV, *Visite*, b. 1, n. 13, 10 September 1522, Visitatio Sancti Martini de Bibano (Sacile).
132. See *Constitutiones et privilegia patriarchatus*, primae par. Tit. tert., cap. XXIX, pp. 50–1.
133. Systematic scrutiny of the curial registers from the years 1420–1478 and 1492–1493 has not revealed any judicial action against consensual separation: see ASPV, *AMP*, regs. 2–36 and 46.
134. ASPV, *CM*, vol. 12, Margherita de Amicis *vs* Alvise battil'auro, 1512.
135. See *infra*, ch. 5, §§ 3 and 4.
136. See *Constitutiones et privilegia patriarchatus*, n. 122, cap. III, "De sacramento penitentiae," pp. 13–16.
137. ASPV, *CM*, vol. 9, Marco Antonio de Stefani *vs* Lucretia q. Simonis Vacha, 1506–1507: the patriarch ordered that Lucrezia be taken to the monastery of San Daniele and that she be interrogated there, "beyond the power of her relatives" (extra suorum consanguineorum potestam).
138. That the consent of parents was not necessary for the constitution of the marital bond was reiterated in instructions to confessors: see BNF, P.7.2, Antonino (S.) Vescovo di Firenze, *Confessionale: Omnis mortalium cura (1470 ca.)*, ch. eii.

139. D. Lombardi, *Fidanzamenti e matrimoni*, pp. 216–217.
140. ASPV, *CM*, vol. 16, Marino di Giovanni cercherius *vs* Serena, 1515.
141. "È stà alcuno deli toi parenti che cum minaze o cun alcun altro modo te abia cercà de indur o persuaderti che tu debi dir altrimenti che la verità?"
142. See ASPV. *CM*, vol. 7, Nicolò q. Dominici Cortesii *vs* Angela Sebastiani Cavazza, 1503–1508: "Again warned that she should freely tell the truth." (Iterum monita quod debeat libere dicere veritatem).
143. "Parendome per iustitia che per qualche ziorno tu debbi star sequestrata nel monastero di San Servulo o in qualche altro monastero de oservantia, aciò che tu sii fuora de la potestate de li tuoi parenti, et che tu puossi più liberamente e fuorsi cum più siceritade responder la verità circa le cose predicte, è tu contenta de obedirme?" See the document cited *supra*, note 137.
144. See *supra*, § 4.
145. The cause is found in ASPV, *CM*, vol. 6, Giovanni di Luchino a Serico *vs* Cassandra de Marconibus, 1492–1493.
146. "Se tuoi fradelli ti dirà che tu vadi munega, dili che loro vadano frati, et che tu non voi andar munega perché tu ha marido." She "responded nothing, but receded laughing." (Nihil respondit, sed ridens recessit.) ASPV, *FC*, vol. 1.
147. See *supra*, ch. 3, § 3.
148. That the party directly interested had to ratify the appeal presented in his or her name is also attested in ASPV, *AMP*, reg. 34, Antonia q. Alegreti *vs* Giorgio da Cattaro, 16 January 1475, where Antonia, in a published sentence, presented herself to the vicar to declare that the appeal following the sentence was requested against her will and that she did not intend to ratify it. The vicar accommodated her request.
149. As we have noted, both inquisitors and authors of confession manuals maintained that a period of solitude favored confession.
150. In ASPV, *CM*, vol. 32, Menega *vs* Iohannis Blanco, 1532: the declarations of a husband who declared himself disposed to appear in the tribunal to prove the death of his first wife "for the exoneration of the conscience of donna Ana, his wife," allow us to understand the importance of the control of women's conscience for the control of marriage. (Pro exoneratione conscientie done Ane, uxoris sue).

151. C. Casagrande, *La donna custodita*, p. 118.
152. See also ASPV, *CM*, vol. 32, Cecilia Stella *vs* Gaspare Tuscano, 1532: The vicar arranged for Cecilia to spend eight days in the monastery of Sant'Anna "to the end and effect that the reverend lord can have from her her free consent," and ordered the abbess not to let her talk with anyone without the express permission of the vicar. (Ad finem et effectum ut sua reverenda dominatio possit habere ab ea liberum suum consensum).
153. See the document cited *supra*, note 145 and note 137.
154. It should be noted that, if the judge mostly questioned the woman, men were not always examined alone.
155. "Vardar l'anima," "descargar la coscientia." See the document cited *supra*, note 85. For the interrogation of the wife (Clara Marcello), see *supra*, § 4. Francesco (the husband), instead, was only interrogated on the facts, and the examination became simply with an "interrogatus quod dicat veritatem de his que interrogabitur."
156. Corporal oath: taken with the hand on the Sacred Scripture.
157. See the document cited *supra*, note 37. The original text was in Latin, but was translated into Italian by Cecilia Cristellon for the Italian publication of this book and is here rendered into English.
158. "Fia, varda ben l'anima tua che tu non sia periura et che tu non sia causa che questo Hieronimo, s'el fosse tuo marido, tolesse una altra, ché li fioli sariano illegittimi, et similiter, si tu tolessi uno altro, saresti in peccato mortalissimo, et li fioli sariano bastardi, et non potaresti recever i sagramenti de la giexia, et veneristi a star continuamente excommunicata et poteresti etiam padir assai pena temporale cum grande tuo danno et vergogna." ASPV, *CM*, vol. 9, Elena de Stefani *vs* Hieronimo Marangon, 1513.
159. See *supra*, ch. 2, § 9.
160. See the documents cited *supra*, notes 118 and 137.
161. "Ne error peior fieret." ASPV, *CM*, vol. 11, fasc. 11, Elisabeth di Eustacchio tessitore *vs* Jacopo dalla Zotta, 1510.
162. About the fear that the party who had consented to give testimony could commit the mortal sin of perjury see Thomas Aquinas, *Summa Theologica*, tomus II, pars II, quest. 69, art. 1.
163. See c. 13, C.XXII q. V. On the theological plane, Abelard's *Etica* contains the theory that intention assumes a central role in the definition of sin. See P. Prodi, *Il giuramento e il tribunale della coscienza*, in particular p. 480 and Idem, *Una storia della giustizia*, pp. 54–57.

164. P. Prodi, *Il sacramento del potere*, p. 292.
165. See c. 5, C. XXII q. V.
166. C. 6, C. XXII q. V.
167. C. Casagrande-S. Vecchio, *I peccati della lingua*, p. 276.
168. M. Turrini, *Il giudice della coscienza*, pp. 288–289.
169. The actual language used was *secundum allegata et probata*. Explicit declarations of the magistrate on the necessity of basing their own judgment on a probable truth, for example in ASPV, *CM*, vol. 9, Martino q. Baptiste Cursi *vs* Giovanna filia Johannis Liberalis de Arteno, 1507–1508; and ASPV, *CM*, vol. 7, Andrea de Ballinio da Brixia *vs* Helisabeth filia Petri de Flandria, 1504; *CM*, vol. 9, Ludovica de Comitibus *vs* Hieronimo da Verona, physicus, 1507, and the document cited *supra*, note 37. See also *supra*, note 92.
170. "Pro exoneratione conscientie sue."
171. A. Calore, "*Tactis Evangeliis.*" On the Scriptures as relic see O. Niccoli, *La vita religiosa nell'Italia moderna*, p. 21. The acts of a litigation that occurred in Zara attest instead to different uses, such as an oath sworn on the image of the Virgin or of Christ crucified. ASPV, *CM*, vol. 11, f. 9. The oath on the image of the Virgin was decidedly unusual: in the moment of swearing, the Gospel, the blessed cross, the relics of the saints, and the altar became privileged as tangible signs of the presence of the divine. See A. Prosperi, *Fede, giuramento, inquisizione*, pp. 158–159, which speaks of the "magic power" (valore magico) of the oath.
172. See C. Casagrande-S. Vecchio, *I peccati della lingua*, pp. 275 and 288, note 86.
173. ASPV, *CM*, vol. 14, Margherita da Traù *vs* Alessandro Aurio.
174. See *supra*, ch. 3, § 6 and n. 112 for examples of oaths requested of minors. Regarding the regulation about the age of the oath taker, see c. 14, C XXII q. V. See also L. Sorrenti, *L'Autentica 'Sacramenta puberum.'* An example of not imposing the oath on a child because he was a minor in the course of an interrogation by the Signori di Notte is in E. Orlando, *Morire per gioco*, p. 43.
175. ASPV, *FC*, vol. 1, Pasqua da Cherso *vs* Giovanni Corner, 1494.
176. "Al sangue de la verzene Maria." ASPV, *CM*, vol. 16, Angela q. Bertolini *vs* Innocentio Murario, 1515.
177. "Iurando al sangue de Dio." ASPV, *FC*, vol. 3, Damiano Masarachia *vs* Marieta f. Bone, 1525.

178. S. Piasentini, *Indagine sulla bestemmia*. In some texts of the sixteenth century feminine blasphemy was considered evidence that the practice of blasphemy had reached its greatest intensity: see J. Delumeau, *La paura in Occidente*, p. 624: "It was no longer only the men who blasphemed, but also the women."
179. ASPV, *CM*, vol. 7, Bernardina de Guzonibus *vs* Bernardino conte di Collalto, 1500–1501.
180. "Un biastemador de Dio e de' santi [che] tuoria uno sacramento falso per un bagatino." A bagatino was a small coin worth one twelfth of a Venetian soldo. ASPV, *CM*, vol. 15, Helisabeth Gurgura *vs* Francisco de Nigris, 1514–1515.
181. "Si blasfemant aut maledicant Deum vel sanctos". See the document cited *supra*, note 137.
182. "Il peccato di taser la verità." See the document cited *supra*, note 134. This same understanding is in ASPV, *AMP*, reg. 26, 16 January 1466, Caterina (Rosa) *vs* Matteo Paralono. See also *AMP*, reg. 33, Isabetta Pachello *vs* Hieronimo Marangon, 1 November 1474 where, following the deposition of a witness is noted that "this witness did not say anything but the truth, because she loves her soul." ["Ipsa testis non dixit nisi veritatem, quia amat animam suam."]
183. "Per el sagramento che vi ho dato de sopra," "ho dicto la veritade como si fosse davanti el mi' confessor." ASPV, *CM*, vol. 32, Baptistina de Bossis *vs* Marino Trono, 1532.
184. "Nulla alia de causa testificata est nisi quod citata fuit et sacramentata per (...) archipresbiterum...". ASPV, *CM*, vol. 14, Graziosa Badoer *vs* Agostino Minio, 1514. "cusì Dio mi adiuti che son per dire e dirò la verità como se adesso fuosi al punto dela morte." ASPV, *CM*, vol. 12, Caterina de Teodoris *vs* Francisco Rubeo, 1512. An analogous case from Feltre is cited in S. Seidel Menchi, *I processi matrimoniali come fonte storica*, p. 79: "I came here to tell the truth about what I know, as if I had gone to confess."
185. The use of the term *sacramentum* for *iuramentum* after the clarification of sacramental theology in the twelfth and thirteenth centuries is noted also in P. Prodi, *Il sacramento del potere*, p. 65.
186. "Solum conscientia sua," "super conscientiam suam."
187. "Quod re vera nunquam contraxit matrimonium cum M. A. ...et quod si verum esset quod ex sua fragilitate passa fuisset se labi in taliter contrahendo, vellet exonerare conscientiam suam et dicere veritatem" See the document cited *supra*, note 37: also ASPV, *CM*, vol. 14, Graziosa Badoer *vs* Agostino Minio, 1514. In a study of the causes of separation in Navarre in the sixteenth and seventeenth

centuries, one of the most frequent models of female self-representation is of a woman "fearful of God and of her conscience." [Timorosa de Dios y de su conciencia.] In the corresponding male model, conscience is not mentioned: the man presented himself as "fearful of God." [timoroso de Dios] See M.J. Campo Guinea, *Comportamientos matrimoniales*, p. 141. See also *supra*, note 150.

188. See the document cited *supra*, note 134; also ASPV, *CM*, vol. 12, Lucretia Fosco *vs* Angelo Cima, 1512–1513.

189. For example, a judge granted separation to a woman simply because in his presence she said to [her husband's] face that he procured her to prostitution: see ASPV, *AMP*, reg. 17, Bartolomea *vs* Andrea, 3 October 1455. In ASPV, *AMP*, reg. 6, Jacopo da Vicenza *vs* Lucia 17–27 July 1437 the judge withdrew a mandate sent to a woman with the order to return to her husband because she swore – and she was the only one to swear – that she had married another man before him. In ASPV, *AMP*, reg. 9, Maria da Alessio *vs* Giovanni da Mencastro, 12 August–1 October 1442, the magistrate declared a marriage annulled after having examined some witnesses in favor of Maria because she swore that the marriage had not been consummated.

190. "*varia ac mutabilis semper*".

191. The situation was different, for example, in the tribunal of Xanten, in the archiepiscopal principate of Cologne, where the oath was generally demanded of men: see J. Löhr, *Die Verwaltung des Kölnisches Großarchidiaconats Xanten*, p. 218, note 2. See also L. Roper, *The Holy Household*. On women in the tribunal see L. Gowing, *Domestic Dangers*, pp. 30–58; for Venice, L. Guzzetti, *Women in Court*.

192. There is for example the case of taking the hand as an expression of nuptial consent: if during the Quattrocento the tribunal sought to substitute the gestural expression with a verbal expression of consent, in the Cinquecento they gave it the same value attributed to it by the laity. See *infra*, ch. 5, § 2.

193. A. Esposito, *Convivenza e separazione*.

194. G. Romeo, *Recensione*, pp. 381–383, which highlights how the "generalized disaffection to the sacrament of penitence in medieval Europe" that endured at least until the second half of the Cinquecento was conquered thanks to a "great silent revolution promoted by the Company of Jesus and made clear in the turn of a few decades by a large part of Italian confessors, including parish

priests." See Idem, *Ricerche su confessione dei peccati e Inquisizione*, in particular pp. 35–61.
195. On reserved cases see E. Brambilla, *Alle origini del Sant'Uffizio*, pp. 495–513.
196. See S. Luperini, *La promessa sotto accusa*, J. Ferraro, *Marriage Wars*, pp. 57–91.
197. See the bibliography cited *supra*, note 191.

CHAPTER 5

"Maybe so": Marriage and Consent in Pre-Tridentine Venice

In the 1520s when a certain Agostino Penzino discovered that Marietta, to whom he had secretly "given his hand," had publicly married another man, he did not hesitate to claim a sort of natural right over the woman. But when a neighbor asked him if they were married, he could only respond: "maybe so" (*forse che sì*).[1] Where did this uncertainty derive from?

In the eleventh century, strengthened in its authority during the Gregorian reform, the Church affirmed its own judicial monopoly over marriage. Through conciliar legislation, papal decretals, canonical collections, and diocesan synods, canon law on the institution of marriage was formalized,[2] a system that intertwined with common law and had to confront and sometimes conflicted with lay statutory and customary law. The simultaneous management of marriage according to different juridical systems made marriage a bond with an undefined outline. What custom considered a marriage could assume the traits of concubinage by canon law, while what the laity considered an imperfect union could be considered "true marriage" by ecclesiastical sentence.[3] This created uncertainty about the contracting of the bond, its essence, and its end, which allows us to understand the embarrassed response of Agostino Penzino.

The dialectic among the different juridical systems that regulated marriage oriented (and often created) the principal documentation used in this work. "A multivalent and dialogic source" by definition, the marriage litigation presents two versions of contrasting facts, adapted as much to the decrees of canon law as to the unwritten laws of custom.[4] The judge who was supposed to choose the most convincing of these two constructs was simultaneously an expert canonist and familiar with the language of customary law. In his role he exercised a certain judgment, as he had ample margins of liberty "to interpret canon law according to the customary law of the community."[5] We thus find flexible magistrates who sentenced in favor of a marriage for which the celebration had not been proven, because the alleged groom had acted like a husband with the woman he defined as a concubine.[6] We also chance upon rigid interpretations of canonical norms that declared non-existent a marriage contracted before numerous witnesses, where the bride could prove the taking of the hand – which constituted for the laity the clearest sign of nuptial consent – but not the verbal expression of consent, which the Church sought to confirm.[7]

During the suit ecclesiastical judges showed themselves to be attentive observers of marital practices. In the exercise of their office they did not limit themselves to recording marriages; they also intervened to modify the ritual, promote the doctrine of pure consent and of the indissoluble bond, and affirm the competence of the patriarchal tribunal over marital conflicts. They were aware they were confronting a lay marital code that was for the most part autonomous. Even when they denied any legal value to unions formed according to lay expectations, they had to recognize the existence of these unions in fact.[8]

Ecclesiastical judges were confronted with claimants in court who sought for the most part to adapt their own version of facts to the decrees of canon law, but who instead sometimes naively shared or consciously sustained a lay ethic about marriage, to the point of making impassioned defenses for the civil administration of sacramental marriage.[9]

Before Tridentine decrees quelled the debate over marriage to require it be celebrated by the parish priest in order to be valid, the laity felt they could legitimately validate or censure a union according to the parameters fixed by a code of signs and by communal values. Two women determined to validate the community's role in the formation of a couple concluded their deposition by saying: "It seemed proper to me that dona Perina should win, because she had the right, because this marriage is public and manifest" and "she wants whoever is right to win, and she believes that Salomona is in the right."[10] Often impassioned defenders of customary law, those who appeared in court were also aware of the fact that, in the field of marriage, a different and stronger system of law was being imposed. And if they generally maintained that dialogue and reconciliation might be possible, sometimes they perceived this law solely as a crushing weight. To avoid validating its authority, they refused to present themselves to testify. They would be forced to do so with the help of the secular arm.[11]

This chapter seeks to analyze the dialectic relationship between the conception of marriage held by the laity (and often shared with the secular clergy) and the conception of marriage held by the ecclesiastical hierarchy, which was established in the court. At the center of this analysis is the idea of consent – and thus the expression and the conditions of consent, as well as its limits, its duration, and its repeatability – since consent formed the foundation and the essence of both canonical and lay notions of marriage, though with very diverse interpretations.

1 "Consent Makes Marriage"
(*Consensus facit nuptias*)

In 1546 the nobleman Hieronimo Mudazzo presented himself before the patriarch of Venice claiming to have contracted a marriage with the noblewoman Lucrezia Bondumier. Between them, as between their relatives and friends, all the solemnities required by Venetian customs were respected. For the stipulation of the dowry contract, in fact, Hieronimo and Lucrezia found themselves in the presence of relatives in the house of Francesco Priuli, Lucrezia's uncle. Having obtained the blessing of her father (which would have been followed by her mother's blessing, if she were alive),[12] the young people had taken each other's hands and kissed in a sign "of true marriage *per verba de presenti* (by words in the present)." Their relatives and friends had celebrated with them and about ten days later they were reunited in the same place, to do "the kin (*el parentà*)" as they said. The relatives, mutually congratulating them, had openly recognized Hieronimo and Lucrezia as husband and wife (*palam publice et notorie*). The young woman was then often led from the "bedroom to the living room or the portico" with music and dancing, so that all could see her and recognize her as Hieronimo's wife. The next night, finally, the solemn wedding was celebrated, with banquets and dancing.[13]

Concluding his petition, Hieronimo affirmed that "by the most ancient and approved custom in Venice, marriages are contracted according to this method, and bonds thus created are considered legitimate, canonical, and *per verba de presenti* marriages, certainly without doubt, and contracted before the church (*in face ecclesie*), whether a priest or anyone else pronounces the words *de presenti*."[14]

Hieronimo Mudazzo made this closing argument a few years before the Council of Trent reconvened to make new regulations regarding marriage. A few years later his affirmations would have at least seemed inopportune to the judge, given that he was making claims based on the weight of tradition, asking and obtaining that this be confirmed by witnesses and the bride; the same patriarch considered Hieronimo's argument it completely legitimate.[15] His discourse, in effect, touched upon some key points of pre-Tridentine practices of marriage: first of all, the fact that a marriage contracted without the presence of a priest could still be considered a marriage before the church (*in facie ecclesiae*); and second, the fact that a marriage contracted without words of consent could be a marriage *per verba de presenti*. Recalling a timeless tradition, the Venetian nobleman did not seem aware how the attitude of the ecclesiastical tribunal and the sensibility of the laity had changed regarding these practices. We seek here to retrace this evolution.

With the affirmation of the sacramental nature of marriage – sanctioned by the ecumenical council of Lyon in 1274[16] – the Church had sought to favor the publication and solemnization of the event, primarily through proclamations and the priest's blessing.[17] In the fifteenth century and for the entire pre-conciliar period the laity did not comply with this obligation and the Church, though continuing to recommend the practices of proclamations and priestly blessings, seems to have decided not to enforce it.[18] Venetian marriage litigations clearly reveal the ecclesiastical hierarchy's complete acceptance of marriage celebrated with a reciprocal exchange of consent, regardless of whether the minister of the rite was an ecclesiastic or layperson. The free consent of the couple was the only thing required for the validity of the marriage and consent gave it sacramental value. Not only did the ecclesiastical judge abstain from adopting punitive measures against those who had contracted a marriage without a priest or indeed without witnesses; he did not even use a reproving tone in declaring the validity of such unions (which came rather to be depicted in churches),[19] and defined them in his sentences as legitimately and canonically contracted before the church (*legittime et canonice contracte, et in facie ecclesie*). Only lawyers used expressions like "clandestine marriage" or *ecclesie odiosus* (distasteful to the church).[20] To contest the validity of such unions, however, they did not recall canonical norms, but stressed the absence of qualified witnesses at the weddings: they therefore underlined the importance of the contractual aspect of the marriage bond more than its sacramental aspect.[21]

The attitude of the tribunal towards marriages contracted without a priest was not limited to those celebrated based on the extremely formalized ritual followed by Hieronimo and Lucrezia: the cases examined here document the existence and acceptance of extremely diverse marriage practices. The locations of marriages could be the most varied: the church,[22] the attic, the portico,[23] the place where the hearth was, the bedroom, the study,[24] the window,[25] the gallery, the stairs,[26] the garden,[27] the street, the threshold, the tavern,[28] the boat,[29] even the jail.[30] The choice of the place is sometimes explained by its symbolic value:, for example, among the lower-middle classes marriage near the hearth celebrated the role of the woman in managing the house[31]; the fire, too, was a symbol of family and life.[32]

The minister of the rite could be a relative – generally the father, a brother, an uncle, but sometimes also the mother,[33] or even the bride's employer; or those who were the young girl's guardians or were responsible for her honor, if they were not family.[34] Women were not absolutely excluded from this office,[35] but the presence of a man was held to be more reassuring: "You know that I have no man in this house, I beg you to come here to my house because this evening *misser* Zuan Baptista del Ferro comes here to give me his hand and take me as his wife," said Franceschina Lando to her neighbor (1519).[36] The minister of the rite did not have to be Catholic: in the case of the nobles Alvise Caravello and Diana Minio it was the woman's doctor, a Jew, who solicited the expression of consent "according to the command of God and your holy law."[37]

The role of officiant could naturally be filled by a priest, but his presence was not felt necessary to bring the marriage into a sacral dimension: an image of the Virgin,[38] an open tabernacle,[39] a crucifix,[40] an oath (better if taken while touching the Gospels),[41] a sign of the cross traced on the bride's front,[42] an invocation of the Father, Son, and Holy Spirit, and the simple expression "according to the command of God and the Holy Mother Church,"[43] were elements that the faithful usually considered capable of bringing a marriage into the sphere of the sacred.[44] Only if a strong blood tie united a priest to one of the spouses was he given priority in officiating the rite: if the bride's brother was a friar, for example, he would substitute for their father during the request for consent.[45] More frequently it was the case that marriages were celebrated by the confessor, who was often the intermediary between the spouses and the relatives in the case of secret marriages, encouraging and sometimes imposing on them the solemnization of the bond.[46] That the role of officiant was often filled by a layperson (man or woman) or by a priest was not very relevant in the eyes of the observers, such that a witness who was asked who had celebrated a marriage could not remember "if it were the priest or one of their girls who was there."[47]

In the sixteenth century the presence of a priest at weddings became more frequent and legitimizing. This was probably connected to the growing importance the parish priest assumed in his territory thanks to the recognition of the fiscal and sanitary roles entrusted to him by the Republic. It was also likely a consequence of the synodal disposition that prescribed the license of the parish priest to contract betrothals,[48] and also the provision of the Great Council, dating from 1506, that entrusted the parish priest with the registration of noble marriages. This is clear in cases where a husband's friend declined the offer of officiating the rite: "I don't have enough soul," said one of them, asking to be replaced "by a priest from the neighborhood" even if the spouses did not know any.[49] The presence of the priest could reassure the bride about the groom's intentions: "You are my wife, as I have said other times, and to remove any suspicion I called the priests here from S. Provolo to make it clear to you."[50] More frequently they also gave nuptial sermons on the subject of marriage, "which is a noble sacrament," symbolic of the union between Christ and the Church,[51] of which one should not "make jokes."[52] The priest slowly replaced the laity in the celebration of marriage: in 1546 Hieronimo Mudazzo felt the need to explicitly explain that a marriage contracted without a priest was still a marriage in *facie ecclesie*, which he did not need to have explained or confirmed by witnesses. This was evidently a principle that was beginning to be discussed, even though the Bolognese session of the Council of Trent, which would officially open the debate on marriage among the conciliar fathers, had not yet begun.[53]

2   The Expression of Consent

Another notable aspect of Hieronimo Mudazzo's closing speech was that he claimed a marriage contracted with the touching of hands and a kiss between spouses was a marriage *per verba de presenti*, notwithstanding the lack of verbal expression of consent. This was an affirmation which made use of a very long and strong tradition that the ecclesiastical tribunal, after having opposed it for the entire fifteenth century, finally had to validate.

For the entire pre-conciliar period, the simple touching of hands became for the laity a symbol of marriage and, in common language, "to give the hand" signified – and generally substituted for – the expression to marry. The day "that I gave her the hand,"[54] "without otherwise giving the hand"[55] were the expressions with which the parties commonly introduced their discourse about their own marriage. By sticking a hand out of a hole in the wall of the house to unite it with that of the groom, a young woman who was kept segregated sought to conclude her marriage without being seen by her relatives. A ceremony without the touching of hands did not seem, in the eyes of the laity, sufficient to begin a marriage.[56] A hand pulled back in an impulsive gesture became a symbol of denied consent in cases of "fearful" (*meticulosum*) marriage.[57] The impossibility that hands had been united rendered a union unlikely: "if one says that Michiel had touched [Virida's] hand," insinuated one neighbor woman, "how did he do so? From the balcony with a rod?"[58] This statement quickly silenced the suspicions of a certain Lucrezia.[59]

Even though doctrine recognized both gestural and verbal expressions of consent as valid, for the entire fifteenth century, the Venetian tribunal denied the touching of hands the ability to express free consent, even if it was accompanied by ceremony celebrated in the presence of witnesses, which guaranteed a certain publicity for the event.[60] A marriage contracted by touching hands (*per tactum manuum*) would inevitably be declared invalid in favor of a later contract made with words (*per formam verborum*).[61] Nevertheless, whoever wanted to see the validity of his own marriage recognized by a judge did not always claim that it had been celebrated with words of consent, instead attempting to obtain a favorable sentence simply by declaring that the bride had taken his hands.[62] Sometimes they did not even remember if words of consent had been expressed, and they asked that witnesses be interrogated for greater clarity.[63] There were also those who did not understand the importance of formulas of consent, and calmly repeated them to the judge, even claiming that there had not been a marriage. In one case, the interjection by a lawyer who sought to attribute the error to his client's testimony and claimed that they were not talking about consent but only about the touching of hands, arrived late.[64]

In the first decades of the sixteenth century the ecclesiastical tribunal began to assume a different attitude towards the taking of hands, probably considering the symbolic value that this gesture continued to enjoy among the faithful. (Ottavia Niccoli records that it was commonly believed, even in 1592, in Senigallia (near Ancona) that "after having taken the hand one cannot turn around".)[65] Not only did magistrates begin to value the use of this gesture as an expression of nuptial consent, they considered the expressions "to give the hand" and "to marry" as equivalent: the vicar of Torcello, in an injunction to the parish priest of Burano to stop a marriage between two youths, ordered the vicar not to allow them to take hands, either in the church of Burano or in their parish. In 1508, a judge reminded the "Greek" Arsenio, who wanted to leave his "dishonest" wife, that "if he had given her his hand" he could not "separate himself from nor leave" her.[66]

From the fifteenth century onward, there were other gestures that also characterized nuptial ceremonies which began, in the sixteenth century, to spark the interest of magistrates particularly attentive to customs. Magistrates seemed not only to attach circumstantial value to these gestures but also considered them constitutive of the marital bond. Such was the case with the nuptial kiss, an important confirmation of spousal consent and that alluded to the consummation of marriage, which in fact the spouses exchanged with embarrassment and only because they were induced to do so by their relatives.[67] Sometimes the family protected the gesture from the indiscretion of onlookers by making a curtain (*cortina*), lowering the curtain of the bed on which the spouses were seated.[68] The kiss also assumed a role in peacemaking and in sealing an alliance. The spouses affirmed this, and the groom demonstrated it when he kissed the bride's family as well.[69] The great importance of the common meal and the sharing of a chalice of wine was also recognized. The symbolic value of this drink, probably attributable to the moment when contracts were concluded,[70] meant that it was used in nuptial ceremonies even in those regions of Germany where beer was the usual drink.[71] With the nuptial banquet (made up mostly of sweets, of traditional "round and twisted" cookies, and sometimes of wild birds captured by the groom[72]) they began a relationship based on faith (*fides*), of which the bride was the guardian.[73] The care of meals was her responsibility, a role that made her recognized as wife even if her husband had a concubine.[74] Only separation – not coincidentally defined as the separation of bed and table – sanctioned the end of this bond of fidelity.

3 "The Bond Between Man and Woman That Cannot Be Dissolved Except by Death"

While testifying in 1514 a witness had to answer the question "what is marriage?" By then three centuries had passed since the fixing of canonical norms about the institution, but such a question was still legitimate because of the fluidity of contemporary marital practices. This variety of practices also meant that the witness's answer – which affirmed that "it deals with the bond between man and woman that cannot be dissolved except by death" – should not have been taken for granted by the magistrate who asked the question.[75]

Since the sixth century the ecclesiastical hierarchy had tried to affirm the principle of the indissolubility of marriage. Even if at the beginning of the thirteenth century it had not yet penetrated civil law, it became "law for all the Church" with the Decretals of Gregory IX in 1234.[76] However, Venetian marriage conflict clearly reveals how the process of internalizing and sharing this principle was strongly resisted by the laity. By the fifteenth and sixteenth centuries, however, the doctrine of indissolubility had been widely spread and moreover had become an undeniable fact. In the tribunal those who contracted a second marriage while the first spouse was still alive advanced as justification their belief that their first spouse had died. They thus recognized the indissolubility of marriage at least as a principle of canon law and knew it was better to make their version of facts conform to this principle.[77] The discomfort of indissoluble marriages was, however, evidenced by the high percentage of causes for the annulment of a previous marriage, which often led to the contracting of new marriages.[78] These litigations mostly involved foreigners, whose distance from their place of origin favored the contraction of a new union and rendered them better able to hide a preexisting bond.[79]

The range of reactions raised by the imposition of indissolubility went from unaware bewilderment to true and real ideological hostility. In the eyes of the laity marriage was a union that could be embraced or dissolved according to the social context in which one found him or herself living in various moments. One husband, captured by the Turks, persuaded his wife to remarry and make a family with another man.[80] Another man's servile condition made it possible for his wife to obtain an annulment of her first marriage and the subsequent recognition of the second one as valid – but, as she declared during the suit, it was the continued absence of her husband that led her to remarry.[81] In some cases, certainly, a second marriage stipulated *per verba de presenti* before witnesses had an exclusively formal value for the couple, intended to protect the honor of the woman so that she would not seem like "a whore or his concubine,"[82] even if the parties were aware that this did not create a "true marriage."[83] The spouses did not always formally shape the establishment of a new union so that it would correspond with the canonical model of marriage. They did not value the legitimacy of a second marriage based on the criteria of Church law but on variable parameters according to the condition and matrimonial behavior of the spouse. Thus, a woman was convinced that she had legitimately contracted a second marriage because her new husband was also already married; another felt it was legitimate to contract a new marriage as her first husband had already done so. To their eyes the parity of marital status and legal reciprocity between the parties rendered the dissolution of one marriage and the contraction of another perfectly legitimate.[84] Even the infidelity of a wife was considered sufficient grounds to end a marriage and contract a second one, as we have already seen[85] and as was also attested by the schemes of a husband who sought to induce his wife to adultery in order to contract another marriage himself.[86] These cases reveal the persistence of a conception of marriage – conforming to a minority interpretation of the Gospel of Matthew (19.9) and respectful of ancient legislation – that allowed divorce *quoad vinculum* in case of female adultery.[87]

If, on an ideal level, the Church firmly maintained the principle of marriage's indissolubility, in reality it administered divorce by applying the theory of matrimonial impediments, which allowed certain factors like consanguinity, coercion, impotence, and minority, to render the bond null. The discrepancy between the lay conception (of dissolvable marriage) and ecclesiastical conception (of indissoluble marriage) was resolved in court through a practical compromise: those who turned to the ecclesiastical judge could advance canonical motivations to guarantee the dissolution of a bond that had become burdensome without having these actually coincide with the real motives for the suit.[88] On a theoretical level, however, this discrepancy remained unbridgeable. The diverse terminology with which the laity and the ecclesiastical hierarchy designated the nullity or annulment of a marriage is a clue to how far apart these two sides were regarding marriage's indissolubility. Canon law did not adopt the use of the term "annulment," which implied the existence of a legitimate bond that became null with the magistrate's sentence. Instead it used the concept of "nullity," which was simply declared by the ecclesiastical judge, who was limited in the litigation to verifying it.

The marriage was either indissoluble or non-existent. For the laity this was inconceivable. The language is also revealing in this case. Successive declarations not directly relevant to some of these suits, in fact, clearly reveal the difficulty the laity had in understanding that the bond could be null from the beginning (*ab initio*) and that the role of a judge, who could not be legitimately substituted by the will and rationality of the parties, even in the most striking cases (marriage with a hermaphrodite, for example), could be necessary and at the same time not active, but simply declarative. Language did not allow for this possibility: the Veronese Caterina de Medici, who obtained an annulment of her marriage with Giulio Maffei for having had sexual relations with his brother before the marriage, indicated many years later that she was already the wife (*olim uxor*) of the latter.[89] Michele Leoni, whose bond with a hermaphrodite was judged non-existent, would be recognized by a witness years later as "he who had a wife who was half man and half woman."[90] In both of these cases there was no doubt that the couple was no longer married, but it was considered equally certain that they had been previously: marriage, then, was dissoluble but had a factual existence.

4 From Plural Marriage to Polygamy

We have seen how laity considered the loosening of the marital bond by their own initiative a legitimate practice, at least if the social condition of the spouses was equal, through mutual consent, or when one of the parties felt that his or her spousal rights had been infringed upon. That the dissolution of marriage was not perceived as a sin is attested to by the declarations of those who confessed that they had contracted a second marriage in disregard for a preexisting bond. In 1512 Alvise Battilauro discovered after nine years of marriage that his wife Margherita was married 14 years earlier to another man, so he threw her out of the house and opened a case for annulment. After an examination of witnesses the vicar proceeded to interrogate the woman *ex officio*. It was not even necessary to have her swear an oath because she confessed the previous marriage and her long cohabitation with a certain Pignata, abandoned because she "grew tired of taking care of him"[91] after he was injured. Freed from her husband, Margherita had lived for a while on her own, then married Alvise *per verba de presenti* before witnesses. She had not known, though, to maintain absolute silence about her first marriage, and years later, the news had reached Alvise.[92]

After having told her story to the vicar, Margherita explained that she had been silent about the truth until that moment because she hoped that Alvise would be obligated to "bear the costs and take care of her" due to the public ceremony by which she had married Alvise as well as the long cohabitation that had followed. However, convinced that "the sin of hiding the truth" would harm her more than abandonment – and probably considering that her constructed story was threatened by the presentation of an eyewitness – she now preferred to confess.[93] She thus hinted at her remorse for having hidden the truth (and lied) in court, aware that this was a sin, but she did not show herself absolutely unsettled for having abandoned her first husband and having lived in adultery. Above all, she did not show herself to have any understanding of the fact that, by contracting a second marriage, she had abused a sacrament. It should also be noted that the behavior of the woman, far from bringing social blame, was accepted by all those who knew the facts, so much so that the vicar could interrogate them only after repeated threats of excommunication and fines, and thanks to the intervention of the secular arm, as witnesses refused to present themselves in court, persuaded by the "tears and prayers of Margherita."[94]

The absence of guilt in the confession of a double marriage corresponds to a significant silence in the marriage litigations until the second decade of the sixteenth century: in the innumerable documents relative to the practice that today we would call polygamy the term does not appear at all – an absence that indicates a still indistinct perception of the crime.[95] In effect the sin of polygamy – which in the period after Trent was punished by the Inquisition as the abuse of a sacrament – was never invoked by the parties in Venetian marriage causes. Venetians, when speaking of a second union, defined it as "marriage in fact" or "adultery." It was not imputed or punished by the tribunal either, which limited itself to determining if a marriage was valid or not, and declaring whether a successively contracted marriage were existent or non-existent.[96] The bigamist, even if he or she won the suit, was usually – but not necessarily – responsible for the litigation costs, which typically fell on the loser of the case.[97] The sentence sometimes deplored the "reckless" behavior of the party who had contracted a new marriage without being certain of the death of his or her first spouse[98]; it recognized the full dotal rights of the injured party[99]; and, in perfect harmony with canonical norms, it declared the offspring of the annulled marriage to be legitimate.[100] In other cases, the sentence assumed an exculpatory tone towards the deceived rather than an accusatory tone towards the deceiver.[101]

Beginning in the second decade of the sixteenth century, the court began to develop a different sensibility regarding cases of plural marriage. In 1513 a sentence ordered that Giandomenico Ceti, guilty of having taken three wives, be punished and castigated "for his own correction and as an example to others."[102] The clearly exceptional daring of Giandomenico – who had publicly married these three women in the space of four years – was not enough on its own to explain the unusual, although not completely unique, tenor of the sentence.[103] Two years earlier, in fact, during a suit that involved Francesco Rizardi and Franceschina di Matteo, the woman's procurator – certainly aware of the elements capable of influencing the magistrate's decisions[104] – accused Francesco of rape (*stuprum*), adultery, and abuse of the sacrament, calling for him to receive the humiliating punishment reserved for heretics.[105] The lawyer's request is notable since he both connected the act of "having more wives" to rape and adultery (according to the common interpretation of the glossators and thirteenth-century commentators) and exposed it as an autonomous crime and sin (in line with a concept that had begun to make inroads within criminal law in the fifteenth century but which anticipated the doctrinal developments in canon law at the end of the sixteenth century). In fact, strengthened by the dispositions of the Council of Trent, canon law at the end of the sixteenth century placed on the bigamist the suspicion of heresy.[106] The greater severity of the ecclesiastical tribunal regarding plural marriage was in line with general changes of the ecclesiastical management of marriage beginning in the sixteenth century, which, in Venice as elsewhere, heralded the dispositions of Trent. In Florence the 1517 synodal constitutions condemned bigamists to be publicly dishonored, to ride through the city with a miter on their head, and to be jailed for five years. In Venice a synodal disposition imposed the registration of betrothals with the parish priest, and marriage litigations attest to the growing presence of priests at weddings as well as the assumption of a more active role by ecclesiastical judges in managing a marriage suit.[107] The attitude of the tribunal towards those who contracted multiple marriages in disregard for canonical norms became more strict beginning in the second decade of the sixteenth century, but towards those who showed themselves to be unaware of the norms – a phenomenon recognized as perfectly plausible even in 1514 – they instead proceeded with benevolence. Elena de Stefani, for example, asked for the annulment of a marriage contracted with Hieronimo Marangon because her first husband, Domenico, whom she had married in great secrecy, had returned to Venice after having spent four years in the "Levant as a merchant."[108] In the sentence that granted the woman's request, the judge, drawing on a long juridical tradition, attributed her behavior to feminine *fragilitas* that would have stopped her from opposing the new marriage desired by her kin (although they had not placed her under any pressure) and justified Elena's actions with ignorance of canonical norms forbidding a second marriage without certain knowledge of the first spouse's death.[109] It was not until the early seventeenth century that women could no longer claim ignorance of the law (*ignorantia iuris*) about plural marriage: "since everyone knows that a man cannot have two wives," affirmed Prospero Farinacci († 1618), it should be presumed that even women know "what everyone knows."[110]

5 Separation Between a Private Fact and "the Gravest Thing" (*res gravissima*)

While in the pre-Tridentine era the indissolubility of marriage was rarely respected, the legal restrictions regarding separation were followed even less often. Separation was supposed to be granted only for motives considered "most grave" by canon law – adultery and violence – and only by the sentence of an ecclesiastical judge.[111] The laity for the most part considered separation a private matter or as a process that should be managed by a network of kin and neighbors.[112] Among the conjugal behaviors censured by lay morality were the squandering of a dowry by the husband, a husband who did not adequately provide for his wife or guarantee her a lifestyle adequate to her status, or that he did not allow her to take charge of the household or denied her the honor and respect due to a wife. These were all considered almost as grave as physical violence or adultery, at least when the latter did not compromise the social position and authority of the woman.[113] Whenever the husband tarnished himself with such faults, the judgment of the community recognized the wife's right to leave him and to return to her natal family, bringing with her her own goods, dresses, and jewels. If the husband showed himself to be seriously repentant, this kind of separation could be temporary: in May 1548, Caterina de Medici fled the house where she lived with her husband and brother-in-law, bringing with her part of her belongings and going to stay with her mother's cousins. Her brother-in-law, in his own name and on his brother's behalf, agreed to draw up a document in which he recognized that Caterina had gone "for just and legitimate cause." Affirming to love her as a "daughter" just as her husband had loved her as a "good wife," he invited her to return without "fear or suspicion" for the things which she had taken with her, as she would "never be bothered regarding these goods." Reiterating the legitimacy of her flight, he pledged to guarantee this promise with all of his possessions, thus convincing Caterina to return.[114]

Female recourse to the ecclesiastical tribunal generally happened after the failure of repeated attempts to reconcile; for men, the tribunal was an instrument they could use to restore marital cohabitation.[115] The ecclesiastical judge inserted himself in mediation by the family and community by imposing, on one side, respect for the canonical principle according to which separation could only be granted following very serious violence or adultery, but requiring on the other side the husband to guarantee – under penalty of an enormous fine – to "treat his wife well": to not use violence, to trust her to govern the house, and guarantee her a socially congruous lifestyle.[116] To arrive at this type of accord the judge made use of other intermediaries, who had to give surety for the husband and guarantee with their own belongings that he would respect the conditions imposed by the tribunal.

Many marriage litigations attest that the behaviors the laity considered to be valid motives for separation were different from those provided for by canon law. The many *de facto* separations which the judge ended simply with an order to respect the obligation of cohabitation (given after the request of one of the two parties without developing into a cause) are clues to the understanding of separation as a substantially private matter. Whoever removed herself from cohabitation – almost always the woman[117] – probably considered married life so onerous that she (or he) sought to remove herself from its burdens. However, under the threat of excommunication, she would not hesitate to rejoin her spouse, either because she did not have valid motives to obtain a legal separation or because she had not yet reached a point of exasperation or unscrupulousness to be induced to use questionable legal constructs. The fact that the tribunal never proceeded *ex officio* against the unobservance of cohabitation left ample space for consensual separations to take place. These are widely documented in the notarial records, but left no trace in the curial register except when they took place in the middle of a litigation, before the judge's sentence. In such cases the magistrate opposed the free initiative of the parties with excommunication.[118]

From the general picture of marital separation as understood by the laity, some particular cases emerge that simultaneously legitimate the jurisdiction of the ecclesiastical judge to decide on matters of separation and reiterate how the laity considered it more a natural epilogue to an unpleasant union than an extreme solution to an unsustainable situation. As we have seen, a woman felt authorized to present herself to the vicar, declaring simply that she did not want her husband, and a couple requested separation without providing other motives except that, after 40 days of marriage, the wife was "unhappy."[119] In both of these cases the judge imposed the continuance of cohabitation on the couples.

Notwithstanding that the tribunal maintained a constant and generally passive attitude about separation for the entire period under investigation, in 1462 the patriarch Andrea Bondumier sought to combat the practice of *de facto* separation with a synodal disposition that excommunicated spouses who had separated without judgment or ecclesiastical license and forbade priests from administering the sacraments to them, under penalty of suspension of their ecclesiastical benefice and payment of a fine (of one ducat) every time they transgressed this rule.[120] At this stage we are not able to determine the long-term effects of this disposition. Some procedural documents attest to the developing role of confessors in promoting the authority of the ecclesiastical judge regarding marriage through the application of discipline for reserved cases. Some documents instead show confessors who exercised *de facto* jurisdiction over marriages that eroded the vicar's jurisdiction.[121] We can say that, at least in the years immediately following Andrea Bondumier's synodal disposition, the customs regarding separation did not undergo significant changes: there is no recorded increase in recourse to the tribunal for separation, and the registers of the curia also do not document proceedings against transgressing priests.[122]

Effective control over *de facto* separation would probably be achieved only long after the Council of Trent, when discipline of cases reserved to the bishop could be applied efficiently. To reach this goal it was necessary that the practice of annual confession with one's own parish priest was well diffused and that the confessors were capable of distinguishing between sins reserved to the bishop and those that could be absolved in confession.[123] The first objective was reached by coordinating the application of coercive measures and the explanation of pastoral functions.[124] The second objective was only possible through indoctrination of the secular clergy, and in particular by educating them about cases of conscience.[125] Still, this did not eradicate the practice of consensual separation, which is amply documented in Venice (as elsewhere) until at least the eighteenth century.[126]

6   Conditions and Errors

The doctrine according to which marriage was established solely by consent allowed for consent to be subjected to particular conditions as long as they were explicitly and freely expressed before the bond was constituted.[127] The marriage would be final as soon as the agreed-upon condition was verified; if it was not, a new expression of consent was required.[128]

The concrete cases considered here, however, demonstrate that some ecclesiastical judges were extremely reluctant to accept the principle that marriage require anything other than a pure and simple expression of consent. And if someone who agreed to a conditional marriage could declare it null only with difficulty (invoking a lack of respect for the required condition), a person who adduced errors in evaluation or complained before the judge about alleged deceptions he or she had suffered would receive neither understanding nor a favorable sentence.

In all of these cases the proceedings were extraordinarily fast. They could last from only a few minutes – the time used by the vicar to listen to the summary versions of the two parties and send them home – up to a maximum of five months, in a completely exceptional case.[129] These proceedings did not always become formalized as a suit.

6.1   *Virginity and Fidelity*

In a society like that which we are examining, strongly characterized by agnatic connections, a woman's role consisted in guaranteeing the "continuity of the group and the coherence of its genealogy" through her chastity and purity.[130] Pre-marital virginity and conjugal fidelity were thus fundamental requirements, and they were also monetarily valuable.[131] A woman's honor depended in great part[132] on the perception of her sexual conduct, while a man's honor depended on the perception of the sexual conduct of the women he was supposed to control, who might be daughters, wives, or sisters.[133] In the ecclesiastical tribunal female virginity was not as highly valued as it was by lay morality. The protests of Andrea Filocampo that he was not bound to a contracted marriage with Isabella since she had confessed that she was not a virgin were valued before the tribunal only as a bitter outburst: the vicar, in fact, briefly heard the parties and immediately discharged the couple, recommending that the husband treat his wife "with marital affection."[134]

A sailor named Teodoro asked for an annulment after having married before witnesses Lucia, daughter of a caulker, because he wanted a wife who was "a virgin maiden" and not a "widow and corrupt," as Lucia had revealed herself to be. The judge imposed the obligation to solemnize and consummate the marriage.[135] In the first case the judge did not have any legal reason to make a different decision. It had nothing to do with the fact that the parties had subordinated the validity of the marriage to Isabella's virginity. In the second case the magistrate was not limited to assume a completely passive attitude toward the declarations by the parties, but he exercised a certain judgment since he did not consider Teodoro's expressed demand that his wife be a virgin at the moment of the ceremony as absolutely binding.[136] Unmoved, the judge did not interrogate the witnesses present; he based his sentence only on the confessed exchange of consent. Three years after the publication of the sentence he did not hesitate to excommunicate Teodoro, who still refused to accept Lucia as a legitimate spouse.[137] When a magistrate established that Luca da Cattaro was married to a certain Margherita whom he considered an ex-concubine, he acted in perfect harmony with applicable juridical norms and in respect to one of the foundational principles of pre-Tridentine marital doctrine. Luca, in fact, claimed that he had promised the woman that he would marry her when he returned from a trip, provided that she, in the meantime, "lived honestly."[138] On his return, however, he discovered that Margherita had fled with another man. Interrogated by the vicar if the promise of marriage was followed by sexual relations, Luca admitted it without any hesitation.[139] These being the facts, the judge could not do anything but issue a sentence in favor of the marriage: based on canon law, sexual relations not only transformed the promise of marriage into a marriage in all its effects but had also rendered null any conditions placed on the validation of the marriage.[140] The abandoned young man was evidently unaware of the norm or else did not consider it binding.[141]

6.2 *Dowry Promises*

Another reason a man could consider that a marriage was not binding and refuse to have it solemnized and begin cohabitation was if dowry promises were not respected. As much as in the fifteenth century the dowry constituted simply an "element of property relations between the spouses," it also demonstrated the "legitimate character of the union." In marriage cases the dowry contract was an extremely effective instrument for demonstrating the celebration of a marriage.[142] In Venice, however, this was rarely cited to prove a marriage. This was likely because the marriages whose existence was in question were rarely formalized in written contracts. The dowry agreements – if they were not respected – were instead sometimes presented in court as a proof against marriage. This strategy was destined to fail, even though canonical norms allowed for contractors to subordinate the validity of the marriage to the respect of dotal promises.[143]

Some husbands declared themselves disposed to solemnize the marriage and begin cohabitation as long as their wives respected the dotal agreements, but an "oarsman [named] Giovanni," for example, asked for an annulment of his marriage to Maria as she had married him with the agreement that she would place at his disposition, in addition to her dowry, a house in which they could live without rent as long as he did not obtain a house from the procurators of San Marco.[144] The condition was not respected and Giovanni asked to be able to contract a new marriage.[145]

In all the cases examined here the judge declared the marriage valid without taking into account the expression of any condition that had been stipulated. To obtain the respect of dotal promises, a husband who considered himself deceived had to turn to another magistrature, without being able to make this deception have any weight in negotiating a favorable sentence from the ecclesiastical judge; legally dissolving the bond that tied him to a defaulting wife turned out to be impossible.[146]

6.3 Mistaken Identity

We have seen how in practice the validity of marriage was not generally subordinated to conditions that had to do with honor (the virginity of the bride or the faithfulness of the wife) or with economic considerations (respect for dotal promises), even if doctrine considered these conditions capable of nullifying a marriage if they were expressed before the wedding and not respected later. In doctrine and in practice these were not errors about the fortune or the quality of a person; if committed they did not invalidate the marriage. In the legal texts and the halls of the tribunal it should not surprise us to find occasional deceptions so pervasive as to give rise to the adage "on the subject of marriage, he who is able, deceives."[147]

Still, there were some errors considered capable of invalidating a marriage: these regarded the physical identity of a person and his or her condition (free or servile).[148] Mistaken identity was clearly exclusive from consent but rarely presented as a motive for annulment.[149] This was utilized – in Venice as in Kostanz – as a legal expedient to circumvent the principle according to which errors about fortune had no capacity to annul a marriage.[150] In this way Mattea di Antonio Zambono sought to end the marriage that united her to Giovanni of Corfù. Giovanni presented himself before the vicar claiming that he had married Mattea five years before following the mediation of a certain "slavic Elena."[151] On that occasion a marriage contract was drawn up, based on which the mother of the young girl was required to give her a patrimony of 100 gold ducats, partly in money and partly in goods.[152]

The woman's procurators (the printer Giovanni Taccuino and her brother) did not react to the opponent's petition only with ritual objections[153]; they declared themselves ready to demonstrate that the marriage between Mattea and Giovanni was a case of mistaken identity and therefore null *ab initio*. According to their version, "sixteen or twenty years ago" two citizens from Corfù lived in Venice who both called themselves Giovanni, and they lived in a house in service to a nobleman of ca' Barbarigo. The only difference between the two was their socioeconomic condition: one was in fact the administrator of Barbarigo's business, and the other was a servant in the office of the Capi of the neighborhood (*Capi di sestier*), adept, among other things, in flogging and torture. Only the former could have aspired to a marriage with a woman of good condition and a dowry equal to that of Mattea. She, not knowing of the existence of the two Giovannis, had married one thinking she was marrying the other, whom she considered the only one.

The real motive and the result of the suit are unknown.[154] The cohabitation of Giovanni and Mattea for six months following the marriage throws a shadow of doubt on the woman's version of the story. Barbarigo's administrator was not presented to testify; all the witnesses from ca' Barbarigo, including Barbarigo himself, were recused by Mattea's lawyers. Thus, anyone who could have given better information on the event and on the two Giovannis was excluded from testimony. Full of gaps about the case's motives and results, the documentation is nevertheless extremely eloquent about the attitude of the judge towards this type of impediment to marriage. As soon as Mattea's procurators brought up exceptions about mistaken identity, the vicar made it the focal point of the case, transferring the burden of proof from the plaintiff – who should have had to prove the marriage – to the defendant, who would now have to prove the mistaken identity. He also explicitly declared that such an exception had the capacity to invalidate (*destruere*) the case and render judgment null. Before proceeding, the magistrate imposed on Mattea's procurators an oath against false testimony (*iuramentum calumnie*) – he wanted to be sure that they had not raised the exception only to prolong the litigation – but, in accommodating Mattea's positions, he recognized the entity of a person's goods and his social status as valid criteria to establish someone's identity.

6.4 *"Error of Condition"* (error conditionis)

The error of condition (that is, a mistake about the free or servile condition of a person) could also render a marriage null. This principle was complicated by the teaching of Saint Paul, by which there was no distinction in Christ "between Barbarian and Schytian, between slave and free." (Col 3, 9–11).

Roman law prohibited marriage between a free person and a slave.[155] Civil law, which did not recognize a slave as a person, therefore did not give slaves juridical capacity or the possibility of contracting a marriage without their master's consent.[156] Though not unanimously,[157] canon law, because of the words of St. Paul, allowed slaves to receive the sacraments and thus the possibility of freely contracting a marriage.[158] Probably due to the fact that customary norms expected the loss of liberty for anyone who married someone in a servile condition[159] and that children born of a marriage with a slave were considered illegitimate,[160] canon law elaborated the doctrine of nullity of marriage regarding error of condition.[161] Based on this principle the free spouse could request annulment of a marriage contracted with a non-free person if, at the moment of marriage, the person's servile condition was not known,[162] and if, once it was known, he or she avoided sexual relations with the unfree spouse.[163] The canonical justification of this impediment consisted in the impossibility of realizing, in the presence of servile condition, the good connected to marriage: this, in fact, impeded the benefit of the sacraments (*bonum sacramenti*) and the exercise of cohabitation because the slave had to live in the house of his master, and could be sent anywhere and sold; it impeded the benefit of faith (*bonum fidei*), as the slave was not able to pay the conjugal debt (*debitum coniugale*) when requested[164]; it did not allow for the benefit of progeny (*bonum sobolis*), because the slave was not able to raise his offspring, as all that he had belonged to his master.[165]

Among the acts of the Venetian ecclesiastical tribunal there are six – maybe seven[166] – cases regarding nullity of marriage based on error of condition. It was generally a free woman who requested the annulment of a marriage contracted with a slave[167] or defended herself from a case of alleged marriage by invoking the servile status of the alleged husband.[168] However, we also chance upon one man, Antonio da Cividale, who presented some witnesses to the vicar intended to establish the future liberation of a certain Anna, *pro causa matrimoniali inter eos.*

The scarce and fragmentary information relating to these proceedings, the fact that the complaints presented by the parties did not generally develop into a litigation,[169] the absence of sentences in most cases,[170] and finally, the unhappy results of archival research[171] reduce our considerations on the origins and motivations of these disputes to hypothesis.

While in the cases examined earlier – when a husband presented himself before the judge because his wife had not been a virgin when they married or had not respected the terms of the dowry agreement, or when a wife simply expressed her irritation towards her husband[172] – we see an improper and moreover naïve use of the ecclesiastical tribunal, in annulment cases regarding mistaken identity parties carried themselves in a very knowledgeable way. Servile status – sometimes proven by documents – was a juridical expedient to which people could resort to end a marriage that had become burdensome. The version agreed upon by both parties[173] or the fact that a slave husband was absent for a long time made *error conditionis* a canonical justification capable of starting a litigation, but it was not the true motivation for the cause. The request to place the wife in a "secure place" where she could freely declare her will reveals a family that opposed a marriage and sought to influence their daughter.[174] The case of Antonio da Cividale, however, who wanted to prove the future liberation of Anna for the cause of marriage between them (*pro causa matrimoniali inter eos*), is completely obscure. The hypothesis that this was a case of alleged marriage from which the defendant sought to escape by putting forward her own servile condition is not supported by juridical norms, which allowed the free person to marry the servile person if they knew, and if the condition was unknown at the moment of the wedding, they could continue in the marriage once it came to their attention.[175]

All the cases brought for error of condition are from the 1450s. With only one exception, I'm not aware of proceedings of this type for the later period either in Venice or elsewhere.[176] In the later period such an impediment probably became an argument of mere doctrinal speculation. In the first decade of the sixteenth century a Venetian judge mentioned it when comparing it to the impediment of impotence, affirming that consent was implicitly subordinated to the potential for sexual intercourse (*potentia coeundi*), just as it was to a person's free condition. Thomás Sánchez amply treated it in his *De sancti matrimonii sacramento*, but in a copy of the important and widely used confessor's manual by Martín de Azpilcueta (Navarro), conserved in the library of the venetian parish of Santi Aspostoli, one hand from the end of the sixteenth century had postiled with objections and annotations all the sections relating to impediments of marriage, except that which dealt with conditional marriage and, in particular, the servile condition, as evidence that this was not of practical application.[177]

7   The Age of Consent

This book began with a case that involved two young nobles, Marietta Barbaro and Matteo Giustinian. In spite of what appeared in the nuptial contract drawn up by the notary, (which registered a union that apparently conformed to the restrictions of canon law and noble ideals of marriage), it was a socially transgressive marriage that would be declared invalid by ecclesiastical sentence. There was doubt, in fact, that the groom was over 14, the minimum age required by canon law for a man to get married.[178] This was also very early compared to normal marriages of Venetian noblemen, who, by the end of the fifteenth century, generally married around the age of 33.[179] A debate about the minority of the groom is unique among the cases examined, though there are many cases that debate the minority of the bride.[180] Though unusual, it offers an occasion to introduce an argument on a differing perception, both cultural and judicial, of masculine and feminine puberty.

During the cause the bride's family claimed that Matteo was not only over 14, but in fact was 15, 16, or possibly even 17. The family of the groom, on the other hand, maintained that at the time of the wedding he had not yet reached the canonical age.

To prove Matteo's legal majority, Marietta's father went to depose the ship captain who had brought Matteo's parents from Corfù to Venice 11 years earlier, along with a child who in his judgment was no younger than two and no older than four years old. The witness was uncertain, however, of the identity of the child[181] as was another witness who in 1504 had met the Giustinian family in Sicily with a child of about three.[182] To demonstrate that the groom had reached and surpassed the canonical age of marriage, Marietta's father drew attention to the young man's face, more mature than a 14-year-old's. Marietta's nurse also affirmed that Matteo was in fact taller than the bride's brother, who was 17.[183] These were weak arguments, substantially personal opinions expressed by witnesses who were strongly tied to the plaintiff.

Beyond the fact that in the pre-modern period it was not easy to prove a person's age, it should also be considered that the boundary between childhood (the period between 7 and 14) and adolescence was not well defined and could be lowered or raised according to the physical or psychological maturity of the youth. Marietta's family therefore sought to demonstrate that Matteo had frequented prostitutes. They evidently wanted to bring up the norm of canon law by which, for the purpose of approximating puberty, carnal *malitia* makes up for age in marriage.[184] Even if Matteo were not yet 14, sexual activity would have lowered the threshold of puberty and signaled his entrance into adolescence.

Matteo's family instead presented him as a *mente captus* (fool). His mental frailty would be revealed through speeches "suitable for imbeciles" and by the fact that he did not know how to read or write. This was particularly important because he had underwritten a marriage contract and it was revelatory of an intrinsic weakness, as his social status and breeding should have guaranteed him the mastery of reading and writing.[185] To try and become literate he had lived for four months in the house of pre' Francesco Ritio, but he had had little success as he was a "little animal without intelligence, unstable, and whatever he says today he will deny tomorrow."[186] He was at the level of a nine-year-old child. At the moment the contract was stipulated, as Marietta's witnesses admitted, he had revealed to the notary "I don't know how to write very well," asking the notary to sign for him.[187]

If the fact that a noble of his age could be incapable of reading and writing raised suspicions that he was weak-minded, his being "insane" and deprived of "good intellect" would be clearly manifest in his reprehensible and revolting behavior, such as stealing meat, beating and insulting servants, attacking them with firebrands, staining the walls with his own excrement, making it into balls and ingesting it, and urinating on his shoes and washing them in the canal.

This argumentative strategy sought to increase the threshold of legal puberty, which signaled the beginning of responsibility. For penal law, in fact, mental infirmity reduced the criminal to the status of a child (*puer*). Children were generally not punishable because they were unaware and thus irresponsible.[188] The fact that Matteo's teacher attributed to him the intellect of a nine-year-old is not insignificant as it insinuated not only the suspicion that he was a child, but also that he was, at least mentally, in the phase of childhood that extended from infancy until age ten and during which the pre-pubescent was deprived of will.[189] Matteo's representatives preoccupied themselves with demonstrating that he had not reached social maturity, the full perception of which involved marriage for a Venetian nobleman "which consisted of, in the end, commitments which the contractors were obligated to fulfill, both with respect to the marriage and with respect to the dowry." It is important to note that for a nobleman marriage should not initiate, but rather complete the passage to adulthood, the end of a long process signaled by various experiences in the public sphere.[190] This should not have interested the ecclesiastical judge – and in fact it often did not interest him, as we have seen[191] – but it could certainly contribute to rendering the union invalid in his eyes. It is important to remember that, in dubious cases, it was the judge's prerogative to decide if the child was responsible. In his sentence the vicar mentioned only the principles of canon law, declaring that between Matteo and Marietta there was no marriage in consideration of the minor age of the groom and that, as indicated in court, carnal *malitia* had not made up for age. As expected by canonical norms, the union was to be considered a betrothal (*sponsalia per verba de futuro*).[192]

The threshold of marriageability for men fixed by canon law and that which was regulated by custom were separated, at least among nobles, by a gap of about 20 years. On the other hand, the canonical threshold of female marriageability, fixed at 12, effectively approached social norms, coincided with them, and could even be preceded by them. Early marriageability for girls, which was functional for family strategies that had as their goal "the good positioning of their own reproductive, productive, and symbolic resources,"[193] was widespread and well documented in pre-Tridentine Italy.[194] It has left traces in the marriage litigations,[195] which often also attest to episodes of duress and violence, both physical and psychological, that could accompany the marriages of young girls. While the only case of male minority I have found, presented above, revolved for the most part around the psychological, physical, and social immaturity of the boy – according to a model common to other, very rare cases found in other archives,[196] as will be underlined in the statistical portion of this work – only a third of the requests for annulment for female minority relied on the immaturity of the girl. The others brought up that she had been forced or suffered violence, or were based on the lack of the marriage's consummation. One clichéd image of child brides is that of the rich, pre-pubescent heiress who was a victim of deceit, duped by the groom and his family. One who denied the validity of marriage did not linger on the childish attitudes and behaviors that cast suspicion on the age of the bride but only insisted that she was not yet 12 years old. Another common model was that of the girl forced to marry by her family, who then challenged the validity of the marriage because of the minority of the bride. Even in this case, they did not bring up particulars that demonstrated the girl's immaturity; instead, they focused on the details of coercion – an aspect that I will explore more below.

A groom who wanted to prove a marriage with a girl whose age was in doubt focused, for the most part, on the consummation of the marriage, proven by calling upon midwives or, as might be claimed by the groom's procurator, hidden in its physical effects by medical and magical practices. These cases gave rise to writings about the female body and its perception that were sometimes extraordinarily precocious and eloquent.[197]

Proof of sexual relations was of primary importance for the purposes of marriage's indissolubility. Only when a marriage was not consummated, in fact, could a bride enter the convent without her husband's consent[198] – and when the child bride was a rich heiress, the husband and the convent often competed over her. As I have already outlined, sexual relations constituted an element capable of lowering the threshold of nuptial age for canon law. However, the Venetian tribunal does not seem to have held to this principle, to the extent that I have never found a trace in the sentences (if not in the only case of male minority), not even when spouses had cohabited for a certain period. In 1488, for example, the judge declared a marriage contract null with a minor bride, even though the couple had lived together for eighteen months. The sentence did not make any allusion to the consummation of the marriage, evidently not considering this to be a sufficient condition to validate or invalidate the union. A similar position is revealed in an annulment sentence from 1491, in which the husband had paid for the food of the wife with whom he lived. The magistrate, moreover, demonstrated that he did not give weight to the norms by which a marriage *per verba de futuro* – which, we recall, could be assimilated to marriage *per verba de presenti* with a prepubescent – could be transformed into a marriage in all respects with a renewal of consent once the parties reached the legal age. This renewal could even be silent when the spouses had had sexual relations or lived together.[199]

To the extent that important studies allow us to affirm that late medieval society did not encourage the pre-pubescent consummation of marriage, marriage litigations "crack open the assumption that preadolescent marriage, so frequent among aristocratic Europeans of the late medieval period and the Renaissance, was respectful of physiological times of the female body and avoided exposing prepubescent girls to the trauma of defloration."[200] The juridical value of sexual relations, the primary role that they developed in the indissolubility of marriage, and their patrimonial consequences[201] were sometimes sufficient reasons to induce a groom to consummate a marriage with a physically pre-pubescent bride, often with her parent's blessing.[202] That for the child bride this constituted a traumatic event was a detail that male honor could boast of and, in court, it was a useful indication of the marriage's consummation. When Giorgio Zaccarotto declared that he had consummated his marriage with Maddalena di Sicilia, not yet 12 years old, he sought to demonstrate this by mentioning the girl's turmoil and fear – evidently considering that a judge familiar with the custom could immediately place these signs among the customary reactions of the defloration of a very young bride.[203]

For the daughters of the middle and lower classes, marriage and its consummation occurred later than for the daughters of the nobility, though the feelings of an Enrico Teutonico, who preferred to postpone the marriage of his 15-year-old daughter for three years, considering her still a "little girl" (*garzona*), were decidedly unusual.[204] Marriage often also constituted for them the final phase in lengthy negotiations between kins. Families (regardless of social class) were disposed to impose their own politics with an iron fist, if they were not able to obtain the consent of their children.[205] In general, however, agreements between families show parents who wanted a good life for their children. Such agreements valued both economics and the elements capable of creating an enjoyable and harmonious union, according to a sensibility encouraged by both humanists and medical treatises.[206] The choice of a spouse for one's children did not discount attractiveness (especially in the choice of a bride, but also in the choice of a groom),[207] considering this an element that could benefit the union and probably also the couple's fertility. Among merchants and artisans the practice of encouraging (or at least allowing) the intimacy of young couples is documented, as in the case of Niccolò di Domenico Cortesii and Angela di Sebastiano Cavazza, who were betrothed when they were both nine years old. By an agreement between the fathers of the "bride" and "groom," which provided for the marriage of the two children when they had reached a legitimate age, Niccolò was sent to his future father-in-law's house. He then left the house and his bride at age 16. The couple, wanting to break the promise, went to the vicar, who, in order to ensure that the young people had not exchanged consent, nor followed the promise with sexual relations, interrogated the girl, who revealed some episodes of their intimacy:

> When the said Niccolò requested carnal copulation and Angela refused him, the said Niccolò said: You don't want to be my wife? And I responded to him: But yes, when I am your wife I will do what you want. Interrogated, she also said: This Niccolò kissed me and touched me as betrothed people do together, and we slept in one bed, and sometimes we were left alone, and he sought to use me as a husband does with a wife, but it does not seem to me that he went so far that he took my virginity. Interrogated, she said: [When] these things [happened] I could have been twelve, thirteen or fourteen and even older, because when he left our house he was by my judgment sixteen....I let him do these things to me because I considered him to be my husband. Then she was warned that she should freely say the truth if this Niccolò had gone so far with her that he had taken her virginity, and she responded: It seems to me no.[208]

The nearly contemporary experience of the daughter of a Flemish merchant, named Elisabeth, is in some ways similar but more painful in her awareness of a strong contrast between her age, the marriage desired by her father, and the first sexual overtures. At 13 her father promised her in marriage to Andrea, a year older than her. Her father committed to taking them both in his house with their eventual children and furnishing them with food and lodging, in addition to a dowry of 100 gold ducats, as long as the young man committed to work for his father-in-law. Though bending to the will of her parents, the girl was not enthusiastic about the agreement, which seemed premature to her – as she explained to her family and her groom, when she was asked "if she was content." When the young man insisted on sleeping with his bride, her mother allowed it after he promised "not to touch her." He did not maintain his promise. The two slept together for about a month, during which Andrea admitted that "carnal copulation... was not completed because the said Elisabeth said it hurt and could not suffer the completion of carnal copulation." This was confirmed by Elisabeth, who "asked about the carnal copulation responded: he has touched me a lot, but he has not taken my virginity." At the time of the wedding Elisabeth was at least a year older than the canonical nuptial age, and when she was interrogated by the vicar, she was already 14. During her deposition she reaffirmed with regret what she had declared before the wedding, to the extent that the argument was lacking in juridical value: "My father sent me [to a husband] too early – if only I had at last been 20 years old!"[209] Her self-perception and ideas about her stage of life induced Elisabeth to project marriage into a far-off age. Her voice cannot leave the historian indifferent, even if it does not have any statistical significance.

8   Consent and Parental Coercion

8.1   *"I Wanted to Take Whomever My Father Gave Me"*

The problem of parental consent to marriage ran through the entire preconciliar period and would be brought up again, with force, at the Council of Trent, continuing to incite debates among the conciliar fathers.[210] The foundation of marriage on the consent of the couple alone was potentially destabilizing, as it took the union out of parental control in a period when marriage was principally considered a means to promote or consolidate alliances between families.[211] Canonical norms were in conflict with secular arrangements, which provided severe penalties – ranging from loss of dowry to imprisonment – for those who contracted marriage without parental approval.[212] In Venice, between the medieval and early modern periods the Republic abstained from legislating on the subject of marriage with the exception of regulating marriages of patricians and *cittadini originari*, the control over which was entrusted to the Avogaria di Comun.[213]

The majority of pre-Tridentine marriage litigations dealt with cases of alleged marriage. Among these, many were begun because the family of one of the parties, knowing that their son or daughter had contracted a socially incongruous marriage, opposed it with the firmest resolution.[214] The ecclesiastical tribunal offered a concrete opportunity to subvert parental control.[215] In York as in Castille, young people rendered their marriages as solemn during the suit, as soon as they appeared before the ecclesiastical judge. In Venice one couple in love prevented the negative outcome of a judicial proceeding by choosing as an officiant of their marriage the patriarchal vicar in person and asking that the act be recorded in the registers of the curia; a young woman enclosed in a monastery under the strict control of her two sisters used the interrogation put to her by the ecclesiastical judge to confess that she had gotten married and to demonstrate her desire to be united with her husband.[216] These were exceptional cases that sometimes signaled the end of any relationship with their family of origin.[217] Women as much as men were subjected to very strong pressures (of material and psychological nature) by their relatives, which generally caused them to subordinate their own desires to those of the family. Giovanna de Liberalis, asked about her relationship with Martino Cursio, who claimed her as his wife in court, did not deny her tender feelings for the young man, even highlighting the traits of their romance:

> It is true that, as lovers do, I have talked with the said Martin many times during the day,[218] openly and publicly, because I loved him and he loved me... Our love began on All Saint's Day, and it will be three years on the next All Saint's Day... and this love lasted between us until the last feast of St. Victor, and all this time our love continued. Yes, many times I have spoken in secret with the said Martin... he came here to this village for my love, to see me and speak to me, and speaking to me in the street passing people, and our conversations were that I loved him and he loved me.[219]

There had been plans and promises of marriage, but the young woman was not disposed to respect them: "because I intend to take the man my father gives me, and if he had asked my father for me, I would have thus taken him as another," Giovanna stated.[220] When submission to paternal authority did not emerge naturally, other factors came together to bend the will of children or wards: the fear of being "yelled at and abandoned" by uncles; the fear of sending one's own soul "to the house of the devil"; a mother's curse; and the exclusion from their parents' wills.[221]

Abandonment and exclusion from the will represented a concrete threat which could be carried out.[222] The mother of 13-year-old Lucrezia Vacca, for example, did not even come to the sentencing that declared the marriage between the young girl and Marco Antonio de Stefani as valid – a marriage the woman had strongly opposed. She gave her last will without mentioning her only daughter (who had already lost her father), although she had claimed during the entire suit to only want "what my kin want."[223] While the fear of abandonment, particularly in the case of very young girls, is clear in an age when a woman's very subsistence was endangered when deprived of familial support, it is less immediately decipherable how submission to parental will emerged from the fear of eternal damnation. At this time the Church proposed that marriage relied on pure consent and both in texts of canon law and instructions to confessors it was reiterated that it was not necessary to respect the will of one's parents in the choice of a spouse.[224] However, it is likely that while the ecclesiastical hierarchy made themselves advocates of the principle of consent, the lower clergy, who lived in direct contact with the laity, shared their ethics and ignorance of doctrinal subtleties and that they supported parental authority over marriage.[225] It should also be considered that the curse of one's parents, which appears primarily as an instrument used by mothers against both daughters and sons, would have had a very strong impact not only in virtue of widespread superstitious beliefs but also because it undermined the pre-Tridentine matrimonial ritual, which assigned a very important role to paternal and maternal blessings.[226]

If in the pre-Tridentine era the theory of consent established legal premises by which the aspirations of young lovers, the intrigues of dowry hunters, and the ambitions of bold (*audaci*) women could be realized,[227] after the council requirements that a union be publicized through banns, and that it be celebrated in the church and in the presence of at least two witnesses rendered it more difficult to remove marriage from parental control. Young people firmly determined to be husband and wife could turn to one of those "tumultuous" marriages, celebrated by surprise and by deception before the parish priest. This kind of marriage was amply documented across Europe. It was valid for all purposes but condemned by the Church, as immortalized by Alessandro Manzoni in *The Betrothed*.[228] Younger sons of patrician families to whom kin politics denied access to marriage could marry according to a secret rite (which came to be celebrated following an episcopal dispensation and registered in a specific curial register).[229] This type of wedding constituted an expedient to obtain or protect a state of sexual and affective stability at a personal level and eventually soothe the conscience, without compromising relations with one's family. In a period that tended to limit access to marriage in order to guarantee patrimonial integrity,[230] the interests of the family of origin were protected to the detriment to the family in formation. Sometimes an instrument of family strategies, secret marriage became insidious, causing grave repercussions in the public sphere. As we have already noted,[231] based on Venetian laws only those whose parents were both nobles and had had their marriage recorded with the Avogaria di Comun could be admitted among the ranks of the nobility and aspire to be part of the Council (and thus to be part of the government) because they were registered in the *Libro d'Oro*. If a noble destined to perpetuate his lineage married according to the secret rite, he precluded his children from access to his own class, and, in fact, placed the survival of the ruling class in danger. To avoid this danger patrician families formed particular institutions. As "a family of noble families,"[232] the Republic intervened in the life of its members through the arm of the Inquisitors of State, the highest Venetian tribunal, to prevent and eventually repress those actions which could bring damage and dishonor to the aristocratic body in its entirety, and first among these was a marriage opposed to class rules. Young nobles who intended to formalize *mesalliances* risked being sequestered and brought before the Inquisitors to be severely warned – an experience that had a notable deterring effect – or, if they sought to obtain their goal by fleeing beyond the confines of the Republic, they risked being followed by the *sbirri*.[233] Until the beginning of the eighteenth century, families and the state sought to keep marriages contracted against the rules of the patriciate under control, and in the course of the eighteenth century they found much greater difficulty in controlling their members.[234] Influenced by developments in customs and aspirations, and sensible to the weakening role of the patriciate in a state that was increasingly less influential on the international stage, in numerous cases they avoided recording their marriages with the Avogaria even when they had the right to do so because they had contracted a bond between nobles. They thus indifferently – if not deliberately – provoked the extinction of their own lineage.[235]

8.2 *"Fearful Marriage"*

Matrimonium meticulosum or fearful marriage, which was contracted by coercion and therefore considered null by canon law, also fell in the realm of family control over marriage.[236]

Among the cases examined here, those brought for annulment based on lack of consent are rare.[237] The typology of this kind of litigation varied according to whether the supposed victim of fear was a man or a woman, but beyond that, they were very standardized. Suits for feminine fear generally involved young or very young brides, who had often contracted marriage before the legitimate age. They were generally fatherless,[238] entrusted to the guardianship of paternal uncles or a stepfather, and were often strongly influenced by their mothers.[239]

Unlike other cases, in which the complainant found a way to explain his or her free initiative and individuality in the ecclesiastical tribunal, these suits left the interested party in the shadow and instead featured their relatives and tutors. These authority figures claimed they had constrained the young girl with physical violence to make a marital bond that now they wanted to declare null, probably in favor of a new, more advantageous union or to confine the girl in a monastery.[240] To add credibility, the parents, relatives, and tutors did not hesitate to admit threats and violence nor to describe the displays of embarrassment of the young girls or the rebellions of brides. The one's will was bent by the fear of being burned alive, while the resistance of another – who, when her future husband's name was announced at the table, abandoned the meal – was overcome with that her stepfather might break her arms.[241]

Because threats were considered in court as a source of just fear (*iustus metus*), it was necessary to demonstrate that whoever had made the threat would not have hesitated to carry it out.[242] Thus the case in which a paternal aunt told the court how her brother, a "fierce [man], who for little cause would threaten and beat" his daughter and wife, dragging them by their long hair through the alley, to the extent that the same witness had to intervene many times tearing at him with her hands for fear that he would kill them.[243]

Violence preceding marriage was generally accompanied by pressure at the ceremony. The girl often prayed to God or her family not to force her to marry the man chosen by her family, cried "a great deal" (*grandemente*), or declared herself disposed to take the path of the cloister instead. Incapable of saying "no," after remaining silent, she finally expressed her assent only after repeated requests, sometimes only with a timid nod of the head, and took the hand of her groom because her stepfather or uncle united their hands by force.[244]

In the most frequent cases, in which force and fear (*vis et metus*) mostly consisted of physical violence, young women had to demonstrate that they had openly shown their dissent to the marriage before the ceremony began to obtain a favorable judgment. They declared that they had never agreed to the choice made in their stead by their relatives; they demonstrated repugnance towards their future spouse and abandoned the table every time he was named; they sought to flee or hide themselves in the kitchen before the ceremony, or they committed self-destructive acts, scratching at their faces.[245] However, they also had to demonstrate that, after the wedding, they had not lessened their refusal. Based on doctrine, in fact, marriage contracted by force became valid with spontaneous cohabitation.[246] Beyond unanimously invoking the absence of consummation, then, the protagonists of these litigations generally sought to demonstrate that the violence and the blows that had forced them to accept the marriage continued after it, preventing them from rebelling against such tyranny. The persistence of dissent was externalized: kissed against her will, the bride got angry.[247] If her husband was in the house she obstinately avoided his presence, never making a "nice face" at him, nor gratifying him with the title "husband." She never wore his ring nor the clothes made for her; she did not obey him. If he became ill, she did not take care of him or give him anything to drink.[248] If he found himself "in town" she refused to write to him. If he were mentioned she behaved as if someone had mentioned "the one from hell."[249] It was thus clear that this was not a true marriage, as the rituality of consent and the semiotics of affection (*affectus*) were overturned or distorted.[250]

Cases of annulment in which the impediment of fear was adopted by men presented a very different typology. In most cases, the suit was revealed as an expedient for a seducer to get out of the obligations he contracted to the seduced, appealing to the doctrine of consent. The canvas of the story is consistent: a man of elevated social position, or at least higher than that of the woman involved in the story, was forced to marry her by her parents, who were usually armed when the man and woman were surprised *in flagrante*. In the presence of relatives – and sometimes a priest who was fetched in a hurry – the groom had to uphold a promise of marriage which validated his intimate access to the young girl, or to render solemn vows made in secret before the bride's pregnancy was overshadowed with the shame of illegitimacy.[251] In the eyes of the community her family had the right and the duty either to force her seducer to marry her or to wash the shame of dishonor away with blood.[252] Canon law offered the man a difficult escape.

In these litigations the men never appeared as plaintiffs: they only advanced the impediment of *metus* as a last resort in order to remove themselves from the imposition of solemnizing the marriage. Presenting themselves as victims of fear, in fact, implied an admission that there had been a nuptial ceremony. A ceremony that had occurred rendered the position of the "groom" difficult: to convince a judge to declare the marriage null these men had to demonstrate that they would have paid with their lives if they had refused to contract the bond. No lesser risk would have convinced the judge. In the case that involved Alvise Cavazza and Elena Simoni, for example, Alvise got out of the marriage as he was able to demonstrate that he had been lured into the house of the young woman at night by deceit and had been assaulted with a "dagger"[253] by Elena's father, flanked by two armed men, after which he was disarmed and threatened repeatedly with an unsheathed sword. He had then resisted, holding his hand behind his back so as not to give it to Elena, affirming that he had never married, and then was offered money because he would not proceed to the ceremony. Ultimately incapable of resisting, at the end of the ceremony he had fled with his weapons, not to be seen again until the suit in court.[254] But in some cases, if the family had laid down their arms at the request of a friar who came from a nearby convent to remind them that "these things must be done voluntarily and not forced"; or if, even worse, the marriage had been celebrated after the groom, threatened with death and beaten by the brother of the seduced and by his thugs near the Rialto, spontaneously presented himself at the girl's house to proceed with the wedding, the seducer had no hope of a favorable sentence.[255]

The Council of Trent established that the promise of marriage followed by sexual relations no longer constituted a valid marriage. Cases of alleged marriage that before the council were within ecclesiastical jurisdiction became criminal cases for rape in the jurisdiction of the *Esecutori sopra la bestemmia* after Trent.[256] Men no longer had to turn to the impediment of force to get out of an unequal marriage.[257] In secular tribunals with jurisdiction not over marriage but over rape, women ceased to refer to the words and gestures of *affectus*, which in the pre-conciliar period constituted a presumption of consent (and thus of marriage), and they began to speak about sudden violence rather than a common life in construction.[258]

Even if the Council of Trent denied the value of a marriage that had been promised and was then followed by consummation, the promise continued to have binding value.[259] Theologians, however, tried to oppose unequal marriages and sought to deny women who had recklessly fallen prey to the advances of men of higher social status the possibility of taking such men to court to enforce their promises.[260] Martin de Azpilqueta, called the Navarro († 1586), specified in his very popular confessors manual that the promise of marriage could be dissolved in cases of excessive social inequality between the contractors. According to Sánchez († 1610), moreover, a man was not held to the fulfillment of his promise in the event of great social disparity, or if the woman could sense that the promise was a joke,[261] and Sánchez stated that any such promise by a man of a much higher rank should be interpreted as a joke.

Notes

1. ASPV, *FC*, vol. 3, Damianus Masarachias *vs* Marieta filia domine Bone sclavone, 1525.
2. J. Gaudemet, *Il matrimonio in Occidente*, pp. 105–112.
3. See *infra*, §§ 2–3.
4. For the citation see E. Orlando, *Il matrimonio delle beffe*, p. 234.
5. E. Brambilla, *Dagli sponsali civili al matrimonio sacramentale*, p. 969. Regarding judgment see the observations *supra*, ch. 1, point 9.
6. ASPV, *CM*, vol. 7, Bernardina de Garzonibus *vs* Bernardino conte di Collalto, 1500–1501.

7. ASPV, *CM*, vol. 1, fasc. 11, Isabetta *vs* Jacobo da Marignano, 1454. See *supra*, ch. 3, § 6.
8. In the instances of lawyers or in the sentences that declare a marriage non-existent *de iure*, the expression "Marriage was contracted, even if only *de facto*." ("Contraxit, licet de facto, matrimonium"). An example of the use of this terminology is found also in a letter sent by the patriarchal vicar to the podestà of Vicenza recorded in the registers of the curia in ASPV, *AMP*, reg. 46, 14 December 1492.
9. An example of the defense for lay administration of sacramental marriage is in ASPV, *CM*, vol. 45, Lucretia Bondumier *vs* Hieronimo Mudazzo, 1546.
10. "El me pareria per el dover che dona Perina dovesse venzer, perché l'à raxon, perché questo matrimonio è pubblico e manifesto." " vellet iusticiam habentem vincere et credit domina Salomona habere ius." See ASPV, CM, vol. 16, Perina relicta q. ser Varisci Samitarii *vs* Benedictum Barbitonsorem 1515; ASPV, CM, vol. 15 Salomona Salomono *vs* Filippo Minio, 1514.
11. Ibid.
12. ASPV, *CM*, vol. 17, Marietta Barbaro *vs* Matteo Giustinian, 1515–1517.
13. "El parentà," "palam publice et notorie," "camera alla sala seu portico." See the document cited *supra*, note 9.
14. "Ponit quod de consuetudine antiquissima et approbata in ista inclita civitate Venetiarum contrahuntur matrimonia modis formis et solemnitatibus premissis, et huiusmodi matrimonia habentur et tenentur et reputantur legittima et canonica et per verba de presenti contracta, firma et indubitata et in facie ecclesie contracta preter id et absque eo quod per aliquem sacerdotem vel alium proferantur verba aliqua de presenti per huiusmodi contractum."
15. The suit in fact focused on the annulment of the bond for the impotence of the husband. The celebration of the marriage was not a subject of contention on its own.
16. H. Denzinger – P. Hunerman, *Enchiridion*, pp. 488–489, note 860.
17. For a synthesis of the construction of Christian marriage see C. Deutsch, *Ehegerichtsbarkeit im Bistum Regensburg*, pp. 29–38, and M. Korpiola, *Between Betrothal and Bedding*, pp. 89–118.
18. C. Klapisch-Zuber, *La famiglia e le donne*, pp. 128–131, and regarding pre-Tridentine marriage rituals, pp. 109–151; D. D'Avray,

Marriage Ceremonies, pp. 107–115; and D. Lombardi, *Matrimoni di Antico Regime*, pp. 35–41.
19. See for example the painting of Antonio Vivarini, *Il matrimonio di santa Monica* (c. 1441), now held in the Accademia Gallery in Venice, originally part of a series of stories placed around the statue of St. Monica in the Venetian church of St. Stefano. See also the *Matrimonio di san Giuliano*, in the cycle of the *Leggenda di san Giuliano* (14th century), placed in the northern transept of the Cathedral of Trent, and the *Sposalizio della Vergine* in the church of the Annunciation of Borno in Val Camonica (1474–1475). This last example is mentioned by J. Traeger, *Renaissance und Religion*, p. 84.
20. ASPV, *CM*, vol. 2, fasc. 2, Johannis de Deodatis *vs* Isabetta Bondumier, 1458.
21. ASPV, *CM*, vol. 25, Diana Minio *vs* Aloysium Caravello, 1526–1527: "…cum omnis contractus celebratus cum testibus reprobatis a iure sit nullus."
22. ASPV, *CM*, vol. 2, fasc. 5, Petri de Amatis *vs* Laura de Triultiis, 1461: the priest "opened the sacrament" ("aperuit sacramentum").
23. ASPV, *AMP*, reg. 7, Antonio Sarasino *vs* Isabetta Trivisan, 21 November 1438.
24. ASPV, *CM*, vol. 7, Bernardina de Garzonibus *vs* Bernardino conte di Collalto, 1500–1501.
25. ASPV, *CM*, vol. 9, Marco Antonio de Stefani *vs* Lucretia q. Simonis Vacha, 1506–1507.
26. ASPV, *CM*, vol. 6, Giovanni di Luchino a Serico *vs* Cassandra de Marconibus, 1492–1493.
27. ASPV, *CM*, vol. 5, Regina de Colbrusato *vs* Ioanne Cornelio de Como, 1484.
28. ASPV, *AMP*, reg. 8, Anna *vs* Rigo veludario, 29 April-9 May 1440. E. Orlando, *Sposarsi nel medioevo*, p. 132 considers the tavern as a "location *par excellence* for hidden and false marriage." On the tavern as a "counter-church" see G. Cherubini, *La taverna nel basso medioevo*, p. 204.
29. ASPV, *FC*, vol. 1, Catarina q. Iacob Zanchanarii *vs* Nicolai Mancini de Ragusio, 1468–1469.
30. ASPV, *CM*, vol. 9, Dominicus Spurco *vs* Marietta, 1507.
31. ASPV, *CM*, vol. 13, Giovanni Mammoli *vs* Lucia d'Este, 1513.
32. R. Sarti, *Vita di casa*, p. 116.

33. ASPV, *AMP*, reg. 26, Petrus a Lacu *vs* Catarucia filia Bone, 1465.
34. ASPV, *CM*, vol. 13, Giovanni Mammoli *vs* Lucia d'Este, 1513.
35. ASPV, *AMP*, regs. 26 and 27, Caterina Tommasina *vs* Alfonso di Sicilia, 13 February–18 February 1465; *AMP*, reg. 26, Pasqualina *vs* Guidone (Vito) Trevisano, 13 May 1465.
36. "Voi savé che no ho homo algun in caxa, vi prego che vegnati qui a caxa mia perché questa sera misser Zuan Baptista del Ferro diè vegnir qui per darme la man e tuorme per moglier." ASPV, *CM*, vol. 19, Franceschina Lando *vs* Joanne Baptiste Ferro, 1519.
37. "Secondo commanda Dio et la vostra santa lege." ASPV, *CM*, vol. 25, Diana Minio *vs* Aloysium Caravello, 1526–1527.
38. ASPV, *CM*, vol. 11, Zinevra filia Nicolai barbitonsoris *vs* Hieronimo Baldigara, 1509–1510.
39. ASPV, *CM*, vol. 2, fasc. 5, Petri di Amatis *vs* Laura de Triultiis, 1461.
40. ASPV, *CM*, vol. 18, Lucietam filia q. Hieronymi Nigro *vs* Hieronimum filium ser Antonii centuraii, 1520–1521.
41. ASPV, *CM*, vol. 15, Hieronima Compostella *vs* Francesco da Mosto, 1514: "And he took sacraments that he took her as his wife, and he swore on the saints and the Holy Spirit" ("E feva sacramenti che la toleva per moier, et zurava li santi et el Spirito Sancto.")
42. On both the oath on the Gospels and the sign of the cross traced on the bride's front see ASPV, *CM*, vol. 18, Paule filie q. Boni *vs* Victore barbitonsore, 1516.
43. "Secondo comanda Dio e la Santa Madre Ghiexia." ASPV, *FC*, vol. 2, Valeria figlia di Marco Rio *vs* Francesco aurefice, 1501.
44. G. Paolin, *Monache e donne*, p. 204 mentions a marriage celebrated by carving a cross in the trunk of a tree (1554).
45. ASPV, *FC*, vol. 2, Daniele di Padova *vs* Lucia q. Luce de Carboniris, 1510.
46. For the celebration by the confessor (the woman's), see ASPV, *CM*, vol. 15, Salamona Salomono *vs* Philippo Minio, 1514.
47. "S'el fusse el piovan overo una loro zovine che era lì." ASPV, *FC*, vol. 2, pro dona Lucieta de contracta Sanctae Trinitatis et ser Rocho, 26 June 1517.
48. In 1506, the patriarch required that "no one can presume to baptize or make betrothals" (niuno presuma baptizare vel agere sponsalia) without a license from the parish priest "or one of the titled priests then celebrating the Sabbath" (vel unius ex presbyteris titulatis tunc

facientis hebdomadam). See Giovanbattista Gallicciolli, *Delle memorie venete*, book II, pp. 9–10.
49. "Non mi basta lo animo... da uno prete, de contra'."
50. "Se' mia moier, como vi ho dicto altre volte, e per cavarve de suspetto chiame' i pretti de S. Provolo che ve chiarirò." ASPV, *CM*, vol. 25, Catherina de Brochardis de Schio *vs* Bartolomeo cerdone bergomense, 1526.
51. "Quod erat nobile sacramento." ASPV, *CM*, vol. 17, Marietta Barbaro *vs* Matteo Giustiniano, 1515.
52. "Far beffa."
53. Regarding the Council of Trent see H. Jedin, *Storia del concilio di Trento*. On the debate about marriage see G. Cozzi, *Il dibattito sui matrimoni clandestini*; H. Jedin-K. Reinhard, *Il matrimonio*; R. Lettmann, *Die Diskussion über die klandestinen Ehen*; G. Zarri, *Recinti*, pp. 210–226.
54. "Che li detti la man." ASPV, *CM*, vol. 12, Camilla de Dardanis *vs* Alovisio Donati, 1512.
55. "Senza darge altrimenti la man."
56. ASPV, *CM*, vol. 18, Paula q. magistri Boni Veronensis *vs* Victore barbitonsore, 1516; *CM*, vol. 18, Maria Laurentii *vs* Francisco de Thomasiis, 1516. In the first case the man declared that he had promised to marry his concubine, but he did not give her his hand, in the second the man had expressed proposals of marriage before witnesses "but never took her hand, nor did he accept her as his wife." [tamen numquam illi tetigit manum, nec eam in uxorem accepit.] See S. Seidel Menchi, *Cause matrimoniali e iconografia nuziale*, p. 683.
57. ASPV, *CM*, vol. 2, fasc. 3, Vittore de Sanctis *vs* Maria, 1459.
58. "Se dixe che Michiel ge ha tochà la man [a Virida]...a che modo, dal balchon con un baston?"
59. ASPV, *CM*, vol. 27, Michaelis Salamono *vs* Virida Superantio, 1529.
60. ASPV, *CM*, vol. 1, fasc. 11, Isabetta *vs* Jacopo da Marignano, 1454.
61. ASPV, *AMP*, reg. 11, Maria di Canareggio *vs* Battista cerviate, 26 May 1446. In ASPV, *S*, reg. 1, Pietro de Dulcino *vs* Filippa, the marriage was declared invalid both because of the force and fear (*vim et metus*) "before and after the giving of hands" (ante et post dationem manuum) and because of the fact that the parties had not exchanged words of consent.

62. ASPV, *AMP*, reg. 9, Zanino Tomei Togazi *vs* Maria q. Nicolai de Villa, 30 January–27 November 1441.
63. ASPV, *AMP*, reg. 18, Paola di Benedetto d'Armano *vs* Giorgio Monta. In ASPV, *CM*, vol. 3, fasc. 4, Paolo Gabrieli *vs* Isabetta Bartolomei, 1470, Paolo presented himself before the patriarch recalling that nine years earlier a woman had made him touch the hand of Isabella without however expressing words of consent. He considered himself married to her but Isabella did not. They were fighting about this ("in lite") with "precepts and decrees" ("precetti e mandati") before the vicar, and now the plaintiff asked for clarity and that the marriage be declared invalid. His request was granted.
64. ASPV, *AMP*, regs. 3–4, Lazzaro da Scutari *vs* Caterina Cortese, 20 February 1426–27 and June 1427.
65. M. Bonvini Mozzanti, *L'opera pastorale*, p. 147, also O. Niccoli, *Baci rubati*. For a more general treatment see J.C. Schmitt, *La raison des gestes*.
66. "Greco," "inhonesta," "se lui li aveva dado la man," "separarse né partirse." See on this case also *supra*, ch. 4, § 2.
67. ASPV, *CM*, Nicolò q. Dominici Cortesii *vs* Angela Sebastiani Cavazza, 1503–1508.
68. ASPV, *CM*, vol. 12, Clara Marcello *vs* Francesco de Orlandis, 1512. A long juridical tradition "considered the kiss as one of the signs of nuptial consent." The kiss was also considered a sign of the mimetic consummation of the marriage. See O. Niccoli, *Baci rubati*, p. 225. In English marriage causes the term "to kiss" came to be used to allude to sexual relations. See L. Gowing, *Domestic Dangers*, pp. 190, 249–51; M. Ingram, *Church Courts*, p. 240–242, B. Capp, *When Gossips Meet*, p. 245, and Idem, *Live, Love, and Litigation*, p. 81. On the nuptial kiss see also N. Tamassia, *Osculum interveniens* and S. Seidel Menchi, *Cause matrimoniali e iconografia nuziale*, pp. 692–696.
69. In 1551 in a ritual of peace between two families from the Bolognese countryside, which concluded with a betrothal between two of their members, there was a taking of hands and a kiss of peace between the men of the two houses. See L. Ferrante, *Il matrimonio disciplinato*, p. 915. In Innsbruck, in 1529, the solemn peace between two families from Trent was stipulated "by the taking of hands and the kiss of peace" (per tactum manus et osculum pacis). See M. Bellabarba, *Racconti familiari*, p. 125. On rituals of pacification

in general see O. Niccoli, *Rinuncia, pace, perdono* and Eadem, *Perdonare*.
70. This is particularly true of contracts of sale. See E. Chénon, *Recherches historique*, p. 649, and more generally, on the symbolic importance of drinking wine at a wedding, p. 648–650.
71. ASPV, *CM*, vol. 9, Nicolosa Calderaria *vs* Pietro Girardi, 1507. L. Schmugge, *Ehen vor Gericht*, p. 68. Schmugge argues that the use of wine was evocative of the marriage of Cana.
72. "Bozolai e storti." ASPV, *CM*, vol. 11, Isabetta *vs* Jacopo da Marignano, 1454. "Bozolao" or "buzzola" is the Venetian term for ciambelle, doughnuts or other similarly shaped confections. On the symbolic value of bird see A. Grieco, *From Roosters to Cocks*.
73. On the nuptial banquet see S.F. Weiss, *Medieval and Renaissance Wedding Banquets*. On the symbolic significance of the banquet and the offer of food see A.M. Nada Patrone, *Il cibo del ricco e il cibo del povero*, in particular pp. 455–473.
74. See *supra*, ch. 2, § 9.
75. "Se tratta del ligamen infra l'homo e la dona che non si può desligar noma per morte." ASPV, *CM*, vol. 14, Margherita da Traù *vs* Alessandro Aurio, 1514. The same question was put to a witness in *CM*, vol. 18, Lucretia scaletaria *vs* Domenico Varotario 1517. The witness responded that marriage was "when a man and a woman take each other as husband and wife" ("quando uno e una se tuol per marido e moier").
76. Regarding civil law see G. Marchetto, *I glossatori*, p. 68. For the affirmation of indissolubility as law for all the Church J. Gaudemet, *Il matrimonio in Occidente*, p. 89, p. 181.
77. See for example ASPV, *AMP*, Bartolomeus Alovixii draperius *vs* Maria de Andrea, 1465, ASPV, *CM*, vol. 12, Margherita de Amicis *vs* Aloixio batilauro, 1512. Canon law, moreover, explicitly excluded the possibility of remarrying if the death of the first spouse could not be certified, for cases in which one had not had any news of the spouse in a long time (at least seven years): see X 4. 1. 19. Regarding the juridical debate about nullification by the presumed death of the spouse, see J. Brundage, *Law, Sex and Christian Society*, pp. 292–294.
78. See the data *infra*, ch. 6. It is also understood that anyone accused of having contracted a preceding marriage affirmed that the first marriage was not valid because the first spouse was already married.

An example is found in ASPV, *AMP* 33, Sententia separationis matrimonialis inter Stranam de Antibaro et Georgium de Pastronich, 11 July 1474.

79. The foreign origin of parties did not impede the judges from conducting scrupulous investigations in their place of origin, with the help of vicars of that place. After the Council of Trent, to extirpate the practice of multiple marriages, foreigners who wanted to marry were required to present a declaration of their free state. On bigamy as a product of social mobility see also P. Scaramella, *Controllo e repressione*, T. Dean, *Fathers and Daughters*, p. 102. Also A. Parma Cook-N.D. Cook, *Good Faith*; K. Siebenhüner, *Bigamie und Inquisition*, and Eadem, *Conversion*.

80. ASPV, *AMP*, reg. 11, Orlando da Montefior *vs* Margherita da Lago, 19 May 1447. See the similar case analyzed by K. Meek, *"Simone ha aderito alla fede di Maometto."*

81. ASPV, *AMP*, reg. 14, Caterina di Antonio *vs* Daniele famulo, 15–22 September 1452. On the condition of slavery as a cause for annulment see c. 3, C XXIX, q. II.

82. "Putana vel eius femina." ASPV, *AMP*, reg. 8, Anna *vs* Rigo veludario, 29 April–9 May 1440.

83. "Vero matrimonio." ASPV, *AMP*, reg. 10, Nicoletta (Coletta) *vs* Giorgio da Candida, 27 May – 31 July 1443.

84. See respectively ASPV, *AMP*, reg. 6, Giovanni di Alessio *vs* Maria, 3 June 1437–17 July 1437 and reg. 26, Bartolomeo Alovixii draperius *vs* Maria di Andrea, 1465, also the case mentioned by P. Scaramella, *Controllo e repressione*, p. 468 (1618): "At the second marriage I did not say that I had another wife, and Livia did not say this, because she had renounced me as her husband, and I had renounced her, and because I believed and held that the said marriage made with Livia was no longer valid and that I could take another wife."

85. ASPV, *FC*, vol. 2, Jacobina *vs* Giovan Battista Donati, 1508. See *supra*, § 2.

86. ASPV, *CM*, vol. 12, Johannis Dominici Ceti *vs* Camilla e Angelica, 1512–1513.

87. Divorce was allowed by Hebrew, Greek, and Roman law. See J. Gaudement, *Il matrimonio in Occidente*, pp. 32–35, also regarding the scriptural foundations of indissolubility, and pp. 146–165 on the impediments that allowed for annulment of the bond. Regarding the bibliography relative to separation see *infra*, § 4.

88. See the documents cited *supra*, notes 80–81.
89. On this affair and on the nature of the impediment see *supra*, ch. 1, note 97.
90. "Quello che aveva una moglie metà uomo e metà donna." For the annulled marriage see ASPV, *CM*, vol. 9, Michele Leoni *vs* Faustina Foscarin, 1507, for the definition of the witness *CM*, vol. 10, Paola de Mastellis *vs* Michele Leon, 1508–1510, and on this case, C. Cristellon, *Two genders, one body.*
91. "Vene in fastidio…guernarlo."
92. ASPV, *CM*, vol. 12, Margherita de Amicis *vs* Alvise battilauro, 1512.
93. "Farle le spese e governarla," "il pecado di taxer la verità."
94. "Lacrimis et suasionibus."
95. See G. Marchetto, *"Primus fuit Lamech."*
96. Regarding the phenomenon of bigamy and its repression, see the work of Scaramella and Siebenhüner cited *supra*, note 79. For Troyes see S. McDougall, *The Punishment of Bigamy*. For a treatment of the Hebrew world see C. Galasso, *"La moglie duplicata."* For Cordova see J. Cobos Ruis de Adana, *Matrimonio*. On the attitude of the Spanish Inquisition to bigamy, see E. Gacto, *El delito de bigamia*. For an example of the use of the indicated terminology see ASPV, *AMP*, reg. 5, Menega *vs* Giorgio Greco, 17 November 1427. On the reflection of German and Dutch jurists on polygamy in the early modern era, see S. Buchholz, *Erunt tres aut quattuor*; also G. Bullough, *Polygamy among the Reformers*. See also the observations of L. Roper, *Oedipus and the Devil*, pp. 79–103.
97. For an example of a sentence that did not condemn the bigamist to pay the litigation expenses, but that respected the traditional practice of charging the loser see ASPV, *AMP*, reg. 33, Sententia matrimonialis pro Caterina filia ser Jacobi preconis et aromatarii Sanctis Johannis Bragore *vs* Johannem Franciscum de Longsi de Manta, 1474.
98. "Temerario." ASPV, *AMP*, reg. 29, Maria Sanador e Giorgio (Alegretto) da Sibinico *vs* Dionisio Gabrieli, 7 March 1466; *AMP*, reg. 33, Rada da Trebigna *vs* Nicolaum q. Eustachii, 24 January 1474.
99. ASPV, *AMP*, reg. 31/a (not inventoried), Giorgio Fuscareno *vs* Berucia Lando, 23 June 1469.
100. ASPV, *S*, reg. 1, Ursula de Valentia *vs* Tommasina Superantio, 16 September 1465: the cause was started by Ursula for the recognition of her marriage with the deceased Leonardo Superantio; ASPV, *S*,

reg. 3, Paolo Memo *vs* Lucia, 22 March 1482. The canonical norm referred to is X 4. 16. 14.
101. ASPV, *AMP*, reg. 31/a (not inventoried), Lazaro de Soledo *vs* Samaritana, 3 February 1468. In the case of York, Donahue hypothesizes even that the court may have connived with perjury in cases of preceding marriage. See C. Donahue jr, *Law, Marriage and Society*, p. 60.
102. "Ad sui correctionem et aliorum exemplum." In the sentence it does not mention the nature of the punishment. ASPV, *CM*, vol. 12, Johannis Dominici Ceti *vs* Camilla et Angelica, 1512–1513.
103. Other than the example reported here, consider the concerned peroration in favor of the indissolubility of marriage, made by the patriarchal vicar before a man who requested the annulment of a bond that had tied him to an unfaithful wife so that he could marry another woman. See *supra*, § 2.
104. It was held, as we noted in ch. 3, that procurators and lawyers who provided advocacy during marriage litigations were generally the same for many causes.
105. ASPV, *CM*, vol. 11, Francesco Rizardi *vs* Franceschina Mathei de la lanna de Portogruaro, 1511–1512. See also *CM*, vol. 18, Lucieta q. Hieronimi Nigro *vs* Hieronimum filium ser Antonii Centurai, 1521, where, in one of the *positiones* put forward by the woman's lawyer, the behavior of Hieronimo, who had contracted a marriage in a public form with another woman was defined as implicating "his soul in a grave sin of multiple scandals and abuse of sacraments" ("anime sue gravem periculum plurimorum scandalorum et sacramenti vilipendium").
106. G. Marchetto, *"Prius Fuit Lamech."*
107. See *supra*, ch. 4, § 1. For Florence see D. Lombardi, *Matrimoni di Antico Regime*, p. 83. Different from what happened in Italy, in France, in line with a policy of greater control over marriage, the ecclesiastical tribunal severely punished bigamy, comparing it to heresy. See S. McDougall, *The Punishment of Bigamy*.
108. "Levante como mercadente."
109. ASPV, *CM*, vol. 13, Elena de Stefani *vs* Hieronimo Marangon, 1514. On the construction of female *fragilitas*, see *supra*, ch. 4, note 11.
110. "Quia communiter ab omnibus sciatur non posse virum habere duas uxores, hoc ideo presumptio est., quod mulier sciat quod ab omnibus scitur." See P. Farinacci, *Praxis et theorica criminalis*, Pars quarta, Delictis carnis, Poena ducentis duas uxores, c. 459A, n. 31.

111. For a review of the norms of separation and the reconstruction of the institution according to the lines of development of civil and canon law in the intermediate era, see the bibliography cited *supra*, ch. 4, note 34.
112. See for example, ASPV, *CM*, vol. 1, fasc. 14, Clara Matafar *vs* Michele Giustinian, 1455. Cfr also B. Borello, *Trame sovrapposte*, pp. 156–194, and C. La Rocca, *Tra moglie e marito*.
113. According to lay moral code marital adultery was not considered an outrageous behavior on its own. It became so if the husband treated his concubine with honors equal to those expected for a wife. For example, ASPV, *FC*, vol. 1, Lucia de Molino *vs* Girolamo Memo, 1463. For marital behavior censured by lay morality see also ASPV, *CM*, vol. 6, f. 15, Maddalena Fontana *vs* Andrea e Fragona', 1497–1498. ASPV, *FC*, vol. 1, Flornovella di Niccolò *vs* Vittore Strazarolo, 1458–1459, and the documents cited in the two notes following. See also L. Roper, *The Holy Household*, pp. 194–205, and in particular p. 196.
114. "Per giusta e legittima causa," "figliola," "buona moglie," "timore o sospetto," "mai [sarebbe] molestata in li detti beni." AIRE VE, Zit. E 31, 3, c. 4.
115. See *infra*, Appendix. Regarding cases of separation brought by women only after repeated attempts to reconcile, see also the document cited in note 112 and ASPV, *CM*, vol. 4, fasc. 1, Teologia Baffo *vs* Francesco Baffo, 1475.
116. "Bene tractando". ASPV, *AMP* 28, Nicolosa Nicolai cristallarii *vs* Niccolò, 22 January 1466. See *supra*, ch. 4, § 2.
117. See *infra*, ch. 6.
118. ASPV, *AMP*, regs. 13–15, Lazzaro di Niccolò *vs* Lorenza, 29 November 1451 – 21 March 1453. Consensual separations are documented for the period under examination in Rome, Lucca, and at least in the fourteenth century also in Venice in the notarial registers, for example. See A. Esposito, *Convivenza e separazione*; C. Meek, *Liti matrimoniali*, p. 141; and L. Guzzeti, *Separation and Separated Couples*. Regarding the eighteenth century see C. La Rocca, *Tra moglie e marito*.
119. "Male contenta." Cfr, *supra*, ch. 4, § 2.
120. See *Constitutiones et privilegia patriarchatus et cleri Venetiarum*, primae par. Tit. tert., cap. XXIX, pp. 50–51.
121. See *supra*, ch. 4, § 6.

122. ASPV, *AMP*, regs. 2–37 (1420–1479) and 46 (1492–1493).
123. On the fact that parish priests were not always able to distinguish between sins that could be absolved in confession and those that brought excommunication, those reserved to the bishop, see *supra*, ch. 4.
124. See *supra*, ch. 4.
125. See *supra*, ch. 4 and note 136.
126. See for Venice G. Cozzi, *Note e documenti sulla questione del "divorzio,"* p. 351; for Siena in the seventeenth century see O. di Simplicio, *Peccato, penitenza, perdono*, p. 314. Regarding Livorno in the eighteenth century, half of separations granted by the ecclesiastical tribunal were granted based on simple questions accompanied by a notarial document that attested to the free and reciprocal will of the spouses to separate. The judge granted the separation, which was "the formal and bureaucratic recognition of a private agreement." See C. La Rocca, *Tra moglie e marito*, p. 374.
127. See X 4. 5. 1.
128. See on this point R. Weigand, *Die bedingte Eheschließung*; M. Zurowski, *Le développement de la nation canonique*; R. Helmholz, *Marriage Litigation*, pp. 47–57; J. Gaudement, *Il matrimonio in Occidente*, pp. 135–137.
129. See respectively, ASPV, *AMP*, reg. 20, Isabella di Giovanni Thadei barcaiolo *vs* Andrea Albanese Filocampo, 6 April 1459 and reg. 19, Elena sclavona *vs* Enrico teutonico 22 March–11 August 1458. It should be considered that marriage litigations were often very long; it was normal for them to last at least a year.
130. C. Povolo, *L'intrigo dell'onore*, p. 361.
131. G. Alessi, *Il gioco degli scambi*.
132. For an analysis of female honor that does not limit itself to the sexual honor of the woman see G. Walker, *Expanding the Boundaries*, which underlines in particular the importance of the management of the house for female honor. See also A. Poska, *Elusive Virtue*.
133. The relevance of the theme of honor for the comprehension of the sexual division of social roles in the Mediterranean is demonstrated in the first place by anthropology: see regarding this the bibliography cited by S. Cavallo – S. Cerutti, *Onore femminile*, p. 378. Among the historical works see L. Ferrante, *Differenza sociale e differenza sessuale*; L. Roper, *The Holy Household*; C. Casagrande, *La donna custodita*, pp. 88–128; S. Burghartz, *Geschlecht, Körper, Ehre*, pp. 214–234, C. Povolo, *L'intrigo dell'onore*, in particular pp. 355–393.

134. "Maritali affectu." ASPV, *AMP*, reg. 20, Isabella di Giovanni Thadei barcaiolo *vs* Andrea Albanese Filocampo, 6 April 1459.
135. "Domicella et virgo," "vidua et corrupta" ASPV, *AMP*, reg. 13, Teodoro di Giovanni *vs* Lucia Parisini, 19 October–18 November 1450.
136. See also R. Helmholz, *Marriage Litigation*, p. 51, where a man subordinated his marriage to the condition that his wife conceived a son with him on the same night.
137. ASPV, *AMP*, reg. 15, 11 July 1453. The threat and declaration of excommunication came after a request made by Lucia's mother.
138. "Honeste viveret".
139. ASPV, *AMP*, reg. 14, Benedetta q. Antonii da Padova *vs* Luca da Cattaro, 6 March–22 May 1452. The cause was begun by Benedetta, who asked that her marriage be annulled because Luca was already married to Margherita. The defendant defended himself affirming the validity of his marriage to Benedetta, maintaining that he had not married Margherita, with whom he had made a conditional (*sub conditione*) promise. Margherita, absent, did not take part in the litigation.
140. The fact that the promise of marriage followed by consummation was marriage in all its effects is unanimously recognized by the canonists. For this motive in the cases examined here the husbands underlined that they had "learned" (*appreso*) that their wives were not virgins. See J. Dauvillier, *Le Mariage*, pp. 33–39, 122. See also C. Valsecchi, *"Causa matrimonialis est gravis et ardua,"* p. 463 and note 143. About the fact that sexual relations rendered the conditions placed on a marriage invalid, see J. Gaudement, *Il matrimonio in Occidente*, p. 136. For the juridical norm see X 4. 3. Another example of conditional promise followed by sexual relations declared a valid and legitimate marriage is in ASPV, *AMP* 19, Elena sclavona *vs* Alberto teutonico, 22 March – 11 August 1458.
141. It is instead possible to trace cases of dissolving marriages *per verba de futuro* following the discovery that the betrothed woman was not a virgin in the archives of the Penitenzieria Apostolica. See L. Schmugge, *Ehen vor Gericht*, pp. 155–157.
142. For the citations L. Ferrante, *"Consensus concubinarius,"* pp. 107–132; see also M. Bellomo, *Dote nel Diritto intermedio*; P. Rasi, *La conclusione del matrimonio*, pp. 267–268, and Idem, *La conclusione del matrimonio nella dottrina prima del concilio di Trento*, p. 121,

note 98; D. Howen Huges, *Il matrimonio nell'Italia meridionale*, p. 38. For examples of dotal contracts presented as proof of marriage during marriage litigations, see ASPV, *AMP*, reg. 13, Maria Mauroceno *vs* Giorgio Arimondo, 19 March 1451–24 November 1451, where the defendant defended himself with success from a pretense of marriage by presenting a dotal contract stipulated by him with a certain free woman Anna; ASPV, *CM*, vol. 10, Elena relicta Aloysii barbitonsoris *vs* Aloysio a Brachio aurifice, 1508, where the sentence that declared the union valid spoke of "marriage…contracted and enforced by a dowry." ("matrimonio…contracto, dotali instrumento roborato.")

143. Regarding the canonical norm see X 4. 5. 3.
144. "Giovanni rematore." See respectively ASPV, *AMP*, reg. 9, Anna di Giorgio *vs* Michele da Corfù, 26 November 1442; *AMP*, reg. 23, Paolo Gerogii da Cividale *vs* Gentilina Amedei de Lando, 13 May 1462; ASPV, *S*, reg. 3, Giovanni di Cattaro *vs* Maria, 3 June 1482.
145. It should be noted that this last cause was not started by the man's initiative, but followed a mandate of the vicar that, on the woman's request, imposed on him respect of his marriage, according to a very common procedure in marital litigations.
146. In Venice the Giudici del Proprio had jurisdiction over the subject of dowries. Regarding the dotal system of Venice, see S. Chojnacki, *Women and Men*, in particular pp. 95–111, with ample bibliography. See also L. Guzzetti, *Dowries*; J. Sperling, *Dowry or Inheritance?*; and A. Bellavitis, *Identité, mariage, mobilité sociale*, pp. 140–154, 167–171, 315.
147. "In materia matrimoniale chi può inganna", cited by J. Gaudement, *Il matrimonio in Occidente*, p. 138.
148. See Bernardi Papiensis, *Summa decretalium*, book IV, tit. I, *De sponsalibus et matrimonio*. Cited by G. Marchetto, *I glossatori*, p. 83, note 109.
149. A single case among those examined: ASPV, *CM*, vol. 11, Giovanni q. Arsenii de Corcyra *vs* Mattea q. Antonii Zambono, 1510–1511. For another case discussed by the Congregation of the Council see ASV, CC, *Positiones sessiones*, b. 5, c. 380.
150. For Kostanz see L. Schmugge, *Ehen vor Gericht*, p. 155.
151. On the role of mediators in marriage contracts, see. Seidel Menchi, *Marriage Mediation* and Orlando *Pratiche di mediazione*.

152. "Elena sclavona." The marriage contract, from 2 February 1505, is copied among the acts of the litigation.
153. According to the ritual objections the petition was "variously vague, dubious, obscure..." ("varia vaga, dubia, obscura").
154. The part of the cause containing the sentence was lost and it is not possible to know the result using any other sources.
155. See G. Marchetto, *I glossatori*, p. 82. Ancient law did not recognize the union between slaves as a marriage, but rather as a concubinage ("contubernium").
156. The fact that the slave was married was considered a "tacha," that is a "defect that could devalue the product." See A. Bernardo, *Le logiche del profitto*, p. 383.
157. Antonino da Firenze, for example, considered that "baptism, which is not requested by the slave but imposed, cannot be sufficient to make him a true Christian." See P. Guarducci – V. Ottanelli, *I servitori domestici*, p. 78. On marriage of slaves see F. Broomfield (ed.), *Thomae de Chobham Summa Confessorum*, p. 177; M.M. Sheeman, *Choice of Marriage Partner*, p. 24. D. D'Avray, *Slavery, Marriage and the Holy See*. On slavery and conversion see G. Fiume (ed.), *Schiavitù e conversioni nel Mediterraneo*. See also Eadem, *Schiavitù mediterranee*.
158. See X 4. 19. 1: the slave could contract marriage against the wishes of his master but could not by this be released from his obligations to his master.
159. J. Gaudemet, *Il matrimonio in Occidente*, p. 164.
160. N. Tamassia, *La famiglia italiana*, p. 360. In 16th-century Sicily "the children of slaves born in captivity and baptized were considered partly slaves themselves." See R. Sarti, *Bolognesi schiavi*, p. 453, and the bibliography cited there on page 469, note 132.
161. J. Gaudemet, *Il matrimonio in Occidente*, pp. 161–164.
162. See c. 3, C. XXIX q. II.
163. See c. 2, C. XXIX q. II.
164. According to Spanish law, for example, "The master calling the slave to order him to do some service if, in the same moment his wife calls him to do his duty with her the slave first has to response to the commands of his master." This norm is cited by A. Bernardo, *Le logiche del profitto*, p. 388, note 27. In Seville in the seventeenth century the master had to "let [his married slaves] conduct conjugal

life... for the time imposed by law, which is from Saturday night until Sunday morning." Ibid., p. 389, note 29.
165. I cite on this point Sánchez because his doctrine, although developed in a period after that under examination here, is explicitly based in this case on the authority of judges operating earlier: Graziano, Durant, Tommaso, and Bonaventura. See T. Sánchez, *De sancto matrimonii sacramento*, lib. 7, disp. XIX, An error conditionis dirimat matrimonium et quo iure.
166. ASPV, *AMP*, reg. 14, Maria Mauroceno *vs* Giorgio Arimondo, 19 March 1451–24 November 152. The documentation relative to this case is particularly spotty, given that the registers of the curia only note the appearance in court of the parties for a marriage case. The fact however that Maria was defined as a freedwoman allows us to suppose that she wanted to clarify in court that her condition was free or servile at the moment of her marriage.
167. ASPV, *AMP*, reg. 15, Marina Signolo *vs* Niccolò Rosso, 11 May 1453–12 December 1453; *AMP*, reg. 20, Magdalucia *vs* Damiano, schiavo, 17 August 1459.
168. ASPV, *AMP*, reg. 14, Daniele *vs* Caterina di Antonio, 15–22 September 1452; *AMP*, reg. 17, Jacopo da Carpana *vs* Giustina di Giovanni da Piacenza, 13 February – 23 February 1456.
169. All of these proceedings were recorded in the registers of the curia.
170. Only two causes for error of condition end with a sentence.
171. Witnesses for the parties involved in these cases were not locatable in the Archivio di Stato (see inventario Notarile Testamenti, *ad vocem*), the missing indications of the parish of residence did not allow me to look for information about them in the tax records; in the only case in which a woman presented as proof the contract that established the enfranchisement of her spouse (ASPV, *AMP*, reg. 14, Daniele *vs* Caterina di Antonio, 15–22 September 1452), only the production of the document was recorded, without indication of the notary who had produced it; in the registers of the curia the recording of the nomination of the procurator was not accompanied by indication of the notary who had formalized the procuratorial order, from which, even hypothesizing that the notary who recorded the order had also recorded other documents relative to the couple in question, it is not possible to extend research into the notarial archives.
172. See *supra*, § 2.

173. ASPV, *AMP*, reg. 15, Marina Signolo *vs* Niccolò Ross, 11 May 1453– 12 December 1453.
174. "Loco tuto". ASPV, *AMP*, reg. 17, Jacopo da Carpana *vs* Giustina di Giovanni, 13 February 1456 – 23 February 1456. It is, however, at least plausible that the eventual opposition of relatives or the changed opinion of Giustina could be due to the discovery of the servile condition of her husband, who asked for six months' time to present a contract of enfranchisement but – based on the curial registers – did not appear in the tribunal again.
175. X 2. 2. 3.
176. For other cases of annulment for servile condition in the medieval period, see *supra*, ch. 1, note 16. A case from 1698, for which at this phase of research I have not yet identified the origin, is in ASV, *CC*, *Synopsis*, vol. 2, c. 77. For the documentation of ASV, CC explored for this project see *supra*, note 149.
177. ASV, Biblioteche, S. Apostoli, 009 G 003: Martin de Azpilqueta, *Enchiridion, sive Manuale confessariorum*, foll. 320–337v, 333r–335r.
178. On the canonical age of marriage see A. Esmein, *Le mariage en droit canonique*, pp. 211–216; J. Dauvillier, *Le mariage*, pp. 43–49, 140–141; and J. Gaudemet, *Il matrimonio in Occidente*, pp. 197–198.
179. S. Chojnacki, *Women and Men*, p. 195.
180. See *infra*, ch. 6.
181. ASPV, *CM*, vol. 17, Marietta Barbaro *vs* Matteo Giustiniani, 1516, c. 167.
182. Ibid., c. 164.
183. Ibid., c. 171.
184. "In matrimonio carnalis malitia suppleat aetatem." Gl. "Nubilis" ad X 4. 2 14.
185. On literacy and school in Renaissance Italy, and in particular in Venice, see V. Baldo, *Alunni, maestri e scuole*; P. F. Grendler, *Schooling in Renaissance Italy*; G. Ortalli, *Scuole e maestri*; E. Becchi, *L'istruzione di base*.
186. "Un bestiolo et senza inzegno, et instabile, et quello ch'el dixe ozi el niega doman."
187. "Io non so tropo ben scriver."
188. On the impunibility of *puer* in penal law of the era, see G. F. Falchi, *L'omicidio*, pp. 30–34; T. Gatti, *L'impunibilità*, pp. 131–132; G. Zordan, *Il diritto e la procedura criminale*, pp. 47–48, 211–212; T. Dean, *Crime and Justice*, p. 100; E. Orlando, *Morire per gioco*,

pp. 32–46, and Idem, *Gioco, violenza e punibilità*. On the many erosions of the principle of the impunity of pre-pubescents, see O. Niccoli, *Il seme della violenza*, pp. 10–14.
189. *Ibid.* p. 10.
190. S. Chojnacki, *Women and Men*, pp. 186–205 and 227–243.
191. Regarding dowries, see *supra*, § 6.
192. X 4. 2. 14.
193. L. Ferrante, *Il matrimonio disciplinato*, p. 914.
194. S. Chojnaci, *Women and Men*, pp. 186–205; D. Herlihy-C. Klapisch-Zuber, *I Toscani e le loro famiglie*, pp. 541–547; J. Kirshner-A. Molho, *Marriage Alliance*. For the minor cities of the Veneto James Grubb argues instead that the "child brides" were very rare, only 4 % married at 16 and none before that age. J. Grubb, *La famiglia*, p. 26.
195. L. Ferrante, *Il matrimonio disciplinato;* K. Meek, *La donna la famiglia e la legge*; S. Seidel Menchi, *La fanciulla e la clessidra*; P. Benussi, *Oltre il processo*; C. Cristellon, *La sposa in convento*; E. Orlando, *Pubertà e matrimonio*; U. Parente- P Scaramella, *I processi matrimoniali napoletani*.
196. See the case from Vicenza cited by S. Seidel Menchi, *La fanciulla e la clessidra*, p. 155. Also L. Ferrante, *Il matrimonio disciplinato*, p. 919, mentions the marriage of a boy (who was between 10 and 12 at the time of his marriage).
197. The document, analyzed by E. Orlando, *Pubertà e matrimonio*, previously noted by P. Benussi, *Oltre il processo*, p. 169, is exceptional for both its thoroughness and date (1455).
198. X 3. 32. 2.
199. J. Gaudemet, *Il matrimonio in Occidente*, p. 124.
200. S. Seidel Menchi, *I tribunali del matrimonio: bilancio di una ricerca*, pp. 32–33.
201. M. Bellomo, *Ricerche sui rapporti patrimoniali tra i coniugi*, pp. 187–222, and Idem, *Dote nel diritto intermedio*, pp. 24–31; J. Kirshner, *"Maritus lucretur dotem uxoris sue premortue"*; G. P. Massetto, *Il lucro dotale*; C. Valsecchi, *"Causa matrimonialis est gravis et ardua,"* pp. 431–462; G. Marchetto, *Matrimoni incerti*.
202. In the period under investigation the age of menarche is not documented, except in isolated cases. The best reference available, although it is rough, would be the median age of menarche in eighteenth-century France, which was 15 years and 9 months. It should be noted that this refers to the daughters of the patriciate, that is a

privileged category in terms of diet and lifestyle. See E. Shorter, *L'age des premières règles en France*, p. 497; and S. Seidel Menchi, *La fanciulla e la clessidra*. p. 143.
203. See *supra*, ch. 2, § 8.
204. ASPV, *CM*, vol. 3, fasc. 5, Angela Martini *vs* Enrico Bruno Teutonico, 1471; also S. Seidel Menchi, *La fanciulla e la clessidra*, p. 153.
205. See *infra*, § 8.
206. On the opinions of theorists regarding free choice and the importance of following one's own inclinations to reach happiness, see R. Ago, *Giovani nobili*, in particular pp. 192–193. Some medical treatises from the sixteenth century identify the lack of pleasure experienced by women in the sexual act as the principle cause of sterility. For doctors like Paré and Liebault, those fathers who "even though warned by science and experience" force their daughters into a marriage against their will were guilty "in the eyes of nature herself." See E. Berriot-Salvatore, *Il discorso della medicina*, in particular p. 379.
207. For an example of attention to the attractiveness of the bride, see in particular ASPV, *CM*, vol. 15, Pietro Dandolo *vs* Querina Bollani, 2 May 1515. The attractiveness of the groom is particularly exalted in ASPV, *FC*, vol. 3, Hieronimo Valaresso *vs* Marietta di Jacopo Michiel, 1532.
208. "Dum dictus Nicolaus requireret copulam carnalem et ipsa Angela recusaret, dictus Nicolaus dicebat: Non vostu' esser mia moier? Et mi ge respondeva: Ma de sì quando sarò vostra moier e farò ciò che vui vole'. Dicens etiam interrogata: Questo Niccolò me ha basà et tocà come fano i novici et le novice insieme, et havemo dormido in un lecto, et qualche volta semo romasi soli lui et mi, et lui ha cercato de usar cun mi come fa el marido cum la moier, ma non me par ch'el sia anda' tanto avanti ch'el me habia tolta la mia verginità. Dicens interrogata: Queste cosse e podeva haver da anni dodese in tredese over quatordese et anche più, perché quando lui se partì de casa nostra e' podeva havere a mio iuditio circa anni sedese, subdens etiam interrogata: el lassava far queste cosse cerca la mia persona perché el tegniva per mio marido. Iterum monita quod debeat libere dicere veritatem se questo Niccolò è anda' tanto avanti cum lei ch'el ge habia tolto la sua verginità, respondit: mi me par de no." ASPV, *CM*, vol. 7, Niccolò q. Dominici Cortesii *vs* Angela filia Sebastiani Cavazza, 1503–1508.

209. "Che fosse contenta," "de non toccarla," "copulam carnalem... non perfecit quia dicta Helisabet se dolere dicebat et non posse pati perfectionem copule carnalis," "interrogata de copula carnale respondit: el me ha ben tocha', ma el non me a tolto la verginità," "Mio padre el me ha manda' [a marito] tropo a bonora, almen ch'io avesse habuto vent'anni." ASPV, *CM*, vol. 7, Andrea de Ballinio de Brixia *vs* Helisabeth filia Petri de Flandria, 1504.
210. On the debate relative to marriage at the Council of Trent, see the bibliography cited *supra*, note 53.
211. A. Molho, *Marriage Alliance*. On the question of clandestine marriages as a threat to parental authority, see A.J. Finch, *Parental Authority*, in particular p. 196, for examples of parents who disobeyed the dispositions of the ecclesiastical tribunal about the marriages of their children.
212. T. Dean, *Fathers and Daughters*, p. 91; and D. Lombardi, *Matrimoni di Antico Regime*, pp. 35–59.
213. G. Cozzi, *Padri, figli e matrimoni clandestini*, pp. 184–185. On the politics of regulation and control of noble marriage, see S. Chojnacki, *Women and Men in Renaissance Venice*, pp. 53–75.
214. See in particular, ASPV, *CM*, vol. 9, Marco Antonio de Stefani *vs* Lucretia q. Simonis Vacha, 1506–1507; *CM*, vol. 9, Martino q. Baptiste Cursi *vs* Giovanna de Liberalis de Arteno, vol. 15, Pietro Dandolo *vs* Quirina Bollani, 1507. On the quantitative data from the Venetian marital causes see *infra*, ch. 6. On parental opposition to marriages as the cause of a litigation, see also R. Houlbrooke, *Church Courts*, p. 62.
215. ASPV, *CM*, vol. 6, Giovanni di Luchino a Serico *vs* Cassandra de Marconibus, 1492–1493; ASPV, *AMP*, reg. 34, Antonia q. Alegreti *vs* Giorgio da Cattaro, 16 January 1475; C. Cristellon, *La sposa in convento*, pp. 140–146. See also *supra*, ch. 4, § 5.
216. See for York F. Pedersen, *Marriage Disputes*, pp. 129–133, for Castille F. J. Lorenzo Pinar, *Actitudes violentas*, p. 170, for Venice ASPV, *AMP*, reg. 11, Ventura di Francesco *vs* Jacopo Polo, 1446; also *supra*, ch. 4, § 7.
217. For examples, see ASPV, *CM*, vol. 6, Giovanni di Luchino a Serico *vs* Cassandra de Marconibus, 1492–1493; ASPV, *AMP*, reg. 24, Antonia q. Alegreti *vs* Giorgio da Cattaro, 16 January 1475.
218. The phrase "et de nocte" follows this but is crossed out. Nocturnal encounters would have made the relationship suspicious. On the

negative connotation of nocturnal actions cfr, more in general, R. Erich, *In der Stunde der Nacht*. For Venice S. Piasentini, *Alla luce della luna*.

219. "L'è vero che como fano li inamorati molte volte io ho parlato de dì con el dicto Martin palam et publice, perché io li voleva ben a lui e lui a mi… El nostro amor comenzò el zorno de Ogni Santo, et serano ani tre a la festa de Ogni Santo proximo… et questo amor è durato tra lui e mi fino alla festa di S. Victore proximo passato, et al continuo tuto questo tempo è continuato el nostro amor… Sì che molte volte ho etiam parlato in secreto cum dicto Martin… il qual veniva lì a quela villa per amor mio, per vedermi e parlarmi, e parlavami in su la strada passando la zente, et li parlamenti nostri erano che io voleva ben a lui e lui a mi."

220. "Perchè havea intention de tuor quelli che mio padre me daria, et s'el mi havessi facto domandar a mio patre, haveria cusì tolto lui como uno altro." ASPV, *CM*, vol. 9, Martino Cursio *vs* Giovanna di Giovanni de Liberalis de Arteno, 1507.

221. "Cridata e abbandonata." "A cà del diavolo." See respectively ASPV, *CM*, vol. 12, Clara Marcello *vs* Francesco de Orlandis, 1512; vol. 9, Marco Antonio de Stefani *vs* Lucrezia q. Simonis Vacha, 1506–1507; *CM*, vol. 12, Domenico a Lectis *vs* Andriana Bono, 1507–1509. Disinheritance of daughters younger than twenty-five who had had sexual relations without the responsibility of their father was allowed by Venetian law. See D. Hacke, *"Non lo volevo per marito in alcun modo,"* p. 202 and note 22. See also *infra*, note 223.

222. See beyond the documents cited in the following notes, N. Zemon Davis, *Il dono*, p. 93, which mentions a case of a Tuscan bachelor merchant resident in Lyon who excluded his sister, guilty of marrying "without my consent and against my will," from her inheritance and declared that he wanted to annul an inheritance destined for another sister if she lived with the erring relative; also A. Sorbelli, *Il comune rurale*, p. 174, note 67, cited in J. Kirshner, *Baldus de Ubaldis*, p. 144 and note 69, which mentions a daughter disinherited by her father because she had contracted a marriage he did not like. For examples of statutes that allowed for disinheritance for marriages contracted against parental will, see Ibid., p. 136. The motives for which children could be disinherited authorized parents also to deny them alimony. Ibid., p. 134 and note 37. About the norms and practices of disinheritance for lack of respect for parental authority

regarding marriage, see for Sweden M. Korpiola, *Between Betrothal and Bedding*, p. 167–175.

223. "Quello che vogliono li mei." ASPV, *CM*, vol. 9, Marco Antonio de Stefani *vs* Lucrezia q. Simonis Vacha, 1506–1507. ASVe, *Notarile testamenti*, b. 271, n. 569, Testamentum domine Paule relicta q. Symonis Vacha, 7 April 1507, Atti Bernardus de Cavaneis. Silent disinheritance "was hazardous, for the permitted party would likely bring an action to have the testament nullified." See J. Kirshner, *Baldus de Ubaldis*, p. 122. On the law and successive practices in Venice see A. Bellavitis, *Famille, Genre, Transmission*, in particular pp. 35–53 and pp. 44–46 on *ab intestato* succession. Another example of a mother who sought to control the marital life of her daughter through her will is in ASVe, *Notarile testamenti*, b. 271, n. 583, Testamentum domine Perine uxor ser Johannis Vidutii, atti Bernardus de Cavaneis, 19 April 1515 (Pierina's daughter, Polissena, was involved in a marital cause conserved in ASPV, *CM*, vol. 13, Iohannis de Masonibus *vs* Polissena Vidutiis.)

224. BNF, P.7.2, Antonino (S.) Vescovo di Firenze, *Confessionale omnis mortalium cura (1470 c.)*, ch. *eii*.

225. On the shared common lay marital ethic with secular clergy, see *supra*, ch. 4, § 6 and the bibliography cited there.

226. See in particular ASPV, *CM*, vol. 45, Lucretia Bondumier *vs* Hieronimo Mudazzo, 1546. For an example of a maternal curse thrown against a son if he married the girl she did not like, see *CM*, vol. 9, Domenico a Lectis *vs* Andriana Bono, 1507–1509; an example of a maternal curse is also in F. Pedersen, *Marriage Disputes*, p. 109, note 6.

227. E. Brambilla, *Dagli sponsali civili al matrimonio sacramentale*, p. 983. Regarding the figure of the *mulier audax* see L. Ferrante, *Gli sposi contesi*, p. 348.

228. C. Cristellon, *Does the Priest Have to Be There?*

229. V. Hunecke, *Der venezianische Adel*, p. 15. Based on the data furnished by the author, from the mid-seventeenth century an eighth of patrician marriages were celebrated according to the secret rite. See also L. De Biase, *Amore di Stato*.

230. In the sixteenth century the institute of primogeniture was common across all the aristocratic families of western Europe and from the second half of the century continually augmented the number of

bachelors, who in the seventeenth century constituted, in Italy and France, more than half of all adult men. See J. P. Cooper, *Patterns of Inheritance*; also R. Ago, *Giovani nobili*, p. 376. For a Venetian example of the strategies intended to guarantee the unity of the patrimony, see J. C. Davis, *A Venetian Family*.

231. See *supra*, ch. 1.
232. L. Di Biase, *Amore di Stato*, p. 15.
233. The *sbirri* were a proto-police force. Ibid., pp. 21–22, 32–40.
234. Ibid.
235. V. Hunecke, *Der venezianische Adel*, pp. 238–252. In general, on the new eighteenth-century sensibility regarding customs and on its repercussions for family and political life, see R. Bizzocchi, *A Lady's Man*.
236. On *meticulosus* marriage in post-conciliar Venice, see D. Hacke, *"Non lo volevo per marito in alcun modo."* For Castile see F.J. Lorenzo Pinar, *Actitudes violentas*; for Navarre M.J. Campo Guinea, *La fuerza*; for Regensburg C. Deutsch, *Ehegerichtsbarkeit in Bistum Regensburg* and Eadem, *Konsensehe oder Zwangheirat?* Cases from the German empire in L. Schmugge, *Ehen vor Gericht*, pp. 166–169. See also J. Kermode-G. Walker, *Women*; L. Gowing, *Domestic Dangers*. J. Ferraro, *Marriage Wars*.
237. Only 6 of the 706 cases indexed for the period from 1420 to 1500. See *infra*, ch. 6. All these cases were brought by the women, and 5 were cases for annulment for absence of consent and minority.
238. The exceptions are ASPV, *AMP*, reg, 26, Giorgio Bruna *vs* Trevisana figlia di Francesco da Monfalcon, 25 June 1465; *AMP*, reg. 33, sententia seperationis matrimonialis Agnexine Sancti Angeli filie Georgii de Lacu *vs* Victorem Nigro Sancti Nicolai, 6 May 1474.
239. In particular ASPV, *AMP*, reg, 26, Petrus a Lacu *vs* Catarucia filia Bone, 1465, where it was the mother who celebrated the marriage. *AMP*, reg. 32, Blasio Tubicini *vs* Jacoba filia Dominaci, 19 August 1472.
240. According to C. Donahue Jr., *Law, Marriage and Society*, p. 100, this type of litigation reveals "an arranged marriage that has for some reason gone awry."
241. See ASPV, *CM*, vol. 11, Vincenzo Quirino *vs* Caterina Mauro, 1509–1512; ASPV, *AMP*, reg, 26, Giorgio Bruna *vs* Trevisana figlia di Francesco da Monfalcon, 25 June 1465 and *AMP*, reg. 26, Petrus a Lacu *vs* Catarucia filia Bone 16 May 1465.

242. This for example is sustained by Bartolo. See G. Marchetto, *Il "matrimonium meticulosum"*
243. "Grintoso, che per puocha cosa el mena zoso."
244. ASPV, *CM*, vol. 9, Domenico a Lectis *vs* Andriana Bono; *CM*, vol. 12, Caterina de Teodoris *vs* Francisco Rubeo. On the reactions of brides before the unwanted groom, see also F.J. Lorenzo Pinar, *Actitudes violentas*, pp. 169–170. On the fact that ritual allowed for the bride to not express her assent to the marriage immediately, see S. Chojnacki, *Valori patrizi nel tribunale patriarcale*; M. Seidel, *Hochzeitsikonographie im Trecento*.
245. ASPV, *AMP*, reg. 26, Petrus a Lacu *vs* Catarcia filia Bone.
246. X 4. 1. 21.
247. ASPV, *CM*, vol. 2, fasc. 15, Franceschine Britti *vs* Francisco Agnusdei, 1465–1466.
248. "Buon viso." ASPV, *AMP*, reg. 26, Giorgio Bruna *vs* Trevisana di Francesco da Monfalcone.
249. "In villa," "quel dal inferno." ASPV, *CM*, vol. 12, Clara Marcello *vs* Francesco de Orlandi.
250. On the rituality of consent and *affectus* see *supra*, ch. 2 § 9.
251. ASPV, *CM*, vol. 2, fasc. 7, Ursina Basso *vs* Alvise Soncin, 1462. Also A.M. Lazzari- S. Seidel Menchi, *"Evidentemente gravida."* For the presence of priests see ASPV, *CM*, vol. 11, Ambrosina de Blasonibus *vs* Marco Antonio Bacinetto.
252. See *supra*, ch. 4, § 6, and note 128.
253. "Squartino."
254. ASPV, *CM*, vol. 2, fasc. 12, Helena *vs* Alvise Cavazza, 1462–1463. See also *supra*, ch. 4, § 2.
255. For the intervention of the friar see ASPV, *CM*, vol. 11, Ambrosina de Blasonibus *vs* Marco Antonio Bacinetto, 1509–1510, for the appearance of the groom in the house of the bride after the aggression of her brother, see *CM*, vol. 16, Cornelia Zabarella *vs* Buzacarino de Buzacarinis, 1515. Aggression cost Cornelia's brother and his thugs a trial in the Avogaria di Comun, part of which is conserved in a copy among the documents for the marriage trial.
256. On the Esecutori contro la Bestemmia see *supra*, ch. 1 and note 9.
257. To demonstrate that the nuptial ceremony had been celebrated only by *vim et metum* became superfluous because of the conciliar disposition that deprived any marriage performed without a priest, witnesses, and required publication of validity.

258. About the words and gestures of *affectus* see *supra*, ch. 2, § 9. Regarding strategies and cause language in post-conciliar cases of "rape," see G. Arrivo, *Seduzioni, promesse, matrimoni.*
259. See *supra*, ch. 4, § 2.
260. See G. Alessi, *Il gioco degli scambi.*
261. D. Lombardi, *Matrimoni di Antico Regime,* pp. 135–137.

CHAPTER 6

Venetian "Matrimonialia": A Quantitative Analysis (1420–1500)

In the following pages are the results of my work indexing and cataloguing data from the Venetian marriage litigations for the period 1420–1500.[1] In the analysis of the data presented here it should be noted that the material used is not entirely constituted by causes but also includes all those cases of marital conflict under the jurisdiction of the ecclesiastical judge, many of which did not reach suit but were instead resolved by the magistrate's mandate.

CLASSIFICATION

The 706 cases of marital conflict under the jurisdiction of the patriarchal tribunal of Venice can be classified according to this table:

Classification	Total number of cases	Male plaintiff	Female plaintiff	Plaintiff not specified
Marriage	270	145	125	–
Annulment	133	47	85	1
Separation	118	72	46	–
Betrothal	10	4	6	–
No classification	175	85	75	15
Total	706	353	337	16

© The Author(s) 2017
C. Cristellon, *Marriage, the Church, and its Judges in Renaissance Venice, 1420–1545*, Early Modern History: Society and Culture, DOI 10.1007/978-3-319-38800-7_6

The high percentage of non-classifiable cases is due to the fact that the majority of fifteenth-century litigations are preserved in the registers of the curia. The curial registers for the most part document only the procedural part of the case, which includes the citation and the appearance of the parties, procurators, and lawyers, the presentation of witnesses, and the dispositions of the magistrates, but they do not always specify the subject of the conflict, only noting that the parties presented themselves "for the marriage litigations between them" (*pro causa matrimoniali inter eos*). In addition, sometimes the documentation does not make it possible to distinguish between the plaintiff and the defendant.

Quantitative analysis of the data has revealed a clear prevalence of cases of alleged marriage. The high percentage of cases of this type is connected to the fact that in the pre-Tridentine period, the expression of nuptial consent was not bound by a certain ritual formula nor by the presence of witnesses. The celebration of a marriage – sometimes difficult to prove – could be easily contested in court, just as a union that assumed the marks of a nuptial bond in the eyes of the community was likely to be recognized as a marriage by ecclesiastical sentence, regardless of whether they could prove that it had been celebrated.[2]

Men and women brought suits for alleged marriage beginning with a declaration of the validity of the bond in equal numbers. But in requests for cessation of defamation (a technical term to indicate that the opposing party spread rumors that he or she had contracted a marriage with the plaintiff), men were the primary initiators. In both of these cases this typology was more often resolved in favor of the men.

Among the annulment cases the most prominent type is annulment for a previous marriage. This type of litigations is connected to social and geographic mobility (only 4.7% of the parties in these cases were born in Venice).[3]

Causes for annulment are characterized by the prevalence of female initiative. The juridical construction of *fragilitas sexus*,[4] which attributed to women a weakness and consequently an innate need for protection, sometimes gave women more agency in the court. In suits for annulment for *vis et metus*, for example, the women could use the fact that the tribunal considered the type and intensity of violence capable of constraining a woman to an unwanted marriage was much broader and more diverse that what was capable of inducing a man to marry.[5]

A considerable percentage of annulment litigations (9%) concerned the minority of the bride, that she was younger than 12 years old when she was married. To the extent that minority was sufficient motive to annul a marriage, only four of the 12 requests appealed to the immaturity of the girl. The others brought up the fact that she was forced and subjected to violence, or they claimed the absence of consummation[6]- a factor that, as was noted, had juridical relevance because the occurrence of sexual relations could contribute to lowering the legal threshold for marriageable age.[7] Unlike what happened in other dioceses that have been subjected to quantitative investigation,[8] cases for separation in Venice reveal a clear prevalence of male initiative. If, however, the complaint presented by the plaintiff is considered, the data relative to Venetian *matrimonialia* are in harmony with those of source bases previously analyzed. Even in Venice, in fact, it was generally women who asked for separation, while men most often came to the tribunal to get their wives back. It should also be considered that requests to restart cohabitation led the judge to issue a mandate that required absent spouses to go back to their partners or to present themselves in court to explain why they would not do so. If the receiver of the mandate came to court to contest it and began a marriage litigation, or if instead the parties began living together again or came to a private accord, the proceeding ended and only traces of it remain in the curial registers. As the cause documents record the request for separation but not necessarily the preceding request to reinstate cohabitation (which was often the motive of the litigation), it is possible that the prevalence of male-initiated cases of separation is not a Venetian peculiarity, but a characteristic common to other dioceses that lack curial registers.

Separation was only granted for adultery and violence. Regarding separation, canon law considered male adultery the same as female adultery. It should be noted, however, that while men requested separation only for adultery, women generally requested separation because of violence and the misuse of their dowries.[9]

Litigations regarding betrothals, which debated the legitimacy of dissolving a marriage that had been promised but the promise of marriage that was not followed by consummation, were generally resolved quickly, sometimes without even a debate. The median duration of these causes was two to four months: the longest lasted six months and the shortest only consisted of the presentation of the request to the magistrate and his immediate dissolution of the promise. The sentences that have been preserved always pronounced in favor of dissolving the betrothal, even though doctrine had established the obligation to maintain the sworn promise of marriage as well as the simple promise of marriage.[10]

Sentences

Litigations with sentences	253
Litigations without sentences	453

Phases of Judgment

Litigations of the first grade	530
Litigations of the second grade (appeals)	22
Not classifiable	145

Classification

1. Marriage (270 cases)

Male plaintiff: 145

Petition: declaration of validity of marriage	96
Sentence: declaration of validity of marriage	24
Sentence: declaration of nullity of marriage	19
Sentence: none	53
Petition: declaration of nullity of marriage (cessation of defamation)	32
Sentence: declaration of nullity of marriage	20
Sentence: declaration of validity of marriage	2
Sentence: none	10

Female plaintiff: 125

Petition: declaration of validity of marriage	96
Sentence: declaration of validity of marriage	25
Sentence: declaration of nullity of marriage	30
Sentence: none	41
Petition: declaration of nullity of marriage (cessation of defamation)	22
Sentence: declaration of nullity of marriage	10
Sentence: declaration of validity of marriage	4
Sentence: none	8
Noble plaintiff and defendant	9
Noble plaintiff	12
Noble defendant	15

2. Annulment: 133 cases (19 cases of annulment with a non-classifiable petition)

Male plaintiff: 47

Petition: annulment for preceding marriage	36
Sentence: declaration of nullity of marriage	17
Sentence: declaration of validity of marriage	3
Sentence: none	16
Petition: annulment for sacred orders	2
Sentence: declaration of nullity of marriage	2
Sentence: declaration of validity of marriage	–
Sentence: none	–
Petition: annulment for affinity alone	3
Sentence: declaration of nullity of marriage	1
Sentence: declaration of validity of marriage	–
Sentence: none	2

Female plaintiff: 85

Petition: annulment for preceding marriage	48
Sentence: declaration of nullity of marriage	23
Sentence: declaration of validity of marriage	1
Sentence: none	24
Petition: annulment for lack of consent	3
Sentence: declaration of nullity of marriage	1
Sentence: declaration of validity of marriage	–
Sentence: none	2
Petition: annulment for absence of consent and minority	4
Sentence: declaration of nullity of marriage	3
Sentence: declaration of validity of marriage	–
Sentence: none	1
Petition: annulment for minority alone	4
Sentence: declaration of nullity of marriage	1
Sentence: declaration of validity of marriage	–
Sentence: none	3
Petition: annulment for minority and absence of consummation	3
Sentence: declaration of nullity of marriage	1
Sentence: declaration of validity of marriage	–
Sentence: none	2
Petition: annulment for minority and sacred orders	1
Sentence: declaration of nullity of marriage	1
Sentence: declaration of validity of marriage	–
Sentence: none	–

(continued)

(continued)

Petition: annulment for sacred orders	2
Sentence: declaration of nullity of marriage	2
Sentence: declaration of validity of marriage	–
Sentence: none	–
Petition: annulment for affinity alone	4
Sentence: declaration of nullity of marriage	1
Sentence: declaration of validity of marriage	1
Sentence: none	2
Petition: annulment for affinity and consanguinity	1
Sentence: declaration of nullity of marriage	1
Sentence: declaration of validity of marriage	–
Sentence: none	–
Petition: annulment for consanguinity alone	1
Sentence: declaration of nullity of marriage	1
Sentence: declaration of validity of marriage	–
Sentence: none	–
Petition: annulment for servile condition	1
Sentence: declaration of nullity of marriage	1
Sentence: declaration of validity of marriage	–
Sentence: none	–
Petition: annulment for impotence	5
Sentence: declaration of nullity of marriage	–
Sentence: declaration of validity of marriage	1
Sentence: none	4
Noble plaintiff and defendant	2
Noble plaintiff	4
Noble defendant	2

3. Separation: 118 cases (2 cases with non-classifiable petition)

Male plaintiff: 72

Petition: separation	**12**
Sentence: separation	9
Sentence: obligation of cohabitation	1
Sentence: none	2
Petition: restoration of cohabitation	59
Sentence: restoration of cohabitation	3
Sentence: separation	5
Sentence: none	51

Female plaintiff: 46

Petition: separation	32
Sentence: separation	11
Sentence: obligation of cohabitation	3
Sentence: none	18
Petition: restoration of cohabitation	13
Sentence: restoration of cohabitation	2
Sentence: separation	–
Sentence: none	11
Noble plaintiff and defendant	7
Noble plaintiff	7
Noble defendant	9

4. Betrothals: 10 cases

Male plaintiff: 4

Petition: dissolving of betrothal	3
Sentence: dissolving of betrothal	2
Sentence: respect of betrothal	–
Sentence: none	1
Petition: respect of betrothal	1
Sentence: respect of betrothal	–
Sentence: dissolving of betrothal	–
Sentence: none	1

Female plaintiff:

Petition: dissolving of betrothal	5
Sentence: dissolving of betrothal	1
Sentence: respect of betrothal	–
Sentence: none	4
Petition: respect of betrothal	1
Sentence: respect of betrothal	–
Sentence: dissolving of betrothal	–
Sentence: none	1
Noble plaintiff and defendant	1
Noble plaintiff	1
Noble defendant	1

Notes

1. The quantitative data presented here were compiled through a systematic exploration of the four series that constitute the Venetian source base (cfr. *supra*, ch. 1, point 1). For the period 1420–1465 this is the series *Actorum, mandatorum, praeceptorum* (regs. 2–27), for the period 1452–1500 the series *Causarum matrimoniorum* (vols. 1–6) and *Filciae causarum*, (vol. 1), 1464–1465, 1482 also have the series *Sententiarum* (regs. 1 and 3).
2. See ch. 2, § 9 and ch. 5, § 2.
3. See ch. 3, § 4.
4. See ch. 4, § 1.
5. See ch. 5, § 9.
6. The same thing happened in Lucca. See C. Meeck, *La donna, la famiglia e la legge*, pp. 140–143. See also the observations of S. Seidel Menchi, *La fanciulla e la clessidra*, in particular pp. 153–155.
7. See ch. 5, § 7.
8. See G. Ciappelli, *I processi matrimoniali*, and in the same volume, V. Chilese, *I processi matrimoniali veronesi;* M. Poian, *I processi matrimoniali dell'Archivio Vescovile di Feltre;* U. Parente - P. Scaramella, *I processi matrimoniali napoletani;* L. Faoro, *Il ricorso alla carcerazione*.
9. Request for separation only for adultery was presented by women in 4 cases, corresponding to 27%, while for men it was the reason for 11 cases, corresponding to 73%.
10. See ch. 4, § 2.

CHAPTER 7

Conclusions

This work focused on the ecclesiastical tribunal and on marriage understood both as an institution and as an event experienced by the protagonists in the causes as well as by the community called to testify in court. The attention paid to the procedure, beyond filling a gap about the hermeneutics of marriage litigations, has allowed me to analyze the dialogue between the ecclesiastical hierarchy and the faithful on a subject that was regarded as central to society and that touched upon the most intimate sphere of the individual.

This dialogue was not limited to the couples involved in the conflict, but to a wide swath of the population that was called to intervene in the suit and was interested in its outcome, either directly or indirectly. This, in fact, had important economic and social consequences for the community that watched over the formation and dissolution of the bond. It could also affect the decisions of the magistrate both through the testimony he heard (and we have noted how broad and socially diverse the list of those who were admitted to testify was) and by influencing the stories told by witnesses, as what they debated in the halls of the tribunal came to be discussed outside of it and then brought up again, with the tacit acceptance of the court.

While the voices of the community influenced the decisions of the marriage tribunal, the actions of the court radiated through a swath of the population much wider than those who used it. Those who were called to depose about a controversial union – as well as those who listened to the stories told outside the halls of the tribunal, or who were informed about the outcome of the conflict – reflected on the nuptial rites and practices with which they were familiar and were sometimes prompted to modify them.

What becomes clear in the course of this research is a dimension of flexibility in pre-modern marriage and consequently of the family, which the historiography is sometimes reluctant to acknowledge, even though these results have already been reinforced by recent research.[1] With this information a comparison could be made between pre-Tridentine and post-Tridentine marriage that would allow us to understand the enormous effort made by the Church to assume control over marriage and the practices connected to it. The Church set out to fix a clear distinction between concubinage and marriage, to prohibit sexual relations between the affianced, and to censure bigamy. The persistence of some phenomena (e.g., cohabitation of the betrothed) allows us to describe this effort, at least in part, as in vain.[2]

In addition to cause documents, this work has also systematically used the registers of the acts of the curia which have previously only been explored in small samples. This new documentation has allowed for a deeper analysis of procedure and also for a reconstruction of the phases of recourse to the ecclesiastical judges before, after, or alternative to a litigation, illuminating some aspects of mediation conducted by the vicar in the conflict. Data taken from serial exploration of the acts of the curia – and this is probably their primary contribution – contradicts a common argument in the historiography, according to which women more frequently prompted causes for separation than men, confident of addressing themselves to a "filo-female" institution. However, as emerged in the course of this research, requests for separation were mostly begun as requests by husbands to reinstate cohabitation, launched only by a minority of women who had abandoned the conjugal bed and were determined to face the court – although with little probability of success – rather than to go back to their husband.

The subject of marriage was regulated by diverse sets of laws, distinct expressions of power and ideals that could interact, agree, and collide with one another. The judge had a large margin of discretion to use one more than another, and his action varied according to the types of litigations he found before him, whether they were for alleged marriage, annulment, or separation.

During the litigation, the vicar assumed for the most part a passive role, avoiding doing research on the truth and limiting himself to record a processual truth negotiated by the parties. The judge sometimes assumed an active role during the interrogation of women, who were given the responsibility of mediating between their family and ecclesiastics. The practices and the tenor of the dialogue between judges and women allow us to backdate, at least to the fifteenth century, the origins of the privileged rapport between men of the Church and women, which historiography generally attributes to the politics of controlling individuals' and families' behavior after the Council of Trent. But the attention of ecclesiastics to the sphere of female conscience also reveals – in contrast with the tenor of rare male interrogations – the deep roots of a culture that tended to attribute to women and not to men a responsibility for the existence of a marriage and the cohesion of a family.

In the course of this work I have sought to compare the practices of the Venetian tribunal with those of other tribunals previously analyzed. The constant point of reference is naturally the work of Charles Donahue, who analyzed five tribunals (two English and three from the Franco-Belgian area), identifying in the diverse systems of property transmission the origins of various procedures among different courts. The pioneering work of Richard Helmholz and those dedicated to the tribunals of the German Empire (Thomas Albert, Christina Deutsch, Ludwig Schmugge) also constitute essential material. In the conclusions of this work I will thus limit myself to presenting the largest differences between the Venetian documentation and that of the tribunals previously studied.

Some differences are immediately perceptible. First of all, the serial production of Venetian marriage litigation records (and Italian cause records in general) clearly begins later than it does in the Franco-Belgian area, England, or German territories. While in these regions litigations were systematically recorded among acts of the curia beginning in the fourteenth century, in Venice this only happens after 1420, and in other dioceses even later. This discrepancy can be explained by the different organization of the tribunals and the different methods of production and conservation of documents. The chancery model of the churches on the other side of the Alps is contrasted in Italy with a Church marked by notaries,[3] which entrusted the recording and conservation of its acts to notaries both in the curia and in its own private benches. To the extent that in some episcopal seats we find episodes of the serial documentation of suits before the fifteenth century, only after that point did curias generally have a chancery entrusted with drafting, authenticating, copying, and archiving the documentation produced by the ecclesiastical forum.[4] For the preceding centuries Italian marriage litigations (the celebration of which is amply documented in treatises and frequent references in collections of canon law) are mostly available in notarial archives and occasionally in parish or cathedral chapter archives as, up through most of the thirteenth century, marriage cases were sometimes delegated to the cathedral canons or curates of the city.[5]

Italian documentation also diverges from the transalpine records in terms of quantity. The number of cases discussed in Venice is much smaller than the number in other regions of Europe that have been systematically studied.[6] There are strong reasons to believe that the resolution of marriage conflicts sometimes happened in an internal forum: the same marriage litigations, as we have seen, attest to this. Probably the role developed by confessors did not significantly influence the numeric scope of marriage litigations, since the practice of confession was not extremely widespread before the Council of Trent. Moreover, confession does not explain the peculiarity of Italy, as there are no reasons to believe that confession was more popular in Italy than in France, England, or Germany. The same confessors, however, that appear in this book sometimes made themselves promoters of the patriarchal tribunal's authority on the subject of marital conflict.

An explanation of the quantitative disparity found between Italian and French marriage causes could be found in the role of the Italian notary: it is plausible that, beyond supplying the function of the episcopal chancery up to the fifteenth century, Italian notaries competed with the ecclesiastical tribunal for jurisdiction over nuptial cases, recording the private regulation of conflicts both in terms of the bond's establishment and in terms of separating and identifying the line between concubinage and marriage.

The difference between French and Venetian documentation (but also – to a lesser degree – German and English) is not only quantitative but also qualitative. A relevant piece of data that emerges from my research is the richness of the Venetian documentation: the precision, refinement, and flexibility of recording, which has no comparison anywhere else (not even in England, where the documentation is much more lively than German and French records). In the Holy Roman Empire as in France, the political push to respect the norms that required a marriage be celebrated in public translated, in the tribunal, to the exclusion of social recognition of the marriage as proof: proof of the marital bond had to instead be based on the demonstration of its celebration according to canonical norms. Rituals of affection, that series of clues and presumptions of a conjugal bond's existence, which in Venice playing a fundamental role in proving the bond and which were abundantly described and minutely referenced by witnesses, were not worth mentioning in Paris – or, at least, not worth being recorded. Something else happened in England, where a long tradition of common law guaranteed that the voice of the community had determinative weight in court.

The richness of Venetian documentation also comes from the ecclesiastical judge's attention to the individual soul, which translated to extremely intimate interrogations. I believe this may also have been connected to pre-Tridentine marriage practices; that is, to the difficulty of ascertaining the moment of consent, which only the couple could be certain about since it was an intimate occurrence. In regions where more formal and more objectively verifiable parameters determined the validity of a marriage bond, and where there was a political agreement in place intended to discourage the establishment of marriages in forms not allowed by the canons, this attention to the inner dimension of the faithful did not develop – just as it would be gone by the end of the sixteenth century in Italy, when the Tridentine decrees imposed a single and objectively identifiable nuptial celebration.

In closing I will suggest three new approaches to matrimonial documentation, corresponding to some prospective investigations that seem particularly promising to me.

1. The Venetian procedural documentation makes reference to various lexicons that marriage could apply, both in its constants (touching of the hand, the kiss) and in its variables, determined by the social and geographic provenance of the parties: a marriage established before an image of the Virgin, for example, was generally celebrated by immigrants of Greek origin and evoked the Greek Orthodox custom of swearing oaths on an image of the Virgin instead of the Gospel.

Marriage litigations allow us to reconstruct the language of symbols, signs, and rituals of pre-Tridentine marriage, which were completely different from those of the post-Tridentine marriage with which we are familiar. The analysis of this semantic sometimes brings us to deceptive conclusions when they are conducted based on a post-Tridentine framework. The long debate on the "Arnolfini couple" of Van Eyck is an example. In recent times an illustrious researcher has denied that the scene painted by the Flemish artist was a marriage portrait,[7] while those who are familiar with pre-Tridentine marriage trials would not hesitate to associate the scene with a nuptial celebration, identifiable as much in the gestures of the protagonists as in the place in which the scene is set; in the objects present in the room – the clogs, the fruit, and so on, and in the attestation of the painter of having been present at the event.[8]

The production of the Venetian school in themes of love and marriage is intense and of the highest level. No work exists, however, that interprets these figurative documents. I argue that the combination of a plurality of figurative and verbal sources – primarily the marriage causes, indispensable for accessing concrete lived experience, but also treatises, notarial sources (nuptial and dowry contracts), and epistolary sources (it should be noted that cause documentation itself often preserved love letters[9]) – would allow us to fill this gap.

In recent art history an interpretive line has been developed that connects a series of paintings to marriage that were previously interpreted in a metaphoric or philosophical sense ('Amor sacro e Amor profano' (Sacred and Profane Love) in the Galleria Borghese)[10] or associated with mercenary love (the "Due dame veneziane" (Two Venetian women) of Carpaccio).[11] Paintings with explicit erotic content like "Venere e Amore" (Venus and Cupid) by Lotto or the Venus of Giorgione are now associated without hesitation with marriage and interpreted in the light of epithalamic poetry, considered epithalamia in painting form.[12] The attractiveness of the woman, rather than inhibiting the nuptial interpretation of the painting, reinforces it: based on the documentation we have examined, the erotic-amorous component assumed an important role in the definition of nuptial consent and in marriage; the attractiveness of the bride – upon which witnesses were called to testify – was adopted by her to prove the bond in the case of controversial marriages.[13] I argue that Venetian marriage litigations could allow the deciphering of some paintings of great importance and to correct the interpretative deformation of Renaissance marriage, deprived of its erotic-amorous component because it has been read through a post-Tridentine lens.[14]

2. We have seen how marriage litigations attributed a predominantly arbitrating position to the judge and assigned the direction of the proceeding to the parties involved, putting the burden of proof on the plaintiff and the responsibility for implementing the sentence on

the conscience of the parties. But we have also seen how the magistrate sometimes assumed the traits of the inquisitor and confessor.

The history of confession has produced a vast historiography,[15] playing on the fascination of an experience that is by its nature inscrutable and stretching to grasp its influence on western culture and the elaboration of its models in justice, education, and even psychoanalysis.[16] Historians of confession have had to use mostly normative or literary sources, which were often inspired by practice: hagiographic literature, stories of "exempla" for use by preachers, novels, iconographic sources, penitential books, canonical collections, confession manuals, and penitential *summae*.[17] The results of this book propose a source base exceptionally close to current debates on confession.

As we have seen, in marriage litigations the assumption of an active role by magistrates was principally manifested in interrogations of women. In their conduct, judges demonstrated that they were experts in the art of interrogation and in the practice of expedients that favored confession, as well as capable of establishing a dialogue with their interlocutrix, of gaining her faith, and of closing the distance between interrogator and interrogated. They were supported by notaries who recorded the questions and answers, noting even blushes and sudden displays of "audacity."[18] The joint actions of the magistrates and the extremely scrupulous notaries, both products "of a juridical-chancellory culture of humanistic imprint, endowed with a strong attention for language as a vehicle of signification," provide us with documents of extraordinary richness and density.[19] These interrogations are the closest thing to confession that has been documented[20]: the young woman who asked the vicar to suspend the recording of her declarations, to reveal herself to him in confidence, conferred on the judge the role of confessor and signaled the limits of what remains hidden to the historian.

3. The theory of consent, by which marriage was validated by the simple will of the couple, independent of the manner in which it was expressed, encouraged jurisprudential creativity and often the reconciliation between customary and canonical legal practices. As noted above, after a passionate debate the Council of Trent imposed the celebration of marriage by the priest, banns for three Sundays preceding the wedding, the presence of two or more witnesses at the marriage, and the registration of the act in parish registers.[21] The absence of the priest and of witnesses rendered the parties

unable to establish the marriage, nullifying the bond. With the obligatory presence of the priest and witnesses at weddings, questions relative to the existence of marriages were still far from being resolved. Often, in fact, the new norms, which were capable of being interpreted in different ways and of being manipulated, produced new problems. As Benedict XIV lamented, the conciliar fathers, in assigning the exclusive competence to celebrate marriages to the parish priest, had failed to establish with precision who this priest was.[22]

At the end of the council a dedicated congregation – the Congregation of the Council – was established, entrusted, among other things, with resolving questions that arose from the interpretation of Tridentine decrees. The Congregation's documentation is held in the Archivio Segreto Vaticano. For the most part it deals with – at least in terms of doubts about marriage – questions raised by bishops from around the Catholic world about the exercise of their function as judges of the diocesan tribunal, or cases sent to the bishop by parish priests and confessors: we find, in other words, cases of concrete management on the subject of marriage, and sometimes a report of confession.

The acts of the Congregation reveal the difficulty of adapting a magmatic subject like marriage to the rigidity of norms issued by Trent – a difficulty that interested laity and ecclesiastics, although in different ways, as well as the cardinals of the Congregation and the pope, who did not always express a unified opinion on the resolution of a particular case. The Congregation found itself confronted with diverse questions on the freedom of consent and parental authority; with the problems of marriages celebrated by a false priest, by one insubordinate to a bishop, or before a non-consenting priest, and so on. In the course of our survey of the documents of the Congregation of the Council, we have also found controversies that attest to the strong persistence of a pre-Tridentine conception of marriage: the periphery asked the center if a marriage celebrated without the priest, but before witnesses, and then consummated was truly null. Was it really possible that a rite of this type was not equivalent to a betrothal? Page after page clearly shows that not only the laity, but also a part of the ecclesiastical world that shared its values, had not enthusiastically adhered to the application of the council's decrees. The researcher who opens a trail of investigation through this rich documentation will see, not without surprise, how Tridentine norms that prescribed the presence of a priest at weddings were in turn perceived, endured, used, circumvented, and manipulated – as much by laity as by ecclesiastics – in order to establish an end to an already disagreeable marriage or to establish a socially transgressive union that was opposed by families, or even "heretical," in response to a pastoral request.[23] This documentation, barely explored now, should not be excluded from future studies on marriage.[24] The knowledge of pre-Tridentine marriage practices will allow us to evaluate and interpret their complexity.

Notes

1. W. Reinhard, *Lebensformen Europas*, pp. 199–226.
2. M. Pelaja, *Matrimonio e sessualità*.
3. R. Brentano, *Due chiese*, p. 309.
4. G. Chittolini, *"Episcopalis curiae notarius,"* pp. 221–232. C. Donati, *Curie, tribunali, cancellerie episcopali*.
5. E. Orlando, *Tribunali di curia*.
6. C. Donahue Jr., *Law, Marriage and Society*, pp. 625–632, has identified a median of 137 trials per year in Paris, the city closest to Venice in terms of population among those he examined. See for Venice, the data *supra*, Appendix, remembering that it is difficult to establish a median annual count of trials because the four documentary series in which marriage cases are found do not always overlap chronologically.
7. L. Campbell, *The Fifteenth Century Netherlandish Schools*, p. 198.
8. S. Seidel Menchi, *Cause matrimoniali e iconografia nuziale*.
9. J. M. Usunáriz, *'Volved ya la riendas, porque no os perdáis.'*
10. www.galleriaborghese.it/amorsacro. H. Borggrefe, *Titians sogenannte Himmlische und Irdische Liebe*.
11. http://www.archiviodellacomunicazione.it/Sicap/OpereArte/17 81/?WEB=MuseiVE. B. Aikema - B.L. Brown, *Pittura veneziana*.
12. www.metmuseum.org/art/collection/search/436918 and http:// skd-online-collection.skd.museum/de/contents/showSearch?id= 294844. R. Goffen, *Le donne di Tiziano*, and in the same volume, G.J.M. Weber, *Velata dal tempo*l; K. Christiansen, *Lorenzo Lotto*.
13. ASPV, *CM*, vol. 7, Bernardina de Garzonibus *vs* Bernardino conte di Collalto, 1500–1501.
14. Stimulating observations in S. Seidel Menchi, *Introduction*, http://www.skd.museum/uploads/pics/AM-185-PR01_x.jpg.
15. See the texts cited *supra*, ch. 4.
16. P. Brooks, *Troubling Confessions*, pp. 1–7.
17. For a list of sources used to investigate the history of confession, see R. Rusconi, *L'ordine dei peccati*, pp. 16–55.

18. "Audacia." See respectively, ASPV, *CM*, vol. 9, Michele Leoni *vs* Faustina Foscarin, 1507 and ASPV, *FC*, vol. 2, Antonio Busatto *vs* Raimunda Sicula, 3 June 1510.
19. S. Seidel Menchi, *I processi matrimoniali come fonte storica*, pp. 81–82, and more in general, pp. 68–82. The documentation of transalpine tribunals, for example, is for the most part constituted by protocols that record in summary manner the contents of the sessions of the tribunal. In the English and Franco-Belgian documentation, interrogators did not pay attention to the individual soul in a way comparable to Venice. See the bibliography *supra*, ch. 1 note 4. Seidel Menchi underlines the value of these sources as "ego documents." For more on this see W. Schulze (ed.) *Ego-Dokumente*, K. von Greyerz, *Selbstzeugnisse in der Frühen Neuzeit*, and more recently, G. Ciappelli (ed.), *Memoria, famiglia, identità*.
20. See *supra*, ch. 3, §§ 7–8.
21. On the debate over marriage see the bibliography cited *supra*, ch. 5, note 53. Here we limit ourselves to remembering that the Tametsi decree was voted in with one fourth of the assembly voting against it, the only time that happened at the council. See G. Zarri, *Recinti*, p. 209.
22. Benedicti XIV *Institutionum ecclesiasticarum*, Institutio 33, n. 3, p. 215.
23. C. Cristellon, *Does the Priest Have to Be There?* See for examples ASPV, CC, *Positiones sessiones*, b. 2, cc. 198–240; b. 58, c. 326, *Libri decretorum*, vol. 2, cc. 25–27.
24. On the Congregation of the Council see F. Romita, *Le origini della S.C. del Concilio;* on the archive of the Congregation, P. Caiazza, *L'archivio storico della Sacra Congregazione del Concilio*; F. Blouin, *Vatican Archives*, pp. 21–27; J.T. Noonan, *Power to Dissolve* above all for a valuable introduction to the varies series of the archive. A. Jacobson Schutte, *La Congregazione del Concilio*. Relative to marriage see also D. D'Avray-W. Menski, *Authenticating Marriages*, and B. Albani, *In universo christiano orbe*. The interest in this documentation relative to the subject of marriage is already noted by D. Lombardi, *Matrimoni in Antico Regime*, and G. Zarri, *Recinti*, pp. 232–234, 244–247. An important project directed by Benedetta Albani on the Congregation of the Council is in progress at the Max Planck Institute for European History of Law in Frankfurt am Main, which will include an inventory and systematic catalog of the Congregation's documents.

Abbreviations

ACV	Archivio della Curia Vescovile di Padova
AIRE, Ve	Archivio dell'Istituto di Ricovero e Educazione, Venezia
AMP	Actorum, mandatorum, praeceptorum
ASCVr	Archivio Storico della Curia Vescovile di Verona
ASPV	Archivio Storico del Patriarcato di Venezia
ASV	Archivio Segreto Vaticano
ASVe	Archivio di Stato di Venezia
ATE	Atti del Tribunale Ecclesiastico
BNF	Biblioteca Nazionale di Firenze
CC	Congregazione del Concilio
CM	Causarum matrimoniorum
FC	Filciae causarum
PM	Processi matrimoniali
S	Sentenziarum
S. Apostoli	Biblioteca di S. Apostoli
Synopsis	Synopsis variarum resolutionum ex selectioribus decretis Sacre Congregationis Concilii collecta per materias ordine alphabetico disposita, vol. 2

Manuscript Sources

Archivio Storico del Patriarcato di Venezia

Curia
Sezione Antica
Actorum, mandatorum, praeceptorum, regs. 2- 33 (1420–1476) and 46 (1492–1493)
Causarum matrimoniorum, vols. 1–45 (1451–1545)
Filciae causarum, vols. 1–3 (XV–XVI secc.)
Sententiarum, regs. 1 (1464–1465) 3 (1482) e 4 (XVI sec.)
Patriarcato di Grado
Atti, b. 1.
Archivio Segreto
Criminalia SS. Inquisitionis, vol. 1 (1461–1558)
SS. Visite Pastotrali b. «visite apostoliche, visite 1461–1558»
Biblioteche
S. Apostoli
009G 003

Archivio della Curia Vescovile di Padova

Actorum Civilium
b. 35 (1462)

Archivio Storico della Curia Vescovile di Verona

Atti del tribunale ecclesiastico, Atti civili, Processi, b. 7 (1540–1545)
Matrimoniorum, Processi matrimoniali, b. 4 (1540–1542)

Archivio di Stato di Venezia

Inventari
Avogaria di Comun, 86 ter 2, *Matrimoni patrizi per nome di donna*
Testamenti virorum
Testamenti mulierum
S. Uffizio
Corporazioni religiose soppresse
S. Zaccaria, bb. 4 e 76 (1414- sec. XVIII)
Notarile
Testamenti
b. 218, n. 327, Medea Dardani, vedova di Marino
b. 1237, n 170, Benedetto Marcello q. Cristoforo
b. 272, n. 827, Marco Antonio Marcello q. Benedetto
b. 1258, n. 492 Isabella Michiel q. Ludovico
b. 66, n. 25, Alvise Bollani di Teseo
b. 43, n. 22, Alvise Bollani di Teseo
b. 272, n. 668, Teseo Bollani q. Iohannis
b. 1229, n. 226, Simeone de cà di Vacca q. Johannis
b. 1229, n. 286, Tommaso Gravoran
b. 271, n. 569, Paola relicta q. Simonis Vacha
b. 271, n. 583, Pierina uxor Ioannis Vidutiis
Cancelleria Inferiore
Notai
b. 28, Atti Gaspare de Burati (1490–1513)
Avogaria di Comun
Penale
b. 181, f 12, Marcello Marco (ferito) 1525
Consiglio dei X
Criminale
fil. 6 (1530)

Archivio dell'Istituto di Ricovero e Educazione, Venezia:

Zitelle
Commissarie
E. 31, fasc. 3 (1541–1582)

Archivio Segreto Vaticano

Congregazione del Concilio
Positiones sessiones, bb. 2, 5, 58
Libri decretorum, vol. 2
Synopsis variarum resolutionum ex selectioribus decretis Sacre Congregationis Concilii collecta per materias ordine alphabetico disposita, vol. 2

Biblioteca Nazionale di Firenze

P.6.10 Antonino da Firenze, *Incipit summula confessionis*

Print Sources

Andreas Tiraquellus, *De legibus connubialibus et de iure maritali*, Lugduni 1554.

Antonino da Firenze, *Opera di Santo Antonino Arcivescovo Fiorentino utilissima et necessaria alla instruttione delli sacerdoti et di qualunque devota persona la quale desidera saper bene confessarsi delli suoi peccati*, Venetiis 1536.

Antonino da Firenze, *Summa*, 4 voll., Lugduni 1529.

Gnesotto A. (ed), Barbaro F., *De re uxoria liber in partes duas*, Padova 1915.

Benedicti XIV, *Institutionum ecclesiasticarum*, Romae 1750.

Cannarozzi C. (ed), Bernardino da Siena, *Le prediche volgari*, Firenze 1934–1940 (5 voll.).

Broomfield F. (ed), *Thomae de Chobham Summa Confessorum*, Louvain, 1968.

Constitutiones et privilegia patriarchatus et cleri Venetiarum illustrissimi ac reverendissimi D. D. Ioannis Trivisani iuris utriusque doctoris patriarci Venetiarum, Dalmatieque primatis etc., iussu edita, Venetiis 1658.

Friedberg E. (ed), *Corpus iuris canonici*, Graz 1959.

Decretales Gregorii IX, Venetiis 1566.

Decretum Gratiani, Romae 1582.

Giovambattista Galliccioli, *Delle memorie venete antiche profane ed ecclesiastiche raccolte da Giambattista Galliccioli, libri III*, Venezia 1795.

Gulielmi Duranti, *Speculum iudiciale*, Basel 1574, rist. anast. 1975.

M. Sanuto, *I Diarii (1496-1533)*, Venezia 1879-1902.

Martin de Azpilcueta, *Enchiridion, sive Manuale confessariorum et poenitentium: complectens pene resolutionem omnium dubiorum, quae in sacris confessionibus occurrere solent, circa peccata, absolutiones, restitutiones, censuras & irregularitates / iampridem sermone hispano compositum, & nunc latinitate donatum, recognitum, decem Praeludijs, & quamplurimis alijs locupletatum, & reformatum, ab ipsomet autore Martino ab Azpilcueta doctore Navarro; materiam hoc volumine contentorum, versa docet pagina* Romae 1573.

Nicolai de Tudeschis (Panormitanus), *Commentaria in quinque libros Decretalium*, Venetiis 1591.

Petrus Pictaviensis, *Summa de confessione, compilatio praesens*, Turnholti 1980.

Prosperi Farinacii, *Praxis, et theoricae criminalis*, Lugduni 1631.

Sanchez, T. *De sancto matrimonii sacramento disputationuum tomi tres*, Venetiis 1635.

Savonarola G., *Cum gratia et privilegio. Confessionale pro instructione confessorum reverendi patri fratris Hieronimi Savonarole de Ferraria ordinis predicatorum*, Venetiis 1507.

Ricci P. G. (ed), Savonarola G., *Prediche sopra l'Esodo*, Roma 1955.

Varischi C. (ed), *Sermoni del beato Bernardino Tomitano da Feltre nella redazione di fra Bernardino Bulgarino da Brescia minore osservante*, Milano 1964.

Tommaso d'aquino, *Summa Theologiae*, Milano 1988.

BIBLIOGRAPHY

Accati L. (1990) Soggetto collettivo, soggetto individuale e conflitto politico (1566–1759), in Società italiana delle Storiche (ed.) *Discutendo di Storia: soggettività, ricerca, biografia*, Turin: Rosenberg & Sellier, pp. 77–101.

Ago R. and Cerutti S. (1999) 'Premessa', *Quaderni Storici*, 101 (2), 307–314.

Ago R. (1994) Giovani nobili nell'età dell'assolutismo: autoritarismo paterno e libertà, in G. Levi and J.C. Schmitt (eds.) *Storia dei giovani, Dall'antichità all'età moderna*, Rome and Bari: Laterza, Vol. 1, pp. 375–426.

Aikema B. and Brown B. L. (1999) 'Pittura veneziana del XV secolo e ars nova dei Paesi Bassi' in B. Aikema and B. L. Brown (eds.) *Il Rinascimento a Venezia e la pittura del Nord ai tempi di Bellini, Dürer, Tiziano*, Milan: Bompiani, pp. 236–239.

Albani B. (2008–2009) *Sposarsi nel Nuovo Mondo. Politica, dottrina e pratiche della concessione di dispense matrimoniali tra la Nuova Spagna e la Santa Sede (1585–1670)*, unpublished doctoral thesis, University of Roma-Tor Vergata.

——— (2009) 'In universo christiano orbe': La Sacra Congregazione del Concilio e l'amministrazione dei sacramenti nel Nuovo Mondo (secoli XVI–XVII). *Mélanges de l'École Française de Rome: Italie et Mediterranée*, 121, 63–73.

Alberigo G., Dossetti G., Perikle P., Joannu J.A., Leonardi C. and Prodi P. (eds.) (1991) *Conciliorum Oecumenicorum Decreta*, Bologna: Istituto per le scienze religiose.

Albert T.D. (1998) *Der gemeine Mann vor dem geistlichen Richter. Kirchliche Rechtsprechung in den Diözesen Basel, Chur und Konstanz vor der Reformation*, Stuttgart: Lucius & Lucius.

Alessi G. (1990) 'Il gioco degli scambi: seduzione e risarcimento nella casistica cattolica del XVI e XVII secolo', *Quaderni Storici*, 75 (3), 805–831.

—— G. (2001) *Il processo penale. Profilo storico*, Rome and Bari: Laterza
Alexander M. (2009) 'Paduans, Procurators, and Episcopal Court', in R. Pierce and S. Seidel Menchi (eds.) *Ritratti. La dimensione individuale nella storia (secoli XV–XX)*, Rome: Edizioni di Storia e Letteratura, pp. 21–44.
Allegra L. (1981) 'Il parroco: un mediatore fra alta e bassa cultura', in C. Vivanti (ed.), *Storia d'Italia Intellettuali e potere*, Turin: Einaudi, vol. 4, pp. 893–947.
Anderson M. (1980) *Approaches to the History of the Western Family 1500–1914*, London: Macmillan.
Arellano I. and Usunaríz J. M. (eds.) (2003), *El mundo social y cultural en la época de la Celestina*, Madrid: Iberoamericana.
—— (eds.) (2005) *El matrimonio en Europa y en el mundo ispánico: siglos XVI y XVII*, Madrid: Visor Libros.
Arrivo G. (1997) 'Legami di sangue, legami di diritto (Pisa, secc. XVI–XVIII)' in *Ricerche Storiche*, 27 (2), 231–261.
Arrivo G. (2004) 'Storie ordinarie di matrimoni difficili. Assunta Tortolini e Giuseppe Mazzanti di fronte al Supremo Tribunale di Giustizia di Firenze', in S. Seidel Menchi and D. Quaglioni (eds.) *Trasgressioni. Seduzioni, concubinato, adulterio, bigamia (XIV–XVIII secolo)*, Bologna: Il Mulino, pp. 597–618.
—— (2006) *Seduzioni, promesse, matrimoni. Il processo per stupro nella Toscana del Settecento*, Rome: Edizioni di Storia e Letteratura.
Ascheri M. (1999) 'Il processo civile tra diritto comune e diritto locale: da questioni preliminari al caso della giustizia estense', *Quaderni Storici*, 101 (2), 355–387.
Bailey J. (2003) *Unquiet Lives. Marriage and Marriage Breakdown in England, 1660–1800*, Cambridge: Cambridge University Press.
Bainton R. H. (1958) *La Riforma protestante*, Turin: Einaudi.
Baldo V. (1977) *Alunni, maestri e scuole in Venezia alla fine del XVI secolo*, Como: New Press.
Barahona R. (2003) *Sex, Crimes, Honour and the Law in Early Modern Spain. Vizcaya 1500–1750*, Toronto: University of Toronto Press.
Barbagli M. and Kertzer D. (eds.) (2002) *Storia della famiglia in Europa. Dal Cinquecento alla Rivoluzione francese*, Rome and Bari: Laterza.
Barni G. L. (1949) 'Un contratto di concubinato in Corsica nel XIII secolo', *Rivista di storia del Diritto italiano*, 12, 131–155.
Barthes R. (1984) *Le bruissement de la langue*, Paris: Seuil.
Beucamp J. (1976) 'Le vocabulaire de la faiblesse féminine dans le textes juridique romaines du III au VIe siècle', *Revue historique de droit français étranger*, 54, 485–508.
Becchi E. (2000) 'L'istruzione di base tra Quattrocento e Seicento: scuola laica e occasioni di alfabetizzazione' in M. Sangalli (ed.), *Chiesa e scuola: percorsi di storia dell'educazione tra XII e XX secolo*, Siena: Cantagalli, 33–41.

Bellabarba M. (1997) *Racconti famigliari. Scritti di Tommaso Tabarelli de Fatis e altre storie di nobili cinquecenteschi*, Trent: Società di studi trentini di scienze storiche.
Bellomo M. (1961) *Ricerche sui rapporti patrimoniali tra i coniugi. Contributo alla storia della famiglia medievale*, Milan: Giuffrè.
Bellomo M. (1965) 'Dote nel Diritto intermedio', in *Enciclopedia del Diritto*, Milan: Giuffrè, pp. 8–33.
Belloni A. (1994) 'Die Rolle der Frau in der Jurisprudenz der Renaissance', in P.G. Schmidt (ed.) *Die Frau in der Renaissance*, Wiesbaden: Harrassowitz, pp. 55–80.
Benussi P. (2001) 'Oltre il processo: itinerari di ricerca intorno al matrimonio controverso di Giorgio Zaccarotto e Maddalena di Sicilia (Padova e Venezia 1455–1458)' in S. Seidel Menchi and D. Quaglioni (eds.) *Matrimoni in dubbio. Unioni controversie e nozze clandestine in Italia dal XIV al XVIII secolo*, Bologna: Il Mulino, pp. 149–173.
Bergensen A. (2013) 'Die rituelle Ordnung' in A. Bellinger and D.J. Krieger (eds.) *Ritualtheorien. Ein einführendes Handbuch*, Wiesbaden: Springer VS, pp. 49–75.
Bernhard A. (2002) 'Le logiche del profitto. Schiavi e società a Siviglia nel Seicento' *Quaderni Storici*, 107 (2), 379–389.
Berriot- Salvatore E. (1995) 'Il discorso della medicina e della scienza' in A. Farge and E. Berriot-Salvatore (eds.) *Storia delle donne. Dal Rinascimento all'età moderna*, Rome and Bari: Laterza, pp. 351–395.
Besta E. (1898) 'Gli Antichi usi nuziali del Veneto e gli Statuti di Chioggia', *Rivista italiana per le scienze giuridiche*, 26 (2–3), 204–219.
Bianchi A. (1997) 'La deresponsabilizzazione dei padri (Bologna secc. XVI–XVII)', *Ricerche Storiche*, 27 (2) 263–286.
Bizzocchi R. (2001) *In famiglia. Storie di interessi e affetti nell'Italia moderna*, Rome and Bari: Laterza.
Bizzocchi R. (2014) *A Lady's Man. The Cicisbei, Private Morals and National Identity in Italy*, London: Palgrave Macmillan.
Blauert A. and Schwerhoff G. (1993) 'Vorbemerkungen' in A. Blauert and G. Schwerhoff (eds.) *Mit den Waffen der Justiz. Zur Kriminalitätsgeschichte des späteren Mittelalters und der Frühen Neuzeit*, Frankfurt/M: Fischer, pp. 7–15.
——— (eds.) (2000) *Kriminalitätsgeschichte. Beiträge zur Sozial- und Kulturgeschichte der Vormoderne*, Constance: UVK.
Blouin F. (1998) *Vatican Archives: An Inventory and Guide to the Historical Documents of the Holy See*, New York: Oxford University Press.
Bonvini Mazzanti M. (1984–87) 'L'opera pastorale di frate Pietro Ridolfi da Tossignano, vescovo di Senigallia dal 1591 al 1601', *Picenum seraphicum*, 17, 131–167.

Borello B. (2002) 'Annodare e sciogliere. Reti di relazioni femminili e separazioni a Roma (XVII-XVIII secolo)', *Quaderni Storici*, 111 (3), 617–648.

—— (2003)*Trame sovrapposte. La socialità aristocratica e le reti di relazioni femminili a Roma (XVII- XVIII secolo)*, Naples: Edizioni Scientifiche Italiane.

Borggrefe H. (2001) 'Titians sogenannte Himmlische und Irdische Liebe. Der Beistand der Venus im Hochzeitsbild der Laura Bagarotto', *Zeitschrift für Kunstgeschichte*, 64, 331–363.

Borguière A. (1986) *Histoire de la famille*, Paris: Armand Colin.

Brambilla E. (1997) 'Battesimo e diritti civili dalla Riforma protestante al giuseppinismo', *Rivista Storica Italiana*, 109 (3), 602–627.

—— (1999) 'Confessione, casi riservati e giustizia 'spirituale' dal XV secolo al concilio di Trento: i reati di fede e di morale', in C. Nubola and A. Turchini (eds.) *Fonti ecclesiastiche per la storia sociale e religiosa d'Europa: XV–XVIII secolo*, Bologna: Il Mulino, pp. 491–540.

—— (2000) *Alle origini del Sant'Uffizio. Penitenza, confessione e giustizia spirituale dal medioevo al XVI secolo*, Bologna: Il Mulino.

—— (2003) 'Dagli sponsali civili al matrimonio sacramentale (sec. XV–XVI). A proposito di alcuni studi recenti sulle cause matrimoniali come fonte storica', *Rivista Storica Italiana*, 115 (3), 956–1005.

—— (2004) 'I reati morali tra corti di giustizia e casi di coscienza', in S. Seidel Menchi and D. Quaglioni (eds.) *Trasgressioni. Seduzioni, concubinato, adulterio, bigamia (XIV–XVIII secolo)*, Bologna: Il Mulino, pp. 521–575.

Brambilla E. (2006) *La giustizia intollerante. Inquisizione e tribunali confessionali in Europa (secoli IV–XVIII)*, Rome: Carocci.

Breit S. (1991) *«Leichtfertigkeit» und ländliche Gesellschaft. Voreheliche Sexualität in der Frühen Neuzeit*, Munich: Oldenburg.

Brentano R. (1972) *Due chiese. Italia e Inghilterra nel XIII secolo*, Bologna: Il Mulino.

Broocke C.N.L. (1991) *Il matrimonio nel Medioevo*, Bologna: Il Mulino.

Brooks P. (2000) *Troubling Confessions. Speaking Guilt in Law and Literature*, Chicago: Chicago University Press.

Brucker G. (1986) *Giovanni e Lusanna. Love and Marriage in Renaissance Florence*, Berkeley and London: University of California Press.

Brundage J. (1987) *Law, Sex and Christian Society in Medieval Europe*, Chicago and London: University of Chicago Press.

Bucholz S. (1987) 'Erunt tres aut quattuor in carne una. Aspekte der neuzeitlichen Polygamiediskussion' in H. Monhaupt (ed.) *Zur Geschichte des Familien- und Erbrechts. Politische Implikationen und Perspektiven*, Frankfurt/M.: Klostermann, pp. 71–91.

Buganza G. (1991) 'Il potere della parola. La forza e le responsabilità della deposizione testimoniale nel processo penale veneziano' in J. C. Maire -Viguer and A. Paravicini Bagliani (eds.) *La parola all'accusato*, Palermo: Sellerio.

Bullough G. (1966) 'Poligamy Among the Reformers', in G.R. Hibbard (ed.) *Renaissance and Modern Essays. Presented to Vivian de Sola Pinto in Celebration of his Seventieth Birthday*, London and New York: Routledge and Kegan Paul, pp. 5–24.

Burghartz S. (1992) 'Jungfräulichkeit oder Reinheit? Zur Änderung von Argumentationsmustern vor dem Basler Ehegericht im 16. und 17. Jahrhundert', in R. van Dülmen (ed.) *Dynamik der Tradition. Studien zur historischen Kulturforschung*, Frankfurt/M.: Fischer, pp. 13–40.

—— (1995) 'Geschlecht, Körper, Ehre. Überlegungen zur weiblichen Ehre in der Frühen Neuzeit am Beispiel der Basler Ehegerichtsprotokolle' in K. Schreiner and G. Schwerhoff (eds.) *Verletzte Ehre. Ehrkonflikte in Gesellschaften des Mittelalters und der Frühen Neuzeit*, Cologne, Weimar and Vienna: Böhlau, pp. 214–234.

—— (1999) 'Zeiten der Reinheit, Orte der Unzucht. Ehe und Sexualität in Basel während der Frühen Neuzeit' Paderbon, Munich and Vienna: Schöningh.

—— (2006) 'Tribunali matrimoniali nell'Europa della Riforma: Svizzera e Germania meridionale' in S. Seidel Menchi and D. Quaglioni (eds.) *I tribunali del matrimonio (secoli XV–XVIII)* Bologna: Il Mulino, pp. 211–235.

Caiazza P. (1992) 'L'archivio storico della Sacra Congregazione del Concilio (primi appunti per un problema di riordinamento)', *Ricerca di storia sociale e religiosa*, 42, 7–24.

Calabrese O. (2003) 'La Venere di Urbino di Tiziano Vecellio' in O. Calabrese (ed.) *Venere svelata: La Venere di Urbino di Tiziano*, Cinisello Balsamo, Milan: Silvana, pp. 29–45.

Calore A. (1995) 'Tactis Evangeliis' in S. Bertelli and M. Centanni (eds.), *Il gesto e il rito nel cerimoniale dal mondo antico ad oggi*, Florence: Ponte alle grazie, pp. 53–99.

Calvi, G. (2004) 'Chiavi di lettura', in G. Calvi (ed.) *Innesti. Donne e genere nella storia sociale*, Rome: Viella, pp. VII–XXXI.

Campbell L. (1998) *The Fifteenth Century Netherlandish Schools*, London: National Gallery Publications.

Campo Guinea M. J. (1995) 'La fuerza, el otro lado de la voluntad. El matrimonio en Navarra en los siglos XVI-XVII' *Revista de la Asociación Gerónimo de Uztáriz*, 11, 71–87.

—— (1998) *Comportamientos matrimoniales en Navarra, (siglos XVI–XVII)*, Pamplona: Gobierno de Navarra.

—— (2004) 'El matrimonio clandestino. Procesos ante el tribunal Eclesiástico en el Archivio Diocesano de Pamplona siglos XVI–XVII', *Príncipe de Viana*, 231, 205–221.

Capp B. (2003) *When Gossip Meet. Women, Family and Neighbourhood in Early Modern England*, Oxford: Oxford University Press.
—— (2004) 'Live, Love and Litigation: Sileby in the 1630s', in *Past and Present*, 182 (1), 55–83.
Cappelletti M. (1974) *La testimonianza della parte nel sistema dell'oralità*, Milan: Giuffrè.
Casagrande C. and Vecchio S. (1987) *I peccati della lingua Disciplina ed etica della parola nella cultura medievale*, Rome: Istituto della Enciclopedia italiana.
—— (1991) '«Non dire falsa testimonianza contro il tuo prossimo»: il decalogo e i peccati della lingua' in D. Romagnoli (ed.) *La città e la corte. Buone e cattive maniere tra Medioevo ed Età moderna*, Milan: Guerini, pp. 83–107.
Casagrande C. (1995) 'La donna custodita' in C. Klapisch Zuber (ed.) *Storia delle donne. Il Medioevo*, Rome and Bari: Laterza, pp. 88–128.
Castane N. (1980) *Justice et repression en Languedoc à l'époque des Lumières*, Paris 1980.
Cavallar, O. and Kirshner J. (2004) 'Making and Breaking Betrothal Contracts («Sponsalia») in Late Trecento Florence' in O. Condorelli (ed.), *'Panta rei': Studi dedicati a Manlio Bellomo*, vol. 1, Rome: Il cigno, pp. 395–452.
Cavallo S. and Cerutti S. (1980) 'Onore femminile e controllo sociale della riproduzione in Piemonte tra Sei e Settecento', *Quaderni Storici*, 44 (2), 346–383.
Cavallo S. (2006) 'L'importanza della "famiglia orizzontale" nella storia della famiglia italiana' in I. Fazio and D. Lombardi (eds.) *Generazioni. Legami di parentela tra passato e presente*, Rome: Viella, pp. 69–92.
Cavallo S. (2007) *Artisans of the Body in Early Modern Italy*, Manchester and New York: Manchester University Press.
Cavazzana Romanelli F. (1994) 'Archivio storico del Patriarcato di Venezia' in V. Monachino, E. Boaga, L. Osbat and S. Palese (eds.) *Guida agli archivi diocesani d'Italia*, vol. 2, Rome: Ministero per i beni culturali e ambientali, pp. 285–300.
—— (2006) 'Matrimonio tridentino e scritture parrocchiali. Risonanze veneziane', in S. Seidel Menchi and D. Quaglioni (eds.) *I tribunali del matrimonio, (secoli XV–XVIII)* Bologna: Il Mulino, pp. 731–766.
Cerutti S. (2003) *Giustizia Sommaria: pratiche e ideali di giustizia nella Torino del XVIII secolo*, Turin: Einaudi.
Chavarría Múgica F. (2001) 'Mentalidad Moral y Contrarreforma en la España Moderna (Fornicarios, confesores e inquisidores: el tribunal de Logroño, 1571–1623)', *Hispania Sacra*, 53 (108), 725–759.
Chénon E. (1912) *Recherches historique sur quelques rites nuptiaux*, in «Nouvelle revue historique de droit français et étranger», 36, 1912, pp. 573–660.
Chilese V. (1999) 'La coppia, la famiglia l'onore nella documentazione di un tribunale ecclesiastico nel Cinquecento veneto', *Studi storici Luigi Simeoni*, 8, pp. 81–106.

—— (2000) 'Considerazioni su una causa matrimoniale discussa presso il tribunale vescovile di Verona (1541)', *Annali dell'Istituto storico italo germanico in Trento*, 26 pp. 781–803.

—— (2006) 'I processi matrimoniali veronesi (secolo XVI)', in S. Seidel Menchi and D. Quaglioni (eds.), *I tribunali del matrimonio (secoli XV–XVIIII)*, Bologna: Il Mulino, pp. 123–139.

Chittolini G. (1993) '«Episcopalis curiae notarius». Cenni sui notai di curie vescovili nell'Italia centro-settentrionale alla fine del Medioevo', *Società, istituzioni, spiritualità. Studi in onore di Cinzio Violante*, Spoleto: Centro italiano di studi sull'alto Medioevo.

Chojnacki S. (2000), *Women and Men in Renaissance Venice. Twelve Essays on Patrician Society*, Baltimore and London: Johns Hopkins University Press.

—— (2000) 'Il divorzio di Cateruzza: rappresentazione femminile ed esito processuale (Venezia 1465)', in S. Seidel Menchi and D. Quaglioni (eds), *Coniugi nemici. La separazione in Italia dal XII al XVIII secolo*, Bologna: Il Mulino, pp. 371–416.

—— (2001) 'Valori patrizi nel tribunale patriarcale: Girolamo da Mula e Marietta Soranzo (Venezia 1460),' in S. Seidel Menchi and D. Quaglioni (eds.), *Matrimoni in dubbio. Unioni controverse e nozze clandestine in Italia dal XIV al XVIII secolo*, Bologna: Il Mulino, pp. 199–245.

Christiansen K. (1986) 'Lorenzo Lotto and the Tradition of Epithalamic Paintings', *Apollo*, 124, 166–173.

Ciappelli G. (2006) 'I processi matrimoniali: quadro di raccordo dei risultati della schedatura (Venezia, Verona, Napoli, Feltre e Trento, 1420–1803)', in S. Seidel Menchi and D. Quaglioni (eds.) *I tribunali del matrimonio (secoli XV–XVIIII)*, Bologna: Il Mulino, pp. 67–100.

Cobus Ruis de Adana J. (1985) 'Matrimonio, amancebamiento y bigamia en el reino de Corduba durante el siglo XVII', *Hispania Sacra*, 37 (76), 673–716.

Cohen T. V. and Cohen E. S. (1993) *Words and Deeds in Renaissance Rome: Trials before the Papal Magistrates*, Toronto: University of Toronto Press.

Corazzolo G. and Corrà L. (1981), *Esperimenti d'amore. Fatti di giovani nel Veneto del Cinquecento*, Vicenza: Odeonlibri.

Corrain C. and Zampini P. (1970), *Documenti etnografici e folkloristici nei sinodi diocesani italiani*, Bologna: Forni.

Cowan A. (2007) *Marriage, Manners and Mobility in Early Modern Venice*, Aldershot and Burlington: Ashgate.

Cozzi G. (1976) 'Padri, figli e matrimoni clandestini (metà sec. XVI – metà sec. XVIII)', *La cultura*, 14 (2–3), 169–213.

—— (1980) 'La politica del diritto nella Repubblica di Venezia', in G. Cozzi, *Stato, società e giustizia nella Repubblica veneta* (secoli XV–XVIII), Rome: Jouvence, pp. 15–152.

—— (1981) 'Note e documenti sulla questione del «divorzio» a Venezia (1720–1788)', *Annali dell'Istituto storico italo germanico in Trento*, 6, 275–360.

—— (1985–1986) *Il dibattito sui matrimoni clandestini. Vicende giuridiche, sociali religiose dell'istituzione matrimoniale tra medio Evo ed Età moderna*, unpublished manuscript, university of Venice.

—— (1991) 'Religione, moralità e giustizia a Venezia: vicende della magistratura degli Esecutori contro la bestemmia', *Ateneo veneto* 178 (29), 7–95.

Cracco, G. (1981–1982) 'Il periodo vicentino di San Lorenzo Giustiniani', *Odeo Olimpico*, 17–18.

—— (1982) 'Prefazione', *Sancti Laurentii Iustiniani opera omnia*, Florence: Olschki, 4–7.

—— (1989) 'Esperienze di vita canonicale e Lorenzo Giustiniani', in G. Vian (ed.) *La Chiesa di Venezia tra medioevo ed età moderna*, Venezia: Edizioni Studium cattolico veneziano, pp. 91–145.

Cristellon C. (2001) 'La sposa in convento (Padova e Venezia 1455–1458)', in S. Seidel Menchi and D. Quaglioni (eds.) *Matrimoni in dubbio. Unioni controverse e nozze clandestine in Italia dal XIV al XVIII secolo*, Bologna: Il Mulino, pp. 123–148.

—— (2001) 'Ursina Basso contro Alvise Soncin: il «consilium» respinto di Bartolomeo Cipolla e gli atti del processo (Padova e Venezia 1461–1462)' in S. Seidel Menchi and D. Quaglioni (eds.), *Matrimoni in dubbio. Unioni controverse e nozze clandestine in Italia dal XIV al XVIII secolo*, Bologna: Il Mulino, pp. 279–303.

—— (2004) 'La percezione del matrimonio prima del concilio di Trento', *Popolazione e Storia*, 2, 33–40.

—— (2003) 'L'ufficio del giudice: mediazione, inquisizione, confessione nei processi matrimoniali veneziani (1420–1532)' *Rivista Storica Italiana*, 115 (3), 850–897.

—— (2008) 'Marriage and Consent in Pre-Tridentine Venice: Between Lay Conception and Ecclesiastical Conception, 1420–1545', *Sixteenth Century Journal*, 39 (2), 389–418.

—— (2009) 'Does the Priest Have to Be There? Contested Marriages before Roman Tribunals (Italy Sixteenth to Eighteenth Centuries)', *Österreichische Zeitschrift für Geschichtswissenschaft*, 20 (3), 10–30.

—— (2009) 'Ritratto di una cortigiana del Cinquecento: Caterina de Medici da Verona e le sue vicende (1518–1582)' in R.A. Pierce and S. Seidel Menchi (eds.) *Ritratti. La dimensione individuale nella storia (secoli XV–XX)*, Rome: Edizioni di Storia e Letteratura, pp. 147–176.

—— (2010) 'Public Display of Affection: The Making of Marriage in the Venetian Courts before the Council of Trent (1420–1545)' in S. Matthews Grieco (ed.) *Erotic Culture in Renaissance Italy*, London: Farnham and Burlington: Ashgate, pp. 173–197.

―――― and Seidel Menchi S. (2011) 'Rituals before Tribunals in Renaissance Italy: Continuity and Change, 1400–1600' in M. Korpiola (ed.), *Regional Variation of Matrimonial Law and Customs in Europe 1150–1600*, Leiden: Brill, pp. 275–287.
D'Avray D. L. (1998) 'Marriage Ceremonies and the Church in Italy after 1215' in T. Dean and K.J.P. Lowe (eds.) *Marriage in Italy, 1300–1650*, Cambridge: Cambridge University Press, pp. 85–106.
―――― (2005) *Medieval Marriage: Symbolism and Society*, Oxford and New York: Oxford University Press.
―――― (2012) 'Slavery, Marriage and the Holy See: from the Ancient World to the New World', *Rechtsgeschichte-Legal History*, 20, 347–351.
―――― and Menski W. (2016) 'Authenticating Marriage: The Decree Tametsi in a Comparative Global Perspective', *Max Planck Institute for European Legal History. Research Paper*, 3, http://papers.ssrn.com/sol3/papers.cfm?abstract_id=2754003
Damaska M. (1991) *The Faces of Justice and State Authority*, New Haven: Jale University Press.
Dauvillier J. (1933) *Le Mariage dans le droit classique de l'Eglise depuis le «Décret de Gratien» (1140) jusq'à la mort de Clément V (1314)*, Paris: Recueil Sirey.
D'Elia A. F. (2004), *The Renaissance of Marriage in Fifteenth Century Italy*, Cambridge MA and London: Harvard University Press.
De Biase L. (1992) *Amore di Stato. Venezia. Settecento*, Palermo: Sellerio.
De Boer W. (2001), *The Conquest of the Soul: Confession, Discipline, and Public Order in Counter-Reformation Milan*, Leiden: Brill, 2001.
Dean T. (1998) 'Fathers and Daughters: Marriage Laws and Marriage Disputes in Bologna and Italy, 1200–1550', in T. Dean and K.J.P. Lowe (eds.) *Marriage in Italy, 1300–1650*, Cambridge: Cambridge University Press, pp. 85–106.
―――― (2004) 'Domestic Violence in Late-Medieval Bologna', *Renaissance Studies*, 18 (4), 527–543.
―――― (2007) *Crime and Justice in Late Medieval Italy*, Cambridge: Cambridge University Press.
Degrandi A. (1993) 'Problemi di percezione e rappresentazione del gioco d'azzardo', in G. Ortalli (ed.) *Gioco e giustizia nell'Italia di Comune*, Rome: Viella, pp. 109–120.
Del Col A. (1994) 'Alcune osservazioni sui processi inquisitoriali come fonti storiche', *Metodi e ricerche*, 13 (1–2), 85–105.
―――― 2000 L'inquisizione romana: metodologia delle fonti e storia istituzionale' in A. De Col and G. Paolin (eds.) *Atti del seminario internazionale, Montereale Valcellina, 23–24 settembre 1999*, Trieste Montereale Valcellina: Edizioni Università di Trieste – Circolo Culturale Menocchio, pp. 51–72.
Delarun J. (1995) 'La donna vista dai chierici' in C. Klapish Zuber (ed.), *Storia delle donne. Il Medioevo*, Rome and Bari: Laterza, pp. 24–55.

Delille G. (1985) *Famille et propriété dans le royaume de Neaples*, Paris and Rome.
Della Misericordia M. (2001) 'Giudicare con il consenso. Giustizia vescovile, pratiche sociali e potere politico nella diocesi di Como nel tardo medioevo', *Archivio Storico Ticinese*, 38 (130), 179–218.
Delumeau J. (1990) 'La confession pour tranquilliser' in J. Delumeau (ed.) *L'aveu et le pardon*, Paris: Fayard pp. 37–45.
―――― (1995), *La paura in Occidente*, Turin: Einaudi.
Denzinger H. and Hunerman P. (2009) *Enchiridion symbolorum definitionum et declarationum de rebus fidei et morum*, Bologna: EDB.
Derosas G. (1980) *Moralità e giustizia a Venezia nel '500 – '600. Gli Esecutori contro la bestemmia*, in G. Cozzi (ed.), *Stato, società, giustizia nella Repubblica Veneta (sec. XV–XVIII)*, Rome: Jouvence, pp. 431–528.
―――― (1992) 'La crisi del patriziato come crisi del sistema familiare: i Foscarini ai Carmini nel secondo Settecento' in G. Benzoni, M. Berengo, G. Ortalli and G. Scarabello (eds.) *Studi veneti offerti a Gaetano Cozzi*, Venezia: Il Cardo, pp. 309–331.
Deutsch C. (2005) *Ehegerichtsbarkeit im Bistum Regensburg (1480–1538)*, Cologne, Weimar and Vienna: Böhlau.
―――― (2005) 'Konsensehe oder Zwangheirat? Zur mittelalterlichen Rechtsauffassung «consensus facit matrimonium»', *Zeitschrift für Geschichtswissenschaft*, 53 (10), 677–690.
Di Renzo Villata G. 'Separazione personale dei coniugi (Storia)', *Enciclopedia del diritto*, 41, Milan: Giuffrè, 1989, pp. 1350–1376.
Di Simplicio O. (1994) *Peccato, penitenza, perdono, Siena 1575–1800. La formazione della coscienza nell'Italia moderna*, Milan: Franco Angeli.
Dinges M. (2001) 'Usi della giustizia come elemento di controllo sociale nella prima età moderna, in M. Bellabarba, G. Schwerhoff and A. Zorzi (eds.) *Criminalità e giustizia in Germania e in Italia. Pratiche giudiziarie e linguaggi giuridici tra tardo medioevo ed età moderna*, Bologna and Berlin: Il Mulino and Duncker & Humblot, pp. 285–324.
Dixon S. (1984) 'Infirmitas sexus: Womanly Weakness in Roman Law', *Tijdschrift voor Rechtsgeschiedenis*, 52 (4), pp. 343–371.
Dominici G. (1927) *Regole e governo di cura familiare*, Florence: A. Garinei.
Donahue Ch. Jr. 1989 (ed.) *The Records of the Medieval Ecclesiastical Courts*, vol. 1., *The Continent. Reports of the Working Group on Church Court Records*, Berlin: Duncker & Humblot.
―――― (1981) 'Proof by Witnesses in the Church Courts of Medieval England: An Imperfect Reception of the Learned Law' in M. S. Arnold, T. A. Green, S. A. Scully and S.D. White (eds.) *On the Laws and Customs of England*, Chapel Hill, North Carolina: University of North Carolina Press, pp. 127–158.
―――― (2007) *Law, Marriage, and Society in the Later Middle Ages. Arguments about Marriage in Five Courts*, Cambridge: Cambridge University Press.

Duby G. (1981) *Le chevalier, la femme, et le prêtre. Le marriage dans la France féodale*, Paris: Hachette littérature générale.
Duer C. J. (1951) *The Judicial Notary*, Washington: The Catholic University of America Press.
Duni M. (1999) *Tra religione e magia. Storia del prete modenese Guglielmo Campana (1460?–1541)*, Florence: L.S. Olschki.
Duval A. (1976) 'Contrat et sacrement de mariage au Concile de Trente', *La Maison-Dieu*, 127, pp. 34–63.
Dyer A. (2003) 'Seduction by Promise of Marriage: Law, Sex and Culture in Seventeenth-Century Spain', *The Sixteenth Century Journal*, 34 (2), pp. 439–455.
Eibach J. (2004) 'Das Haus: zwischen öffentlicher Zugänglichkeit und geschützter Privatheit (16.-18. Jahrhundert)', in S. Rau and G. Schwerhoff (eds.) *Zwischen Gotteshaus und Taverne. Öffentliche Räume in Spätmittelalter und Früher Neuzeit*, Cologne, Weimar and Vienna: Böhlau, pp. 183–205.
——— (2007) 'Der Kampf um die Hosen und die Justiz – Ehekonflikte in Frankfurt im 18. Jahrhundert', in S. Kesper Biermann and D. Kippel, (eds.) *Kriminalität im Mittelalter und in der Früher Neuzeit. Soziale, rechtliche, philosophische und literarische Aspekte*, Wiesbaden: Harassowitz, pp. 167–188.
——— Schmidt-Voges I. (2015) (eds.) Das Haus in der Geschichte Europas. Ein Handbuch, Oldenburg: De Gruyter.
Eisenach E. (2004) *Marriage, Family, and Social Order in Sixteenth Century Verona*, Kirksville, Mo.: Truman State University Press.
Erdö P. (1986) 'Eheprozesse im mittelalterlichen Ungarn', *Zeitschrift der Savigny Stiftung für Rechtsgeschichte, Kanonistische Abteilung*, 72 (1), 250–276.
Esmein A. (1891) *Le mariage en droit canonique*, Vol. 1, Paris: L. Larose et Forcel.
Esposito A. (2000) 'Convivenza e separazione a Roma nel primo Rinascimento', in S. Seidel Menchi and D. Quaglioni (eds.) *Coniugi nemici. La separazione in Italia dal XII al XVIII secolo*, Bologna: Il Mulino, pp. 499–517.
Esposito A. (2004) 'Adulterio, concubinato, bigamia: testimonianze dalla normativa statutaria dello Stato pontificio (secoli XIII–XVI)', in S. Seidel Menchi and D. Quaglioni (eds.) *Trasgressioni. Seduzioni, concubinato, adulterio, bigamia (XIV–XVIII secolo)*, Bologna: Il Mulino, pp. 21–42.
Fabbri L. (1996) 'Trattatistica e pratica dell'alleanza matrimoniale', in M. De Giorgio and C. Klapisch Zuber (eds.) *Storia del matrimonio*, Rome and Bari: Laterza, pp. 91–117.
Falchi G. F. (1927) *L'omicidio in Alberto da Gandino e nella tradizione romana*, Padova: Zannoni.
Faoro L. (1996–1997) *Processi matrimoniali dell'Archivio Arcivescovile di Trento 1657–1669*, unpublished degree thesis, University of Trent.
——— (2000) 'Il giudice e il principe. Diritto canonico e responsabilità di governo nella vicenda di Matthias Stelzhamer e Giulia Linarolo (Trento

1664–1666)' in S. Seidel Menchi and Diego Quaglioni (eds.) *Coniugi nemici. La separazione in Italia dal XII al XVIII secolo*, Bologna: Il Mulino, pp. 191–334.

——— (2006) 'Il ricorso alla carcerazione nei processi matrimoniali di Trento (secoli XVII–XVIII)' in S. Seidel Menchi and D. Quaglioni (eds.), *I tribunali del matrimonio (secoli XV–XVIIII)*, Bologna: Il Mulino, pp. 189–209.

Farr J. R. (1995) *Authority and Sexuality in Early Modern Burgundy (1500–1730)*, New York: Oxford University Press.

Fasano Guarini E. (1996) 'Gli «ordini di polizia» nell'Italia del Cinquecento: il caso toscano' in M. Stolleis (ed.) *Policey im Europa der Frühen Neuzeit*, Frankfurt/M: V. Klostermann, pp. 55–95

Fazio I. and Lombardi D. (2006) (eds.) *Generazioni. Legami di parentela tra passato e presente*, Rome: Viella.

Fedele P. (1978) 'La responsabilità del giudice nel processo canonico', in A. Giuliani and N. Picardi (eds.) *L'educazione giuridica*, vol. 3, *La responsabilità del giudice*, Perugia: Libreria editrice universitaria, pp. 158–184.

Ferrante L. (1987) *La sessualità come risorsa (Bologna secolo XVII)*, in «Melanges de l'École Française de Rome», 99, pp. 989–1116.

——— (1989) 'Differenza sociale e differenza sessuale nelle questioni d'onore (Bologna sec. XVII)' in G. Fiume (ed.) *Onore e storia nelle società mediterranee*, Palermo: La Luna, pp. 105–127.

——— (1994) 'Il matrimonio disciplinato: processi matrimoniali a Bologna nel Cinquecento', in P. Prodi (ed.) *Disciplina dell'anima, disciplina del corpo e disciplina della società tra medioevo ed età moderna*, Bologna: Il Mulino, pp. 901–927.

——— (1996) 'Il valore del corpo, ovvero la gestione della sessualità femminile' in A. Groppi (ed.) *Il lavoro delle donne*, Rome and Bari, pp. 206–228.

——— (1998) 'Legittima concubina, quasi moglie, anzi meretrice. Note sul concubinato tra medioevo ed età moderna' in A. Biondi (ed.) *Modernità: definizione ed esercizi*, Bologna: Il Mulino, pp. 123–141.

——— (2001) 'Gli sposi contesi. Una vicenda bolognese di metà Cinquecento' in S. Seidel Menchi and D. Quaglioni (eds.) *Matrimoni in dubbio. Unioni controverse e nozze clandestine in Italia dal XIV al XVIII secolo*, Bologna: Il Mulino, pp. 329–362.

——— (2004) «Consensus concubinarius»: un'invenzione giuridica per il principe?' in S. Seidel Menchi and D. Quaglioni (eds.) *Trasgressioni. Seduzioni, concubinato, adulterio, bigamia (XIV–XVIII secolo)*, Bologna: Il Mulino, pp. 107–132.

Ferraro J.M. (1995) 'The Power to Decide: Battered Wives in Early Modern Venice' in *Renaissance Quarterly*, 48 (3) pp. 492–512.

——— (2000) 'Honours and the Marriage Wars of Late Renaissance Venice', *Acta Histriae*, 9, 41–48.

———— (2000) 'Coniugi nemici: Orsetta, Annibale ed il compito dello storico (Venezia 1634)', in S. Seidel Menchi and D. Quaglioni (eds.) *Coniugi nemici. La separazione in Italia dal XII al XVIII secolo*, Bologna: Il Mulino, pp. 141–190.

———— (2001) *Marriage Wars in Late Renaissance Venice*, Oxford and New York: Oxford University Press.

Ferri G. (2012) *L'arbitrato tra prassi e sistemazione teorica nell'età moderna*, Rome: Aracne.

Finch A. J. (1990) 'Parental Authority and the Problem of Clandestine Marriage in the Later Middle Ages', in *Law and History Review*, 8 (2), 189–204.

Fiorelli P. (1961) 'Confessione (storia)', in *Enciclopedia del diritto*, vol. 8; Milan: Giuffrè pp. 864–870.

Fiume G. (2007) (ed.) *Schiavitù e conversioni nel Mediterraneo*, special issue, *Quaderni Storici*, 126 (3).

Flandrin J. L. (1975) *Les amours paysannes (XVIe- XIX siècles)*, Paris: Gallimard/Julliard.

———— (1976) *Parenté, maison, sexualité dans l'ancienne société*, Paris: Hachette.

Fournier P. (1880) *Les Officialités au Moyen-Age*, Paris: E. Plon et cie.

Fowler L. (1972) 'Recusatio iudicis in civilist and canonist Though', *Studia Gratiana*, 15, 717–785.

Gacto E. (1987) 'El delito de bigamia y la Inquisicion española', *Anuario de Historia del derecho Español*, 57, 465–492.

Galasso C. (2004) '«La moglie duplicata». Bigamia e levirato nella comunità ebraica di Livorno (secolo XVII)' in S. Seidel Menchi and D. Quaglioni (eds.) *Trasgressioni. Seduzioni, concubinato, adulterio, bigamia (XIV–XVIII secolo)*, Bologna: Il Mulino, pp. 417–442.

Gambier M. (1980) 'La donna e la giustizia penale veneziana nel XVIII secolo', in G. Cozzi (ed.), *Stato società e giustizia nella Repubblica veneta (secc. XV–XVIII)*, vol. 1, Rome: Jouvence, pp. 529–575.

Garnot B. (1996) (ed.), *L'infrajudiciaire du Moyen Age à l'époque contemporaine*, Dijon: Editions Universitaires de Dijon.

Gatti T. (1930) *L'impunibilità, i moventi del reato e la prevenzione criminale negli statuti italiani dei secc. XII–XVII*, Padua: CEDAM.

Gaudemet J. (1989) *Il matrimonio in Occidente*, Turin: SEI.

Geremek B. (1973) 'Il pauperismo nell'età preindustriale' in R. Romano and C. Vivanti (eds.) *Storia d'Italia, I documenti*, vol. 5, Turin: Einaudi, pp. 667–698.

———— (1986) *La pietà e la forca. Storia della miseria e della carità in Europa*, Rome and Bari: Laterza.

Gergen M. (1994) 'The Social Construction of Personal Histories: Gendered Lives in Popular Autobiographies', in T. R. Sarbin and J. I. Kitsuse (eds.), *Constructing the Social*, London: Sage, pp. 19–44.

Gillen N. (2014) «*Nur Gott vor Augen*». *Die Strafgerichtsbarkeit des Patriarchen von Venedig (1451–1545)*, Cologne, Weimar and Vienna: Böhlau.

Ginzburg C. (1966) *Stregoneria e culti agrari tra Cinquecento e Seicento*, Turin: Einaudi.

——— (1976) *Il formaggio e i vermi. Il cosmo di un mugnaio del '500*, Turin: Einaudi.

——— (1984) 'Prove e possibilità, postfazione' in N. Zemon Davis *Il ritorno di Martin Guerre. Un caso di doppia identità nella Francia del Cinquecento*, Turin: G. Einaudi, pp. 129–154.

——— (1989) 'L'inquisitore come antropologo', in R. Pozzi and A. Prosperi (eds.) *Studi in onore di Armando Saitta dei sui allievi pisani*, Pisa: Giardini, pp. 23–33.

——— (1992) 'Unus testis. Lo sterminio degli ebrei e il principio di realtà' *Quaderni Storici*, 80 (2) 529–548.

——— (1994) 'Aristotele, la storia, la prova', *Quaderni Storici*, 85 (1), 5–17.

——— (1999) *History, Rhetoric, and Proof*, Hannover and London: University Press of New England.

Giuliani A. (1971) *Il concetto di prova. Contributo alla logica giuridica*, Milan: Giuffré.

Giuliani A. and Picardi N. (1995) *La responsabilità del giudice*, Milan: Giuffré.

Gleixner U. (1994) «*Das Mensch*» *und* «*der Kerl*». *Die Konstruktion von Geschlecht in Unzuchtsverfahren der Frühen Neuzeit*, Frankfurt/M and New York: Campus.

Gleixner U. (1998) 'Sexualisierung der Geschlechterverhältnisse? Zum Unzuchtsdiskurs in der Frühen Neuzeit. Die Deutung von «Unzucht» zwischen dörflicher Vorermittlung und herrschaftlichem Gericht' in H. Wunder and G. Hengel (eds.), *Geschlechterperspektiven. Forschungen zur Frühen Neuzeit*, Königstein – Taunus: Helmer, pp. 358–367.

Goeffen R. (2003) 'Le donne di Tiziano' in O. Calabrese (ed.) *Venere svelata: La Venere di Urbino di Tiziano, Catalogo della mostra*, Milan: Cinisello Balsamo: Silvana editoriale, pp. 93–107.

Goody J. (1983) *The Development of Family and Marriage in Europe*, Cambridge and New York: Cambridge University Press.

Gottlieb B. (1980) 'The Meaning of Clandestine Marriage' in R. Weaton and T. K. Hareven (eds.), *Family and Sexuality in French History*, Philadelphia: University of Pennsylvania Press, pp. 43–83.

Gowing L. (1996) *Domestic Dangers: Women, Words and Sex in Early Modern London*, Oxford and New York: Oxford University Press.

Grendi E. (1980) 'Per lo studio della storia criminale' *Quaderni Storici*, 44 (2), p. 579.

——— (1987) 'Premessa', *Quaderni Storici*, 66 (3), pp. 695–700.

—— (1990) 'Sulla «storia criminale»: risposta a Mario Sbriccoli', *Quaderni Storici* 73 (1), pp. 269–275.

Grendler P. F. (1989) *Schooling in Renaissance Italy. Literacy and Learning, 1300–1600*, Baltimore and London: Johns Hopkins University Press.

Grossi P. (1995) *L'ordine giuridico medievale*, Rome and Bari: Laterza.

Guarducci P. and Ottanelli V. (1982) *I servitori domestici della casa borghese Toscana nel basso medioevo*, Florence: Libreria editrice Salimbeni.

Guzzetti L. (1997) 'Separation and Separated Couples in Fourteenth-Century Venice' in T. Dean and K.J.P. Lowe (eds.) *Marriage in Italy, 1300–1650*, Cambridge: Cambridge University Press, pp. 249–274.

—— (2002) 'Dowries in Fourteenth-Century Venice', *Renaissance Studies*, 16 (4), 430–473.

—— (2010) 'Women in Court in Early Fourteenth-Century Venice', in J. Sperling and K. Wray (eds.) *Across the religious divide: women, property, and law in the wider Mediterranean (ca. 1300–1800)*, New York and London: Routledge, pp. 51–66.

Hacke D. (1999) '«Non lo volevo per marito in alcun modo». Matrimoni forzati e conflitti generazionali a Venezia fra il 1580 e il 1680' in S. Seidel Menchi, A. Jacobson Schutte and T. Kuhen (eds.) *Tempi e spazi di vita femminile tra medioevo ed età moderna*, Bologna: Il Mulino, pp. 195–224.

—— (2001) 'La promessa disattesa: il caso di Perina Gabrieli (Venezia 1620)' in S. Seidel Menchi and D. Quaglioni (eds.) *Matrimoni in dubbio. Unioni controverse e nozze clandestine in Italia dal XIV al XVIII secolo*, Bologna: Il Mulino, pp. 395–413.

—— (2001) 'Von der Wirkungsmächtigkeit des Heiligen: magische Liebeszauberpraktiken und die religiöse Mentalität venezianischer Laien der Frühen Neuzeit', *Historische Anthropologie*, 9 (3) pp. 311–332.

—— (2004) *Women, Sex and Marriage in Early Modern Venice*, Burlington: Ashgate.

Harringhton J. (1995) *Reordering Marriage and Society in Reformation Germany*, Cambridge: Cambridge University Press.

Helmholz R. (1974) *Marriage Litigation in Medieval England*, Cambridge: Cambridge University Press.

—— (1982) 'Excommunication as a Legal Sanction: the Attitudes of the Medieval Canonist', *Zeitschrift für Rechtsgeschichte, Kanonistische Abteilung*, 68 (1), 202–218.

—— (1990) *Roman Canon Law in Reformation England*, Cambridge: Cambridge University Press.

Herlihy D. and Klapisch Zuber C. (1978) (eds.) *Le Toscans et leurs familles. Une étude du catasto florentin de 1427*, Paris: FNSP Presses de Science Po.

Herlihy D. (1985) *Medieval Households*, Cambridge: Harvard University Press.

Hespanha A. M. (2003) *Introduzione alla storia del diritto europeo*, Bologna: Il Mulino.
Houlbrooke R. (1979) *Church Courts and the People During the English Reformation 1520–1570*, Oxford: Oxford University Press.
Howen Huges D. (1996) 'Il matrimonio nell'Italia meridionale' in M. De Giorgio and C. Klapisch Zuber (eds.) *Storia del matrimonio*, Rome and Bari, pp. 5–61.
Hunecke V. (1995) *Der venezianische Adel am Ende der Republik 1646–1797. Demographie, Familie, Haushalt*, Tübingen: Max Niemeyer.
Ingram M. (1987) *Church Courts, Sex, and Marriage in England*, 1570–1640, Cambridge: Cambridge University Press.
Jachobson Schutte A. (2002) 'Perfetta donna o ermafrodita?' Fisiologia e gender in un monastero settecentesco', *Studi storici*, 43 (1), 235–246.
Jacobson Schutte A. (1988), *Consiglio Spirituale e controllo sociale. Manuali per la Confessione stampati in volgare prima della Controriforma*, in M. Berengo (ed.) *Città italiane del '500 tra Riforma e Controriforma, Atti del Convegno internazionale di Studi, Lucca, 13–15 ottobre 1983*, Lucca: Maria Pacini Fazzi, pp. 45–59.
Jacobson Schutte A. (2003) 'Review: J. Ferraro, Marriage Wars in Late Renaissance Venice', Sixteenth Century Journal, 34 (1), pp. 243–244.
Jachobson Schutte A. (2006) 'La Congregazione del Concilio e lo scioglimento dei voti religiosi. Rapporti tra fratelli e sorelle', *Rivista Storica Italiana*, 118 (1), pp. 51–79.
Jedin H. and Reinhard K. (1981) *Il matrimonio. Una ricerca storica e teologica*, Brescia: Morcelliana.
Jedin H. (1957–1961) *A History of the Council of Trent*, London: T. Nelson, 2 vols.
Kelly J. (1984) *Women, History and Theory*, Chicago: University of Chicago Press.
Kermode J. and Walker G. (1994) *Women, Crime and the Courts in Early Modern England*, Chapel Hill and London: University of North Carolina Press.
Kirshner J. (1991) '«Maritus lucretur dotem uxoris sue premortue» in Late Medieval Florence', *Zeitschrift der Savigny Stiftung für Rechtsgeschichte. Kanonistische Abteilung*, 77, 111–155.
—— (1999) 'Donne maritate altrove. Genere e cittadinanza in Italia' in S. Seidel Menchi, A. Jacobson Schutte and T. Kuehn (eds.), *Tempi e spazi di vita femminile tra medioevo ed età moderna*, Bologna: Il Mulino, pp. 377–429.
—— (2000) 'Baldus de Ubaldis on Disinheritance: Context, Controversies, Consilia', *Ius commune. Zeitschrift für Europäische Rechtsgeschichte*, 27, 119–214.
—— (2002) 'Li emergenti bisogni matrimoniali in Renaissance Florence' in W. J. Connel (ed.) *Society and Individual in Renaissance Florence*, Berkeley: University of California Press, pp. 79–109.

—— (2015) *Marriage, Dowry and Citizenship in Late Medieval and Renaissance Italy*, Toronto: University of Toronto Press.
Klapisch Zuber C. (1990) *La maison et le nom. Stratégie et rituels dans l'Italie de la Renaissance*, Paris: Éditions de l'EHESS.
Koch E. (1991) *Maior dignitas est in sexu virili. Das weibliche Geschlecht im Normensystem des 16. Jahrhunderts*, Frankfurt/M: V. Klostermann.
—— (1997) 'Die Frau im Recht der Frühen Neuzeit. Juristische Lehren und Begründungen', in U. Gerhard (ed.) *Frauen in der Geschichte des Rechts*, Munich: C.H. Beck, pp. 73–93.
Köhler W. (1932) *Das Zürcher Ehegericht und seine Auswirkung in der deutschen Schweiz zur Zeit Zwinglis*, Leipzig: Heinsius.
—— (1942) *Das Ehe- und seine Sittengericht in den süddeutschen Reichsstädten, dem Herzogtum Württemberg und in Genf*, Leipzig: Heinsius.
Kuehn T. (1989) 'Reading Microhistory: the Example of Giovanni and Lusanna', *The Journal of Modern History*, 61 (3), 512–534.
—— (1999) 'Figli, madri, mogli e vedove. Donne come persone giuridiche', in S. Seidel Menchi, A. Jacobson Schutte and T. Kuehn (eds.), *Tempi e spazi di vita femminile tra medioevo ed età moderna*, Bologna: Il Mulino, 431–460.
—— (2002) *Illegitimacy in Renaissance Florence*, Ann Arbor: University of Michigan Press.
La Rocca C. (2000) 'Essendo impraticabile il seguitare a vivere insieme...». Separarsi a Livorno nel '700', *Bollettino storico pisano*, 69, pp. 45–70.
—— (2001) 'Interessi familiari e libero consenso nella Livorno del Settecento', in S. Seidel Menchi and D. Quaglioni (eds.), *Matrimoni in dubbio. Unioni controverse e nozze clandestine in Italia dal XIV al XVIII secolo*, Bologna: Il Mulino, pp. 529–550.
—— (2006) 'Tra due fuochi. Legami tra coppie e famiglie d'origine a Livorno nel secondo Settecento', in I. Fazio and D. Lombardi (eds.) *Generazioni. Legami di parentela tra passato e presente*, Rome: Viella, pp. 93–107.
—— (2009) *Tra moglie e marito. Matrimoni e separazioni a Livorno nel Settecento*, Bologna: Il Mulino.
Labalme P.H. (1995), 'Religious Devotion and Civic Division in Renaissance Venice: The Case of Lorenzo Giustiniani' in A. Vauchez (ed.) *La Religion civique à l'époque médiévale et moderne (Chrétienté et Islam)*, Rome: École française de Rome, pp. 297–308.
——, Sanguineti White L. and Carroll L. (1999) 'How to (and How Not to) Get Married in Sixteenth-Century Venice (Selections from the Diaries of Marin Sanudo)', *Renaissance Quarterly*, 52 (1), 43–72.
Laiou A.E. (1993) *Consent and Coercion to Sex and Marriage in Ancient and Medieval Societies*, Washington.
Lane F.C. (1978) *Storia di Venezia*, Turin: Einaudi.

Latasa P. (2005) 'La celebración del matrimonio en el virreinato peruano: disposiciones sinodales en las archidiócesis de Charcas y Lima (1570–1613)', in I. Arellano and J. M. Usunaríz (eds.), *El matrimonio en Europa y en el mundo hispanico: siglos XVI y XVII*, Barcelona: Visor Libros: pp. 237–256.

Laverie E. and Lamaison P. (1982) *L'impossible mariage: violence et parenté en Gévaudan, XVIIe, XVIIIe et XIXe siècles*, Paris: Hachette Littérature.

Lazzeri A.M. and Seidel Menchi S. (2001) '«Evidentemente gravida». «Fides oculata», voce pubblica e matrimonio controverso in Valsugana (1539–1544)' in S. Seidel Menchi and D. Quaglioni (eds.) *Matrimoni in dubbio. Unioni controversie e nozze clandestine in Italia dal XIV al XVIII secolo*, Bologna: Il Mulino, pp. 305–327.

Le Goff J. (1977) 'Nel medioevo: tempo della Chiesa e tempo del mercante', in Le Goff J. (ed.) *Tempo della Chiesa e tempo del mercante e altri saggi sul lavoro e la cultura nel medioevo*, Turin: Einaudi, pp. 2–23.

Lefebvre C. (1956) *Les origines romaines de la procédure sommaire aux XIIe et XIIIe siècles*, in «Ephemerides Iuris Canonici», 12, pp. 149–197

Lefebvre Teillard A. (1973) *Les officialités à la veille du Concile de Trente*, Paris: Librairie générale de droit et de jurisprudence.

—— (2000) 'Causa natalium ad forum ecclesiasticum spectant: un pouvoir redoutable et redouté', *Cahiers de recherches médiévales (XII–XV s.)*, 7, 93–103.

Lepsius S. (2003) *Der Richter und die Zeugen*, Frankfurt/M: Vittorio Klostermann.

—— (2003) *Von Zweifeln zur Überzeugung. Der Zeugenbeweis im gelehrten Recht ausgehend von der Abhandlung des Bartolus von Sassoferrato*, Frankfurt/M: Vittorio Klostermann.

Lettmann R. (1967) *Die Diskussion über die klandestinen Ehen und die Einführung einer zur Gültigkeit verpflichtenden Eheschliessungsform auf dem Konzil von Trient. Eine kanonistische Untersuchung*, Münster: Aschendorff.

Lischka M. (2006) *Liebe als Ritual. Eheanbahnung und Brautwerbung in der frühneuzeitichen Grafschaft Lippe*, Paderborn, Munich, Vienna and Zürich: Schöning.

Löhr J. (1909) 'Die Verwaltung des Kölnisches Grossarchidiaconats Xanten am Ausgange des Mittelalters', *Kirchenrechtliche Abhandlungen* 59/60, Stuttgart: Enke.

Lombardi D. (1994) 'Il matrimonio. Norme, giurisdizioni, conflitti nello Stato fiorentino del Cinquecento', in *Istituzioni e società in Toscana in età moderna, Atti delle giornate di studio dedicate a G. Pansini (Firenze, 4–5 dicembre 1992)*, vol. 2, Rome: Ministero per i beni culturali e ambientali, Ufficio centrale per i beni archivistici, pp. 787–805.

—— (1994) 'Intervention by Church and State in Marriage in Sixteenth and Seventeenth Century Florence' in T. Dean and K.J.P. Lowe (eds.) *Crime, Society and the Law in Renaissance Italy*, Cambridge: Cambridge University Press, pp. 142–156.

—— (1997) (ed.) *Legittimi e illegittimi. Responsabilità dei genitori e identità dei figli tra Cinque e Ottocento*, special issue, *Ricerche Storiche*, 27.

—— (1996) 'Fidanzamenti e matrimoni dal Concilio di Trento al Settecento' in M. De Giorgio and C. Klapisch Zuber (eds.) *Storia del matrimonio*, Rome and Bari: Laterza: pp. 215–250.

—— (2000) 'L'odio capitale, ovvero l'incompatibilità di carattere. Maria Falcini e Andrea Lotti (Firenze 1773–1777)' in S. Seidel Menchi and D. Quaglioni (eds.) *Coniugi nemici. La separazione in Italia dal XII al XVIII secolo*, Bologna: Il Mulino, pp. 335–367.

Lombardi D. (2004) 'Famiglie di Antico Regime', in G. Calvi (ed.) *Innesti. Donne e genere nella storia sociale*, Rome: Viella, pp. 199–221.

—— (2006) 'Giustizia ecclesiastica e composizione dei conflitti matrimoniali (Firenze, secoli XVI–XVIII)' in S. Seidel Menchi and D. Quaglioni (eds.) *I tribunali del matrimonio (secoli XV–XVIIII)*, Bologna: Il Mulino, pp. 577–607.

Lombardi D. (2001) *Matrimoni di Antico Regime*, Bologna: Il Mulino.

—— (2008) *Storia del matrimonio dal Medioevo ad oggi*, Bologna: Il Mulino.

Lorenzo Pinar F. J. (1999) *Amores inciertos, amores frustrados. Conflictividad y transgresiones matrimoniales en Zamora en el sieglo XVII*, Zamora: Editorial Semuret.

—— (2002) 'Actitudes violentas en torno a la formación y disolución del matrimonio en Castilla durante la Edad Moderna' in J.I. Fortea, J.E. Gelabert and T.A. Mantecón (eds.), *Furos et rabies: violencia, conflicto y marginación en la edad moderna*, Santander: Servicio de Publicaciones de la Universidad de Cantabria, pp. 159–182.

Lottin A. (1975) *La désunion du couple sous l'ancien régime: L'exemple du nord*, Paris: Editions universitaires.

Luhmann N. (1994) 'Inklusion und Exklusion' in H. Berding (ed.) *Nationales Bewusstsein und kollektive Identität. Studien zur Entwicklung des kollektiven Bewusstseins in der Neuzeit*, Frankfurt/M: Suhrkamp, pp. 15–45.

Luebke D.M. and Lindemann M. (2014) (ed.) *Mixed Matches. Transgressive Unions in Germany from the Reformation to the Enlightenment*, New York and Oxford: Berghahn.

Luperini S. (2001) 'La promessa sotto accusa (Pisa 1584)' in S. Seidel Menchi and D. Quaglioni (eds.) *Matrimoni in dubbio. Unioni controverse e nozze clandestine in Italia dal XIV al XVIII secolo*, Bologna: Il Mulino, pp. 363–394.

Maccarone M. (1995) *Nuovi studi su Innocenzo III*, Rome: Istituto Storico Italiano per il Medioevo.

Maire Vigueur J.C. (1991) 'Giudici e testimoni a confronto', in J.C. Maire Vigueur and A. Paravicini (eds.) *La parola all'accusato*, Palermo: Sellerio, pp. 105–123.

Mancuso F. (1999) *Exprimere causam in sententia. Ricerche sul principio di motivazione della sentenza nell'età del diritto comune classico*, Milan: Giuffrè.

Manussacas M. I. (1973) 'La comunità greca e gli arcivescovi di Filadelfia', in M. I. Manussacas (ed.), *La Chiesa greca in Italia dall'VIII al XVI secolo. Atti del convegno storico interecclesiale, Bari 30 aprile – 4 maggio 1969*, vol. 1, Padua: Antenore, pp. 45–87.

Marchetti P. (1994) *Testis contra se. L'imputato come fonte di prova nel processo penale dell'età moderna*, Milan: Giuffrè.

Marchetti V. (2008) *L' invenzione della bisessualità. Discussioni tra teologi, medici e giuristi del XVII secolo sull'ambiguità dei corpi e delle anime*, Milan: Mondadori.

Marchetto A. (1998–1999) *La dote contesa. Il processo matrimoniale di Ludovico Caccialupi, Diana Venier e Pietro Stella (Venezia 1551)*, unpublished degree thesis, University of Trent.

Marchetto G. (2000) 'I glossatori di fronte al diritto canonico: matrimonio e divorzio nella riflessione di Azzone (†1220 ca.)', *Annali dell'Istituto storico italo-germanico in Trento*, 26, 53–109.

—— (2001) *Il «matrimonium meticulosum» in un «consilium» di Bartolomeo Cipolla (ca.1420–1475)*, in S. Seidel Menchi and D. Quaglioni (eds.) *Matrimoni in dubbio. Unioni controverse e nozze clandestine in Italia dal XIV al XVIII secolo*, Bologna: Il Mulino, pp. 247–278.

Marchetto G. (2001) 'Matrimoni incerti tra dottrina e prassi. Un «consilium sapientis iudiciale» di Baldo degli Ubaldi (1327–1400)', in S. Seidel Menchi and D. Quaglioni (eds.) *Matrimoni in dubbio. Unioni controverse e nozze clandestine in Italia dal XIV al XVIII secolo*, Bologna: Il Mulino, pp. 83–105.

—— (2004) '«Primus fuit Lamech». La bigamia tra irregolarità e delitto nella dottrina di diritto comune' in S. Seidel Menchi and D. Quaglioni (eds.) *Trasgressioni. Seduzioni, concubinato, adulterio, bigamia (XIV–XVIII secolo)*, Bologna: Il Mulino, pp. 43–105.

—— (2008) 'Il 'divorzio imperfetto': i giuristi medievali e la separazione dei coniugi', Bologna: Il Mulino.

Mariani B. (1991) 'L'attività della curia arcivescovile milanese e l'amministrazione diocesana attraverso l'operato del vicario generale Romano Barni (1474–1477)', *Società e Storia*, 54 (4), pp. 769–811.

Marongiu A. (1964) 'Divorzio (Storia)', in *Enciclopedia del Diritto*, vol. 13, Milan: Giuffrè, pp. 182–507.

Marshall A.J. (1989) 'Ladies at Law: The Role of Women in the Roman Civil Courts', in C. Deroux (ed.) *Studies in Latin Literature and Roman History*, vol. 5, Bruxelles: Éditions Latomus, pp. 35–54.

Martin R. (1989) *Witchcraft and the Inquisition in Venice*, Oxford and New York.

Massetto G. P. (1996) 'Il lucro dotale nella dottrina e nella legislazione statutaria lombarde dei secoli XIV–XVI' *Ius Mediolani. Studi di storia del diritto milanese offerti dagli allievi a Giulio Vismara*, Milan: Giuffrè, pp. 189–364.

Matthews Grieco S. (1991) 'Corpo, aspetto e sessualità' in N. Zemon Davis and A. Farge (ed.), *Storia delle donne. Dal Rinascimento all'età moderna*, pp. 53–99.

Meccarelli M. (1998) 'Arbitrium iudicis und officialis im Ius comune', Zeitschrift der Savigny- Stiftung für Rechtsgeschichte, germanistische Abteilung, 115, 1998, pp. 552–565.

Meccarelli M. (1998) *Arbitrium. Un aspetto sistematico degli ordinamenti giuridici in età di diritto comune*, Milan: Giuffrè.

Meeck C. (1995) 'La donna, la famiglia e la legge nell'epoca di Ilaria del Carretto' in S. Toussaint (ed.) *Ilaria del Carretto e il suo monumento – la donna nell' arte, la cultura e la società del Quattrocento*, Lucca: S. Marco Litotipo, pp. 137–163.

────── (2000) 'Liti matrimoniali nel tribunale ecclesiastico lucchese sotto il vescovo Nicolao Guinigi (1394–1435)' *Quaderni lucchesi di studi sul Medioevo e sul Rinascimento*, 1, 105–142.

────── (2000) '«Simone ha aderito alla fede di Maometto». La «fornicazione spirituale» come causa di separazione (Lucca 1424)', in S. Seidel Menchi and D. Quaglioni (eds.) *Coniugi nemici. La separazione in Italia dal XII al XVIII secolo*, Bologna: Il Mulino, pp. 121–139.

Megna L. (1985) 'In margine ad alcune carte processuali di area vicentina: sponsali e matrimonio tra XVI e XVII secolo', in C. Povolo (ed.), *Bolzano Vicentino: dimensione del sociale e vita economica in un villaggio della pianura vicentina (secc. XIV–XIX)*, Bolzano Vicentino: Comune di Bolzano vicentino, pp. 309–335.

Meneghetti Casarin F. (1989) '«Diseducazione» patrizia, «diseducazione» plebea: un dibattito nella Venezia del Settecento', *Studi veneziani*, 17, pp. 117–156.

Menegon L. (1997) 'I figli naturali nell'ambito della famiglia patrizia veneziana in età moderna: un primo approccio', *Terra d'Este*, 7, 73–95.

Migliorino F. (1985) *Fama e infamia. Problemi della società medievale nel pensiero giuridico nei secoli XII e XIII*, Catania: Giannotta.

Minnucci G. (1989–1994) *La capacità processuale della donna nel pensiero canonistico classico*, 2 vols. Milan: Giuffrè.

────── (2001) '«Simpliciter et de plano, ac sine strepitu ac figura iudicii»: Il processo di nullità matrimoniale vertente fra Giorgio Zaccarotto e Maddalena di Sicilia (Padova e Venezia 1455–1458): una lettura storico-giuridica' in S. Seidel Menchi and D. Quaglioni (eds.) *Matrimoni in dubbio. Unioni controverse e nozze clandestine in Italia dal XIV al XVIII secolo*, Bologna: Il Mulino, pp. 175–197.

Mitterauer M. and Sieder R. (1977) *Vom Patriarchat zur Partnerschaft: Zum Strukturwandel der Familie*, Munich: Beck.

Mohle S. (1997) *Ehekonflikte und sozialer Wandel: Göttingen 1740–1840*, Frankfurt a.M. – New York: Campus.

Molho A. (1994) *Marriage Alliance in Late Medieval Florence*, Cambridge MA and London: Harvard University Press.

Molmenti P. (1973) *La storia di Venezia nella vita privata: dalle origini alla caduta della Repubblica*, Trieste: LINT.

Moscarda D. (2001) 'Il cardinale Giovan Battista de Luca giudice rotale e la causa matrimoniale tra Michele de Vaez e Giovanna Maria de Sciart (Napoli 1650)' in S. Seidel Menchi and D. Quaglioni (eds) *Matrimoni in dubbio. Unioni controversie e nozze clandestine in Italia dal XIV al XVIII secolo*, Bologna: Il Mulino, pp. 415–429.

Muir E. (1993) *Mad Blood Stirring. Vendetta and Factions in Friuli during the Renaissance*, Baltimore and London: Johns Hopkins University Press.

Muir E. (1997) *Ritual in Early Modern Europe*, Cambridge and New York: Cambridge University Press.

Murray J. (2012) (ed.) *Marriage in Premodern Europe: Italy and Beyond*, Toronto: CRRS.

Nada Patrone A.M. (1981) *Il cibo del ricco e il cibo del povero. Contributo alla storia qualitativa dell'alimentazione. L'area pedemontana negli ultimi secoli del Medio Evo*, Turin: Centro studi piemontesi.

Niccoli O. (1991) 'Introduzione' in O. Niccoli (ed.) *Rinascimento al femminile*, Rome and Bari: Laterza, pp. V–XXVI.

——— (1995) 'Baci rubati. Gesti e riti nuziali in Italia prima e dopo il Concilio di Trento', in S. Bertelli and M. Centanni (eds.) *Il gesto e il rito nel cerimoniale dal mondo antico ad oggi*, Florence: Ponte alle grazie, pp. 224–247.

——— (1995) *Il seme della violenza. Putti, fanciulli e mammoli nell'Italia fra Cinque e Seicento*, Rome and Bari: Laterza.

——— (1998) *La vita religiosa nell'Italia moderna (secoli XV–XVIII)*, Rome: Carocci.

——— (1999) 'Rinuncia, pace, perdono. Rituali di pacificazione della prima età moderna' *Studi storici*, 40 (1), 219–261.

——— (2000) *Storie di ogni giorno in una città del Seicento*, Rome and Bari: Laterza.

——— (2005) *Rinascimento anticlericale*, Rome and Bari: Laterza.

——— (2007) *Perdonare. Idee, pratiche, rituali in Italia tra Cinque e Seicento*, Rome and Bari: Laterza.

Nicolini U. (1995) *Il principio di legalità nelle democrazie italiane. Legislazione e dottrina politico-giuridica nell'età comunale*, Padua: CEDAM.

Niero A. (1980) 'Dal patriarcato di Grado al patriarcato di Venezia', in *Grado nella storia e nell'arte. Antichità altoadriatiche*, 17, pp. 265–284.

Noonan J. T. (1972) *Power to Dissolve. Lawyers and Marriages in the Court of the Roman Curia*, Cambridge: Cambridge University Press.

Nörr K.W. (1967) *Zur Stellung des Richters im gelehrten Prozess der Frühzeit*, Munich: C.H. Beck.

——— (1993) *Iudicium est actus triarum personarum. Beiträge zur Geschichte des Zivilprozessrechts Europas*, Goldbach: Keip.

Novick P. (1988) *That Noble Dream: The "Objectivity Question" and the American Historical Profession*, Cambridge: Cambridge University Press.

Orlando E. (2004) 'Il matrimonio delle beffe. Unioni finte, simulate, per gioco (Padova e Venezia, fine secolo XIV – inizi secolo XVI)' in S. Seidel Menchi and D. Quaglioni (eds.) *Trasgressioni. Seduzioni, concubinato, adulterio, bigamia (XIV-XVIII secolo)*, Bologna: Il Mulino, pp. 231–267.

―――― (2006) 'Tribunali di curia, processi matrimoniali e sedimentazione documentaria. Casi veneziani dai secoli XIII-XIV' in F. Cavazzana Romanelli, M. Leonardi and S. Rossi Minutelli (eds.) *«Cose nuove e cose antiche». Scritti per monsignor Antonio Niero e don Bruno Bertoli*, Venice: Biblioteca nazionale Marciana, pp. 137–152.

―――― (2006) 'Pubertà e matrimonio nella Padova di metà Quattrocento', in S. Seidel Menchi and D. Quaglioni (eds.) *I tribunali del matrimonio (secoli XV–XVIIII)*, Bologna: Il Mulino, pp. 375–410.

―――― (2007) 'Mixed marriages between Greeks and Latins in Late Mediaeval Italy', *Thesaurismata*, 37, 101–119.

―――― (2011) 'Gioco, violenza e punibilità del puer nel basso medioevo. Dalla tolleranza alla repressione, tra caso, colpa e dolo', in Filii, filiae …: položaj i uloga djece na Jadranskom prostro, Poreć, pp. 46–68.

―――― (2014) 'Pratiche di mediazione e controllo del matrimonio in età pre-tridentina', *Acta Histriae* 22 (2), pp. 305–326.

―――― (2014)*Migrazioni mediterranee. Migrazioni, minoranze e matrimoni a Venezia nel basso medioevo*, Bologna: Il Mulino.

Ortalli G. (1993) *Gioco e giustizia nell'Italia di Comune*, Rome: Viella.

―――― (1996) *Scuole e maestri tra medioevo e rinascimento. Il caso veneziano*, Bologna: Il Mulino.

Padoa-Schioppa A. (1999) 'Sur la conscience de juge dans le ius commune européen', in J. Carbasse and L. Depambour Tarride (eds), *La conscience du juge dans la tradition juridique européene*, Paris: PUF, pp. 95–129.

Paolin G. (1984) *Monache e donne nel Friuli del Cinquecento*, in A. Del Col (ed), *Società e cultura del Cinquecento nel Friuli Occidentale. Studi*, Pordenone, pp. 201–228.

Parente U. and Scaramella P. (2006) 'I processi matrimoniali napoletani (secoli XVI–XVII)', in S. Seidel Menchi and D. Quaglioni (eds.) *I tribunali del matrimonio (secoli XV–XVIIII)*, Bologna: Il Mulino, pp. 163–188.

Parma Cook A.P. and Cook N.D. (1991), *Good Faith and Truthful Ignorance. A case of Transatlantic Bigamy*, Durham and London: Duke University Press.

Passeron J.C. and Revel J. (2005) (eds.), *Penser par cas*, Paris: Éditions de l'École des Hautes Études en Sciences Sociales.

Pastore A. (1998) *Il medico in tribunale. La perizia medica nella procedura penale d'antico regime (secoli XVI–XVIII)*, Bellinzona: Casagrande.

Pedersen F. (1994) 'Did the Medieval Laity know the Canon Law Rules on Marriage? Some Evidence from Fourteenth-Century York cause paper', *Medieval Studies*, 56 (1), 111–152.

——— (2000) *Marriage Disputes in Medieval England*, London, Rio Grande, Ohio: Hambledon.

Pelaja M. (1994) *Matrimonio e sessualità a Roma nell'Ottocento*, Rome and Bari: Laterza.

Pennington K. (1991) *Il diritto dell'accusato. L'origine medievale della procedura legale* in J.C. Maire Viguer and A. Paravicini Bagliani (eds.), *La parola all'accusato*, Palermo: Sellerio, pp. 33–41.

Pérez De Herédia Y Valle I. (1977) *Die Befangenheit des Richters im kanonischen Recht* St. Ottilien: EOS.

Pia E. C. (2015) *La giustizia del vescovo. Società economia e Chiesa cittadina ad Asti tra XIII e XIV secolo*, Roma: Viella.

Piasentini S. (1999) 'Indagine sulla bestemmia a Venezia nel Quattrocento', *Studi Storici*, 2, 513–549.

Pizzolato N. (2006) '«Lo diavolo mi ingannao». La sodomia nelle campagne siciliane(1572–1664)', *Quaderni Storici*, 122 (2), pp. 449–480.

Plöchl W.M. (1962) *Geschichte des Kirchenrechts*, vol. 2, *Das Kirchenrecht der abendländischen Christenheit 1055 bis 1517*, Vienna and Munich: Herold.

Poian M. (2006) 'I processi matrimoniali dell'Archivio Vescovile di Feltre (secoli XVI–XVIII)' in S. Seidel Menchi and D. Quaglioni (eds.) *I tribunali del matrimonio (secoli XV–XVIIII)*, Bologna: Il Mulino, pp. 141–161.

Pomata G. (1981) 'Barbieri e comari', in G. Pomata (ed.) *Cultura popolare nell'Emilia Romagna. Medicina, erbe, e magia*, Milan: Silvana Editoriale, pp. 175–178.

Pomata G. (2002) 'Family and Gender', in J.A. Marino (ed.) *Early Modern Italy, 1550–1796*, Oxford: Oxford University Press, pp. 69–86.

Pomata G. 'La storia delle donne: una questione di confine', in *Gli strumenti della ricerca: Questioni di metodo*, Florence: La nuova Italia, 1983, Vol. 2, pp. 1434–1469.

Porqueres I Gené, E. (2006) 'L' autonomia dei figli minorenni. Matrimonio cum fuga a Maiorca tra Seicento e Settecento', in I. Fazio and D. Lombardi (eds.) *Generazioni. Legami di parentela fra passato e presente*, Rome: Viella, pp. 223–240.

Povolo C. (1996) *Il processo Guarnieri*, Koper: Zgodovinsko drustvo za juzno Primorsko.

——— (1997) *L'intrigo dell'onore. Poteri e istituzioni nella Repubblica di Venezia tra Cinque e Seicento*, Verona: Cierre.

Prodi P. (1973) 'The Structure and Organisation of the Church in Renaissance Venice: Suggestion for Research' in J.R. Hale (ed.) *Renaissance Venice*, London: pp. 409–430.

―――― (1992) *Il sacramento del potere. Il giuramento politico nella storia costituzionale dell'Occidente*, Bologna: Il Mulino.

―――― (1997) 'Il giuramento e il tribunale della coscienza: dal pluralismo degli ordinamenti giuridici al dualismo tra coscienza e diritto positivo' in N. Pirillo (ed.) *Il vincolo del giuramento e il tribunale della coscienza*, Bologna: Il Mulino, pp. 475–490.

―――― (2000) *Una storia della giustizia. Dal pluralismo dei fori al moderno dualismo tra coscienza e diritto*, Bologna: Il Mulino.

Prosperi A. (1993) 'Fede, giuramento, inquisizione' in P. Prodi (ed.) *Glaube und Eid. Treueformeln, Glaubensbekenntnisse und Sozialdisziplinierung zwischen Mittelalter und Neuzeit*, München: Oldenbourg, pp. 157–171.

―――― (1996) *Tribunali della coscienza. Inquisitori, confessori, missionari*, Turin: Einaudi.

Provinciali R. (1970) 'Giuramento decisorio', in *Enciclopedia del diritto*, Milan: Giuffrè, Vol. 19, pp. 103–127.

Quaglioni D. and Esposito A. (1991) 'I processi contro gli ebrei di Trento 1475', in J.C. Maire Vigueur and A. Paravicini Bagliani (eds.) *La parola all'accusato*, Palermo: Sellerio.

Quaglioni D. (1989) *Civilis sapientia. Dottrine giuridiche e dottrine politiche fra medioevo ed età moderna. Saggi per la storia del pensiero giuridico moderno*, Rimini: Maggioli.

―――― (2000) '«Divortium a diversitate mentium». La separazione personale dei coniugi nelle dottrine di diritto comune (appunti su una discussione)', in S. Seidel Menchi and D. Quaglioni (eds.) *Coniugi nemici. La separazione in Italia dal XII al XVIII secolo*, Bologna: Il Mulino, pp. 95–118.

―――― (2001) '«Sacramenti detestabili». La forma del matrimonio prima e dopo Trento', in S. Seidel Menchi and D. Quaglioni (eds.) *Matrimoni in dubbio. Unioni controversie e nozze clandestine in Italia dal XIV al XVIII secolo*, Bologna: Il Mulino, pp. 61–79.

Radford Ruether R. (1983) *Sexism and God Talk*, Boston: Beacon Press.

Rando D. (1994) *Una chiesa di frontiera. Le istituzioni ecclesiastiche veneziane nei secoli VI–XII*, Bologna: Il Mulino.

Ranum O. (2001) 'I rifugi dell'intimità' in P. Ariès and G. Duby (eds.) *La vita privata. Dal Rinascimento all' Illuminismo*, Rome and Bari: Laterza, pp. 161–204.

Rasi P. (1941) 'L'applicazione delle norme del Concilio di Trento in materia matrimoniale', *in: Studi di storia del diritto in onore di Arrigo Solmi*, Milan: Giuffrè, Vol. 1, pp. 235–281.

―――― (1943) 'La conclusione del matrimonio prima del Concilio di Trento', *Rivista di storia del diritto italiano*, 16, 233–321.

―――― (1958) *La conclusione del matrimonio nella dottrina prima del concilio di Trento*, Naples: Jovene.

Reinhard W. (2004) *Lebensformen Europas. Eine historische Kulturanthropologie*, Munich: Beck.
Rigo A. (2000) 'Interventi dello Stato veneziano nei casi di separazione: i Giudici del Procurator. Alcuni dati degli anni Cinquanta e Sessanta del XVI secolo', in S. Seidel Menchi and D. Quaglioni (eds.) *Coniugi nemici. La separazione in Italia dal XII al XVIII secolo*, Bologna: Il Mulino, pp. 519–536.
Robin F. (1967) *Kinship and Marriage An Anthropological Perspective*, Harmondsworth: Penguin.
Romeo G. (1997) *Ricerche su confessione dei peccati e Inquisizione nell'Italia del Cinquecento*, Naples: La Città del sole.
—— (2002) 'Recensione a E. Brambilla Alle origini del Sant'Uffizio', *Rivista di Storia e Letteratura Religiosa*, 38 (2), 379–384.
Romeo G. (2003) 'Confesseurs et inquisiteurs dans l'Italie moderne: un bilan', *Revue de l'Histoire des Religions*, 220 (2),153–165.
—— (2008) *Amori proibiti. I concubini tra Chiesa e Inquisizione*, Rome: Laterza.
Romita F. (1989) 'Le origini della S. C. del Concilio' in *La Sacra Congregazione del Concilio. Quarto Centenario dalla Fondazione (1564–1964). Sudi e ricerche*, Vatican City: Tipografia Vaticana, 13–50.
Roper L. (1994) *Oedipus and the Devil. Witchcraft, Sexuality, and Religion in Early Modern Europe*, London and New York: Routledge.
—— (1991) *The Holy Household. Women and Morals in Reformation Augsburg*, Oxford and New York: Clarendon and Oxford University Press.
Rosoni I. (1995) *Quae singula non prosunt collecta iuvant. La teoria della prova indiziaria nell'età medievale e moderna*, Milan: Giuffrè.
Rospocher M. (2004) 'Recensione a S. Cerutti, Giustizia Sommaria: pratiche e ideali di giustizia nella Torino del XVIII secolo', *Ricerche storiche*, 24, 188–192.
Rossiaud J. (1996) *La prostituzione nel medioevo*, Rome and Bari: Laterza.
Rossoni I. (2000) 'Anelli nuziali nel XVI secolo', *Annuario di specializzazione in storia dell'arte dell'Università di Bologna*, 1, pp. 11–23.
Rubin G. (1975) 'The Traffic in Women: Notes on the 'Political Economy' of Sex' in R. R. Reiter (ed.) *Toward an Anthropology of Women*, New York: Monthly Review Press, pp. 157–210.
Ruggiero G. (1980) *Violence in Early Renaissance Venice*, New Brunswick, N.J.: Rutgers University Press.
—— (1985) *The Boundaries of Eros. Sex, Crime, and Sexuality in Renaissance Venice*, New York: Oxford University Press.
—— (1987) 'Più che la vita caro»: onore, matrimonio e reputazione femminile nel tardo Rinascimento', *Quaderni Storici*, 66 (3), pp. 753–775.
—— (1993) *Binding Passions: Tales of Magic, Marriage, and Power at the End of the Renaissance*, New York: Oxford University Press.
Rusconi R. (2002) *L'ordine dei peccati. La confessione tra Medioevo ed età moderna*, Bologna: Il Mulino.

Safley T.M. (1984) *Let No Man Put Asunder: The Control of Marriage in the German Southwest: A Comparative Study, 1550–1600*, Kirksville, Mo.: Sixteenth Century Journal Publishers, Northeast Missouri State University.

Salvioli G. (1927) 'Storia della procedura civile e criminale', in P. del Giudice (ed.) *Storia della diritto italiano*, vol. 3 (2) Milan: Hoepli.

Sarti R. (2001) 'Bolognesi schiavi dei «Turchi» e schiavi «turchi» a Bologna', *Quaderni Storici* 107 (2), 437–473.

Sarti R. (2003) *Vita di casa. Abitare mangiare vestire nell'Europa moderna*, Rome and Bari.

Sbriccoli M. (1974) *Crimen laesae maiestatis. Il problema del reato politico alle soglie della scienza penalistica moderna*, Milan: Giuffrè.

—— (1988) 'Fonti giudiziarie e fonti giuridiche. Riflessione sulla fase attuale di studi di storia del crimine e della giustizia criminale', *Studi Storici*, 29 (2), pp. 493–501.

—— (1991) 'Tormentum, idest torquere mentem' in J.C. Maire Viguer and A. Paravicini Bagliani (eds.) *La parola all'accusato*, Palermo: Sellerio.

—— (2001) 'Giustizia negoziata, giustizia egemonica. Riflessioni su una nuova fase degli studi di storia della giustizia criminale' in M. Bellabarba, G. Schwerhoff and A. Zorzi (eds.), *Criminalità e giustizia in Germania e in Italia. Pratiche giudiziarie e linguaggi giuridici tra trardo medioevo ed età moderna*, Bologna and Berlin: il Mulino and Duncker & Humblot, pp. 345–364.

—— (2004) 'Deterior est condicio foeminarum. La storia della giustizia penale alla prova dell'approccio di genere', in G. Calvi (ed.), *Innesti. Donne e genere nella storia sociale*, Rome: Viella, pp. 73–91.

Scaramella P. (1999) 'Il matrimoni legato: l'«impotentia ex maleficio» in un caso napoletano di fine Cinquecento', in *Munera parva. Studi in onore di Boris Ulianich*, Vol. 2, Naples: Fridericiana editrice universitaria, pp. 317–348.

—— (2004) 'Controllo e repressione ecclesiastica della poligamia a Napoli in età moderna: dalle cause matrimoniali al crimine di fede (1514–1799)' in S. Seidel Menchi and D. Quaglioni (eds.) *Trasgressioni. Seduzioni, concubinato, adulterio, bigamia (XIV–XVIII secolo)*, Bologna: Il Mulino, pp. 443–501.

Schlinker S. (2008) *Litis contestatio. Eine Untersuchung über die Grundlagen des gelehrten Zivilprozesses in der Zeit von 12. bis zum 19. Jahrhundert*, Frankfurt/M.: V. Klostermann.

Schmidt H.R. (1998) 'Hausväter vor Gericht. Der Patriarchalismus als zweischneidiges Schwert' in M. Dinges (ed.) *Hausväter, Priester, Kastraten. Zur Konstruktion von Männlichkeit in Spätmittelalter und Früher Neuzeit*, Göttingen: Vandenhoeck & Ruprecht, pp. 213–236.

Schmitt J.C. (1999) *Il gesto nel medioevo*, Rome and Bari: Laterza.

Schmugge L. (2008) *Ehen vor Gericht. Paare der Renaissance vor dem Papst*, Berlin: Berlin University Press.

Scott J. (1986) 'Gender: a Useful Category of Historical Analysis', *American Historical Review*, 91 (5), pp. 1053–1075.

Segre R. (1996) 'La Controriforma: espulsioni, conversioni, isolamento' in C. Vivanti (ed.), *Storia d'Italia. Gli ebrei in Italia*, Vol. 1, Turin: Einaudi, pp. 709–778.
Seidel M. (1994) 'Hochzeitsikonographie im Trecento', *Mitteilungen des Kunsthistorischen Instituts in Florenz*, 38 (1), 1–47.
Seidel Menchi S. (1999) 'A titolo di introduzione' in S. Seidel Menchi, A. Jacobson Schutte and T. Kuehn (eds.) *Tempi e spazi di vita femminile tra medioevo ed età moderna*, Bologna: Il Mulino, pp. 13–18.
—— (1999) 'La fanciulla e la clessidra. Note sulla periodizzazione della vita femminile nelle società preindustriali' in S. Seidel Menchi, A. Jacobson Schutte and T. Kuehn (eds.) *Tempi e spazi di vita femminile tra medioevo ed età moderna*, Bologna: Il Mulino: pp. 105–155.
—— (2000) 'I processi matrimoniali come fonte storica' in S. Seidel Menchi and D. Quaglioni (eds.) *Coniugi nemici. La separazione in Italia dal XII al XVIII secolo*, Bologna: Il Mulino, pp. 15–94.
—— (2001) 'Percorsi variegati, percorsi obbligati. Elogio del matrimonio pretridentino', in S. Seidel Menchi and D. Quaglioni (eds.) *Matrimoni in dubbio. Unioni controverse e nozze clandestine in Italia dal XIV al XVIII secolo*, Bologna: Il Mulino, pp. 17–60.
—— (2003) 'La svolta di Trento. Ricerche italiane sui processi matrimoniali', in I. Arellano and J. M. Usunáriz (eds.) *El matrimonio en Europa y en el mundo hispánico: siglos XVI y XVII*, Madrid: Visor Libros, pp. 145–166.
—— (2004) 'Marriage Mediation in Early Modern History' in B. P. F. Wanrooij (ed.) *La mediazione matrimoniale. Il terzo (in)comodo in Europa fra Otto e Novecento*, Rome: Edizioni di storia e letteratura, pp. 1–17.
—— (2006) Cause matrimoniali e iconografia nuziale. Annotazioni in margine a una ricerca d'archivio, in S. Seidel Menchi and D. Quaglioni (eds.) *I tribunali del matrimonio (secoli XV–XVIIII)*, Bologna: Il Mulino, pp. 663–703.
—— (ed.) (2016) *Marriage in Europe, 1400–1800*, Toronto: Toronto University Press.
—— (2016) Introduction, in S. Seidel Menchi (ed) *Marriage in Europe, 1400–1800*, Toronto: Topronto University Press, pp. 3–30.
Sheeman M.M. (1978) 'Choice of Marriage Partner in the Middle Ages: Development and Mode of Application of the Theory of Marriage', *Studies in Medieval and Renaissance History* 1, pp. 1–33.
Shorter E. (1975) *The Making of Modern Family*, New York: Basic Books.
—— (1981) 'L'age des premières règles en France, 1850–1950', *Annales ESC*, 36, pp. 495–511.
Sibeth U. (1994) *Eherecht und Staatsbildung. Ehegesetzgebung und Eherechtsprechung in der Landgrafschaft Hessen*, Darmstadt and Marburg: Hessische Historische Komm.
Siebenhüner K. (2004) '«M'ha mosso l'amore»: bigami e inquisitori nella documentazione del Sant'Uffizio romano (XVII secolo)' in S. Seidel Menchi and

D. Quaglioni (eds.) *Trasgressioni. Seduzioni, concubinato, adulterio, bigamia (XIV–XVIII secolo)*, Bologna: Il Mulino pp. 503–533.

——— (2006) *Bigamie und Inquisition in Italien 1600–1750*, Paderborn: F. Schöningh.

——— (2008) 'Conversion, Mobility and the Roman Inquisition in Italy around 1600', *Past and Present*, 200 (1), pp. 5–35.

Sissa G. (1990) 'La verginità materiale, evanescenza di un oggetto', *Quaderni Storici* 75 (3), 739–756

Sorbelli A. (1910) *Il comune rurale dell'Appennino emiliano nei secoli XIV e XV*, Bologna: Arnaldo Forni Editore.

Sorrenti L. (1991) 'L'Autentica 'Sacramenta puberum' nell'esegesi dei dottori bolognesi del Duecento. Guizzardino e Iacopo Baldovini' *Rivista internazionale di diritto comune*, 2, pp. 69–121.

Sperling J. (2004) 'Marriage at the Time of the Council of Trent (1560–70): Clandestine Marriages, Kinship Prohibitions, and Dowry Exchange in European Comparison' *Journal of Early Modern History* 8 (1) 67–108.

——— (2007) 'Dowry or Inheritance? Kinship, Property, and Women's Agency in Lisbon, Venice and Florence (1572)', *Journal of Early Modern History*, 11 (3), 197–238.

Stone L. (1979) 'The Revival of Narrative. Reflection on a New Old History', *Past and Present*, 85 (1) pp. 3–24.

——— (1990) *Road to Divorce: England 1530–1987*, Oxford and New York: Oxford University Press.

——— (1995) *Uncertain Unions and Broken Lives: Intimate and Revealing Accounts of Marriage and Divorce in England*, Oxford and New York: Oxford University Press.

Strasser U. (2004) *State of Virginity. Gender, Religion and Politics in an Early Modern Catholic State*, Ann Arbor MI: University of Michigan Press.

Stretton T. (2008) *Marital Litigation in the Court of Requests (1542–1642)*, Cambridge: Cambridge University Press.

Tamassia N. (1885) *Osculum interveniens (Contributo alla storia dei riti nuziali)*, in «Rivista Storica Italiana», 2, pp. 241–264.

——— (1971) *La famiglia italiana nei secoli decimoquinto e decimosesto*, Rome: Multigrafica.

Tentler T.N. (1977) *Sin and Confession in the Eve of Reformation*, Princeton: Princeton University Press.

Thompson E.P. (1990) *Whigs and Hunters*, London: Penguin Books.

Traeger J. (1997) *Renaissance und Religion. Die Kunst des Glaubens im Zeitalter Raphaels*, Munich: C.H. Beck.

Tramontin S. and Donaglio F. (ed.) (1981) *Venezia e Lorenzo Giustiniani*, Venezia: Comune di Venezia, ufficio affari Istituzionali – patriarcato di Venezia.

——— (1989) 'Dall'episcopato castellano al patriarcato veneziano', in G. Vian (ed.) *La Chiesa di Venezia tra Medioevo ed età moderna*, Venezia: Edizioni Studium cattolico veneziano, pp. 55–85.

Turchi L. (2004) 'Adulterio, onere della prova e testimonianza. In margine a un processo correggese di età tridentina' in S. Seidel Menchi and D. Quaglioni (eds.) *Trasgressioni. Seduzioni, concubinato, adulterio, bigamia (XIV-XVIII secolo)*, Bologna: Il Mulino, pp. 305–382.

Turrini M. (1991) *La coscienza e le leggi. Morale e diritto nei testi per la confessione della prima età moderna*, Bologna: Il Mulino.

―― (1994) *Il giudice della coscienza e la coscienza del giudice*, in P. Prodi (ed.), *Disciplina dell'anima, disciplina del corpo e disciplina della società tra medioevo ed età moderna*, Bologna: Il Mulino, pp. 279–294.

Ulbricht O. (1995) (ed.) *Von Huren und Rabenmuttern. Weibliche Kriminalität in der Frühen Neuzeit*, Cologne, Weimar and Vienna: Böhlau.

Usunáriz J.M. (2003) 'Volved ya la riendas, porque no os perdáis: la transformación de los comportamientos morales en la España del XVI siglo', in I. Arellano and J. M. Usunáriz (eds) *El mundo solcial y cultural de La Celestina*, Madrid and Frankfurt am Main: Iberoamericana and Vervuert, pp. 295–321.

―― (2004) 'El matrimonio y su reforma en el mundo hispánico durante el Siglo de Oro: la promesa matrimonial' in I. Arellano and E. Godoy (eds.) *Temas del Barroco Hispánico*, Madrid and Frankfurt am Main: Iberoamericana and Vervuert, pp. 293–312.

―― (2005) 'El matrimonio como ejercicio de libertad en la España del siglo de oro', in I. Arellano and J. M. Usunáriz (eds.) *El matrimonio en Europa y en el mundo hispánico: siglos XVI y XVII*, Madrid: Visor Libros, pp. 167–185.

―― (2016) Marriage and Love in Sixteenth and Seventeenth Century Spain, in S. Seidel Menchi (ed) *Marriage in* Europe, *1400–1800*, Toronto: Toronto University Press, pp. 201–224.

Valsecchi C. (1999) *'Causa matrimonialis est gravis et ardua. 'Consiliatores' et matrimonio fino al concilio di Trento' Studi di Storia del diritto*, 2, Milan: Giuffrè, 407–513.

van der Heijden M. (1998) *Huwelijk in Holland. Wereldlijke rechtspraak en kerkelijke tucht 1550–1700*, Amsterdam: Bert Bakke.

―― (2016) 'Marriage Formation: Law and Custom in the Low Countries 1500–1700', in S. Seidel Menchi (ed.) *Marriage in Europe 1400–1800*, Toronto: Toronto University Press, pp. 115–175.

Vecchio S. (1995) 'La buona moglie' in C. Klapisch Zuber (ed.) *Storia delle donne. Il Medioevo*, Rome and Bari: Laterza, pp. 129–165.

Walker G. (1996) 'Expanding the Boundaries of Female Honour in Early Modern England', *Transaction of the Royal Historical Society*, 6, 235–245.

Watt J. R. (1992) *The Making of Modern Marriage. Matrimonial Control and the Rise of Sentiment in Neuchatel, 1500–1800*, Ithaca, N.Y.: Cornell University Press

Weber G.J.M. (2003) 'Velata dal tempo: La Venere di Giorgione' in O. Calabrese (ed.) *Venere svelata. La Venere di Urbino di Tiziano, Catalogo della mostra*, Milan: Silvana, pp. 47–55.

Weigand R. (1963) *Die bedingte Eheschließung im kanonischen Recht*, Munich: Max Hueber.

Weinstein R. (2003) *Marriage Rituals Italian Style: An Historical Anthropological Perspective on Early Modern Italy*, Leiden: Brill.

——— (2006) 'Genitori e figli nelle comunità ebraiche italiane della prima età moderna: continuità e cambiamenti' in I. Fazio and D. Lombardi (eds.) *Generazioni. Legami di parentela tra passato e presente*, Rome: Viella, pp. 185–203.

Weiss S.F. (1998) 'Medieval and Renaissance Wedding Banquets and Other Feast' in M. Carlin and J.T. Rosenthal (eds.) *Food and Eating in Medieval Europe*, London and Rio Grande: Hambledon Press, pp. 159–174.

White A. (1978) 'The Fiction of Factual Representation' in A. White (ed.) *Tropic of Discourse: Essays in Cultural Criticism*, Baltimore: Johns Hopkins University Press.

Wunder H. (1997) 'Herrschaft und öffentliches Handeln von Frauen in der Gesellschaft der frühen Neuzeit', in U. Gerhard (ed), *Frauen in der Geschichte des Rechts*, Munich: Beck, pp. 27–54.

——— (1998) *He Is the Sun, She Ist the Moon. Women in Early Modern Germany*, Cambridge and London: Harvard University Press.

——— (2016) 'Marriage in the Holy Roman Empire of the German Nation from the Fifteenth to the Eighteenth Century: Moral, Legal and Political Order' in S. Seidel Menchi (ed.) *Marriage in Europe, 1400–1800*, Toronto: Toronto University Press, pp. 61–93.

Zarri G. (1996) 'Il matrimonio tridentino' in P. Prodi and W. Reinhard (eds.), *Il concilio di Trento e il moderno*, Bologna: Il Mulino, pp. 437–483.

——— (2000) *Recinti. Donne, clausura e matrimonio nella prima età moderna*, Bologna: Il Mulino.

Zemon Davis N. (1976) 'Women History in Transition: the European Case', *Feminist Studies*, 3 (3/4), 83–103.

——— (1987) *Fiction in the Archives: Pardon Tales and Their Tellers in Sixteenth-Century France*, Stanford: Stanford University Press.

——— (2000) *The Gift in Sixteenth-Century France*, Oxford: Oxford University Press.

——— (2004) *l'Histoire tout feu tout flamme. Entretiens avec Denis Crouset*, Paris: Albin Michel.

Zimbalist Rosaldo M. and Lamphere L. (1975) (eds.) *Women, Culture and Society*, Stanford: Stanford University Press.

Zordan G. (1976) *Il diritto e la procedura criminale nel Tractatus de maleficis di Angelo Gambiglioni*, Padua: CEDAM.

Zorzi A. (1993) *Battagliole e giochi d'azzardo a Firenze nel tardo medioevo: due pratiche sociali tra disciplinamento e repressione*, in G. Ortalli (ed.), *Gioco e giustizia nell'Italia di Comune*, Rome: Viella, pp. 71–107.

Index

A
abandonment, 5, 14, 128, 134, 169, 188
accusatorial, 120
adultery, 2, 14, 19, 21n9, 114, 115, 168, 170–3, 203n113, 221, 226n9
advocates, 188
affinity, 34, 40, 124
age, 1, 2, 16, 20, 35, 44, 47, 50, 52, 78, 88, 90, 94n3, 98n40, 100n59, 106n116, 106n117, 135, 142n34, 181–6, 188, 190, 210n202, 221
agency, 6, 7, 12, 220
Ago, Renata, 10, 27n76, 211n206, 215n230
Albert, Thomas, 63n27, 229
Alexander III, 54, 116
Alexander of Hales, 133
alimony, 21n9, 50
alliance(s), 9, 80, 85, 166, 187
Altieri, Marco Antonio, 55, 56
Ancien Regime, 15

annulment, 7, 13, 19, 38, 48, 50, 69n95, 81, 85, 86, 89, 97n39, 109n139, 115, 120, 121, 123, 126, 138n5, 142n34, 167–9, 171, 175, 177, 179, 180, 183, 184, 190, 192, 194n15, 202n103, 209n176, 215n237, 220, 223, 228
apostoli, 6, 59, 60
appeal(s), 4, 7, 33, 38, 59–60, 82, 100n57, 117, 119, 120, 129–31, 135, 192, 221
Aquinas, Thomas, 89, 133, 153n162
arbitrium, 15–18, 47
archive
  episcopal, 5
  notarial, 1, 3, 208n171, 230
  state, 4
Archivio Segreto Vaticano, 234
Archivio Storico del Patriarcato di Venezia, 2
authority, 2, 14, 15, 30n119, 84, 86, 89, 96n26, 96n28, 99n55, 103n93, 104n101, 113, 115,

125, 127–9, 136, 137, 147n92,
    159, 161, 172, 174, 188, 190,
    208n165, 213n222, 230, 234
Avogaria di Comun, 2, 3, 21n9,
    21n11, 117, 118, 187, 189
Azpilqueta, Martin de, 193

B
banns, 189, 233
    proclamation of, 162
Barbaro, Francesco, 1, 20n2
bed, 34, 54, 89, 166, 186, 228
Benedict XIV. *See* Prospero Lambertini
bethrothal. *See* matrimonium per verba de futuro
bigamy, 2, 9, 21n9, 200n79, 228
bishop, 3, 5, 15, 33–5, 37, 40, 41, 52,
    84, 119, 123, 147n92, 148n106,
    174, 204n123, 234
blasphemy, 84, 91, 134, 155n178
Bonaventure, Edward, 133
Burano, 166

C
Calvi, Giulia, 13, 29n102, 29n105
Capi di Sestier, 178
Castello
    bishop of, 3, 5
    diocese of, 3
Castille, 187
Catholicism, 6
Cerutti, Simona, 10, 27n76, 30n131, 31n138, 204n133
church, 2–4, 6, 7, 9, 15–18, 35–8, 51,
    54, 57, 59, 60, 91, 92, 113,
    126–8, 131, 137, 143n44,
    159–64, 166–8, 188, 189, 228,
    229
Cipolla, Bartolomeo, 35, 62n17, 119, 145n74

citation, 36–8, 61, 220
classes, 3, 8, 9, 11, 55, 163, 185
Clement V, 17
clergy
    regular, 79, 124, 125, 127, 136
    secular, 16, 125–7, 136, 161, 174
community, 7, 9, 14–19, 29n116, 36,
    38, 51, 53, 54, 85, 86, 91, 125,
    127, 160, 172, 173, 192, 220,
    227, 231
concubinage, 7, 9, 51, 52, 57, 58,
    70n119, 92, 159, 228, 230
concubine(s), 21n11, 51, 54, 57, 58,
    73n165, 86, 91, 92, 125, 126,
    160, 166, 167, 176, 197n56,
    203n113
condition(s), 13, 35, 39, 46, 50, 80,
    91, 92, 103n94, 112, 115, 129,
    130, 161, 167–9, 173–81, 184
confession(s), 16, 47–9, 57, 58, 91,
    92, 111–57, 170, 174, 204n123,
    230, 233, 234
Congregation of the Council, 4, 53, 54, 234
conscience(s), 59, 86, 113, 120, 123,
    125, 127, 129–37, 152n150,
    156n187, 174, 189, 229, 233
consent
    expression of, 18, 50, 51, 87, 116,
        156n192, 160, 163–6, 175
    future, 40, 50, 116, 179, 180, 185, 190
    present, 53, 116, 161, 176
consummation, 43, 45, 50, 52, 56,
    124, 166, 183–5, 191, 193, 221
Contarini, Maffeo, 40
contumacious, 37, 38, 78
contumacy, 37–9, 141n26
convent(s) 13, 40, 41, 45, 58, 82, 83,
    100n57, 129, 130, 147n92, 184,
    192
copula, 50, 124, 126

cost and fees, 11, 17, 59, 60, 84, 117, 118, 126, 169, 170
council
    of Lyon, 162
    of Trent, 2, 9, 16, 20, 53, 92, 113, 137, 162, 164, 171, 174, 187, 193, 229, 230, 233
Council of Forty, 117
crucifix, 163

D

Dalla Minutaria, Giovanni, 43, 45, 46
Dandolo, Fantino, 40, 41, 92
daughter(s), 1, 13, 55, 60, 82, 86, 87, 123, 131, 135, 150n126, 172, 175, 180, 185–8, 191
Decretum, 96n26
defendant, 35–9, 42, 43, 46–8, 59, 77, 78, 83, 87, 91, 92, 111, 141n26, 178, 180, 220
defloration, 9, 50, 184, 185
De Groppis, Matteo, 40
Delle Croci, Niccolò, 40
deposition(s), 5, 20, 46, 49, 77–80, 82, 85, 87, 94n9, 99n53, 104n101, 106n116, 118, 122, 133–5, 145n68, 150n126, 155n182, 160, 186
diocese, 2–4, 22n13, 33, 34, 37, 61n10, 78, 80, 112, 116, 126, 136, 143n44, 221, 229
Di Sassonia, Enrico. *See* Saxony, Henry of
Di Sicilia, Maddalena, 40, 43, 50, 65n55, 105n112, 106n116, 107n118, 107n120, 185
divorce, 168
divortium. *See* separation
Donahue, Charles Jr., 21n4, 21n6, 22n16, 26n62, 62n11, 62n12, 63n24, 68n86, 68n93, 69n99, 98n43, 100n58, 106n113, 215n240, 229, 235n6
dowry, 1, 12, 19, 40, 84, 86, 91, 117, 161, 172, 176–8, 180, 183, 186, 187, 189, 232

E

Eisenach, Emlyn, 7, 25n49, 72n144, 73n167, 108n129
error(s), 78, 91, 132, 165, 174–81
Esecutori sopra la Bestemmia, 21n9, 193
Esposito, Anna, 73n167, 126, 151n130, 156n193, 203n118
Europe, 4, 58, 156n194, 189, 214n230, 230
evidence, 9, 14, 18, 39, 47, 48, 77, 79, 81, 111, 118, 119, 127, 181
exception(s), 39–43, 46, 60, 61, 77, 105n104, 118, 178, 180, 187
excommunication, 34, 35, 38–40, 48, 59, 60, 83, 85, 86, 117, 130, 131, 141n26, 170, 173, 204n123
expenses, 18, 38, 85, 99n53
expert(s), 9, 89, 160, 233

F

faith. *See* fides
fama, 46, 103n93
family
    dissolution of, 3, 113
    formation of, 6, 7, 51, 80, 113, 129
favor matrimonii, 14, 18, 19, 36, 47, 48, 59, 87, 92, 114–15, 138n5
fear, 12, 19, 41, 45, 46, 78, 81, 86, 93, 97n39, 114, 117, 120, 121, 128, 129, 133–7, 172, 185, 188, 190–2
feminine
    individuality, 113
    self consciousness, 113
fidelity, 166, 175–6

fides, 53, 166
flexibility, 4, 9, 33, 123, 228, 230
Florence, 7, 55, 56, 143n44, 171
formal joiner of issue. *See* litis contestatio
fornication, 69n109, 70n119
forum (internal, external), 84, 125, 133, 147n92, 230
fragility, 14, 18, 19, 112, 122, 125, 135
France, 210n202, 215n230, 230

G

gender, 6, 7, 12–14, 19, 20, 88
Gergen, Mary, 7, 25n47
Germany, 109n139, 166, 230
Giorgione, 232
Giustiniani, Lorenzo, 3, 100n57
God, 38, 45, 46, 58, 59, 99n53, 114, 122, 130, 132–5, 163, 191
Gospel(s), 133, 154n171, 163, 168, 231
Greek(s), 78, 114, 134, 166, 231
Gregory IX, 95n23, 167
Guzzetti, Linda, 126, 151n130, 156n191, 206n146

H

Hacke, Daniela, 7, 23n25, 25n42, 25n48, 28n94, 29n109, 29n111, 31n146, 108n121, 213n221, 215n236
handkerchief, 56, 57
heart(s), 55, 113, 121, 122, 132
Helmholz, Richard H., 20n4, 22n16, 23n18, 30n133, 61n1, 61n10, 62n11, 63n24, 65n47, 69n100, 69n110, 74n178, 87, 94n9, 100n58, 102n90, 104n101, 204n128, 205n136, 229

herbaria, 90, 107n120, 107n121
Holy Roman Empire, 6, 230
honor, 6, 51, 84–6, 88, 91, 115, 126, 149n114, 150n127, 163, 167, 172, 175, 177, 185, 203n113, 204n132, 204n133
humanitas, 39, 123
husband, 1, 12, 13, 35, 41, 43, 48, 49, 51, 53–7, 60, 73n165, 81, 85, 87, 89, 91, 97n34, 98n40, 100n57, 113–15, 117, 121–4, 126, 128, 129, 131, 134, 140n26, 142n41, 150n126, 152n150, 156n189, 160, 161, 164, 166–73, 175, 177, 179, 180, 184, 186, 187, 189–91, 194n15, 199n75, 200n84, 203n113, 205n140, 209n174, 228

I

impediment
  affinity, 28n97
  consanguinity, 168
  crime, 19
  force and/or fear, 81, 192, 193
  honesty, 51
  incest, 13
  of minority, 39, 168
  preceding marriage 38–9
  servile condition, 179–81
  vow(s), 192
in facie ecclesiae, 162
inquisition, 4, 84, 111–57, 170
inquisitor(s), 20, 112, 118, 120, 135, 189, 233
inquisitorial, 16, 80, 84, 90, 96n26, 100n62, 107n121, 118–20
instance, 33, 38, 39, 194n8
institution(s), 4, 6–8, 10, 11, 15, 27n77, 33, 53, 142n34, 159, 166, 189, 227, 228
interrogation(s) 11, 47, 58, 78, 80, 82, 96n25, 111–15, 118–20,

122, 127, 129–31, 133, 135, 137, 187, 229, 231, 233

J
Jew, 93, 163
jurisdiction, 2–4, 15, 17, 19, 21n9, 30n123, 33, 34, 40, 41, 84, 100n60, 117, 120, 136, 143n44, 173, 174, 193, 206n146, 219, 230
justice
  bureaucratic, 14, 19
  hegemonic, 14, 15
  negotiated, 14, 15, 19, 30n119

K
kin(s), 129, 161, 171, 172, 185, 188
kiss, 53, 54, 71n140, 121, 161, 164, 166, 186, 191, 198n69, 231

L
Lambertini, Prospero, 172
La Rocca, Chiara, 7, 25n50, 27n73, 142n34, 203n112, 203n118, 204n126
law
  canon, 4, 9, 14, 16–19, 23n18, 34, 48, 51, 52, 54, 63n27, 88, 89, 106n116, 112, 123, 132, 134, 159, 160, 167, 168, 171–3, 176, 179, 181–4, 188, 190, 192, 199n77, 203n111, 221, 230
  civil, 19, 34, 51, 167, 179, 203n111
  customary, 3, 18, 19, 91, 159, 160
  German, 6
  Roman, 179, 200n87
lay
  ecclesiastical, 5, 7, 19, 51, 86, 168
  secular, 2, 86, 161
libro d'oro, 189
litigantes, 104n100

litis contestatio, 36, 38, 42, 66n63
Lombardi, Daniela, 7, 22n16, 25n41, 25n46, 25n52, 26n59, 27n73, 29n107, 31n148, 56, 71n131, 72n155, 72n157, 97n30, 101n68, 101n70, 113, 140n22, 140n24, 141n30, 143n43, 143n44, 145n71, 147n92, 151n128, 152n139, 195n18, 202n107, 212n212, 217n261, 236n24
London, 108n125
Lotto, Lorenzo, 232, 235n12
love, 44, 52–5, 58, 82, 91, 123, 172, 187, 188, 232
Lutheran, 93

M
madonna, 82
magistratures, 2, 21n9, 101n68, 177
Malice, 41
Manzoni, Alessandro, 189
marriage
  alleged, 35, 51, 81, 88, 89, 91, 117, 126, 127, 130, 160, 179, 180, 187, 193, 220, 228
  clandestine, 7, 51, 70n119, 116, 142n37, 162, 212n211
  faked, 7
  formation of, 7, 51, 113, 129, 160
  mixed, 7
  per verba de futuro, 183, 184, 205n141
  per verba de presenti, 161, 162, 164, 167, 169, 184, 194n14
  plural, 23n17, 169–72
  presumed, 15, 42, 51, 54, 55, 81, 89, 97n34, 116
marriage cases, 5, 7, 48, 68n87, 84, 101n68, 107n121, 114, 118, 124, 176, 193, 208n166, 230, 235n6

marriage litigations, 2, 5–8, 11, 12, 17, 22n14, 25n36, 26n62, 33–75, 80, 83, 87–90, 114, 116, 118, 119, 124, 127, 139n13, 141n26, 159, 162, 170, 171, 173, 183, 184, 187, 202n104, 204n129, 206n142, 219–21, 227, 229–33
marriage practices, 2, 20, 50, 136, 163, 231, 235
mediation, 13, 15, 17, 18, 111–57, 173, 178, 228
mediator, 16, 20, 59, 111–15, 117, 124, 125, 135, 136, 206n151
mesalliance, 3, 19, 189
Middle Ages, 68n88, 84, 100n59, 103n94, 135, 142n34
modus operandi. *See* procedure
monastery: *See* convent
morality, 172, 175, 203n113
  parameters of, 93

N
Navarro. *See* Azpilqueta, Martin de
New World, 4, 23n18
Niccoli, Ottavia, 22n16, 29n115, 30n119, 30n127, 71n136, 71n140, 72n157, 105n104, 108n125, 109n132, 109n133, 146n85, 154n171, 165, 198n64, 198n68, 199n69, 210n188
nobility, 3, 20n2, 22n16, 23n25, 34, 185, 189
noble, 1, 19, 164, 181, 182, 189, 212n213
notarial records, 1, 3, 4, 95n20, 147n92, 173, 203n118, 204n126, 208n171, 230, 232
notary(ies), 1, 2, 11, 13, 20n1, 21n11, 22n13, 34, 35, 40, 46, 52, 55, 78, 79, 94n13, 95n20, 99n53, 112, 136, 181, 182, 208n171, 229, 230, 233
nun(s), 40, 41, 45, 83, 128, 129
nuncio, 34, 36, 37, 59, 64n35, 79
nuptial blessing, 55, 56, 161, 162, 186, 189
nuptial bond. *See* marriage

O
oath, 23n17, 37, 39, 42, 43, 46–50, 66n69, 66n71, 67n76, 67n80, 77, 79–80, 82, 83, 90, 95n17, 95n23, 96n26, 99n53, 106n116, 113, 114, 130–7, 137n5, 141n28, 141n29, 154n171, 154n174, 156n191, 163, 169, 178, 196n42, 231
objections, 39, 41, 60, 88, 92, 178, 207n153
Orlando, Ermanno, 7, 22n12, 22n13, 22n17, 23n25, 25n50, 30n135, 69n110, 106n117, 107n118, 108n125, 154n174, 193n4, 195n28, 200n80, 206n151, 209n188, 210n195, 210n197, 235n5
orthodox. *See* greek

P
paintings, 232
papal penitentiary 6, 33, 40, 54, 130, 159
parental authority, 127–9, 188, 213n222, 234
Paris, 231, 235n6
parish, 15, 17, 37, 38, 40, 92, 125, 136, 156n194, 160, 164, 166, 171, 174, 180, 189, 196n48, 204n123, 208n171, 230, 233, 234

INDEX 283

patriarch, 2–4, 12, 34, 37, 40, 41, 79, 84, 86, 100n57, 111, 119, 126, 127, 135, 136, 149n112, 151n137, 161, 162, 174, 196n48, 198n63
Paul, Saint, 179
peritus. *See* expert
perjury, 83–4, 91, 99n55, 100n59, 100n62, 101n68, 119, 131–5, 153n162
petition(s), 6, 36, 42, 61, 63n28, 85, 97n34, 111, 118, 130, 137n5, 161, 178, 207n153
plaintiff, 35, 36, 38–43, 46–8, 59, 61, 66n71, 67n76, 77, 83, 87, 88, 91, 96n28, 97n34, 107n118, 111, 118, 124, 137n5, 178, 181, 192, 198n63, 220, 221, 232
poligamy. *See* bigamy
positions, 13, 14, 40, 42–7, 66n71, 79, 82, 83, 119, 136, 147n92, 172, 178, 184, 192, 232
postponements, 39
post-Tridentine, 9, 52, 57, 93, 137, 143n44, 228, 231, 232
power(s), 2, 17, 47, 55, 83, 113, 116, 118, 125, 127, 128, 130, 133, 134, 228
presumption(s), 16, 18, 47, 49–58, 69n109, 81, 193, 231
pre-Tridentine, 16, 18, 50, 52, 53, 80, 83, 87, 115, 116, 127, 135, 159–217, 220, 228, 231, 232, 234, 235
priest. *See* secular clergy
Priuli, Lorenzo, 56, 65n51, 67n78, 127, 161
procedure
  ex officio, 34, 118
  ordinary, 16, 17
  summary, 15–17, 41, 42, 59–61, 118

procurators, 34, 35, 39, 42, 46, 58, 61, 82, 92, 177, 178, 202n104, 220
Proof(s) 10, 16, 18, 20, 35, 47–58, 68n86, 77, 82, 83, 87, 91, 96n26, 98n40, 105n108, 106n117, 111, 112, 122, 131, 141n28, 176, 178, 184, 206n142, 208n171, 230, 232
Prosperi, Adriano, 96n26, 101n63, 113, 140n25, 146n78, 154n171
Protestant Reformation, 4
psychoanalysis, 233
public, 18, 30n119, 37, 46, 51, 54, 56, 86, 95n20, 116, 123, 125, 128, 132, 150n123, 160, 169, 183, 189, 202n105, 230
publication, 17, 35, 41, 51, 99n53, 153n157, 162, 176, 216n257
publice, 65n49, 213n219

Q
Quaglioni, Diego, 6, 25n44, 26n66, 27n73, 67n75, 68n87, 69n101, 70n119, 142n34

R
rape, 2, 9, 117, 144n55, 171, 193
res iudicata, 41
responsibility, 10, 20, 59, 113, 114, 130, 133, 136, 166, 182, 213n221, 229, 232
right(s), 10, 16, 17, 34, 36–8, 40, 48, 53, 59, 60, 81, 82, 85, 86, 93, 100n60, 128, 159, 160, 169, 170, 172, 190, 192
rite(s), 60, 61, 118, 133, 162–4, 189, 214n229, 228, 234

ritual(s), 7, 16, 18, 22n17, 46, 52, 53, 56, 57, 70n120, 83, 91, 92, 134, 136, 160, 163, 178, 189, 198n69, 207n153, 216n244, 220, 231
Rome, 60, 126, 203n118

S

Saints, 58, 134, 154n171, 196n41
Sánchez, Thomás, 105n108, 180, 193, 208n165
San Jacopo di Murano, 128
  monastery of, 128
San Mattia
  abbes of, 45, 46
  convent of, 41
  nuns of, 45
Saxony, Henry of, 119
Sbriccoli, Mario, 14, 26n55, 29n111, 30n117, 30n119, 31n153, 99n55, 137n4, 145n61
schismatic. *See* greek
Schmugge, Ludwig, 6, 24n33, 62n11, 199n71, 205n141, 206n150, 215n236, 229
secular clergy, 16, 125–7, 136, 161, 174
Seidel Menchi, Silvana, 6, 25n37, 25n44, 26n61, 26n66, 27n73, 67n75, 70n114, 71n137, 72n145, 72n150, 98n48, 99n53, 101n65, 102n83, 109n137, 138n8, 140n22, 142n34, 144n57, 149n110, 149n117, 155n184, 197n56, 198n68, 206n151, 210n195, 210n196, 210n200, 211n202, 211n204, 216n251, 226n6, 235n8, 235n14, 236n19
sentence
  execution of, 60, 117, 143n44
  in judicato, 41

register of, 2, 5, 14, 58, 60, 83, 84, 173, 181, 233
separation, 2, 5–7, 14, 15, 18, 19, 21n9, 48, 114, 115, 122, 126, 136, 142n34, 142n41, 149n112, 155n187, 156n189, 166, 172–4, 203n111, 204n126, 221, 226n9, 228
servants, 34, 45, 57, 73n165, 88, 182
sexual intercourse. *See* copula
sexus
  fragilitas, 14, 19, 112, 220
  quality of, 123, 177
Signori di notte, 154n174
signum, 54
Slave(s), 3, 17, 61, 90, 179, 180, 207n156, 207n157, 207n164
Solution(s), 3, 13, 15, 17, 18, 173
son, 1, 35, 43, 107n118, 141n26, 149n114, 163, 187
soul(s), 2, 12, 55, 112–14, 118, 120, 130–2, 135, 145n59, 155n182, 164, 188, 202n105, 231, 236n19
Spain, vii
Sponsalia, 52
spouse(s), 2, 5, 14, 19, 28n97, 34, 35, 48, 50, 53, 55, 57, 65n60, 86, 88, 89, 111, 114, 116, 117, 124–6, 129, 136, 141n32, 163, 164, 166–9, 170, 172–4, 176, 179, 184, 185, 188, 191, 199n77, 199n78, 204n126, 208n171, 221
status, 3, 6, 7, 20, 52, 54, 57, 73n165, 88, 115, 168, 172, 178–80, 182, 193
Stone, Lawrence, 9, 10, 23n26, 25n36, 27n69, 55
stuprum. *See* rape
stylus curiae, 17
suit(s), 5, 7–9, 11, 12, 14, 15, 18, 20, 34–6, 38–42, 46, 48, 50, 52, 56, 58–61, 65n47, 78, 80, 81, 84,

85, 87, 89, 100n62, 109n139, 111, 113–20, 122, 124, 126, 128, 132, 135, 136, 141n32, 142n34, 160, 167, 168, 170, 171, 175, 178, 187, 188, 190, 192, 194n15, 219, 220, 227, 229

T
Tametsi, Decret, 31n144, 236n21
testimony (formation of, burden of), 80–3, 178
Torcello, 166
tribunal
   ecclesiastical, 2, 5, 6, 8, 13, 33, 37, 49, 51, 83, 84, 87, 123, 125, 128, 136, 137, 139n11, 140n19, 162, 164, 165, 171, 172, 175, 179, 180, 187, 190, 202n107, 204n126, 212n211, 219, 227, 230
   secular, 2, 6, 193
Turks, 90, 93, 167

U
urbanitas, 39, 123

V
Vatican Secret Archive, 4
Venetian, 2–5, 7, 8, 12, 14, 20n2, 21n11, 22n12, 33, 34, 37, 39, 41, 43, 49, 56, 66n66, 73n165, 78–80, 82, 84, 87, 93, 106n116, 106n117, 109n139, 111, 113, 116, 120, 122, 124, 127, 128, 132, 136, 145n67, 146n84, 147n89, 155n180, 161, 162, 165, 167, 170, 179–82, 184, 189, 195n19, 199n72, 212n214, 213n221, 219–26, 229–32

Venice, 1–4, 7, 21n9, 22n16, 22–3n17, 23n25, 31n147, 33, 37, 39–41, 54–7, 59, 60, 66n66, 67n77, 74n171, 78, 82, 84, 85, 97n33, 99n53, 101n68, 104n97, 105n108, 111, 119, 126, 159–217, 219–21, 229–31, 235n6, 236n19
Verbalization, 61n5
vicar, 11, 12, 14, 16, 34, 36–8, 40, 41, 48, 52, 56, 60, 70n123, 78–80, 84, 85, 95n20, 104n104, 111, 112, 114, 117, 120–3, 127–31, 135, 136, 139n19, 142n41, 143n42, 147n93, 148n106, 149n112, 152n148, 153n152, 166, 169, 170, 173, 175–9, 183, 185–7, 194n8, 198n63, 200n79, 202n103, 206n145, 228, 229, 233
virginity, 50, 89, 105n108, 115, 175–7, 186

W
wedding, 31n144, 50–8, 72n155, 79, 82, 121, 125, 136, 161, 162, 164, 171, 177, 180, 181, 186, 189, 191, 193, 199n70, 233, 234
wife, 12, 21n9, 35, 36, 38, 40, 41, 43, 48, 49, 51, 53–8, 73n165, 82, 85, 87, 89, 92, 93, 98n40, 109n139, 113–15, 117, 119, 124–6, 128–30, 142n41, 152n150, 153n155, 161, 163, 164, 166–77, 180, 184, 186, 187, 189, 191, 196n41, 197n56, 199n75, 200n84, 202n103, 203n113, 205n136, 205n140, 207n164, 221

women, 3, 5, 6, 8, 11–14, 19,
    24n35, 29n107, 35, 45, 49,
    55, 73n165, 86, 88, 90, 91,
    97n40, 109n139, 112–15,
    117, 118, 120, 122, 127,
    129–31, 134, 135, 137,
    140n26, 141n29, 146n79,
    152n150, 156n191, 160, 163,
    170, 172, 175, 187, 189, 191,
    193, 203n115, 211n206,
    215n237, 220, 221, 226n9,
    228, 229, 232, 233

Y
York, 187, 202n101

Z
Zaccarotto, Giorgio, 39–41, 43, 50,
    65n55, 73n163, 105n112,
    106n116, 107n118, 107n120, 185
Zarri, Gabriella, 113, 140n25,
    197n53, 236n21, 236n24
Zemon Davis, Natalie, 7, 24n35,
    25n47, 29n102, 71n136, 213n222